HUMAN MANIPULATION

A Handbook

Malcolm Coxall

Edited by Guy Caswell

Cornelio Books

Published by M.Coxall - Cornelio Books
Copyright 1985, 2013 Malcolm Coxall
First Published in United Kingdom, Spain, 2013
ISBN: 978-84-940853-2-1

Contents

Preface

Why would anyone write a book about human manipulation when many of us have little clue as to what manipulation is or why it might be important to us? The answer is that we, the majority of the world's population, the faceless masses who shuffle off to work every morning and hang our coats up when we come home in the evening, are the main targets of a rigorous exploitation by global puppeteers. Therefore, maybe we should take an interest in how we are manipulated and why.

In recent years phrases such as spin doctors, smoke and mirrors, the Teflon man have become commonplace in our media, adding to the already familiar ideas of Big Brother and 1984. Public consciousness and discontent at the shenanigans of our political masters is getting louder every day.

And in another sense, human manipulation has become something of a plague. The bad examples of our leaders have permeated the consciousness of the people where we even manipulate each other as proxies for our government, or even on our own account. It's truly a morally sad state of affairs.

But it wasn't always like this. Until quite recently the very idea of a central government was alien to many societies. Concepts such as a total DNA database of all citizens, ID cards, video monitoring of our movements and the routine surveillance of our telephone and other communications were unheard of. Such ideas were abhorrent and unthinkable. Nowadays, however, we live in a world where all power is vested in government and little is left to the individual. All authority resides with a regulated state. And this state is everywhere, in everything we do, it permeates our life.

And occasionally we do see the truth behind our "civilised", Western, democratic governments: To mix our metaphors and eras, modern capitalist government often shows itself as a towering and threatening brute - feudalism on steroids. Occasionally, we glimpse this violent and armed thug, especially when there is a risk that we might step out of line or challenge its authority.

Fortunately, most of us rarely see the uglier side of this monster, because he prefers us to see him in his well-cut suit, a civilised urbane man, smiling, always reasonable, so trustworthy.

But what we are really seeing is a prime example of a new and virulent form of institutional social control. Because our ever more pervasive governments can no longer rely on traditional feudal methods like coercion and intimidation, a new, efficient and repeatable method of social control has grown up. It is called political manipulation, and it is everywhere.

More frighteningly, the lines between government and commerce have become blurred as government and big capital merge from a popular point of view, into the great "Them". "They" are now in a unique historical position. "They" have access to unlimited economic resources, they control the media, and "they" control all political and military resources and institutions.

A concentration of power between political and economic elites creates an enormous risk to human freedom. These elites have moved on from the messy and violent traditional methods of social control to a much more dangerous paradigm of social manipulation, this time backed up by the end-stop of limitless state violence.

Such a dangerous conjunction of total influence and power has rarely existed in human political history.

Manipulation relies on ignorance, and for our sake, for mankind's dignity and the preservation of our basic freedoms, I believe we all should question our roles as pawns to be conveniently moved here and there according to the wishes of some faceless "grandmaster". Is this the kind of world we want to inhabit?

And so, I now present this humble attempt to define and de-mystify the subject of human manipulation. Everyone has a right to see if they are being manipulated and decide for themselves whether they find it acceptable or not - and if not what they can do to stop it.

Having said all of this, morality, politics, economics and government are not like the weather. What happens isn't inevitable. It's not pre-determined. An economy or a government or a political or economic system does not exist in nature or by the hand of God. We don't have to settle for what we get. And, crucially, it can be changed, by us.

We are now at an important moment in human social and political development which requires serious and universal political reflection and debate. This book is intended to contribute to that debate. It may perhaps even provide the key to unlocking some of the manipulative chains that have been placed upon us by the shadowy manipulators that govern us.

---o0o---

"The Truth shall set you free"

1. Social control and manipulation

1.1 What is social control? Before we can begin to discuss human manipulation in any detail, we must first put the subject into its proper context as a method of social control. But what do we mean by social control?

Social control refers to societal and political mechanisms that regulate individual and group behaviour in a conscious or unconscious attempt to gain compliance with the rules of a given society, state, or social group.

1.1.1 Types of Social control: There are two basic types of social control, enforced in different ways: informal social control and formal social control.

Informal social control works by means of individual socialisation where individuals develop behaviour which conforms to the acceptable rules of the group. Enforcement is by means of interpersonal sanction and reward, with the objective of maintaining "interpersonal stability".

Formal social control involves the use of external sanctions and rewards enforced by some kind of government or authority with the primary objective to prevent the onset of "chaos" or "social fragmentation".

All human societies contain some degree of organisation based on a set of social norms. These external constraints represent forms of social control; they may be written or unwritten laws, taboos against certain physical and sexual conduct, deference to group leaders and revered icons, etc.

A government uses social control institutionally to govern its people whilst social controls from peers within a group are interpersonal. But the two are also interchangeable, for instance where a citizen obliges another citizen to abide by the law, or where a government appeals to the citizenry to "do the right thing". Governments are not the only social controllers, and neither are our social peers.

1.2 Sources of social control: There are two basic sources of social control: interpersonal and institutional.

1.2.1 Interpersonal social control: Unless our societal peers are involved in education or criminal activities such as intimidation, blackmail, fraud or political violence, then they have few opportunities to efficiently control our actions. The exception to this is the use of manipulation, a method of social control much more democratically available to the man in the street. The generalised availability of many methods of manipulation makes it the method of choice of social control in interpersonal relationships.

1.2.2 Institutional social control: Of course, institutions have access to many more resources than private individuals, and this gives them much greater access to all methods of social control. In this context, methods of institutional social control could be defined as, "those actions which permit a government or management to govern and bring about changes without interruption or opposition from those it governs or manages".

We find that there is a wide range of social controls available to modern governments and managements. Manipulation is just one of these methods.

The cocktail of methods of social control available to well organised governments and other well resourced organisations such as companies, gives these institutions a substantial advantage over the poorly resourced individual in society. The exception to this is where individuals form organised groups to oppose an institution.

1.3 Methods of Social Control

There are 7 basic methods of social control:

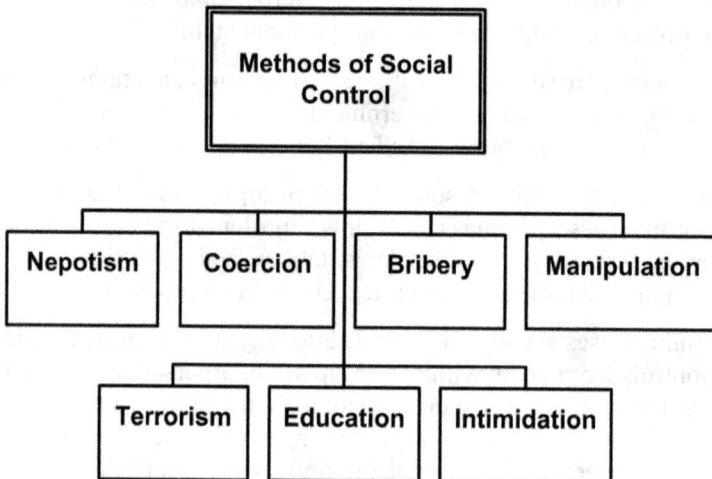

```
                    ┌──────────────────────┐
                    │  Methods of Social   │
                    │      Control         │
                    └──────────────────────┘
                               │
   ┌─────────────┬─────────────┼─────────────┬──────────────┐
┌──────────┐ ┌──────────┐ ┌──────────┐ ┌──────────────┐
│ Nepotism │ │ Coercion │ │ Bribery  │ │ Manipulation │
└──────────┘ └──────────┘ └──────────┘ └──────────────┘
              ┌────────────┬──────────────┐
          ┌───────────┐ ┌───────────┐ ┌──────────────┐
          │ Terrorism │ │ Education │ │ Intimidation │
          └───────────┘ └───────────┘ └──────────────┘
```

1.4 Modern concepts of social control: These days the main players in all forms of social control are governments, corporate entities, independent economic interests and to some extent, private individuals. How is social control manifested in modern society?

1.4.1 Government Control: The deterrence factor of the police and armed forces is coupled with the exercise of civil and criminal law and the bureaucratic functions of government. The iron fist in the velvet glove of government control is always physical violence, the threat of physical pain or material depravation.

At the same time, most governments, including Western democracies, routinely engage in state terrorism by violently interfering in the governance of other sovereign states. There is much evidence that they endorse or ignore the use of bribery in large scale energy and arms deals with other client countries. They interfere in the education of our children so as to sell their particular ideologies and they run their old-boys networks to cover it all up. There is a wealth of evidence to demonstrate all of the above.

1.4.2 Corporate control: In the corporate context we see social control manifested using company rules, disciplinary measures and the ultimate threat of dismissal. Corporate control operates on the basis of offering a limited set of material and social rewards to workers in return for compliance, whilst simultaneously threatening poverty and social exile for failure to comply.

1.4.3 Government versus corporate social control: Corporate and government controls can be complimentary or contradictory, depending on the political attitudes of the government. A strong government-led social security system offsets the primary corporate control of the threat of poverty because it offers an "economic safety net" to the unemployed. Conversely, corporate influence can undermine government policies by reducing investment, cutting jobs and diverting tax revenue to other jurisdictions. When such obvious conflicts of interests arise, the two "estates" respond by making accommodations to each other.

So, in modern Western states, the corporate and government classes have reached a cosy accommodation where the power of one is used to support the initiatives of the other. It is a dangerous combination of economic power and ideological pragmatism, with the civil populations in the middle and the outside world seen simply as an opportunity for plunder, personal, political or corporate enrichment.

1.4.4 Individual control: In interpersonal relationships a dynamic of control may exist where one or more individuals attempt to maintain dominance over one or more individuals. This can be something as formal as a boss-colleague relationship or as intimate as the relationship between married partners, siblings etc. Interpersonal control operates at a more emotional level where the rewards are acceptance, stability, love, respect etc. and the threats against non-compliance range from emotional rejection through material deprivation to physical violence.

1.5 Where does manipulation fit in to the scheme of social control?

Over the centuries, social control has changed and evolved in all cultures. In Western society not very long ago, it was quite rare to find someone who could read[1.1]. Now we have almost universal literacy. Less than 150 years ago, slavery was still being practiced by Western nations. Today forced labour has been almost entirely abolished globally. Examples abound which demonstrate the gradual "liberalisation" of the methods of social control and a move away from overt violence.

The art of government has been refined. Violence is now recognised as a last resort rather than the norm of day to day human and social management. Modern Western nations have thus gradually evolved away from the use of coercion towards the more subtle methods of manipulation and the use of incentives to manage their peoples.

Why has this evolution in methods of government happened? Well simply because it was realised that high densities of urban populations could no longer be controlled by the traditional feudal methods of violence or threats of violence. A better and more efficient alternative was needed - and manipulation was the obvious choice.

This isn't to say that manipulation wasn't always in use to some extent in the past. Indeed it was. Manipulation is as old as man himself and it was in constant use in personal life and in diplomatic activity between nations.

But its use as the mainstream method of domestic political social control is a relatively new phenomenon. Political manipulation is now the central pillar of Realpolitik and has become the single most important component of social control by modern governments.

In addition to their widespread use by governments, manipulative methods are also highly available to all of us. Every one of us has suffered from and probably used some manipulative action sometime in the last 24 hours, and we probably experience manipulation first hand even more frequently than this.

The use of manipulation at all levels of society is now endemic and is actually becoming even more widespread as new uses and new methods of manipulation are discovered and deployed.

---oOo---

2. Manipulation - a new method of control?

2.1 Preamble: So what are the moral and physical implications of this new found method of social control in our daily lives? To answer these questions, we firstly need to understand exactly what it is we are discussing when we talk about "human manipulation". The following is an attempt to dissect the concept by asking the fundamental question "What is manipulation?" To fully explore this topic we have further divided the subject into the following sub-questions and topics:

- A definition of manipulation
- Perceptions of manipulation
- A history of manipulation
- Who manipulates us?
- The effects of manipulation
- What makes manipulation possible?
- Classifying Manipulative Methods
- Evolution of Manipulation
- Human Frailty and manipulation
- Why is manipulation useful?
- Why is manipulation now so prevalent?
- Can manipulation be managed?

2.2 Towards a definition of manipulation: Manipulation is a difficult concept to define clearly and completely. A cursory search of the internet elicits a wide range of perceptions of manipulation ranging from discussions of control freak boyfriends to stories of CIA help with Pinochet's torture chambers. The word is laden with emotion and its meaning varies greatly from person to person and between different social, ethnic, psychological and political cultures and individuals.

Some people would be very insulted to be labelled as "manipulative" and yet to others it would be considered a badge of honour. Some of our contemporary politicians and industrialists make no secret that they consider manipulation an absolute necessity and a valid method in government and business. Others see manipulation as one of the greatest evils of modern capitalism, a source of immorality and a social disease.

When we take some of the emotion out of the word, then the concept of manipulation does start to become a lot more understandable and mundane, more like something that all of us have actually experienced or done ourselves to some extent.

The word has strong connotations in all parts of our society. It is interesting to make a small list of how the public might define manipulation based on a simple, random internet search of the word, just to get a feeling for the differences in perception of manipulation. It is interesting to note that some of these definitions are quite complimentary about manipulation, whereas others are morally damning:

- "Exerting shrewd or devious influence especially for one's own advantage"

- "A behaviour that a person may use in order to get their way... they may say certain things or behave in a certain way as to make someone give them what they want."

- "The difference between persuasion and manipulation lies in: 1. The intent behind your desire to persuade that person, 2. The truthfulness and transparency of the process, and 3. The net benefit or impact on that person"

- "Artful, expert, or skilled handling of an implement or situation"

- "Creating a false or misleading appearance to deceive."

- "Skilful or artful management"

- "Control freaks manipulate and pressure others to change so as to avoid having to change themselves, and use power over others to escape an inner emptiness. When this pattern is broken, 'the controller feels utterly powerless'.

- "In a manipulative event someone else always succeeds, voluntarily or not, to influence you to behave in a way that meets their needs and not yours."

- "Manipulation sometimes operates in a roundabout way, to the detriment of the original and real contact between the victim and the manipulator."

- "Manipulation may also be defined as 'the secret exertion of influence or the imposition of rules by an outside source which would normally be unwelcome to the victim'."

- "In a modern industrial management regime the definition of manipulation can be broadened to include 'the art of secretly setting objectives for an organization and its employees and using covert methods to achieve those objectives, regardless of whether they are contrary to the putative will of others.'"

- "Manipulators seek to make a devious act of trickery seem like a simple act of gentle persuasion."

It's pretty clear from just this small sample that "manipulation" means quite a lot of different things to different people. Some of these definitions see manipulation as totally repugnant whilst others look upon it as almost a virtue, for yet others it can be seen as just a necessary evil.

In fact all realities are partially true. Manipulation can be used as a tool for good in the hands of a benefactor but it can transform into an evil weapon in the hands of a self-seeking profiteer. The use and outcomes from a manipulative act range from benign and good to vicious and evil. Historically, manipulation has been both a subject of human advancement and a source of appalling human misery.

But, let us not confuse the morality of manipulation with the outcome of a manipulative action. We will discuss the morality of the manipulative technique later on.

2.2.1 Perceptions of manipulation: Mundane and Profound: In order to get closer to an understanding of manipulation we should separate the definition of manipulation into two basic sub-definitions:

- **Mundane manipulation:** Actions of close associates, requiring less skill or resources to implement.

- **Profound manipulation**: Actions of external agents, governments, and business interests requiring serious skills and resources to implement.

2.2.1.1 Mundane manipulation: When some of us think about manipulation we have visions of clever politicians and strategists plotting our control. We imagine the personal effects of manipulation but we almost always attribute the manipulative plot to some faceless, clandestine, monolithic secret state organisation such as the KGB, CIA or MI6 etc.

In reality, most manipulation is rather commonplace. Governments and corporations do manipulate and sometimes with appalling consequences. But we should remember that most manipulation is actually the work of people and organisations much closer to home, for instance our employers, local authorities, supermarkets and yes, even our friends and family.

So whether we are in the office with our colleagues and boss, in the local shop picking up the groceries, or even with our own family and friends, we can actually quite easily find ourselves in a manipulative trap. Regardless of the participants, we will experience all the adverse effects that manipulation involves with all the effects that this has on our own plans, our relationships and our self-respect.

Examples of mundane manipulation:

- At the office, a colleague does not give you enough time to complete the report that you are working on for that important meeting tomorrow. Alternatively, you are given a poorly defined, low quality task to complete before tomorrow. Either way you are angry and stuck for time. However, your colleague is charming and humorous and you feel your anger is disarmed.

- You are unhappy at work and you want to discuss your problems with your boss's superior. Your immediate boss reacts immediately by saying that if you're not happy, he can put someone else in your place and that many people would be happy to have your job. Under these veiled threats, you decide to keep your mouth shut.

- At the supermarket your child starts screaming because he wants something he is not allowed. Drained by the torrent of tears and under pressure from the dirty looks of the other customers (who wonder why you are torturing your child and are perhaps thinking of complaining to the children's department about your cruelty), you cave in and give the little fellow what he wants.

- During a regular visit to an elderly parent you have to listen to a litany of complaints about how lonely they are, and to constant mentions that their elderly neighbour gets daily visits from their kids. The conversation implies that everyone would be much better off if the ageing mother or father departed from this world. Despite your initial good intentions, you start to feel guilty and unhappy. You decide to visit your elderly parent again that same evening or the next day, putting aside any of your existing obligations.

2.2.1.2 Profound manipulation: Generally speaking, the most serious forms of manipulation occur at a political or commercial level where manipulative influences are exercised on large groups of people or over entire populations. We refer to these actions as "profound manipulation".

These profound forms of manipulation are ambitious. They operate on a vast scale and they seek to alter popular views about political policy, military actions, consumer products, politicians themselves and even our moral attitudes.

Generally, the manipulators in these cases do not know their victims, the manipulators are normally very well financed in comparison with their victims and very often the manipulator is quite anonymous. Generally, the victim is a large group, up to and including whole cultural groups such as "Western Christendom".

Examples of profound manipulation:

- **Kristallnacht**: Over a period of several years, the works of Joseph Goebbels, the Nazi propagandist, convinced huge numbers of ordinary German citizens that many of their troubles were the fault of Jewish control of capital. The manipulation was so convincing that the Nazi party effectively controlled the fate of the country's Jewish population simply by calling upon the general population to punish or attack them.

  These attacks actually happened continuously over several years but culminated in the infamous Kristallnacht. On this night in 1938, scores of synagogues where burned and hundreds of Jews were assaulted and murdered by German citizens and Nazi members. Goebbels' pathological hatred for Jews and communists drove his propaganda efforts over the years. It led finally to the horror of the mass murder on an industrial scale of millions of Jews, communists, gypsies and political enemies of the Nazis, transported from the whole continent of Europe to the Nazi death camps. Sociologists still ponder how it was possible for the beliefs of almost an entire nation to have been so effectively manipulated as to allow such atrocities to occur.

- **Dresden:** The Nazis were not the only masters of political manipulation. The Allied forces in the Second World War were also highly adept at manipulating public perception of their own war crimes. The deliberate bombing of civilian areas of Dresden in February 1945 when 1200 US and UK bomber planes dropped 4000 tonnes of high explosive munitions on a civilian city was one such crime. The firestorm which resulted destroyed an urban area of 40 square kilometres. Critics noted that Dresden was not important as a military target and indeed few of the infrastructural or industrial targets of the city were hit. It is more likely that Dresden was targeted by the Allied forces because it was a culturally important German city whose destruction would weaken German morale and reduce support for the war effort. The vast majority of the 20,000 people killed in the raid were German civilians.

  This act and the bombing of Hiroshima and Nagasaki are generally considered to be Allied war crimes. However, "the winner gets to write the history" and all of these acts of Allied barbarity have been air-brushed away and re-branded as "necessary acts of defence". Today they are of interest just to the intellectuals who know the truth. The "Allied" public has been largely convinced of the justification for these and other illegal and immoral acts of their governments in this and other wars.

- **Iraq / Afghanistan:** The lead up to the invasion of Iraq in 2003 was a piece of manipulative stage management that failed for the British government of Tony Blair and the US regime of G.W. Bush. Despite this failure to manipulate public opinion, the results of their actions left at least half a million dead in Iraq and Afghanistan, mostly civilians.[2.2]

The final justification of the UK's involvement in the war was a fabricated report of the existence of Iraqi weapons of "mass destruction". The dossier of "intelligence" used by Tony Blair to get the support of the British parliament later proved to be almost completely fabricated.

Despite having retired from public life, many people are still expecting that Bush, Blair et al will stand trial for their war crimes.

The tragic repercussions of the Iraq war and the Afghanistan debacle can be seen with Iraq now under the influence of its neighbour Iran, both militarily and politically. An unintended consequence of the Iraq war was the unleashing of a huge number of battle hardened guerrilla fighters for various anti-Western Islamic causes. Today Iraq barely functions as a modern civil state with the victims of this misguided adventure being ordinary Iraqi civilians. In Afghanistan, meanwhile, the US and allied soldiers are counting down the days to departure, leaving the population at the mercy of the feared Taliban again.

Meanwhile, the manipulation of the public was so poorly managed by Bush and Blair's governments that public opinion in Europe was and is almost entirely negative about both military campaigns. Many citizens see these acts of war as having impoverished their own countries and the relationship between the USA and Europe descended to a historical low at that time. In last ditch attempts to hold onto public support, both parties attempted some of the most bizarre manipulative stunts in modern history, like blaming Al Qaeda for supporting Iraqi resistance. This is an accusation akin to suggesting that Ian Paisley was guilty of financing arms supplies for the provisional IRA.

Premature withdrawal from both theatres was finally demanded by the elected representatives of both USA and UK as the Bush-Blair manipulative plot became so "thin" as to become totally absurd.

Despite the manipulative, upbeat messages of "Mission accomplished" which echo from the wastelands of Afghanistan and Iraq, the public knows that they have been fed a pack of lies on an enormous scale by a pair of the world's most inept, incompetent (and criminal) manipulators.

Had it not been for the tragic volume of bloodshed and horror caused by the Bush-Blair monster partnership, the entire affair would have made a good script for a 19th century comic opera - a comedy of errors!

2.2.2 Approaching a final definition for manipulation: Let us move on from these descriptions of manipulation to a more sophisticated, linguistically tighter, less emotional, and more functional definition of manipulation.

Based on some of the above observations, the following is a possible definition:

-   Manipulation is a strategy or manoeuvre, which gives rise to a plan and an action, which may be voluntary or involuntary.

-   The strategy will include a manipulator who consciously and deliberately develops and implements a plan and an action.

-   The manipulator seeks a change in the behaviour or attitudes of a victim.

-   The manipulator always benefits from the manipulative action.

-   The strategy can target a single victim, a group of victims or multiple groups of victims.

-   The results of a manipulative action may be positive, negative or neutral for the victim.

-   A victim is defined as someone who is manipulated without noticing that he has been manipulated, i.e. their behaviour or attitude has been altered by the manipulator without the victim being consciously aware of it.

-   Emotionally, a manipulator objectifies a "victim" and generally keeps a long-distance relationship with them.

-   A manipulator cannot maintain intimate contact and a relationship with a victim because trust and intimacy are irrevocably compromised by the act of manipulation.

-   Many conscious manipulators have problems with relationships because they fear for their own vulnerability. Manipulators tend to prefer "control" to "symbiosis".

2.2.2.1 Separating real manipulation from "conspiracy theories": There is a very important distinction between manipulation and conspiracy theories, namely, provability. Manipulation in modern society is very much a demonstrable reality and not a theory.

A manipulative action is something which we all experience and practice almost every day of our lives, either in a passive, morally neutral way or sometimes in a more malicious manner. Manipulation is a tangible phenomenon with an almost infinite number of facets. It is very much alive and kicking in modern society, politics, and commerce and indeed throughout all human organisations and institutions. It can be observed from the living room to the cabinet office, from the king's palace to the shop floor and the works canteen. It knows no political boundaries and it is used by socialists, capitalists, believers, atheists and anarchists, everyone in fact.

In other words manipulation is the universal method of choice for non-violent social control. This fact sets the study of manipulation aside from an analysis of conspiracy theories.

A conspiracy theory: On the other hand, a conspiracy theory may actually be true to some extent. We do not know how true until the conspiracy theory is fully proven and it enters into the main body of human history or it is finally proven to be false and hence discarded. We do know that conspiracy theories are often constructed as ad hoc hypotheses to explain personal or political motives or to fill gaps in our knowledge with possible answers. Conspiracy theories are a symptom of a popular lack of trust in political institutions. Often this lack of trust in politicians originates in political chicanery and secrecy rather than any actual misdeeds.

Conspiracy theories tend to arise when political elites refuse to deliver the truth to the general public. The public smells a rat and the public space between people and their politicians rapidly becomes fertile ground for endless theories about what "really happened".

It is understandable that such theories should be constructed in the absence of actual facts. Indeed it is a fascinating subject and sociological phenomenon. However, it is not the subject of this book.

2.2.3 Essential conditions of manipulation: There are several conditions which must be fulfilled to define an action truly manipulative:

-   Deception: The victim must not be aware of the manipulative part of the plan or action. Some parts of the action may be visible but not all.

-   Absolute secrecy and the anonymity of the manipulator are essential. In political terms this anonymity is often referred to as "deniability".

-   The victim must understand much less about the manipulation than the manipulator.

-   Manipulation relies on a victim's inability to recognize and avoid the manipulative action.

-   A manipulative action must be too "expensive" for the victim to recognise, avoid or overturn. "Expensive" refers to economic cost or cost in terms of time or other resources.

- The effects must be contrary to the putative will of the victim.

- The conscious manipulator must be capable of disregarding the moral quality of the modus operandi he uses. He cannot be swayed by short-term moral considerations.

2.3 Perceptions of manipulation: There are a lot of misconceptions about manipulation. Despite its relatively long and colourful history, the subject still remains a bit of a mystery to most of us. Here are a few perceptions of manipulation which many of us have:

- Manipulation is something that we all know exists, that we discuss sometimes, and that we all know is used by powerful forces in government and commerce to get their own way.

- Few of us know really how or why manipulation works.

- Few of us know how to avoid manipulation.

- Most of us see manipulation as just something we should ignore, try to avoid, or just have to put up with.

- For most of us, manipulation is nothing for "us", ordinary folk, but something for "them", the ruling classes. Most of us are unaware that we are personally engaged in some form of low level manipulation almost all the time.

2.3.1 Misconceptions about manipulation: There are many popular misconceptions about manipulation. Here are a few of the most common:

- **Manipulation is exclusive:** Most interesting is the perception that manipulation is exclusive to the powerful. The reality is quite the opposite. In fact, manipulation as a method of control is absolutely democratic. It is certainly not confined to the upper echelons of government or society. It is an endemic form of behaviour available to everyone in some form or other and is in frequent use by most of us on a daily basis.

- **Manipulation is rare:** In modern society, we all manipulate and we are all manipulated on a daily basis. Government and political manipulation is a constant backdrop to our lives: Wars are justified, cigarettes are banned, trials take place in secret, documents are hidden, deals and alliances are made behind closed doors all of the time.

- **I would never manipulate anyone:** In personal or professional life we are all guilty of some level of manipulation. We bitch about a colleague at work without even realising that we are in fact engaged in an exercise to deliberately alienate our work mates against the victim, whilst simultaneously establishing stronger emotional bonds with our co-conspirators. We manipulate our spouses and family in all kinds of subtle and often unconscious ways to maintain the peace or progress a particular personal or family cause, often in the interests of the greater good. Despite the intentions, all these acts may well be manipulative.

- **No-one understands it very well:** In business manipulative management has been warmly adopted in the commercial world from the advertising department, human resource management to the board room. Manipulation now permeates all human relationships both in the workplace and in the home. Books are written about how to manage the "control freak" bosses and husbands. Colleagues vie against each other for recognition, kudos and promotion at work. Our children leverage us with emotional blackmail to buy them the latest gadget which in turn has been sold to them by the beguiling wiles of the marketing department of some faceless mega corporation.

- **It's just a passing phase:** Social media define a new arena of manipulative activity where we struggle to have more "friends" than our friends, where we strive to create positive impressions of our rather tedious existence in order to gain status.

  Everywhere we look today we can see the manipulative method at work: covert actions by unknown players to achieve undiscovered objectives by the implementation of hidden agendas. And we are all somewhat guilty of this. There is no sign of manipulation going out of fashion anytime soon.

2.4 A history of manipulation: The subject of manipulation is so morally overloaded that it's difficult to give an objective history which works for everyone.

If we mean to define a history of political manipulation in the sense of modern political chicanery, then manipulation is a relatively new phenomenon, beginning (in Europe) at the time of the great classical empires. Cases and anecdotes abound of manipulative activities in ancient Rome and Greece[2.1]. After the decline of Rome's influence, manipulation in government begins to be noted again with the spread of feudal systems of government only from the 11th century onwards.

However, if we broaden the concept of manipulation to include the use of any covert influences to achieve any hidden objectives, then the history of manipulation is as old and continuous as mankind itself. Humanity has always been manipulative to some extent whenever it was appropriate in a situation, whether at a personal or tribal level.

2.4.1 Historical influences: Two factors which have influenced the use of manipulation and made it more widespread is the advent of urban living and the relative decline in the use of violence.

In less delicate days, leaders and governments got their own way and enforced rule at the end of a sword. Tribal rulers were absolute and had no need for subtleties like manipulation. Any deviation from their "law" met with instant violence.

Over time, and with the advent of feudalistic government, more subtle means were required. This was not only for government but also for managing relationships with other governments and other members of the aristocracy of a particular fiefdom. These people were often the extended family of a ruler where the use of violence might have created more problems than it solved.

The real beginnings of systematised political manipulation would seem to be best remembered in the works of Niccolo Machiavelli who made the first attempts to formally define the manipulative sub-plot of how to be an effective "Prince".

2.4.2 Machiavelli and the manipulative Renaissance: Machiavelli was one of the first to recognise that government didn't necessarily need violence in order to be effective. He understood the full range of social control techniques available to his employers yet Machiavelli felt coercion was generally a poor tool of government for political control. He dedicated his infamous work "The Prince" to explaining his vision of prudent, less violent government by clever manipulation.

For Machiavelli the diplomat, the use of violence was a crude, primitive, expensive and unnecessary means of control, especially when applied against the masses. Machiavelli recognised that state-sponsored violence tends to generate popular resentment, which in turn destabilises government. This was a revolutionary concept to his post feudal landlords.

However, Machiavelli also makes the proviso that it is important occasionally to exercise the ruler's right to use force, but strictly on a short term and finite basis. The same goes for intimidation. Machiavelli had no moral objections to the use of violence, bribery or nepotism in government, but he didn't think that those who resort to these methods deserved the same admiration as rulers who rely on more subtle techniques. Despite his relatively non-violent approach to government, Machiavelli was still condemned as immoral and duplicitous. It's just as well he didn't advocate the much more common feudal methods of government in his writings like the rack and the garrotte, which were the daily tools of his bosses for maintaining their authority.

So why was Machiavelli so inclined to recommend manipulation instead of the more traditional methods of war, bribery, torture and (threats of) violence?

In Machiavelli's day, education amongst the masses was non-existent or very poor at best. It centred largely on religious indoctrination. Any education which did exist was actually just propaganda used to promote the church or the family of the princes that ruled the wealthy city states of Italy. The masses were largely "putty in the hands of their princes" with church and state working in tandem in a relatively affluent environment.

The renaissance was in full swing in Europe when Machiavelli was a diplomat for the Borgia and Medici families. There was a sense that in the wealthy and sophisticated urban setting of Florence, the traditional tribal violence was somehow out of place. It somehow lacked the intelligence and subtlety of "scientific government".

So, along with the flat earth beliefs and a bunch of other superstitious nonsense, the concepts and methods of government began to undergo a gradual but thorough revision.

One result of these revisions (apart from the Protestant Reformation) was Western Europe's first attempt at a definition of civil government. This was manifested by Machiavelli's literary attempts in "The Prince" and "Discourses" to define a more effective means of government which did not necessarily always include the rack, the cannon or the sword.

2.4.3 From Machiavelli to the industrial revolution: In a discussion of political history it's hard to say with certainty when a particular political development actually came to fruition and when a new set rules of government came into effect. Gradually, after the upheavals of the Renaissance and Reformation, the rules of civil government began to change.

Many feudal governments (and managements that behave in a feudal way) still exist in the world today. But it is possible to say that in the Western world at least, the political methods advocated by Machiavelli have come to be almost universally adopted.

The use of gratuitous violence by governments has been reduced to a minimum. For most ordinary people, state violence has all but disappeared, except on the rare occasions when it is used to reinforce the ultimate military authority of the state. The trend towards manipulation rather than the use of brute force can be seen as rulers of developing nations also begin to adopt less coercive methods, preferring to use the media first and the rifle butt second.

Parallel political developments have also taken place in capitalist industry. Corporations in the more affluent industrial sectors don't talk in terms of "disciplinary measures" they talk "quality circles" and "worker participation".

There is an undoubted link between a high incidence of industrial unrest and the age and poverty of an industry. One doesn't hear of many strikes in the high-tech sector. Are the managers of these companies more conciliatory than their colleagues in the old, "smoke-stack" industries? Are the higher salaries in these new industries the only factor which keeps the workers quiet? Probably not. The reality is that the newer industries have also adopted newer and more effective manipulative methods.

2.4.4 Manipulation today: Today, our governments and corporations are almost entirely dependent on manipulation as a means of getting their own way. In business, manipulative techniques permeate marketing, human resource management, change management, regulatory affairs, training, and accountancy, to name just a few areas, from the lowest level to the boardroom.

In a similar way, governments now rely heavily on manipulative strategies to become elected, stay in power and implement their agendas. Even in the last 3 generations, the overt use of violence to control labour forces or civilian populations has declined dramatically and tends to be the action of last resort.

This doesn't imply that our governments or corporations are more "caring" or humane than they used to be. They have simply realised that they can be more effective using manipulation than sending in the riot squad.

Modern manipulative technique has become a hugely complex subject and a "must have" skill for managers and politicians. This fact alone makes it imperative that we all have a proper understanding of how manipulative methods actually work, and, if we object to them, how we can detect and avoid them.

2.5 Who manipulates us? The simple answer to this question is: Everyone. The use of manipulation is totally democratic. We can all use some form of manipulation against some other person or group in some particular circumstance. Indeed, we all do manipulate other human beings to some extent all the time.

2.5.1 Interpersonal manipulation: Naturally, not all manipulation is equally serious, either for the mortal soul of the manipulator or against the supposed will of the victim. It's a good bit more nuanced than that. There are several levels of interpersonal manipulation:

- **Low level subconscious:** Every sentence we utter is framed to convey lots of covert messages to the listener. It is linguistic manipulation which tailors our mode of communications to that particular listener, albeit sub-consciously.

- **Conscious:** Ascending from sub-conscious linguistic manipulation, we all constantly play interpersonal rhetorical games to achieve our objectives. These objectives may be quite innocent: trying to persuade someone of something or simply trying to create or maintain a good impression.

- **Deliberate:** Some people just can't help themselves and when they can't persuade us they consciously attempt to manipulate us. We have all been guilty of doing this at some time to some extent. But everyone knows that deliberate manipulation is dishonest, regardless of the motives, (which may be very good).

2.5.2 Institutional manipulation: Most private and public institutions are fully equipped for the manipulation of large numbers of people. These institutions range from government departments, commercial enterprises to NGOs.

Almost all organisations exist because they have an agenda they want to project to some other group of people. In all cases, manipulation is part of the core method of achieving this objective.

Here are a few examples of the areas where manipulation is used:

- **Government:** Preventative health advertising, public order and security policies, defence justifications, promotion of environmental responsibility, energy saving etc

- **Commercial:** Product advertising, corporate image management (PR), product safety testing, data management, corporate management of staff and other resources. Written works like "In Search of Excellence" and texts describing "scientific management" are laden with barely disguised manipulative techniques from worker incentive schemes to concepts of "worker participation" in management.

  The psychologists Maslow and Herzberg have had their interpretations of the hierarchy of human needs applied most often in the study and implementation of economic incentives and the exploitation of workers in industrial work situations. They are often the darlings of contemporary man-management "types".

- **NGOs:** Political parties, charities, research organisations, think tanks and lobbying groups all try to alter our opinions and behaviour in a way which is sympathetic to their own agenda. Charities make us pay by showing us distressing images, political parties may appeal to our fears, pride, patriotism, etc. to obtain our votes or money.

2.6 The effects of manipulation: Here is a description of some of the potential effects of manipulation:

- **Effects without limit:** The effects of manipulation are basically limitless. It has been used to start wars, to avoid wars and to end wars. Manipulation has cost millions of lives (a case in point is when Tony Blair manipulated the United Kingdom parliament and people into a war with Iraq based on a completely imaginary risk of weapons of "mass destruction"). This act ultimately cost between 500,000 and 1,000,000 largely innocent lives. We will never know the true number of lives lost because it wasn't "policy" in Iraq to count dead Iraqis.

- **Effects can be good or bad:** Manipulation has also saved probably millions of lives as well, as in the use of advertising to persuade people to stop smoking or to lead a healthier lifestyle. It has therefore also saved many people from enormous suffering as well.

  This dichotomy exists because the effects of manipulation are determined entirely by the moral quality of the manipulator. Evil intent brings evil consequences regardless of how the intentions are implemented and vice versa.

- **Being manipulated upsets us:** Because manipulation is mostly covert it tends to make us feel uncomfortable when used to alter our daily lives. This is an entirely understandable feeling.

  After all who likes the idea that we are being moved around by some external power like simple pawns on a chess-board? No-one does.

The increasing use of manipulation creates another effect; it generates a new imperative in the general public to understand how manipulation actually works. This alters the game somewhat because knowledge of the manipulative technique also reduces its power as a means of social control.

2.6.1 The changing face of manipulation: Look back at an early TV advert from the 1960s or a newsreel from British Pathé from the 1940s. These are great fun to look at and often hilarious. On the other hand, they are also a depiction of an incredibly naïve population when seen by a "modern viewer".

Even though most of us couldn't always precisely verbalise what is wrong with the content of these "documentaries", we would almost all see them as being pathetically manipulative in the most obvious of ways. Probably in 30 years time, our grandchildren will view our present naivety in a similar way.

2.6.2 Future view for manipulation: Projecting forward from the politically "savvy" public of today, we rapidly realise that a sea-change in our understanding of power is happening at the moment. In the Western world we are beginning to understand the vocabulary of power in a way which would have been unknown 50 years ago.

We talk about "control freaks", we are horrified by the manipulation of international inter-bank lending rates, we attack the economic establishment and the corrupt tricks of our politicians, and we use our own social networks to raise virtual revolts or gather millions of signatures in global petitions. We rail against "the system" in a way which is well-defined, organised and effective, in a way unthinkable in our parents' times.

At this moment there seems to be no let up in the use of technology to manipulate enormous numbers of the world's population. However, simultaneously, the human response to this manipulation is also quite impressive; using the same technological tools to discredit and debunk at least some of the manipulative elements facing modern societies.

2.6.3 Future responses to manipulation: More "liberal" government, together with the marketing magic of the Telecoms and IT industries have manipulated us into being totally "connected".

Not only has this brought enormous profits for these industries but it has also released a technological genie of enormous potency. Taken together with the increased use and understanding of manipulation, we, "the people", now have the power not only to use manipulation on our own account; we also have the global reach to apply it to anyone, basically anywhere.

Not only that, but we also now have the ability and knowledge to recognise and neutralise manipulation when it is being used to influence our behaviour. This truly is a game-changer.

So in a sense, the increased use of manipulation has actually begun to make the technique less effective. Manipulation must be partly covert to be effective. If everyone knows how manipulation works, we will constantly be on the lookout for it. It ceases to be covert and thus ceases to be effective.

In 50 years time, will our grandchildren find our adverts and news reports hilarious as well? Is the general public finally beginning to understand how its rulers and rich really work?

2.6.4 "Toxic" persistence: On the subject of manipulation, there is one characteristic which seriously sets it aside from other methods of social control and that is that many manipulative methods tend to be self-perpetuating. Unless consciously "switched off" by the manipulator, they just carry right on, manipulating us.

Whereas coercive methods of social control (police, army, spies, terrorists etc.) are expensive to maintain, manipulation is not. Whilst coercion is unlikely to be long lived, manipulation can be continued without the support of the original instigator at a very low cost.

For instance, consider the manipulative technique of "stating the obvious" in politics. Once an assertion has received the status of "obvious" by the general public, a precedent is set and the statement's status as self-evident is self-reinforcing. No-one ever bothers to challenge it.

Ritualism is similar, because as it becomes more widespread it actually increases and encourages further adherence to the system of beliefs from which it derives its power. Look at Scientology or Christianity for example.

This self-perpetuating property of some kinds of manipulation is a particularly worrying characteristic because it means that long after a manipulator has left the "scene of the crime", the practice or assertion he has passed off on his victims may remain operational, regardless of whether he or his incumbents benefit or not.

This phenomenon also makes recognition and isolation of a manipulator particularly difficult, because the manipulation can become a simple but relentless working of an anonymous and systemic bias. It ceases to be a conscious finite manipulative act of an individual or group. The manipulative payload loses its original reason and context but it continues to be just as toxic as ever. This is potentially dangerous stuff indeed.

2.7 What makes manipulation possible? The most important characteristic of a victim for the manipulator is that the victim must be unaware of the underlying manipulative action. As soon as a victim suspects something is happening, the game changes and sometimes the manipulative act must be abandoned partly or completely.

A potential victim with a good understanding of manipulative methods is fairly immune to many manipulative ploys. It's a bit like a householder who understands the mind of a burglar. Once you know what the burglar needs to be effective, you can do the necessary things to block their action. Generally a burglar can't be bothered with a house that looks too secure or dangerous and simply moves onto the next best opportunity. In a similar way, a manipulator looks for easy opportunities and will avoid a run in with a savvy, well-informed and cautious individual or group.

2.8 Classifying Manipulative Methods: There are several ways of classifying manipulation, depending on whether you are the manipulator, the victim, a sociologist or just a casual observer.

2.8.1 Classification by Opportunity, Accessibility, and Ease of Manipulation: Depending on the objective, the environment and the method of manipulation to be used, a manipulator needs to find an appropriate opportunity. This alters the accessibility of each manipulative method.

Manipulation can be divided into three more or less sophisticated types, ranging from simple, quite accessible "Tricks and Traps" such as deception to the more complex, less accessible "Human bias games" i.e. altering a victim's recollection, finally there is the very complicated, highly specialised "Complex manipulations" like statistical frauds.

Tricks and Traps: In the simplest of the three types, we see the manipulator using techniques like deceit, secrecy and simple language tricks to achieve his objectives. These are techniques which will pretty much work on any victim. The creation and delivery of a workable deceit on a victim is a relatively simple matter. These techniques work without any form of particular psychological weaknesses manifested by the victim. They are in common usage and they are effective against large groups or entire populations. Generally, these methodologies are highly available for use by any manipulator within their class (politician, government, manager etc) because they require less skill to execute than manipulations which rely on human psychological biases. This most basic form of manipulation is just a simple fraud or deceit requiring little skill.

Complex Manipulation: These methods take advantage of the difference in skills and technical knowledge between a manipulator and victim. In this complex form, the perpetrator needs very special skills to manipulate the victim and relies on the victim not having the skills to contradict the manipulative assertions. For example, statistical or scientific knowledge may be used to manipulate the public to use certain medications or treatments. The public is generally ignorant of statistics and lacking in specialist scientific knowledge and unable to contradict the claims of the manipulator.

Human Bias Games: In this most complex scenario, the manipulator relies on specific weaknesses in the cognitive processes of the victims. The method requires the targeting of a particular prejudice in the victim or a common cognitive weakness in either the entire population or a specific group. An alternative opportunity for the manipulator exists in the use of so-called human "heuristic errors". Heuristic errors are inherent failures in the mental "shortcuts" that we all use to process data quickly. These failings in common heuristics leave us open to external manipulation.

These underlying biases in human psychology are a complex mix of assumptions, logical errors, pre-conceptions, fear, greed, laziness, anxiety, tradition, ambition, egoism etc. Most of us exhibit some or all of these so-called "biases" which alter our beliefs or our decision making ability. The manipulator finds victims who display a particular psychological bias. He then uses this to deliver a "payload" such as a change in attitude, behaviour or decision of the victim.

A manipulator just needs to decide the most useful bias to employ against a particular victim. These methods require greater precision and complexity than the basic "Tricks and Traps" and are much more insidious. This is very much "expert level" manipulation.

2.8.2 Classification by Manipulative Environment: The following environments have their own appropriate methods of manipulation:

- Domestic-Personal

- Political and Social

- Corporate - Market

- Corporate - Employee

2.8.3 Classification by Mode of manipulation: A sociologist observing manipulative behaviour also creates various complex classifications of manipulation based on all kinds of criteria and we can classify manipulation in terms of motivation or the type of victim. One useful consideration when evaluating a manipulative action is to understand the mode of manipulation being conducted:

- Crowd manipulation

- Data manipulation

- Market manipulation

- Media manipulation

- Psychological manipulation

- Political manipulation

2.9 Evolution of Manipulation: There are many methods of manipulation but because it is normally a partly secret activity we cannot say for sure just how many sub-types of manipulation really exist. Manipulation is an ancient method of social control which has a complex hierarchy of methods and many hybrids of manipulative methods. It is also a rapidly evolving form, constantly morphing to adapt to technological and demographic changes in our world. The technological revolutions of our present time mean that new means of manipulation are being added to the traditional repertoire almost constantly.

2.10 Human Frailty and manipulation: Manipulators rely on inherent human weaknesses one way or another, whether it is our shortage of time, money, knowledge, skills or self-awareness. Apart from our ignorance, lack of time or resources, all of us are also victims to all kinds of cognitive and emotional weaknesses. These weaknesses are the stock in trade of the manipulator. Let us take a look at these biases / weaknesses.

2.10.1 Heuristics, bias and manipulation: Cognitive research has shown that we all use a large set of rules to interpret the world we live in and to make sense out of what we perceive to be reality. These rules are known as heuristics.

A typical "heuristic" would be the use of examples in a book like this. Here we have to describe abstract ideas. It's much easier to do that with an example. Examples work as a way to simplify and understand complex or abstract problems.

A practical instance would be when we see many stories about obesity in the newspapers. We might conclude that we are all becoming obese, simply because we can remember seeing many negative statistics on the subject.

Unfortunately, heuristics are not universal or universally reliable. In other words these rules of interpretation are sometimes bent or biased in a particular way. One particular memory bias means that most people tend to remember more bizarre data better than more mundane data.

There are three basic classifications of bias defined in sociological and psychological terms:

- Decision-making - Belief - Behavioural biases
- Social biases
- Memory errors and biases

These biases have different origins and effects:

- **Decision-making, belief and behavioural biases:** Many of these biases affect belief formation, material, business or economic decisions, and general human behaviour. An example would be the "wishful thinking bias" in which an investor believes his investment will rise in value because it would be "nice" if it did.

- **Social biases:** Social biases relate to how we interact in a social group. For example, the "in-group bias" is a tendency for people to give preference to other members of their own group, as when someone asks for a recommendation for a particular job. We tend to look to our own close circle of friends first rather than considering the suitability of contacts in our wider professional circle.

Social biases are considered to be types of "attribution bias". An attribution bias is the systematic error people make when determining the cause of a particular event. People constantly make attributions regarding the cause of their own and others' behaviours. However, these attributions do not always accurately reflect reality. Rather than operating as objective perceivers, people are prone to make perceptual errors that lead to biased interpretations of their social world.

- **Memory errors and biases**: A memory bias either enhances or impairs memory recollection (this is either the chance that a memory will be recalled at all, or the amount of time it takes for the memory to be recalled, or both), or the bias may alter the content of a reported memory. So, for instance, with the "Hindsight bias" we tend to see past events as being predictable, even though they weren't.

Cognitive and emotional biases: These biases above can be further classified as follows:

- Emotional bias
- Cognitive bias

2.10.2 Emotional bias: This is a distortion in cognition and decision making due to emotional factors. This means that a person will be usually inclined in the following ways:

- **Attractive**: To believe in something that has a positive emotional effect, that gives a pleasant feeling even if there is evidence to the contrary. Thus, we tend to believe that a friend has been successful because they are decent, intelligent, good hearted and have empathy. This idea is emotionally attractive.

- **Repellent**: To be reluctant to accept unpleasant facts that cause mental suffering. In this case we refuse to believe that a friend is successful because they have cheated, have deceived and have acted dishonourably. These are emotionally repellent.

These biases can be either individual or linked to interpersonal relationships or to group influences, such as when a group has a strong emotional attachment to a person, ideology or symbol.

Emotional biases are often very strong in patriotic or religious environments but the strongest emotional biases occur between members of a family or spouses.

2.10.3 Cognitive bias: This is a pattern of deviation in judgment that occurs in particular situations which may sometimes lead to perceptual distortion, inaccurate judgment, illogical interpretation, or what is broadly called irrationality.

Poor judgement: Implicit in the concept of a "pattern of deviation" or "poor judgement" is a standard of comparison with what is normal or expected. The definition of "normal" may be determined by people outside a particular situation, or it may be a set of independently verifiable facts, like the value of a stock on the stock exchange.

Heuristics: A continually evolving list of cognitive biases has been identified over the last decades of research on human judgment and decision-making. Some cognitive biases are presumably adaptive, because they lead to more effective actions in a given context or enable faster decisions when timeliness is more valuable than absolute accuracy. These biases are then referred to as heuristics: rules of thumb to allow us to function without getting bogged down in too much mental processing.

Other reasons for cognitive bias: Other cognitive biases can result from a lack of appropriate mental mechanisms (bounded rationality), or simply from a limited capacity for information processing. Here are some common causes of cognitive bias:

- **Bounded rationality:** This is the concept where a decision maker deliberately simplifies the available choices because they lack the ability and resources to arrive at an optimal solution. In this way a decision maker feels that they have achieved a satisfactory solution rather than the best solution. This occurs continuously in consumer choice. A consumer will often take advice or tips from friends and colleagues on what model of car to buy and, despite hard evidence from the car salesman that there is a better deal; the buyer will stick to their subjective decision.

  We see bounded rationality at play in the concept of "Adaptive bias" where decisions are based on limited information and a bias based on the costs of a decision being wrong. Similar equations of bounded rationality are found in other cognitive biases such as in the "Prospect theory" of losses and gains, where decisions are made on the basis of some concept of probable losses and gains from a decision. Again, we see it in "Mental accounting" where, people classify and evaluate economic outcomes. For instance people act differently when buying with cash or with a credit card because of some cognitive bias.

- **Attribute substitution:** Attribute substitution is a psychological process thought to be the basis for a number of cognitive biases and perceptual illusions. This is the process where a decision maker, faced with a complex, difficult judgment, unconsciously substitutes it with an easier judgment. It manifests itself, for example, when someone tries to answer a difficult question, and they actually answer a related but different question, without even realizing that a substitution has taken place.

Because of this complexity, the individual replaces the target attribute with a more easily calculated "heuristic" attribute. This substitution is thought to take place at an intuitive level rather than in a deliberate conscious substitution. This explains why individuals can be completely unaware of their own biases, and why biases persist even when the subject is made aware of them.

- **Attribution theory:** This concerns the way in which we attempt to understand our world by attributing reasons for events. These attributions can be explanatory attributions such as attributing our hangover to "bad beer". Attribution can also be related to interpersonal relationships, where we attribute certain behaviour to ourselves or others because we always strive to be seen in a positive light. For instance we may always blame our partner for starting arguments, when this is obviously untrue.

- **Naïve realism:** This psychological phenomenon is another reason why some cognitive biases occur. It is based on the "Three tenets of naïve realism" which state the following big assumptions. Clearly, these assumptions will give rise to some serious cognitive biases for anyone applying any of them to their world view:

  a. I am objective: I see entities and events objectively, as they are in reality. My social attitudes, beliefs, preferences, priorities, and so on follow from a dispassionate and unbiased view of the information or evidence available

  b. Everyone agrees with me: Other rational persons generally share my reactions, behaviours, and opinions so long as they have access to the same information as me, and provided that they too have processed the information in a reasonably thoughtful and open-minded way.

  c. Dissenters are ignorant, lazy, or biased: When an individual or group does not share my views, the reason can only be for one or more of the following three possibilities:

     o The individual or group has been given a different data set than me. In this case, provided that the other party is reasonable and open minded, the sharing of data will resolve this difference of opinion.

     o The individual or group in question may be lazy, irrational, or otherwise unable or unwilling to proceed in a normal way to deal with the objective evidence to reach reasonable conclusions.

- o The individual or group in question may be biased (either in interpreting the evidence or in proceeding from evidence to conclusions) by ideology, self-interest, or some other distorting personal influence.

- **Cognitive dissonance:** This is a powerful psychological phenomenon. The phrase describes the feeling of discomfort felt by a subject when simultaneously holding two or more conflicting cognitions: ideas, beliefs, values or emotional reactions. In a state of cognitive dissonance, people feel a "disequilibrium" which manifests itself as anxiety, frustration, hunger, dread, anger, embarrassment, guilt etc.

We all seek instinctively to avoid cognitive dissonance but this great desire to avoid can also lead to significant cognitive biases. For instance, a person who values financial security forms a strong emotional relationship with someone who is financially insecure and carefree on the subject. This creates a sense of discomfort in the subject which is a symptom of cognitive dissonance. In order to dissipate this dissonance, the subject will either have to rethink their attitude to financial security, their view of their partner's financial security or the future of their relationship.

- **Impression and self-perception management:** Our desire for acceptance within our group can drive us to try and manage the impressions we create and how we are perceived externally. These psychological processes can cause cognitive biases by altering our rational view according to the perceptions of ourselves which we are attempting to project.

- **Availability heuristic**: This is a source of various cognitive biases caused by a mental shortcut that occurs when people make judgments about the probability of events based on the ease with which examples come to mind. We can't always very quickly recall how certain actions and consequences are related. Some are more obvious and easier to recall than others.

The availability heuristic operates on the notion that, "if you can think of it, it must be important." In other words, the easier it is to recall the consequences of something, the greater we perceive these consequences to be. Obviously this is irrational but it is common nonetheless.

- **Representativeness heuristic:** We use this heuristic to make a judgement regarding the likelihood of an event or fact occurring by comparing it to an existing prototype that already exists in our minds. Our prototype is for us the most relevant or typical example of a particular event or object. When people rely on representativeness to make judgements, they are likely to make incorrect judgements; the fact that something is more representative does not make it more likely.

For example, if we know someone is a vegetarian, passionately interested in environmental politics and also a member of the Green Party, would we assume that they were more likely to work as a campaigner for an environmental NGO than for the civil service as a clerk? Most people would guess the person was an environmental campaigner whereas in fact it is much more likely that the person works for the civil service as a clerk. There are after all, many more civil servants than environmental campaigners.

Thus biases arise from judging probabilities on the basis of resemblance. We use the representativeness heuristic because it is an easy computation but the problem is that people often overestimate its accuracy in predicting the probability of an event.

- **Emotional influences:** Emotions play an important part in making decisions even when we think we are being totally rational and logical. Emotions often speed up decision making and indeed emotions can play a critical role in our ability to make fast, rational decisions in complex and uncertain situations. But emotions can also bias the quality of our decisions.

- **Introspection illusion:** This is a cognitive bias in which people wrongly think they have direct insight into the origins of their mental states while treating others' introspections as unreliable. This creates an illusion that we "know why we like the things we like and feel the way we feel". The reality is that the origins of certain emotional states are unavailable to us, and when pressed to explain these emotional reactions, we will just make something up. In certain situations, this illusion leads people to make confident but false explanations of their own behaviour or inaccurate predictions of their future mental states.

- **Misuse of statistics:** The poor application or deliberate misapplication of statistical methods gives rise to all kinds of cognitive biases. The simple 100% correlation between the sale of blankets in Toronto and the temperature in Paris could lead to all kinds of strange conclusions, except that there is no causal relationship. However absurd this example, this indicates just how easily the misuse of statistics can be a source of great cognitive bias despite an apparently scientific origin.

Most people are completely unaware of how statistical methods should be used. This ignorance opens up a huge range of possibilities for a biased understanding of data.

- **Innumeracy:** A poor understanding of numbers can lead to conclusions which are severally biased and unrepresentative. For example, we could headline a story saying "E.Coli counts in drinking water have increased by 400% in just 2 years".

That kind of alarming news could send the average citizen down to the supermarket to stock up on bottled mineral water. But taking a look at the numbers reveals that the headline is misleading because the arithmetic is poorly stated, perhaps for manipulative reasons. In fact, the number of E.Coli cases rose from 2 to 8 in 3 consecutive years. Yes, this is a 400% increase in 2 years. However, given the total national population is 55 million and the number of cases was just 8, the incidence is absolutely miniscule. Suddenly the headline fades into irrelevance. However, many people fail to examine or understand the basic arithmetic behind the headline.

2.11 Why is manipulation useful? If we remove the moral overtones, we begin to understand why manipulation is so very "useful" as a means of social control.

Manipulation can be perceived as "useful" for several reasons depending on whether you look at it as a sociologist or from the point of view of the manipulator:

- **Low Cost:** Manipulation is an efficient method of social control because it achieves its results with relatively low costs.

- **Low Violence:** Manipulation avoids more coercive methods and reduces political violence. It can achieve the same results with much less bloodshed.

- **High Deniability:** Many acts of manipulation are highly deniable. A carefully designed manipulation can be totally secret and can be almost completely covered up and made untraceable.

- **No Consequence:** Manipulation does not usually cause the often unpleasant consequences of coercion such as revenge against the manipulator.

- **Democratic:** Manipulation is a relatively democratic technique, by which we mean that many manipulative techniques are available to many or all of us. Many of us are already using these techniques in some way every day. Manipulation tends to "level the playing field" between those that have a lot of power and those that do not. In this sense manipulation supersedes coercion as a means of social control, and balances the disparity between powerful and powerless

2.12 Why is manipulation now so prevalent? The use of manipulation has increased rapidly in the last few decades. Why is this?

The twentieth century brought enormous social changes to Western society. Primarily these changes involved the concept of universal suffrage, a movement towards a more humanistic society, an increasing emphasis on democratic institutions and a popular demand for accountability.

Political violence still happens, but it occurs less and less within our own societies. Government has tended to become more "scientific", more targeted and more systematic. Their methods of government parallel the development of "scientific management techniques" initiated by Ford, Taylor and the other early 20th century industrial modernisers.

Political manipulation as a sophisticated means of government fits in nicely with the tendency to use more systematised methods in management. Corporate interests have mirrored the increased interest in manipulation as a means of achieving strategic objectives, although it's not entirely sure whether corporate interests lead governments or vice versa.

Either way, manipulation is now fully fledged as a politically "legitimate" method of government which most of our modern politicians, civil servants and managers don't even think twice about.

2.13 Can manipulation be managed? Yes, manipulation can be managed: recognised, neutralised, exposed, avoided and counteracted. Provided the potential victim does his homework and knows what to look for, manipulation is quite a recognisable and manageable phenomenon.

The first step in handling manipulation is for the victim to be able to recognise the manipulation for what it is, identify the manipulator and their objectives, and then understand what is actually happening to them.

This is a difficult "first step" because either most people can't be bothered to try to understand what is actually happening or many forms of manipulation are so secret, subtle and invisible that the victim hardly realises that anything adverse is actually happening.

Only if a victim realises that something unpleasant has just happened do they express any enthusiasm for taking action against the manipulator. By then it is usually too late.

In the management of manipulation, the most important principle is "pre-warned is pre-armed". It's a sensible attitude which is generally ignored by most of us.

Managing manipulation is all about being aware and responsible for what is happening to you. Many people in their busy lives have tended to abdicate this personal responsibility to some other "higher" authority such as their employer, or the government. Not a good idea.

---oOo---

3. The manipulative personality

According to most modern sociologists and psychologists, for manipulation to be successful the manipulator should exhibit the following attributes:

- An ability to conceal aggressive intentions and behaviour.

- Knowledge of the psychological vulnerabilities of the victim to determine what tactics are likely to be the most effective.

- Possess a sufficient level of ruthlessness to have no qualms about causing harm to the victim if necessary.

Consequently, manipulation is likely to be accomplished through covert aggressive means, (aggressive in the sense that it shows no empathy with the victim).

3.1 Manipulative behaviours: Understanding the many types of manipulation which exist and which manipulative methods we are most likely to suffer is helpful in reducing the potentially destructive power of the manipulator. This knowledge also helps us create less destructive relationships and encounters because it warns potential manipulators that we are not very suitable victims. Below we look at a model to describe active and passive manipulative personalities. It is particularly referenced towards interpersonal manipulation, but actually, with just a little imagination, the model also works perfectly well for institutional manipulators and their victims.

Active-Passive Model: There are several definitions of manipulative behaviour but here we will present the model developed by Shostrom. He distinguishes between active and passive manipulators and presents eight kinds of manipulators, four in each category:

Active manipulator: The active manipulator is characterized by an active search for victims. The maintenance of control by an active manipulator must be defended at all costs. This type of manipulator "victimizes" others, and takes advantage of their weakness. The active manipulator finds gratification in the free exercise of control over others.

The four personalities of active manipulator identified by Shostrom are:

- The Dictator
- The Judge
- The Bad and Brutish Type
- The Calculating Type

Passive manipulator: The passive manipulator on the other hand seeks control through passive methods using subversive means. Passive manipulation is designed to never offend the victim and as a technique is more often more successful. The four personalities of the passive manipulator are:

- The Victim
- The Defender
- The Kind and Amiable Type
- The Dependent Addict

The relationship between manipulative types: You'll notice that each active type has its corresponding passive type and vice versa. It is interesting to examine how these opposite personality types are related. An active manipulator of a certain type will often seek out a victim of the opposing passive kind. The same is true in reverse: a passive manipulator, like a "victim" in a controlling marital relationship who casts the spouse as the "dictator", manipulates him or her by subversive means. The diagram below helps us to locate and view these manipulative behaviours and their active or passive complementary behaviour.

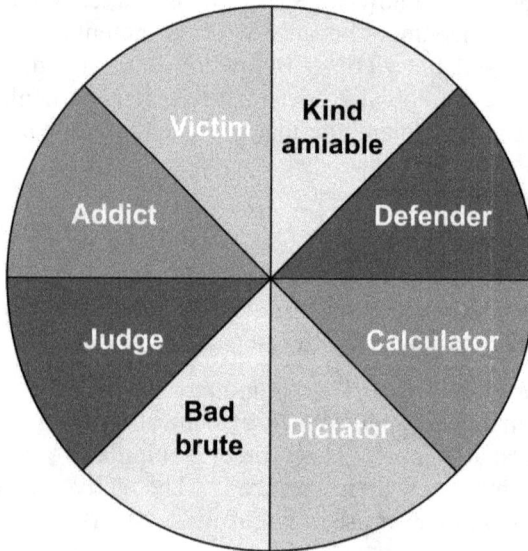

3.1.1 The Dictator and the Victim: While the dictator exaggerates their power, the victim embellishes his or her weakness and sensitivity.

The dictator dominates and gives orders like some spoiled and abusive "child king". They can usually provide extensive references to support their arguments and they claim to speak with high moral principles. A dictator will do anything to control their victim.

The target, usually a victim of the dictator, forgets things, does not seem to listen, but quietly collects these injustices and injuries, about which they can and do speak extensively to outside observers. They will do anything to make the other person appear responsible for their situation as the victim.

3.1.2 The Calculating type and the Dependent addict: The calculating type exaggerates his control while the dependent inflates his addiction and dependency.

The calculating manipulator flatters, lies, and constantly tries to deceive their victim to gain their control. They will claim that the target person is "really the only one who understands me", or "really understands my case".

The target "dependent" will seek to inspire constant pity and a need to be helped, supported, guided and perhaps manipulated. In this way, they will let others do their work for them. The calculating type can be a pressure salesman, a seducer, a gambler or a blackmailer. The addict can be parasitic, eternally childish, a hypochondriac, a helpless individual or a whiner.

3.1.3 The Brutish and the Kind: The brutish type exaggerates aggression, cruelty, and rudeness whereas the kind, amiable type embroiders warmth, love, and kindness.

The brutish type intimidates, and makes direct or implied threats of the kind: "Do not let me down, everything depends on you!", "don't forget, there are plenty of others who would like to be in your position!"

The amiable subject, however, kills by kindness and always wins when it comes to a conflict with a brutish type. "How can he do that? He is such a nice guy!" The Brute can be hateful, spiteful and mean. The amiable type is always non-violent, implies nothing, and is virtuous and inoffensive.

3.1.4 The Judge and the Defender: The judge exaggerates his critical side, is wary of everyone, morally condemns all guilt, bears a grudge and is slow to forgive.

The defender has an inflated supportive and protective attitude and never judges. Even when there is guilt, the defender is sympathetic to the cause of the guilty and even suffers with them. Without the defender, who knows what will happen? The judge knows everything, dishes out blame, gathers resentments and takes an uncompromising moral position.

The defender is a saviour, a martyr, a carer, is embarrassed and hurt for others and the guilty are all in debt to the defender: "After all I've done for you ..." The defender would rather deal with the needs of others than take care of his or her own.

3.2 Role of Manipulators: Apart from the more esoteric definitions of the psychology of manipulative personalities, we also need to qualify the executive role of potential manipulators.

To avoid or manage manipulation it is important to recognize the source of manipulation. This is important because manipulation may not necessarily originate from the agencies by which it is implemented. This is because manipulators often use proxies to act on their behalf. Thus, manipulators roles can be divided into Prime-Movers and Proxy-Manipulators:

Many manipulative techniques employ proxy operators to guarantee the security of the prime-mover. This makes recognition difficult because proxies may be acting in good faith, and it makes avoidance difficult because there may be a number of proxies acting apparently independently, whilst being orchestrated by the prime-mover - the real manipulator.

3.3 Popular justifications for manipulative behaviour: We might argue that in the case of a government the use of manipulation is so immoral as to be unacceptable, but we may wonder if it is really that deplorable or dangerous at street level amongst ordinary people.

One might also argue that everyone is manipulated to a certain extent, that we all manipulate each other to some degree and that, since it usually doesn't put us at the "receiving end" of violence, it is a more acceptable method of social interaction than coercion.

Is it more realistic to simply accept that it happens and will continue happening rather than taking a moral position against manipulation?

Evil intent: The answer to the apologist argument is to be found in the raison d'être of the manipulator.

The amount of power or range of manipulation which an individual is capable of exercising is totally irrelevant to the calculations he makes in deciding to manipulate. Whether he is a manipulative spouse, friend, union official, company executive or the Prime Minister, the same moral trade-offs take place.

The type of manipulation employed is also irrelevant. Whether a manipulator is rigging a board-room vote or deliberately ignoring human rights violations in an allied country is merely a function of the amount and area of power he commands.

The fact is that a decision to take advantage of a victim's weakness is only tested by its likelihood of success, and not by any moral code or humanist considerations. This is the real danger of the manipulative personality and sets aside a real manipulator as a sociopath.

The "manipulative type" who holds the rights of his fellow human beings in complete contempt and seeks to use, bully and control the weak simply to achieve his own objectives is always dangerous. They can never justify their attitudes or actions even when operating under the cover of being humane, "spreading democracy", or protecting the rights of others, like those poor Muslim women in Afghanistan, for example.

3.4 Are manipulators psychopaths? The answer to this is no, not everyone who manipulates someone else is a psychopath - otherwise every member of the Western media would have to be locked up for the sake of public safety.

On the other hand, many subjects who exhibit "psychopathic" personality disorders tend to use very subtle and effective methods of manipulation to achieve their objectives.

Therefore, the use of manipulation tends to be associated with psychopathic disorders and behaviour. This warrants a little bit more analysis because it tends to act as a moral and legal boundary between what are effectively harmless (subconscious) forms of manipulation and the more sinister form of manipulation which is much more deliberate and harmful.

3.4.1 The Basic manipulative strategy of a psychopath: Psychopaths are constantly on the lookout for individuals that they can swindle or manipulate according to the psychologists Robert D. Hare and Paul Babiak. Their view is that psychopathic strategy passes through three basic steps:

3.4.1.1 Assessment step: There are different patterns in psychopathic behaviour with regard to finding victims. Some psychopaths are opportunistic, aggressive predators who will take advantage of almost anyone they meet, while others are more patient. These latter will wait for the perfect, innocent victim to cross their path.

Some psychopaths enjoy a challenge while others prey on people who are vulnerable. In both cases, the psychopath is continuously sizing up the potential usefulness of an individual as a source of money, power, sex, or influence. During the assessment phase, a psychopath is able to determine a potential victim's vulnerabilities and will use those weaknesses to plan their manipulation.

3.4.1.2 Manipulation step: When a psychopath has identified a victim, the manipulation phase begins. During this phase, a psychopath creates a persona or "mask", designed specifically to "work" with that victim.

The psychopath may lie to gain the trust of their victim, and their lack of empathy and guilt allows them to lie with impunity; they do not see the value of telling the truth unless it will help get them what they want.

An interaction with the victim will then proceed. The psychopath carefully assesses the victim's persona. The victim's persona gives the psychopath a picture of the traits and characteristics valued in the victim. The victim's persona may also reveal to an astute observer, insecurities or weaknesses the victim wishes to minimize or hide from view.

An ardent student of human behaviour, the psychopath will then gently test the inner strengths and needs that are part of the victim's private self and eventually build a personal relationship with the victim.

The persona of the psychopath - the "personality" the victim is bonding with - does not really exist. It is built on deceit which is carefully developed to entrap the victim. It is a type of mask, one of many custom-made by the psychopath to fit the victim's particular psychological needs and expectations.

This victimization is predatory in nature; it often leads to severe financial, physical or emotional harm for the individual. Healthy, real relationships are built on mutual respect and trust; they are based on sharing honest thoughts and feelings. The victim's mistaken belief that the psychopathic bond has any of these characteristics is the reason it can be successful.

3.4.1.3 Abandonment step: The abandonment step begins when the psychopath decides that his or her victim is no longer useful. The psychopath abandons his or her victim and moves on to someone else. In the case of romantic relationships, a psychopath will usually seal a relationship with their next target before abandoning his or her current victim.

Sometimes, the psychopath has three individuals on whom they are working at the same time: the one who has been recently abandoned, who is being toyed with and kept in the picture in case the other two do not work out; the one who is currently being played and is about to be abandoned; and the third, who is being groomed by the psychopath, in anticipation of abandoning the current victim.

---oOo---

4. The Manipulated personality

4.1 The Manipulated Type: From the Shostrom model we can see how manipulative types can either be active or passive manipulators and how they can be roughly defined and stereotyped.

We learn that active manipulators have ideal corresponding victims and that these may in fact be passive manipulators. This archetype works well when talking about interpersonal manipulation. It is a useful model to generalise about manipulative behaviour and personality types but it doesn't tell the whole story about the personality of the victim.

What we don't see in the Shostrom model is how a manipulator operates in an environment where they do not necessarily find victims of a particular type. What happens when the manipulator is dealing with a mixed group or with the general public?

A manipulator relies heavily on the ignorance and naivety of the victim or victim group. So what characteristics of a victim does a manipulator need in order to be successful? We can grade potential victims' vulnerability as follows:

- **Extreme risk:** A victim with a delusional personality makes for an excellent subject in a manipulative plot. A victim that refuses to believe that they are being manipulated is perfect. Statements like, "I don't believe in conspiracy theories" is music to the ears of the manipulator, the more naïve the better.

- **Medium-High risk:** Ignorance of manipulation: If the victim or group is completely unaware of the concept of manipulation, this is ideal territory for the manipulator. A large part of the general public in Western Europe falls into this category

- **Medium risk:** Aware of manipulation as a political method, but lacking knowledge of the types or motivations for manipulation means these potential victims lack a detailed understanding of the mechanics of or avoidance of manipulation.

- **Low risk:** This type possesses an acute knowledge of manipulative techniques and is conversant with political and personal uses of manipulation. They understand some types of manipulation and reflect on their own use of manipulation and methods to detect and avoid manipulation.

4.2 Why do we let them manipulate us? There are several reasons why we permit manipulation:

- **Ignorance:** In many cases we do not know that we are being manipulated because it all happens in part covertly and also we have no idea at all that we have been manipulated, even after the event.

- **Harmless enjoyment:** Marketing constantly manipulates us to make us prefer one brand over another. Even though some of us know what is going on, few of us bother to resist the pressure and we all just play along. It is seen as harmless, and we have convinced ourselves that we are rational and above the influences of the marketers.

- **Apathy:** Our views of political manipulation are often similar to those we have of marketing. Most of us suspect politicians to be self-serving deceivers and tricksters. We don't know how exactly but we know that they are up to no good. But we don't have the time to understand what's going on and we can't be bothered to understand their squalid games. We respond by keeping our heads down, not getting involved, and making sweeping statements about "all politicians being the same".

- **Avoidance:** In interpersonal manipulation, we are often covertly manipulated. When the manipulation isn't very subtle, we tend to avoid those whom we know for sure are manipulating us, rather than confronting them. We may play the manipulation back to them but generally we just try to keep away from these people.

- **Lack of Energy:** The fact is that some people are less easy to manipulate than others, particularly those whose thresholds of discomfort or hopes are high. Personalities which are more energetic and sceptical tend to be much harder to manipulate.

- **Comfort seeking:** The person who cannot tolerate much discomfort or is less prone to rational examination of their circumstances will tend to react much more easily and more quickly to a manipulative approach.

- **Laziness:** A mentally lazy and uninformed personality, who is less likely to engage in self-analysis, is much more prone to manipulation than those who are more actively "alive" to the social dynamic of manipulation and their own weaknesses. The latter tend to smell a plot whereas the former often blindly walk straight into the traps that have been set for them.

- **Psychological weaknesses:** Manipulators often take advantage of weaknesses in our personalities (like cognitive biases, for example). Thus, if we feel vulnerable and lack self confidence, a manipulator can easily exacerbate our doubts and fears. Likewise, a manipulator can also play on our fears of being seen in a negative light by others. No one likes to be accused of being selfish, incompetent, ungrateful, greedy or any of a multitude of other sins.

- **Bribery:** Manipulators can also use positive incentives to manage our responses such as hope for some future reward.

- **Dependency:** We can generalise that manipulators tend to be effective when they cause discomfort or an unwanted emotion and/or offer a hope of reward. Indeed, becoming independent of external reward systems is often seen as a first step to becoming immune to the manipulator. After all, if a manipulator has nothing you want and cannot threaten something you already have, then there is little they can do to you. You cease to be a victim.

- **Emotional weakness:** In some cases, a manipulator expects an emotional advantage, like more attention, recognition, status, love or even some material benefit like career advancement, the granting of some objective goals or some other tangible rewards. The victim's motivation is avoidance of discomfort, unpleasant emotions or negative consequences. Perhaps he hopes for gain too.

In some cases we just allow the manipulation because it is the best of a bad lot. Small babies learn very quickly how this works and many a toddler extracts a rapid result at the supermarket checkout when he or she gives their mother the choice between tears and screams or mummy buying their favourite sweets The cost of the tears is much greater than the cost of the chocolate or loss of authority.

What we can see from the above is that those with little education, the poor, the weak are all more susceptible to the guiles of the manipulator. Conversely, confident, independent, well-informed and well-resourced people are a lot harder to manipulate.

---oOo---

5. The morality of manipulation

5.1 Preamble: The morality of manipulation: So far we have only discussed manipulation as an abstract method of social control in government, management and interpersonal relationships. We have concluded that it is universally available in various forms and that its use is widespread and increasingly common.

We now move on to consider the subject in a moral-ethical sense. We will try to decide whether manipulation is something which we should tolerate, encourage, accept, avoid or counteract. Is manipulation always intolerable or is it, perhaps morally tolerable in some cases but not in others?

The moral issues are complex and partly dependent on the moral position of the reader; therefore we will make only general statements about the morality of manipulation in specific circumstances and leave the exact moral judgements to the reader.

5.1.1 Conventional views: The conventional sociological conclusions about manipulation and morality go as follows:

-Manipulation is considered "benign" when the victim has an opportunity to pick or reject a manipulated choice. This implies that the choices are not totally obscured from us. Manipulation is considered "covert" when it uses hidden methods, has hidden intentions and allows only limited hidden choices. It may not be covert in all of these respects.

- Manipulation may be considered "benign" when the manipulator acts with high moral intention. Sometimes manipulation is seen as a short term, harmless and pragmatic way to deliver an otherwise completely altruistic package

- Manipulation may be considered "benign" when the manipulator does not profit or when the manipulator benefits less than the victim from a manipulation. This is the case when manipulation is seen as just a "short-cut" to some important social imperative rather than a conspiracy against a victim.

5.1.2 Benign and moral judgements: To come to hard moral conclusions we would have to define concepts like "benign" and "moral". We would have to set standards of moral judgement, perhaps against a humanistic or other code of morality. This is outside the scope of this book because like lots of other moral issues, it generates more questions than answers.

So we will leave out the hard conclusions about the ethics involved and we will just let the reader decide on the morality of a particular manipulative act.

We will content ourselves with a more functional decomposition of some of the more obvious moral issues.

5.1.3 Dismantling the moral issues: To gain a better understanding of the moral issues surrounding manipulation we have divided the subject as follows:

- Manipulation and its ethical components
- How "democratic" is manipulation?
- The value of freedom
- The value of choice
- The supremacy of the individual
- The exercise of power - Violence versus manipulation
- Does the outcome and scale of manipulation matter?
- Mitigation and qualitative differentiation
- Objectification of the victim
- The will to power: Fascism and manipulation
- Debasement of the manipulator
- Conclusions or more questions?

We have chosen the theme of anti-smoking campaigns to illustrate some of the complexities of the moral issues involved in manipulation in general. We could just as easily have picked anti-alcohol or anti-obesity campaigns.

These all involve governments in complex moral conflicts between the interests of their citizens, the state and various seriously influential capitalist lobbies like tobacco, food, pharmaceuticals and healthcare. In all of these scenarios the subject matter, motivation and manipulative methods used present a fertile ground for a discussion of the moral issues involved in large scale manipulation.

5.2 Manipulation and its ethical components: Manipulation contains two ethical components and it is important not to confuse the two issues:

- The morality of the manipulative act itself (regardless of consequences)
- The morality of the consequences of the manipulative act.

A manipulative act itself may encompass a whole range of human ethics, for example:

- We might persuade an elderly relative into moving in with us because it is "more economical and more convenient for the shops" rather than telling them that we are very worried about their ability to live alone. This is a deceit designed to achieve an objective without hurting someone's feelings. The manipulation here is very effective and the motives are entirely honourable.

- We can have quite devious and mostly covert forms of manipulation delivering benign objectives, such as public health messages. The government's Department of Health obliges health warnings on cigarettes and forbids soft-drinks machines in schools. They want us to avoid cancer and not be obese, partly because they want us to believe that they care about us, and partly because of the cost of handling these medical conditions. The manipulation here is quite obvious but we can never be quite sure about how honourable the motives are. We lack some important information about industry and healthcare lobbies.

- We can also have quite obvious attempts at manipulation which have very unpleasant payloads, for instance incitement to racial hatred. The right-wing press try to manipulate our attitudes to immigration to make us antagonistic to foreigners. Their poorly disguised racism has an evil intent and attempts to manipulate in an obvious and ineffective way.

5.3 How "democratic" is manipulation? It is a repugnant concept but manipulation as a means of getting one's way is also one of the most commonly available means of human interaction. It isn't just the preserve of the large corporation or the government spin doctor, it's also the domain of the colleague at work, the local shopkeeper, and even our friends, spouse and family.

These days, manipulation seems hard-wired into human social interaction and before we take a high moral position on the use of manipulation in our social interactions we must first honestly answer the question: "Have we ever engaged in an act of manipulation against an unsuspecting victim?" I think few of us could sincerely say that we have not sometimes manipulated someone, consciously and deliberately.

The next question we need to address is whether it is ever ethically justified to use manipulation.

5.4 The value and cost of freedom: The ethics of using manipulation is very much bound up with concepts such as honesty, individualism, honour, solidarity and respect for the freedom of our fellow human beings. It affects how we communicate and interact with our peers, our society, and our governments and how they deal with us as individuals. It concerns our perceptions of ourselves in society and how our society and peer group perceive us as individuals with free will, whether we have a fundamental right to control our own destiny or are we just pawns in a grand manipulative chess game? Let us just take a look at our "freedom" for a moment:

5.4.1 Are we free? Generally speaking these days, we consider ourselves to be physically quite free. And yet, a closer examination of modern consumer society in Western capitalist states reveals that we are bound almost as tightly as slaves by our legal obligations, our mortgages, our jobs, our family, our consumer "obligations", maintaining our material status in the world, and our feelings of responsibility to all of the above. Sometimes we even feel a responsibility to the anonymous state itself. Our debts and responsibilities, the threats of poverty and the promises of reward bind us in a web of intimidations and incentives where, for many of us, most of our personal choices are effectively emasculated.

5.4.2 The Stockholm syndrome: The Stockholm syndrome: We could argue that we are all free to walk away from all of this at any time. But in practice, few people are willing to abandon their families solely to escape the reins of debt and responsibility. This reluctance to escape is a reality, even though these responsibilities are obviously designed to entrap and manipulate us into being both "good producers" and "good consumers" for the greater glory of the capitalist system which most of us willingly endorse. To walk away from these "chains" has a cost and for most people, the cost of freedom is just too great. For many of us, the security of enslavement is preferable to the relative exile of freedom.

5.4.3 Capitalist manipulation - Consumo ergo sum: And so, on the subject of our enslavement, on we go, paying our mortgages, enriching the banks, driven by the debts of just having somewhere to live, consuming what they tell us to consume. We work, frightened for our future and our job, living a life divided into 3 equal parts of work, sleep and recovery. It's a narrow existence; largely designed and manipulated on our behalf and for many, the cost to escape is just too high. But the cost dynamic of freedom alters constantly and for some, the cost of sacrificing freedom becomes greater than the benefits of incarceration and they decide to abandon the game.

5.5 The value of personal choice: Manipulation isn't always intended to harm the victim. Encouraging a healthy lifestyle by taxing cigarettes and frightening the public with awful images of lung cancer are surely designed for our own good, aren't they?

Those horrific cancer pictures on your cigarette pack are quite clear in their message but are they telling us the whole story? Perhaps the images are just the obvious component of a more insidious underlying covert manipulation.

If the government is so concerned for our health, why then do army recruiting offices not have posters displayed outside showing young men with their entrails spilled on the ground after being struck down by bombs or bullets? Is there a difference between the risks of dying as a smoker or dying as a soldier? Well indeed there is, the per capita risks to a soldier are indeed much greater. But despite this, the images outside the recruiting station emphasise various attractive reasons to join the army, such as seeing the world and "having a job" and "having mates" (that have jobs).

Every potential soldier or smoker has the right to simply ignore this imagery. Hence this part of their manipulation may be considered benign in both cases, because the imagery is indeed true, attractive and may be disregarded.

The fact that as individuals we may stop smoking or that we may well have a happy, safe career in the army may make the manipulation seem benign. But it does not follow that therefore there is a high moral intention behind the machinations of our governments. On the contrary, it is pretty certain that the intentions of the manipulators are driven by self-interest.

The fact that army recruiters don't deliver honest images of the consequences of war means that quite obviously there is a malign, dishonest intention in the Army's recruiting strategy. They simply prefer to project images of happy, live soldiers with their "mates".

The fact that health ministries do actually deliver honest images of the consequences of smoking just means that they value these images for the purpose; it does not mean that the Ministry of Health is being sincere about its economic motives.

Concepts like "honesty" and "deceit" have no importance in such decisions. We are in the world of expedience not morality.

5.5.1 Goody-goody: Despite the apparently "good" intentions of the health authorities, it is worth noting that cheap and obvious forms of manipulation often have an effect which is entirely contrary to the manipulator's plan. Personally, nothing would make me more antagonistic to a no-smoking or healthy living campaign than the realisation that I was being manipulated. Many of us are inclined to behave in a rebellious way when confronted with "nanny state" interference at this level of personal responsibility. This often causes a manipulative plan to backfire.

5.5.2 Secrecy becomes the problem: Very often we manipulate as an alternative to telling the truth. We do this because we see the truth as a higher risk option than a secret manipulation. In the smoking campaign case referred to here, the real covert manipulation may be about reducing the per capita cost of medical care whilst balancing income from taxes on tobacco products. It is felt to be politically unacceptable to treat a population simply in an "actuarial sense", in terms of morbidity ratios etc. simply to optimise tax income from a killer drug whilst fine-tuning the drug's usage to maintain healthcare costs.

Indeed we may wonder why passive smoking is so strongly targeted by government campaigns. Is it because they are worried about us passive smokers or is it because passive smokers represent the worst of both worlds to the manipulative government? Passive smokers cost healthcare budgets a lot of money but passive smokers contribute nothing to tobacco taxes. Could our governments really be so cynical?

A more honest approach by our governments would be to come clean about the health and economic costs of our social habits in a straightforward way by referring smokers to authoritative documentation where they can read the research papers on the links between smoking and cancer and other diseases and give nicotine users professional help with their attempts to stop smoking. A truly benign act would be to ban tobacco products entirely and set up addiction clinics to provide professional treatment for the victims of tobacco.

The fact that none of this actually happens makes us suspect the worst, .i.e. that we are being manipulated for some ulterior economic motive, that the authorities are not telling the whole truth about their strategy.

And so, these days we have governments using rather crude methods to frighten or socially exclude us in an attempt to control the numbers of passive smokers and the costs of smoking to the health system. This often has the reverse effect because the manipulation is so poorly executed it delivers only one message: "You are being manipulated". It fails to deliver the main payload "Smoking is going to reduce your quality of life and that of those around you and then it will kill you early". Bottom line: most of just keep on smoking and distrust our government even more.

5.6 The right to manipulate: Another moral question remains: does anyone have the right to manipulate us regardless of the goodness of their intentions?

Who, after all, determines what is good for us? Given that a manipulative act almost always benefits the manipulator (like a reduction in medical care costs) the moral issue of choice becomes super relevant. There is, after all, a possibility that a manipulator's motives are driven by self interest rather than the best interests of the victims, as might be the case against smoking with the pharmaceutical or nicotine replacement industry being the beneficiaries of anti-smoking policies - who knows? Only the manipulator.

Why was it, we might ask, that smoking was promoted as a fairly good thing to do until quite recently? It was aggressively advertised and embedded in government endorsed activities like national sporting events until a relatively short time ago. Was this because the revenues from tobacco were still greater than the cost of medical care? Was it because many UK and other European ex-colonies were huge tobacco producers and vested interests were at play? Was there some corruption involved at senior political levels?

Are we now negative about smoking because of the costs of medical care? Have vested interests in the health insurance industry got more political influence than the now extinct colonies and much weakened companies like British American Tobacco?

These are rhetorical questions but they do serve to show that manipulation of choice, even when apparently in our favour carries a negative moral implication.

No-one actually has an absolute right to manipulate us.

5.7 The supremacy of the individual: Political institutions see human populations as groups or statistics rather than individuals. Whether it is a government or a management, our leaders see our world not as a lot of individuals but as a set of statistics that describe, depersonalise and generalise the behaviour of a group.

This approach to government is one result of several historical, demographic and social realities such as the huge increases in population, the concentration of populations in urban areas, demands on economies of scale in industrial manufacturing and demands for essential public services.

The days of government by and for an extended tribal family are largely over in our over-populated world. It is understandable that modern leadership attempts to find new ways to manage the vast numbers of human beings that now live in their fiefdoms. That isn't to say that governments have arrived at the correct answer for managing large populations.

The "institutionalised" approach of Western governments towards society flies in the face of an important contradictory trend in the behaviour of modern urban man, namely, our consumer-driven belief in the supremacy of the individual.

It may seem counter-intuitive but it is certainly the case that as western urban populations have grown and become more affluent, the spirit of communal behaviour has declined rapidly.

In the last two hundred years since the rise of industrialisation and consumer capitalism, the "individual" has become the dominant unit of society and has become much more powerful and much more demanding.

Rates of single living have increased dramatically, marriages and new family size decline year on year, as the dominant economic unit of the individual emerges.

It is now taken as a personal (and legal) right that we may operate outside of our original social group or family, that (within fairly broad limits) we can live in a completely different way to the average of society, and that we do not need to conform to the average social moral norms of a society.

We are highly mobile physically, our lifestyles are highly individualistic. The traditional idea of growing to adolescence and then seeking a long-term heterosexual relationship centred on an extended family in one's village is now just a matter of historical record in the western world.

5.7.1 Manipulation and the "supreme" individual: This rapidly emerging individualism creates some difficulties for our managers and governments because the information they have about us as a group is actually the mean value of the whole group and doesn't actually reflect typical exemplars of the group, but rather the average of several extremes.

Despite all the economic and social analyses carried out by government and business, and the division of our society into an ever greater number of socio-economic types, modern government hasn't solved the basic problem which is that we all want something different. The fragmentation of modern urban society shows no sign of abating.

5.7.2 Square pegs and round holes: It is for this reason that governments and commercial organisations constantly get it wrong when making decisions about what they should deliver to us as a society. Their models of delivery are based on assumptions like "acting for the greater good of society" or "satisfying the majority of people". The result is that government institutions tend to treat us all in a standardised way - simply because they cannot manage to create systems that can treat us as individuals.

This institutional depersonalisation of our society is a constant source of irritation to all of us in modern western consumer-driven society. This treatment is seen as contrary to our rights as an individual, which we now see as being supreme to any concepts of common interest.

Just get a typical urbanite onto the subject of how they are treated by utilities companies, banks, police, social welfare agencies, insurance companies, tax officials, public transport, hospitals, schools, etc. Listen to the tirade of abuse that the average consumer heaps onto these state and private institutions. Why? Because we all hate being treated as "just another number" and we all resent receiving standard treatment despite the fact that we are a "special case".

5.7.3 Manipulation and the evolution of the "Free Spirit": The fiercely independent stance of the citizen makes for a huge human management headache for governments and capitalist organisations. So we come back to the subject of manipulation and whether it fits into our modern perception of what is "morally acceptable".

How does it feel to our fiercely individualistic population to be the subject of manipulation by a state or commercial institution? Needless to say, we don't take kindly to any kind of covert interference in our independence or our freedom of choice...... if we know about it that is.

In feudal times we would have been quite happy to accept our landlords' decisions about where and how we live and work. Today, we get very angry and offended by any attempt to curtail or interfere in our rights as individuals to make free choices unsullied by cheap tricks or unfair or biased influences from outside agencies. We become very indignant when we discover that we have been duped for decades by those whom we had trusted, whether they are our banks, our food producers, our governments or our employers.

The morality of manipulation is a historically moving target.

5.7.4 The Manipulator strikes back: The response by governments and business interests to the rising "supremacy of the individual" has been some clever adaptation of the manipulator's art.

Despite rafts of financial regulation, advertising standards, the regulation of marketing practises, consumer protection laws, and legal mechanisms for recourse, the public are still the victim of acts of gross manipulation on a jaw-dropping scale, by both business and government.

From airlines adding hidden charges to energy companies charging us extra to rent their equipment, from the tricks of the telecoms industry forcing new phones on us and locking us into lengthy contracts to banks pushing us into debt we don't need and can't afford, we all suffer a constant barrage of commercial manipulation every single day of our lives. And this is on top of the constant background noise of commercial advertising which permeates almost all of our daily life. Thus, buying a simple thing like a mobile telephone service requires a team of accountants and economists to make the necessary calculation to find the best deal.

In an apparent attempt to provide solutions "absolutely tailored to your individual needs", private companies have discovered new ways to manipulate the group by manipulating the individuals within the group. Commercial manipulation is not just about misinforming the public; it is often about overloading the public with information in order to deliver a manipulative payload. How often have we bought something like a car or white goods without really knowing whether they were what we actually needed?

5.7.5 Manipulation trumps Individualism: Manipulators have learned to dissocialize us from the rest of our group. In this sense, we are now victims of our own individualism because we no longer have any of the strong sense of solidarity or collective power that we had when we were members of the same village, tribe or extended family.

Now we are all alone in the grips of a number of manipulative forces which we cannot hope to fight by ourselves, so we often don't even bother. Most of us just give in and buy something that may work and never mind if it's what we want or can afford. We consume to sate our desire to be free. The cost of avoiding the manipulation has become greater than the economic or moral cost of accepting a manipulation. We capitulate because we can't afford to fight.

5.7.6 Solidarity trumps manipulation: The development of industrial and urban life into a divided society of individuals is music to the ears of the main capitalist manipulators. They prefer their workers to be disunited and their markets to be uninformed and divided. In the same way it also benefits government because a disunited population is a free-flowing, malleable mass that is easy to control. Solidarity is a dirty word to the manipulator because it means collective resistance.

5.7.7 Social networking and manipulation: There are responses though to our social disintegration. Social networking is just one response to this lack of communal living and solidarity, and it may very well yet alter the dynamics of manipulation.

The social networking phenomenon doesn't just extend to the sharing of information about the price of a new phone contract, it has a much more dramatic and explosive potential as we have seen in the recent history of various Middle East dictators.

In a way social networking is the sociological response to the growing social disunity of human societies. With such tools of communication, the moral and economic cost of manipulation may soon begin to exceed the moral and economic cost of popular defiance, but we will address the subject of social networking in more detail later on.

5.8 The exercise of power: At first sight it seems self-evident that manipulation is generally a more benign method of exercising power than violence. Yet the situation is not quite so simple, either politically or morally. To fully understand the moral issues, we first need to contrast the use of coercion, which is relatively expensive, with the use of manipulation which is relatively cheap.

Of course, we are all horrified by the visible and indiscriminate use of force, torture, terrorism or intimidation. This is because the difference in strength between the strong and the weak is so very obviously and physically exploited to profit the interests of the strong. A military dictator has superior fire power over that of the masses he controls, a torturer has the liberty and pain of his victim in his power, the intimidator commands the fear of his subject and the terrorist has elements of surprise and anonymity to use against his targets. These barbarities offend against our basic humanistic instincts to protect the weak of our own species, even against other predator members of our own group.

But in a sense, the misuse of power in this way is potentially less of a threat than manipulation. How could that be so?

Violence versus manipulation: What differentiates the use of violence and the use of manipulation?

5.8.1 Violence versus manipulation (I): Violence: This is the use of blatant coercion or intimidation by a government, management, a powerful individual or group. It uses physical resources and strength to force victims to act in a way which is against their best interests.

A coercive management may threaten dismissal which is a threat to the livelihood of an employee; a government may threaten execution or imprisonment. These are very visible means of controlling the individual or population and are an obvious source of intimidation to a victim.

Power plays involving force or threats of force are finite, tangible and sometimes avoidable by the victim. Denials of such violence don't generally fool anyone. The gratuitous use of violence often signifies an underlying weakness in governments and management. It tends to be an unconsidered reaction or egotistical demonstration of power rather than an orchestrated and surgical goal-seeking operation. Violence usually just signifies a lack of self-confidence by the powerful.

In addition, physical violence almost always leaves survivors and simmering resentment. These act as potent witnesses and a driving force for some form of future retribution.

5.8.2 Violence versus manipulation (II): Manipulation, on the other hand, is, by definition, a covert method of social control which takes advantage not only of differences in strength, but also of discrepancies in knowledge or influence between the manipulator and his victims. Manipulation often leaves no detectable concrete evidence.

5.8.2.1 Deniability: Manipulation may have the same net effect as coercion in that a victim's will is made subordinate to that of the manipulator, but it is more difficult to detect and much harder to avoid because it is secret. This is why it is at the heart of much modern government and commercial management, because of this "deniability" factor and the lack of tangible evidence of its use.

5.8.2.2 Where is the evidence? A manipulator contrives and orchestrates the control of their victim beforehand and does so with the complete confidence of one who knows that they really are in control and will remain undetected. Unlike the use of violence, when a manipulator goes to work the victims rarely discover the source or method of manipulation used.

Victims often never know that a manipulation has even occurred. They will know and understand nothing of how or why a particular belief has suddenly become implanted in their minds or a certain behavioural change has happened. The victim may feel no sense of outrage or curiosity at what has happened to them. They may not even know. There is often no sense of a need to seek revenge.

5.8.2.3 Persistence: Manipulation can be very persistent. It can last for seconds or it can span generations. The evidence for the long term delusion manipulated victim is well documented in history. Consider the following examples:

- The horrifying behaviour of many ordinary German citizens in the death camps of the Second World War stemmed directly from the powerful manipulative rhetoric and propaganda of their leaders during the 1930s.

- The blind patriotism of many young American soldiers going off to fight in Vietnam was based ultimately on the fraudulent assertion that American ships had been attacked in the Gulf of Tonkin in 1964.

Both of these events are insidious cases of the potency and persistence of some kinds of manipulation.

5.8.2.4 Violence versus manipulation (III): So evaluating the level of persistence, the lack of accountability and potency of manipulation, it is clear that manipulation can be a great deal more effective and dangerous than any finite and obvious incident of physical brutality aimed at a limited group, however atrocious.

Whilst a single coercive act may be brutal, a manipulative strategy can be devastating, long-lasting, hard to detect and even harder to attribute to any guilty party. In these respects manipulation is more insidious than physical violence.

5.9 A summary of the moral issues involved in political manipulation: You have now read some of the arguments about the moral implications of manipulation as a political method. It has generated a lot of ethical questions and here is a brief summary:

5.9.1 Mitigation and qualitative differentiation: Some forms of manipulative interference are less morally offensive than others. What mitigates the perceived seriousness of one manipulative act versus another? The following criteria may help us:

- **Persistence:** How persistent are the effects of a manipulative action? Is something which has only a temporary effect less serious than an action which is life altering?

- **Availability:** What are the limitations which determine if particular individuals or groups can use a given manipulative method? After all, if everyone can use a particular manipulative method it becomes more egalitarian and seems somehow less vicious. A manipulative action appears less morally disturbing if it is more democratically available.

- **Avoidable:** How recognisable and avoidable is a particular manipulative action? If a manipulative action is very obvious and avoidable, blame begins to shift slightly to the victim for failing to be alert to the evils of "human nature". One can argue that we are personally responsible for our own safety and that a plain and clearly recognisable manipulative trick or trap should be easily detected by a victim. We shouldn't be gullible should we?

- **Consequences:** How morally "evil" are the consequences of the manipulation? If a manipulation carries a morally unacceptable payload it is a great deal more repugnant than an act which has some incidental or deliberate beneficial effect. Inciting racist hatred cannot be compared with encouraging a healthy diet or more exercise.

- **Objectification of the victim:** The underlying unacceptable concept which makes manipulation ethically repugnant is the objectification of the victim by those in a position of power. It degrades humans as objects whose putative will is considered irrelevant and is therefore disregarded. For the manipulator, we are simply pawns in a game played for their benefit without our knowledge or consent, we have no status or value as individuals. Seen through the eyes of Maslow, manipulation (as a minimum) represents an affront to our basic need for "status and esteem" in the hierarchy of human needs. It is therefore always an attack on our human rights, with or without serious consequences.

5.9.2 The will to power: Fascism and manipulation: Manipulation relies on the dynamics of a victim's weakness and the manipulator's strength. A strong and well informed subject cannot be manipulated; therefore the manipulator seeks out weak subjects to prey upon. This is traditionally the same political foundation which the extreme right-wing uses to achieve and maintain its power. A weak subject cannot fight a manipulator because the cost of the struggle is too great for the victim and so he succumbs to the more powerful manipulator.

Fascists traditionally find vulnerable groups to attack and use their powerlessness to leverage their own political power. For the Nazis it was the Jews, for Tony Blair and George W. Bush it was Muslim civilisation, for Israel it is now the Palestinians, for the English fascist parties it is the immigrant population, etc.

The system of manipulation used by these fascists always works along the same lines:

-   **First:** identify the target (Jew, Muslim, Palestinian, or immigrant etc),

-   **Second:** Vilify them with all kinds of false accusations,

-   **Third:** Demonise them with the general public,

-   **Fourth:** Destroy them and become the public saviour of "your people".

Sometimes this strategy works for a while as it did with Hitler and Bush-Blair but mostly it ends in ultimate defeat for the fascists as the public gradually realise that they are being misled. From an ethical perspective the use of fascist techniques like manipulation is completely inconsistent with a humanist morality, regardless of the outcome.

5.9.3 Debasement of the manipulator: Manipulation also degrades the perpetrator. It demands a blinkered approach to the sensitivities of our fellows. Manipulation numbs empathy in a similar way to that state of disconnection demanded of soldiers by their military masters.

Manipulators caught out in a manipulative crime will excuse their behaviour with statements like "being realistic" or "just following orders". These are the mundane defences of those who lack the moral spine to be idealistic, humanistic and ethical. Post Nazi Germany echoed with such sentiments for decades after the war and Holocaust.

5.9.4 Do outcome and scale matter in the morality of manipulation? The outcome of a manipulation doesn't alter the ethical or criminal nature of a manipulative act however incidentally beneficial the action may turn out to be for the victim. Likewise, the extent of the manipulation doesn't make the act more or less immoral.

Primarily, what affects the moral quality of a manipulative action is moral intention. Manipulation is often immoral because it benefits the manipulator more than victim. It is often immoral because manipulation is frequently a predatory act - it often shows no signs of symbiotic intention; it is often contrary to accepted humanistic principles of cooperative co-existence. Its methods are sometimes immoral regardless of its outcomes, which might range from the extremely evil to the very pleasant.

However, manipulation is sometimes unintentional and sometimes unconscious and sometime well-intentioned, even when ill-advised. Morally therefore, it is impossible to generalise on the use of manipulation.

5.10 Conclusions or more questions? The discussion of all moral issues is difficult and the use of manipulation is a particularly complex case because it is so commonplace and can have outcomes ranging from almost nothing to true human tragedies. Somewhere in this spectrum, a moral line exists where a manipulative act becomes unacceptable. The position of that line is something very specific to the moral outlook of the individual.

In conclusion, in our opinion, we would contend that the active, conscious and serious manipulator in a government, bureaucratic institution, a management or personal relationship is always acting immorally to some extent. They all share the common ethical excuse that, "the ends justify the means". This principle is morally insupportable from a humanist perspective.

Fortunately, most manipulators possess less potential for damage than Goebbels or Blair. But we believe it is incumbent on all moral peoples to expose and overturn manipulation wherever they encounter it - for a "wrong" conjunction of power could see us rapidly regress to the unthinkable world of 1930s Europe yet again. However, we would also argue that some forms of manipulation are so benign as to be irrelevant and are more in the nature of social shortcuts than plots against our fellow human beings. We need to be able to make the moral distinction between the two.

---oOo---

6. How to detect, avoid and counteract manipulation

Preamble: The next question to follow in this discussion is how to deal with this multi-layered barrage of personal and institutional manipulation. Clearly we can manage manipulation because we do it all the time, one way or another. Equally, most of us do feel quite strongly that we have a right, indeed an obligation to manage any attempts to manipulate us. And that brings us down to an important question "How do we manage manipulation when we are also the subjects of the action?"

This chapter will attempt to provide some strategic and practical answers.

Institutional and Interpersonal manipulation - the continuum: We have deliberately chosen not to separate interpersonal and institutional manipulation too much because there is an important sociological connection between the two.

Abusive behaviour and attitudes tend to be associated with individuals who have particular psychological problems but these behavioural tendencies are also "up-scaleable" to institutions and even entire governments. How does this work in practice? We will take a couple of real world examples from the Christian religious establishment:

A single priest running a religious school can turn a blind eye to abusive behaviour by one or two other clerical members of his staff because he has some psychological problems of his own. Very soon the abuse he ignores becomes a part of the ethos of the school because he not only tolerates the abusive practices, but he also encourages them by favouring participating staff members and only hiring collaborators who will keep the abuse "safely secret". Suddenly, what may have started as an individual with an isolated psychological problem becomes an institutional plague. The huge shockwaves of decades of such criminal abuse continue to reverberate in Ireland and many other countries. The ultimate consequences for Church and State in Ireland for example are still unquantifiable. It is estimated that only a tiny percentage of priests were actively involved in these abuses but that large swathes of the church turned a blind eye.

A similar case is the stealing of newly born babies from poor women in hospitals run by Catholic religious orders of Franco's Spain. It started by zealous members of religious orders wanting to "give these children a chance to grow up in a 'proper' Catholic family". It ended up as a nationwide criminal conspiracy run like an industry in which the Roman Catholic Church kidnapped thousands of new-born babies "to order" to sell to wealthy Franco-supporting families, leaving the real families with lies about their babies' mysterious deaths and many empty graves. These hidden crimes continued for decades into the late 1970s and are still being uncovered, 40 years after Franco's death.

In both situations, individuals with psychotic behavioural problems managed to infect whole institutions. There is a free movement of influence, ethical stance and corruption between the original corrupt, psychotic individuals to the institution and then from the institution on to other individuals

Separation of moral responsibility: We labour these examples because there is an important moral issue at stake here. Our society tends to find it convenient to separate us as individuals in our different roles. This implies that somehow our personal behaviour at home is separate from our behaviour at work or elsewhere, and that our moral responsibilities are dictated by the role we are currently playing.

We tend to compartmentalise our lives according to what we are doing. But it doesn't work like that really. We are after all just single personalities operating in different conditions. So, in fact, bad companies or governments or other institutions are actually just composed of groups of bad (and influential) individuals. Governments have attitudes and behave in a certain way because their leaders have particular attitudes and moral standards. These may be good, bad or indifferent.

So it is important to acknowledge that there is a continuum between our behaviour as individuals and our behaviour as employees, spouses, friends, bosses, or governors. It's logically and ethically insupportable to believe that we can separate our moral attitudes from our behaviour in the workplace.

The Nuremburg defence: The often used argument that we can compartmentalise our morality is (still) called the "Nuremberg defence" and is an attempt to isolate personal responsibility for the actions of an individual in different roles. A soldier following orders was not seen as a human being exercising free will and thus was not considered criminally responsible for the Nazi atrocities.

Whilst the Nuremburg defence may work in a politico-legal sense it is a morally corrupt proposition. From a humanistic perspective, we are always completely responsible for our actions regardless of the work or social role in which we find ourselves. There are always options available and choices which permit us to behave in different ways. It is rare that we have absolutely no choice but to behave in one particular way. It may be uncomfortable to face this rather unpalatable truth. We cannot separate all or any human beings from the consequences of their actions even when we might be able to make allowances. A child soldier in the Congo is not as culpable as a mass murderer in the presidential palace. Nonetheless, without the child soldier, the mass murderer politician would be powerless. Moral corruption is infectious.

The Moral Continuum: There is a strong correlation between individual behaviour in different roles. So a psychotic and manipulative spouse does not somehow morph into a well balanced manager when he or she arrives in the office. In general, domestic behaviour gets transferred to the workplace and vice versa. The control freak spouse is almost certainly also a control freak colleague. The gas chamber operator of Nazi Germany or the American B52 bomber pilot dropping napalm on civilian villages in Vietnam can hardly be an innocent, well-balanced and loving father and husband, having watched thousands of victims, also husbands, wives and children perish at his own hand. Brutality has two victims, and one of them is the perpetrator.

To conclude, for the rest of this book we have deliberately mixed our consideration of interpersonal and institutional manipulation in the belief that the only real difference is that of scale. The motivation of perpetrators and the strategies of victims in trying to manage the process of manipulation are transferable, regardless of the origins of the manipulative act.

We will now take a look at what can be done to manage manipulation in general.

6.1 Options for action: There are four possible steps available to a victim, regardless of whether a manipulation is interpersonal or institutional: Recognition, Acceptance, Avoidance and Counterattack. We will examine each of these possible steps in detail.

6.2 Recognising manipulation: The ability to recognize and understand secret and unwelcome social control is a precursor to any other action, or any kind of counter measure against the manipulator. First we need to know if it is actually happening.

Suspicions aroused: The first question is to determine if we really are being manipulated. Sometimes we may just have an uneasy feeling that we are not getting the whole story or that someone is paying too much attention to our reactions for reasons we cannot explain. Proving that there really is a plot is often almost impossible because of the secret nature of the action. However, it should be possible, with time and investigation, to make a fairly good determination if we really are at the receiving end of a manipulative action.

Testing suspicions: Once we have established a working theory about what may be happening to us, we can test it out by probing the perpetrator and looking for reactions. If we think someone at work is setting us up to take the blame for something, like say, a disgruntled customer, we could casually mention that the customer is unhappy to the person that we suspect and watch the suspect's reactions. We can contact the customer and see how the suspect behaves, for instance. We can bring up the suspicion with other colleagues and see if anyone else has noticed anything suspicious.

When we have determined that there is a strong possibility that we are indeed victims we can then decide what (if any) action to take.

Analysing our suspicions: The key to recognising a manipulation lies in analysing some aspects of what we think is happening to us:

Existence: Recognizing that a manipulation is actually happening or is about to happen to us.

Form: Understanding the form that a manipulation is taking and its origin. Here we try to understand the plot and the players.

Motivation: Now we try to determine the motives of the manipulator and why we are involved.

Weaknesses: We have to try to understand which of our own weaknesses are being used by the perpetrator.

Strategic faults: We understand a manipulative ploy when we comprehend how it works, but we understand it even better when we discern how it may fail.

Very often none of this analysis is an easy task for the victim. Manipulation is normally at least partly secret and so getting information is often very difficult or impossible. In addition, many manipulative techniques rely on the inherent inability of a victim to bear the cost of uncovering the deception and secrecy of the action. So recognizing that a manipulative action is actually in progress or has already happened, even after the event, is sometimes impossible. At best it is difficult.

6.3 Accepting manipulation: Sometimes, when we realise that a manipulation is taking place, we may simply accede to the exploitation without any further immediate action. There are three possible reasons why we might do this:

- **Pyrrhic victory:** Sometimes the energy involved in contradicting a manipulation is just so much greater than the damage caused by the act itself. It may be that it just isn't worth the effort. So, we allow the perpetrator to waste their energy and win a costly, sometimes Pyrrhic victory. Meanwhile we do nothing, and just write it off to experience. Often we walk away from manipulative ploys by loved ones because a full-scale confrontation may have a much higher consequence for us than our acceptance of a small personal slight. In a similar way, we may feel affronted by a government implementing some petty bureaucratic control but it simply isn't worth wasting our time fighting it. We allow the manipulator to waste their time and energy on a worthless fight whilst we save our energy for a more important fight later.

- **Role reversal: Become the manipulator:** A common feature of many manipulative personalities is their unwarranted self-confidence. They may behave arrogantly despite their lack of knowledge of their victims. This provides an opportunity for the victim to take over the manipulative lead role.

It works as follows: Sometimes we may allow or even invite a manipulative ploy to take place simply because we wish to determine the trustworthiness or mindset of someone we don't know very well or don't trust. When we see them beginning to exploit us or trying to manipulate us, we can conclude a great deal about that person and adjust our future plans for them. We may even allow a manipulative act to take place because it is convenient for us at that moment, but with the intention of removing the manipulator later when it doesn't suit us to have them around any longer. We thus reverse the role of victim and manipulator.

This works both in interpersonal and institutional relationships: In a simple example, a supermarket may use a "loss leader" product, for instance a wine, at an absurdly low price to entice new customers whilst increasing the price of all other wines to cover the loss on the offer product. A good strategy for a customer is to go and buy every bottle of the "special offer" wine from the supermarket, ignore all other products and look for similar buying opportunities elsewhere. In this case, the "loss leader" offer is accepted with open arms but the loser is the marketing director and the supermarket. We accept the manipulation and just reverse our roles with the manipulator.

At an interpersonal level, with an abusive employer for instance, it may be better to accept abusive treatment without complaint, gather and document detailed evidence and then launch a fully fledged and properly planned counterattack later on, when you are ready (and they are not).

- **Resignation: Battles versus wars:** Many people in many circumstances acknowledge that they are truly powerless in the face of a manipulation and they simply have to acquiesce fatalistically.

Sometimes we simply cannot do anything when confronted by a really well planned, secret and well resourced action. It may be just too big and too comprehensive for us to oppose or avoid. We may be able to snipe ineffectively from a distance but sometimes we are strategically better off to retreat, admit defeat, and live to fight another day rather than exhaust ourselves in one single battle that we know we cannot win.

These kinds of calculations need to be made by everyone when confronted by manipulation whether it's an abusive spouse, employer, commercial entity or government. We need to remember to focus on the war rather than on the battle. The war, in this context, is our own personal sovereignty, and the battle is just one particular assault on it.

Sometimes, for example, with an abusive employer or spouse, it may be better to accept the manipulation without complaint for now and just look for another job or partner.

6.4 Avoiding manipulation: The easiest way to avoid a manipulative act is to remove oneself from the scope of influence of the manipulator: switch off the television, end that controlling relationship, find a different job, find a new country etc.

But if we don't want to spend our lives in suspicious isolation, frightened that everything that happens to us is part of some plot to use us, then we need to develop commonsense precautions which allow us to steer as clear as possible away from manipulators or make ourselves unattractive as targets. Here are some basic tactics which show us how this can be done.

6.4.1 Risk-awareness: This is about keeping our eyes open to the perils around us. If we believe some person or external agency is interested in us in a manipulative sense, we must first understand the type of manipulation to which we think we are now exposed. This helps us understand what personal weakness or biases have attracted a manipulator to us. Once we have discovered why we are interesting, we may be able to deflect their interest or remove ourselves from their target population by showing them that we are not subject to a particular psychological bias and therefore not useful to them.

6.4.2 Self-awareness: If a potential victim has a clear intellectual understanding of their own personal cognitive biases, there is a good chance that a manipulator will fail in their mission. People who are prone to "self analysis" have a much better chance of avoiding the manipulator's interest because they are better prepared to see that weaknesses in their own personal judgement are being used by a manipulator. Individuals who don't recognize this are obviously most at risk of manipulation. From this we can conclude that it is worth having a healthy interest in and understanding of how human psychology may play tricks on us. We refer to this as self-awareness.

We can immediately start improving our self-awareness by not falling into the "assumption trap". We already discussed the concept of heuristics as mental short-cuts to help us make quick decisions in the absence of complete information. So we make these heuristic "approximations" which we hope are close enough to the truth.

Assumptions are one form of heuristic. We see a man staggering along the street outside a bar so we assume he is drunk. We ignore the possibilities that he has just been assaulted or is having a heart attack. We see a nicely dressed, clean shaven man strolling out of the bank with a mobile in one hand and brief case in the other. We assume this is some respectable businessman returning from a meeting with his bankers. We don't suspect that he has just robbed the bank, the proceeds are in his briefcase and that he is speaking with his colleagues to organise his get-away car. Very often our assumptions work fine but sometimes they can fail in a most spectacular way.

Manipulators take advantage of the assumptions that victims make to alter their perceptions. And so it is with the subject of self-awareness. We are all pretty certain of what we are seeing or hearing and that our analysis is considered and objective. However these assumptions about our own objectivity are often invalid. So to improve self-awareness, we must learn to also mistrust our own emotions and judgements and to learn to add caveats to what we think we are seeing. So, that man is not drunk, he is staggering as if he were drunk, along a street, close to a bar. We do not know what his problem is. That is all we can objectively say.

6.4.3 Understanding personal "weaknesses": Apart from the usual cognitive biases and unreliable heuristics that we all fall prey to, we also all have our own personalised cocktail of personality traits which taken together make us unique individuals. However, some of these traits may be perceived by a manipulator as weaknesses and opportunities to control.

For example, some of us are inclined to avoid confrontation. We like to "keep the peace" at all costs. This might be seen as an admirable trait in some circumstances but it can also be used by a manipulator to control our behaviour. Once we have understood this, we can solve the problem by occasionally demonstrating our ability to be confrontational should the need arise. This adds an element of doubt to the calculation being made by someone planning to manipulate us.

A similar scenario can be applied to a whole range of personality traits, any of which may provide an opportunity for a manipulator to control us:

- **The struggle for perfection**: This admirable characteristic may also present a manipulator with an opportunity to control us. A manager may deliberately keep "raising the bar" to an employee so that the employee is locked in a constant struggle to achieve the boss's expectations. It only works with someone who has a hang-up about achieving perfection. The non-perfectionists amongst us would probably throw in the towel after a while and declare that what we have done is the best we can do.

- **The struggle to be infallible**: This is a characteristic which is quite prominent in the workplace where we are often trained to be competitive with our colleagues. This deliberately manipulated competitive environment can cause conflicts where colleagues struggle to be seen as infallible. It is a way of trying to gain the attention and approval of peers and superiors. It only works for those who actually care about how they are perceived by their peers. The less infallible amongst us will simply say, "Sorry, I don't know the answer to that" or "sorry I obviously made a mistake". These words would be anathema to the "infallibles".

- **Generosity versus selfishness:** We all like to be seen as generous even when the act of generosity is foolish or damaging to us. No-one likes to have a reputation as being selfish. However, being kind simply because it conforms to our preferred self-image can be a problem because it gives the manipulator an opportunity to make us act against our own will by using moral blackmail to oblige us to be generous. Governments downgrade social services to the old or disabled because they assume that relatives and neighbours will be kind-hearted and look after the needs of the old and weak. Generosity is a fine human characteristic but it is especially easy to abuse.

- **Consistency versus inconsistency:** Most of us accept that the world is full of contradictions and dichotomies. Even scientific truths are only valid within specific ranges. A fact which is provable in one set of conditions is untrue in another. Materials behave differently at different temperatures for example. However, despite the fact that we all accept the existence of dichotomies and exceptions many of us still fight very hard to demonstrate how consistent we are. It is a trait of the modern world that personal inconsistency is considered bad and consistency is considered good. But again, a strong desire to be constant puts us at the mercy of the manipulator. For example, we may regularly drive to work at a certain time every day. A colleague may take advantage of this by always walking the same route at the same time. Of course you stop and drive him or her to work. If you adopted flexible working hours, would the colleague continue to walk to work at the same time? Probably not.

- **Self-actualisation:** Maslow's "hierarchy of needs" showed us the relationship between basic needs and the ultimate level of psychological development which he called self-actualisation, which is our desire to reach our full personal potential. Many of the world's population struggle to maintain their basic needs like food and security and for them the concept of self-actualisation is a distant dream. But in the rich western world we now see the desire of many individuals focus not on food or shelter but on the desire for "self-actualisation".

  It is a complex subject, but in the context of personality traits and manipulation, it comes down to a desire to feel comfortable with ourselves, being spontaneous, being autonomous, having strong feelings of human fellowship, being task-centric, self-contained but capable of profound relationships, having an open mind, feeling and being appreciated, being contented with one's life. So we have cases where perfectly healthy, affluent individuals are torn by a struggle for "a more profound experience of life". Especially in a modern, urban setting, the desire for "something more" is both admirable and dangerous. The desire for self-actualisation has provided a fertile ground for a huge range of esoteric fads and cults in the last 200 years, mostly with the basic objective of making money for someone. They have given a new (monetary) meaning to the word "enlightenment".

- **Tolerating discomfort:** In Western society, we live in a world with a low threshold to discomfort. Nonetheless, we are conditioned to believe that we should be capable of tolerating discomfort and "suffering in silence". This is considered somehow virtuous, whereas complaining or refusing to tolerate discomfort is considered decadent and morally weak. This "Spartan" attitude is useful when it comes to managing an emergency situation but it can also leave us in a weak and malleable state. For example, if really extreme weather forces the cancellation of a lot of flights we can understand and deal with this. However, if we become too tolerant and accepting, it doesn't take very long before the airline companies starts expecting us to tolerate cancelled flights and build our tolerance into their schedule.

- **Recognising and accepting personal limitations:** Western capitalist culture has gravitated into a sort of meritocracy where no one is really allowed to admit to having personal limitations. We have to be good at what we do all the time. There are no such things as "off days". We are expected to operate as limitless automatons and never admit our personal limitations, for that would be morally weak. This tendency to ignore personal limitations can be richly mined by potential manipulators. We can, for instance, be trapped into a treadmill existence because we feel a duty to deliver regardless of how exhausted we may be by life, work, family and obligations. Our reluctance to admit that we have reached our limit is a classical way to ensnare an employee or colleague into delivering more than they are paid to do. This happens frequently when a company rationalises its staffing levels and leaves 5 people to do the work previously done by 10. No one wants to admit that they are not up to it.

- **Fear/Dislike of confrontation:** This is a common personal characteristic. We can all admire those who prefer peace to confrontation. However, this tendency opens a manipulative opportunity wherein a victim refuses to confront someone despite evidence that a misdeed has occurred. The fear of confrontation is greater than the crime committed.

- **The struggle for self-confidence, emotional attachment and the desire to be liked and accepted:** Again, we can all sympathise with those seeking to be liked, loved and accepted. These are pretty normal emotions but they can be abused by an external controlling influence. For example, we conform to various social norms of behaviour in order to not be expelled or isolated from our social group. We do this even when we know that the behaviour is complete nonsense or is destructive or immoral. How many members of the military actually believe in what they do? Or are they simply there because they need a job and want the companionship of a group of peers? How many of the six million members of the Masonic lodge actually believe in the bizarre ritualism and philosophy of their association? Most conform to it solely to maintain their membership of this commercially useful organisation.

From the above, we can see that a manipulator may be attracted by certain personality traits considered "weaknesses" in the victim. This works at all levels of manipulation, interpersonal, institutional and political. The "weaknesses" are used in different ways but the concepts are the same.

To avoid manipulation we may need to alter the way we are perceived by a manipulator by not allowing them to see our personal traits as potential "weaknesses". The best way to do this is not to be too predictable.

6.4.4 Vigilance: As an individual victim or group we can help ourselves to recognize and avoid manipulation by being continuously vigilant and regard the words and deeds of those in power and those around us with an appropriate level of scepticism.

6.5 Counteracting manipulation: For many of us, avoidance is not a real option because it's not practical to just leave our jobs, families, hide or alter the way we appear. Instead, we need to find alternative strategies which make us uninteresting or even dangerous to a manipulator.

These alternative strategies revolve around the cost and benefit of a manipulation and our ability to make a manipulation so awkward, dangerous and expensive that the perpetrator just gives up.

We have called this topic and other defensive and active strategies "Counteraction". There are as many countermeasures to manipulation as there are manipulative methods and circumstances, so here we give the general principles of how to develop a counterstrategy. These strategies include targeted attacks on the source of the manipulation; this requires more aggressive forms of subversion against the manipulator.

We have divided the countermeasures into the following actions:

- Identifying the original manipulator
- Personal self-defence
- "Keep your powder dry" strategy
- Sticking together
- Retaliation - play the cards back
- Altering the economics - increase the cost to the manipulator

6.5.1 Identifying the original manipulator: It is very important to find the "prime movers" in a manipulative play. Without knowing the true origin of a manipulation it is impossible to effectively avoid a manipulation or to retaliate.

Most people seeking freedom from manipulation are under the impression that they are looking for "nasty people doing nasty things" to them. But this is not the way to find a manipulative source, especially since a manipulator will have taken good care not to appear particularly interested in or aggressive towards their victim. There may also be many proxies implementing a manipulative action and these proxies will distract the victim from the real manipulator. The existence of proxies is a deliberate method of obfuscating the real identity of the manipulator

Known associates: A better approach to finding the source of a manipulation is to carry out a careful study of the suspects, whether individuals, organisations, or managements. This should reveal obvious attitudes, indications of previous manipulative behaviour and signs of any obvious motives for their interest in the current victim.

For example, if a research department in a university suddenly obtains large grant funding from an industrial company (such as a subsidiary of Monsanto), it would then be reasonable to assume that this research organisation might conceivably show signs of manipulative behaviour in the presentation of its GM research results to farmers and the agricultural research world. It could hardly remain objective when a huge corporate vested interest is paying the salaries.

When the research paper by French scientist Seralini et al was published in autumn 2012 on the subject of whether GM maize used with the herbicide "Roundup", was toxic to consumers it was met with a barrage of criticism.

This is because his paper dared to suggest that there was a significant correlation between the incidences of tumours in rats and their eating NK603 maize. Most of the criticism came from academics associated with GM research, some Monsanto financed research departments and from European Food Safety Organisations whose rather shoddy evaluation of the GM product had given it the green light for human consumption in the first place. The disturbing images of Seralini's horribly disfigured laboratory rats sent the cosy GM industry into a furore. Seralini was subjected to acidic attacks from scientists and institutions around the world. After much abuse and denial, Seralini's team issued a comprehensive defence of their paper. The attacks on Seralini were so apoplectic that one has to wonder why so many normally calm scientists became so emotional and vicious about this one scientific study. Had Seralini accidentally uncovered a body of unpublished health risks? The present situation is that Seralini has challenged Monsanto to publish its safety study data - something which the company has hitherto refused to do.

Of course, there may be coincidental connections with a manipulator, but generally speaking, when one works back to the origins of one particular interest consistently benefiting from a 3rd party act, then a single manipulative individual or organisation emerges as the source. This is the group against which the victim should direct their suspicions and investigation.

Obfuscations: In trying to understand the various modes of manipulation and trace their sources, one must be aware of the obstacles to determining the core manipulator:

- **Proxies:** Almost all manipulative techniques employ impersonal or third-party methods of delivery because this is safer for the manipulator. It is therefore important not to attack the wrong targets when identifying the manipulator. There is no point in shooting the messenger, especially if they are reporting back to the originator of the manipulation.

- **Many targets:** Manipulation is not usually narrowly targeted against just you. Unless it is a simple interpersonal issue, you are probably not alone. Finding other victims may help to identify common motives and maybe even the instigator.

- **Hit and Run:** Don't assume that the manipulator is still involved. Many forms of manipulation, once initiated, become autonomous - i.e. the manipulator leaves the field but the effect of the manipulative act continues until it is finally dismantled by a third party. So don't assume you will find any smoking gun or culprit. They may be long gone.

6.5.2 Learn some self defence: We have already highlighted some of the personal characteristics which may make us targets for the manipulator. These traits, which are generally considered to be morally positive characteristics, are perceived as opportunities by the manipulator. Generosity and a desire for peace and reconciliation are seen as signs of weakness. This may be typical of the amoral psychopathic make-up of a manipulator.

To manage this we have said that we need to gain an understanding of our own personality traits and also of the common psychological biases and heuristics that affect our objectivity and judgement. We need to develop a natural vigilance to being manipulated as a result of our own perceived weaknesses. There are several steps we can take to make ourselves less attractive to a manipulator:

Form a group: The ideal strategy for a targeted number of individuals is the formation of an alliance or group to pool resources. We will deal with this in more detail later, but the basic strategy of self-defence is to develop a high level of solidarity, appear confident, resilient, assertive, well-resourced, energetic, discrete, well organised, independent, and courageous. These are not the characteristics which ideally attract a manipulator.

Personal defences: For the individual this means developing self-confidence and self-esteem to deter the manipulator for he is looking for weak subjects, not subjects who display confidence and a strong will.

It may well be worth investing some time to understand the manipulator's mentality in more detail. Various psycho-analytical techniques may help us with this. Transactional analysis is one such technique and is considered to be particularly adept in modelling interpersonal manipulation and abuse. Transactional analysis was developed in the 1950s to model human behavioural interactions. It is now a central part in mainstream behavioural psychology. It is worth a short digression to explain how this might be useful here. In the underlying theory there are three possible ego states: Child, Parent and Adult:

- **The Child Self:** The Child self is the "me", emotional, spontaneous, intuitive, inventive soul who speaks and acts in an emotional, impulsive way. His or her reactions are generally passionate.

- **The Parent Self:** The "Parent self" feels and acts in a way which mimics authority figures, the individuals adopt the role of the judge evaluating situations based on criteria and ethical values inherited from parents. This is the moral self that handles moral values, judgments, prejudices, opinions and concepts of good and evil.

- **The Adult Self:** Finally, an individual has an "Adult self", responding to a situation which needs decisions, he or she uses facts and a real analysis of possible consequences based on verifiable experiments. This is our rational self. It operates clearly with objectivity, is analytical and relies on honest deduction. This is the state of the person who is in touch with "reality".

- **Manipulative risks:** Transactional analysis studies indicate that some interactions are more likely to present a danger of manipulation: So it is for transactions between the "Parent" aspect of a manipulator and the "Child" aspect of the victim or vice versa. These "transactions" are considered to be problematic because they may give rise to abusive or dominating relationships. The objective of a rational honest relationship should be to establish a rational "Adult to Adult" communication which does not dominate or inflate either party.

Techniques like transactional analysis are not a solution for all cases of interpersonal manipulation but they do shine a light on the way a manipulator and victim see each other. TA might even help in some circumstances to correct and alter the behaviour of both parties.

6.5.3 "Keep your powder dry" strategy: Manipulation works because most victims don't have the time or resources to investigate the truth behind the claims or find hidden manipulative payloads. It's cheaper for a victim just to accept a propagandist's assertion than to check it out themselves.

However, some victims do respond with knee-jerk reactions when they become suspicious that they are being manipulated. They then spend a significant amount of energy trying to investigate the truth of why a particular action is happening or why a particular assertion is being pushed on them. This investigative effort can have an enormous cost and effectively neutralise a victim's resistance. Like a hooked fish, a victim may simply exhaust themselves and their resources struggling to understand and unravel a manipulative act.

Incautiously reacting to a manipulation is not the way to deal with a manipulator. There are some important reasons for this:

- **Keep quiet:** The first rule in dealing with manipulation is NOT to allow the manipulator to know that we know what is going on. So, cool discretion is vital. This may also allow us to gain some time to investigate further.

- **Build allegiances and understand the manipulator:** Use the time to find allies, co-victims, to understand the manipulator's motives, the mechanisms being used and the manipulator's own weaknesses. We need time to fully understand the motives and mechanics of the manipulator.

- **Plan the counter-attack first**: Develop a counter-strategy against the manipulator to either remove you from danger or to remove the manipulator's power over you. This may involve reversing the role of manipulator and victim by taking some control of the manipulator's actions.

6.5.4 Sticking together: Solidarity as a weapon to repel manipulation

At what point does a manipulative act become too expensive for a victim to resist or for a manipulator to maintain?

Socio-economic influences: Attempting to manipulate a well-heeled bunch of city barristers is not the same as covertly persecuting a single striking worker in a lowly paid job. In the same way, an individual citizen trying to influence a government decision is not the same as a government minister making a public statement about an upcoming government decision.

There are 4 key differences between the players in these two examples. Their socio-economic differences alter the economic dynamic of any manipulation for the following reasons:

- **Knowledge:** Difference in knowledge. Barristers are legally well equipped, they understand their legal options expertly, and they have access to methods of free or cheap legal protection. In contrast, a striking worker has no legal training or knowledge.

- **Money:** Differences in access to economic resources. The barristers are rich and can hire helpers; the worker is poor and alone. The "city barristers" may be too expensive to manipulate because they have strong economic resources. The striking worker knows nothing of the law, has no economic resources and access only to impossibly expensive legal protection and advice.

- **Solidarity:** Differences in access to others in the same situation. The barristers can make allies with others similarly persecuted. The "city barristers" are in a group and can pool knowledge, money, influence and morale to protect themselves as a group. The striking worker is completely alone against a manipulative force with no-one to share the technical, economic, or emotional burden. The striking worker has to rely on sympathy from his friends and colleagues.

- **Power and influence:** Relative differences in power between manipulator and victim. A striking, lowly paid worker is close to the bottom of the hierarchy of power and influence. The striking worker is nothing to the manipulator; he has no power, free legal recourse or influence over the media. A "city barrister" is near the top of the social pile of power and influence. The "city barristers" are relatively powerful as a group when compared with their manipulator. They operate on a more level playing field of influence with regards to the law and to the media.

  Obviously the targets of a manipulator have to be manageable in terms of cost and likely success; otherwise a manipulative action can rapidly turn to an expensive disaster. Therefore a suitable victim must not be able to afford a serious challenge to the manipulator. In the above instance, the striking worker is an excellent target but the "city barristers" are a very high risk proposition.

Level the playing field: Despite all these disadvantages, from the poorer victim's perspective, all is not lost. There are ways of re-balancing the differences in economic potential between manipulator and victim. These are relatively simple and cheap to implement:

- **Organise:** The first stage is for the victim to share the cost of fighting the manipulation with others whose interests are also at risk. Well organized, motivated and well informed groups of sceptical individuals are the greatest threat to a manipulator. They can pool their energy and knowledge and share the cost of uncovering any manipulative plays. This involves gathering enough evidence to convince a group of supporters to unite behind a cause. In our striking worker case, the victim could join a union or form a union, and/or gather a militant group of workers together.

- **Mount a resistance:** Having established a group with some degree of solidarity for the victim against the manipulator, the group may be persuaded to take appropriate action. So far all that has happened is that the victim's morale may have been boosted by his new supporters.

  But now they must actually alter the balance of cost to the manipulator to make the action too expensive to continue. A victim can use the press and/or internet to accuse the manipulator of all kinds of other offences and to publicise the case to keep the manipulator busy, on the defensive and undermine the manipulator's reputation and legal standing.

A victim can also look for alternative low cost legal devices to attack a manipulator. When appropriate, a victim may have recourse to national or international courts, such as the European Courts of Justice and Human Rights. A victim can organise economic embargos against a manipulator or engage in industrial action to undermine the economic position of a manipulator. There are endless possibilities here. Anything which distracts and weakens the manipulator should be employed in a coordinated attack. The manipulator must be convinced that the manipulation of this particular victim is coming with too great a cost.

- **Tip the manipulative balance of cost and benefit:** Ultimately, the cost of continuing a manipulation should be made to exceed the benefit for the manipulator. When this finally becomes clear, the manipulator will stop. This may take some time but a cleverly managed attack/campaign against a manipulator will eventually win.

6.5.5 Institutional David and Goliath: An example: Here is a small example to explain how a very large entity can be threatened by a single individual.

Airlines don't like carrying disabled passengers because they are too expensive to handle, needing specialist collection and transport. However, European law[6.1] insists that disabled passengers be accommodated on all airlines at no extra cost. One large European airline conglomerate decided to adopt a covert policy of discouraging disabled passengers.

One day, a disabled (blind) passenger with the help of a family member, attempted to book a ticket on the internet. When the passenger asked for special handling and tried to finalise the booking, the flight was suddenly mysteriously full and the reservation cancelled. A few hours later the family member attempted to make the same reservation and found available seats. She finalised and paid for the booking without mentioning that the passenger was blind.

In a separate email to the airline, the passenger requested special handling. Hours later in a curt and unpleasant email, the passenger was told by customer services that the airline did not accept unaccompanied blind passengers for "security reasons".

This was despite clear European directives which insist that airlines must carry unaccompanied, disabled passengers, including blind passengers. This presented a problem. Neither passenger-victim nor their relative actually had the time or resources for a drawn out legal battle with the airline. A rapid victory but at almost no cost was what was needed. Therefore the victim and her relative proceeded to implement a well planned, lightning strike on the airline. It worked as follows:

Step 1: Construct a Documentary: The first action was to construct a chronological statement of the events leading up to the airline refusing to take the passenger, with copies of the incriminating emails and airline reservations. This document was written in the form of a press release and translated into the three major European languages used in the countries where the airline operated.

Step 2: Make Allies: The victim and relative then contacted the international organisation representing blind people in Europe and forwarded their statement with a complaint about the airline. This was a complaint designed to obtain compensation at a later date. Complementing the cooption of the power of the European Union, the victim enlisted morally powerful organisations like the press and the disabled passenger organisations in a simultaneous attack on the airline's good name and reputation. Whilst this has no legal value it is a serious attack on the moral legitimacy and "decency" of the company.

Step 3: Shots across the bow: They circulated by fax and registered post a letter of complaint to all members of the board of directors of the airline's holding company with a copy of their statement. The letter contained specific threats of legal action in the European Court, and a global press release within 24 hours. All letters were copied to IATA and the appropriate directorate of the European Commission in Brussels. The victim thus enlisted the assistance of European and International law, public outrage, public sympathy, and the threat of significant economic and PR damages to the airline. The victim thus solved the problem of their own impotence against this huge airline corporation by leveraging the power of even more gigantic institutions e.g. the European Commission, ECJ and IATA etc. The coup de grace was the appeal to the international airline regulatory organisation.

This last action slammed the door on any attempt by the directors to avoid their legal responsibilities (pass the buck). It guaranteed that there was no possibility for the airline to claim ignorance of the complaint. Every letter was sent and received by registered mail.

Step 4: The Shooting war begins: As the deadline expired the pair issued 6 press releases, 2 to each of the largest circulation newspapers in each country. Within a few hours, the airline started to receive press enquiries about the story and requests for a statement.

Step 5: Airline begins retreat: Within 14 hours the victim had received an apology from customer services for the "error" in processing and confirmation of the flight.

Step 6: Airline sues for peace: Within 48 hours the company secretary of the airline made a telephone call and personal apology to the passenger for the airline's "oversight", he offered to waive the cost of the flight, provide a seat upgrade and offer a complimentary seat for a further flight at the choice of the passenger.

Step 7: Surrender: 72 hours after being rejected as "unfit to fly" with KLM-Air France, our passenger victim had forced this mega corporation into a full-scale retreat with costs and compensation in favour of the passenger.

Step 8: Take no prisoners: Furthermore, the middle and longer-term attack dogs of the European Commission, IATA and Union of Disabled Passengers had been alerted and formal complaints registered. They continued to legally pursue this airline two years after the event with the aid of the European press, always on the lookout for such stories of poor customer service on the airlines.

Example Summary: This is an example of how 2 basically powerless victims, facing the power and manipulative leverage of one of the world's largest airlines, could force an almost instant reversal in the airline's behaviour. They extracted immediate compensation, an apology, obliged the airline to alter its policies and ensnared a very large company in a very costly and labyrinthine legal battle with the European Union and the International Airline regulator. All of this was done at zero cost to the victims, - well, just a few stamps, faxes and a little stratagem.

How could this work? In this example, we see how the victim offsets their own helplessness by collecting multiple "cards" to "play back" against the manipulative airline company.

Firstly, they overwhelmed the airline with a credible range of tangible legal threats and a PR disaster. Any one of the multiple assaults launched by the victim was enough to generate a real concern for the airline's management. Meanwhile the airline only had one card to play and that was their ability to bully the passenger and refuse them the right to travel. They hoped the cost of legal action would put off any challenge by the victim. They miscalculated.

The victim's strategy contained both a short term solution and a mid and long term retaliatory component. They got their seats and assistance, compensation and the knowledge that the airline was now under investigation at the highest level.

The victim used a multi-layered countermeasure which caused both an immediate reaction as well as medium and long term legal punishments against the airline. Once accepted by the European Commission the complaint against the airline became autonomous. All doors of escape for the airline were thus closed.

Within a few hours the airline faced the first ripples of a combined attack as the faxes of complaint started to arrive at the headquarters, addressed directly to the company's directors. Clearly the directors could see that there would be a follow up from the European Commission which might also mean an un-winnable case in the European Court of Justice for the government for breaches of the European Directive, not to mention a lot of bad publicity. Concurrently with the sending of the letters of complaint to the company directors, the first calls from the international press began.

The directors knew that they faced a coordinated attack which had already moved to the arena of the regulatory authorities, the press and public opinion. A call from the legal department of IATA to the company's legal director closed the discussion. Directors on all sides capitulated. They faced legal sanctions, moral condemnation and economic damage to their commercial reputation which could have incalculable costs to their image as the "caring airline".

Victory for the victim was guaranteed from the moment the customer service desk refused to abide by the law and the victim decided to resist.

6.5.6 The use of Social networking to deter and repel manipulation: One of the precursors that allow manipulators to operate in our modern, individualistic world is a lack of social cohesion, an absence of community and solidarity within their target group where victims may not communicate so closely with each other any more. This is much more of an issue in modern western societies than it is in societies that are still centred on tribe, family, village or district.

Social networking has recently emerged as a possible techno response to the lack of communal living and solidarity. It is early days, but it certainly looks as if high speed communication in tandem with open access to social networking tools, may well provide a counterweight to the increasing isolationism of urban life.

A medium for making allies: Social networking may help to alter the dynamics of manipulation as its effects become more widespread. Obviously this new phenomenon doesn't just extend to the sharing of commercial information, but can also be used to organise demonstrations, send reports and photographic images to conventional and internet press and organise "monster" actions against governments and private commercial organisations.

Even in its infancy social networking has had some spectacular effects including the removal of several dictatorships in the Middle East. It demonstrates the truth of the old cliché that "knowledge is power" and adds the addendum "and communications are how that power is shared".

The balance of power: Users of social networking like the anarchic group "Anonymous" operate without any institutional or group identification or capital. They have a makeshift democratic decision making process for "members", but can turn a proposition into a very damaging "cyber-action" within hours.

It is unstructured but still operates like a single organism with quite a ruthless efficiency. It tolerates dissent and relies entirely on group consensus. It is basically impervious to infiltration or dismantling by any external authority because it has no hierarchy. When it is attacked it simply breaks up and reforms itself again. This ability to perform continuous reincarnations sends shivers down the spine of manipulative governments, traditional security services and corporate planners.

Social action: Social networking has enormous potential to redistribute power to individual victims by allowing them to mobilise large groups of support. This is a daunting prospect for the manipulator, who relies on individuals being weak and isolated.

In February 2012, Tesco in the UK was accused of using unpaid labour from the ranks of the unemployed to fill shelves and do other unpaid work in their supermarkets. They were indeed accused of using slave labour.[6.2] Within a few hours of this story appearing in "The Guardian" newspaper an enormous "Twitter" campaign was mounting worldwide to attack Tesco and boycott their stores. This was on a Friday night. By Saturday morning many Tesco shops were being picketed throughout Britain and weekend sales were reportedly 50% down.

By Monday midday, Tesco had apologised and withdrawn from the "employment scheme". The following day the Conservative government had rescinded the entire scheme which made unemployed people work for nothing doing menial tasks for large mega-corporations.

Social upheaval: Social networking also has the potential to unleash pent up social pressures which are very often the result of institutional manipulation. A case in point was an attempt by the British police to manipulate the truth about the shooting and killing of a young black man during a routine stop and search in London in 2011. The tweeting and Blackberry wielding rioters and looters of 2011 sent literally millions of text messages to each other organising rioting and looting as London burned and they made off with €300 million worth of consumer goods.

The government and police watched in shocked amazement. This mayhem should be a salutary case in point to all governments that a manipulative authority can be circumvented and indeed overwhelmed by a concerted group of victims using technologies such as internet based social media.

It's just beginning: Using social networking tools, the speed and spread of communication is truly spectacular and far exceeds the ability of highly structured institutions of "law and order" to communicate so quickly. Social networking is just in its infancy but must be a source of tremendous worry to some of our politicians, civil servants and the capitalist aristocracy.

6.6 Retaliation against manipulation: Attack is the best form of defence. The example we used earlier of the blind passenger in conflict with the manipulative airline demonstrates several principles about the management and counteraction of manipulative institutions by apparently powerless individuals:

- **Good Planning:** Carefully planned and choreographed counter attack can be a very good way to force a manipulator into full retreat. Planning and preparation is essential and all the necessary offensive actions should be fully prepared and put in place before executing them according to a carefully defined timetable.

- **No holds barred:** The victim's counterattack can and should use whatever countermeasures are necessary (including manipulative techniques) against the manipulator. An innocent victim has a moral right to retaliate against an unprovoked attack on their freedom.

- **Fast and furious:** A counterattack against a powerful manipulator should be concerted and not gradual. Gradually escalating counter measures is counterproductive because it pre-warns the manipulator that something is coming. The element of surprise is important and the attack on a powerful institution should be in the nature of a "Blitzkrieg" rather than a war of attrition. The victim needs to achieve concessions immediately and force quick management decisions. Dragging on a struggle just causes people to dig trenches and this can ultimately be exhausting for a victim.

- **Focus on the target manipulator:** Don't attack the proxies - it's a waste of energy, it alienates possible allies and warns the manipulator. In our case about the blind passenger, there's no point attacking the customer service operator or supervisor. They are only operating on management decisions made much further up the hierarchy. It's much better to use these proxies to leak and reveal documents with incriminating information about the real manipulators.

- **Threaten the manipulator by alienating their allies:** As we have stressed already, it is vital to identify and attack the prime manipulator. Knowing their identity allows the victim to attack this person at a very intimate level by turning other colleagues against them. In the example, the victim threatened the airline's regulatory status and good name. Immediately, this divides the board of directors, the company lawyer, the marketing director and the director of regulatory affairs. They will then turn on the operations director and threaten him. They will demand answers, as indeed will the chairman of the board. They will quickly insist on capitulation and damage limitation.

6.7 Altering the economics - increase the cost to the manipulator: Manipulation is supported by a fundamental power dynamic which assumes that the victim has less power than the perpetrator and that if the victim should find the manipulator, the cost of stopping the manipulation would be too great for the victim. Therefore, one certain way to alter the economics of a manipulative act and deter a manipulator is to make the cost of the action too high for the manipulator to bear. Increasing the cost or reducing the benefit of a manipulation will force a rational manipulator to abandon an action

6.7.1 The cost of contradiction: Standing up to a manipulator costs a lot of time, energy and maybe hard cash. Being "in the right" isn't enough in a propaganda war, you also have to have a loud voice and a deep pocket.

During the US involvement in the illegal dirty war against the elected President of Nicaragua, the government of Daniel Ortega was well aware that the USA was illegally arming and financing the Contra rebels to fight a proxy war against his elected (socialist) government. Although everyone in Central America knew what was really going on, only a relatively small number of people outside the zone really understood the situation and the extent of illegal US involvement; that is, until all hell broke loose with the Iran-Contra scandal so publicly revealed.

The USA's campaign of misinformation was so powerful and well funded that any reply or protest from Ortega was drowned out by the barrage of lies broadcast from the Contras and the CIA. The newly formed state of Nicaragua, poverty stricken by civil war against an enemy financed by the USA, had no resources to fight the lies and propaganda of the US or the Contras.

6.7.2 The various costs: The costs of manipulation come in various forms:

- **Costs can be economic:** Access to expensive legal resources, the use of resource materials or specialist resources may well cost money.

- **Costs can be time in man hours:** It may be possible for a victim to defend themselves against a manipulative action and they may have the skills required, but they simply don't have the time to do so. Their other commitments may make their defence impossible.

- **Costs can be calendar time:** A favourite trick is to force a victim's hand by building in a very tight schedule into a manipulative trap. The victim may have the money and the skills to defend themselves but the timescale is too limited for them to investigate.

6.7.3 Altering the economics in favour of the victim: How can a victim do this?

Firstly get more time: The first priority should be to block time-related constraints imposed by the manipulator. We may be able to do this by overlaying our own schedule on the manipulator to permit us more time; this will allow us to disperse the cost and effort of verification over more than the previously allowed time. It will also give us an opportunity to organize our defences and find allies.

In legal and financial circles "playing for time" is standard behaviour. A lawyer may request further information from a plaintiff or defendant just to cause a series of delays to facilitate a defence strategy. In financial circles an accountant can cause considerable delay to a creditor or tax collector by requesting more information, by formally suggesting negotiated settlements etc. All communications cause delays which might be enough to prepare a defence. A victim can use these tricks to cause delays to all manner of manipulative actions.

Scorched earth: Making the objective of the manipulator's actions worthless alters the economics of the manipulative act. If the target of the manipulator no longer exists or has no value, the perpetrator may soon see that there is no point in wasting more effort or cost on the manipulative action and it will soon cease. Trying to economically impoverish a victim won't work when their resources are already sitting in a Swiss bank account, for instance.

6.7.4 Symmetric and Asymmetric situations and strategies: Here are two descriptions of asymmetric conflict, one military, the other in a manipulative conflict

Military examples: In traditional warfare, participants rely on an asymmetry between themselves and their enemy, allowing them to prevail. In modern warfare, guerrilla tactics are the greatest enemy of the conventional military commander. Guerrilla tactics use light arms, fast movement, surprise and flexibility to attack large lumbering pieces of conventional military hardware such as tanks, battleships, convoys or combat troops draped in kilos of useless hardware.

In Afghanistan small groups of fast moving and badly equipped Mujahideen continue (at the time of writing) to pin down tens of thousands of US and "allied" troops, equipped with the best hardware and training in the world. They do this using just a few old AK47s, some home-made munitions and mines made in their cowsheds with whatever they can find.

The IRA held the British army at bay for nearly 30 years with a couple of hundred of old M16 rifles, some fertiliser and sugar, plus a lot of dustbin banging housewives.

The US sixth fleet in the Persian Gulf is less worried by the deployment of Exocet missiles by Iran than it is by the possibility of an aircraft carrier being attacked by hundreds of tiny Iranian speedboats carrying high explosives. Aircraft carriers are not designed to combat rubber dinghies but small vessels such as these can be deadly to large ships, as witnessed by the attack on the USS Cole by a single small boat laden with high explosives. The giant hardware of the US navy was the subject of Lilliputian attacks by tiny but deadly adversaries.

The British and American military rely on hardware and technology; the guerrilla relies on popular support, inventiveness and asymmetric strategies. Combatants with popular support and an innovative approach tend to win the day.

Examples in manipulative "combat": Similar comparisons exist in the use of manipulative methods, where a powerful manipulator tends to rely on an asymmetry between themselves and the victim. The manipulator has more power, more capital, more time, more technology, more agenda-setting influence and more public voice than the victim. This gives the manipulator an ability to implement their plan against the victim.

However, the same opportunity for asymmetric counter-measures is also available to a victim. A powerful manipulator also has weaknesses and a small flexible victim can create mayhem for a slow-moving adversary. A combination of trans-national legal systems such as the European courts together with the use of social networking technology, web technology and more rapid access to the conventional press, can give a victim with limited resources the opportunity to attack and bring down a corporate or institutional giant that is engaged in manipulation.

The battle of David and Goliath has come of age.

---oOo---

7. Manipulative methods: an analysis

We now come to describe the characteristics, applications, and limitations of the most common manipulative methods which we have researched and defined so far, with some illustrative examples.

We won't discuss the morality too much further; we will simply explain how these methods actually work.

The analytical structure: For each method we have used a fixed format which describes each manipulative method in detail. The format is as follows:

- **Definition:** This is a short definition of the manipulative method.

- **Persistence and Accessibility:** Included in each section are two indicators which may help to demonstrate the degree of seriousness with which each manipulative technique should be taken. The first is persistence and the second is accessibility.

- **Persistence:** This is the likely duration of a manipulative action.

- **Accessibility:** is the term used to define the availability of the technique to the manipulator rather than to other persons. A high accessibility indicates that it is a widely available technique. A low accessibility means that it is available only to very specific groups of manipulators. In some cases, the analysis shows the accessibility in terms of a/ Institutional accessibility and b/ Interpersonal accessibility. Some manipulative methods are very simple for an institution but very difficult to access for an individual, and vice versa.

- **Conditions/Opportunity/Effectiveness:** This section refers to the conditions in which the manipulative method can be used, what opportunities are required and how effective the method is.

- **Examples:** These are included in each section. Here we provide some real or realistic examples of how these methods work in practice.

- **Methodology/Refinements/Sub-species:** This section defines the precise methodologies used to execute this manipulation. It defines any refinements of the basic method and any known "sub-species" of the main method.

- **Avoidance and Counteraction:** A description of how a victim or victim group can recognise, avoid and counteract a manipulative act which uses this manipulative method.

---oOo---

8. Agenda control

8.1 Definition: Agenda control is the manipulation of a voting group by control of the order, content and/or phrasing of the agenda for a discussion of issues upon which a group is required to vote. The manipulation works by using one or more methods to alter the outcome of a vote by limiting the choices, setting the order of voting, manipulating the phrasing of a vote or rigging the voting system.

8.2 Persistence: Short. It only applies for the particular agenda in question, but the effects of a manipulated decision can be very long lasting.

8.3 Accessibility: This depends on the users of agenda control:

- **Institutions:** Low - only those persons who decide on the contents of an agenda can use this method. Usually only a small group decides what a meeting or voting agenda contains. These are the only people that can alter the agenda's content.

- **Interpersonal:** High - anyone of us can force an argument into a simple show of hands, and by some very simple manipulations can alter the agenda to guarantee a pre-determined outcome. It is a common method of manipulating an argument to a particular outcome.

8.4 Conditions/Opportunity/Effectiveness: This method of manipulation is very effective and has been used for centuries in both totalitarian and democratic institutions. It is frequently used in interpersonal manipulation.

Institutional: In an institutional sense, its use is limited to individuals who are "constitutionally" guaranteed the right to construct an agenda for a democratic system, like a meeting culminating in a vote.

In a corporate environment, the method is used by those who are responsible for proposing an agenda for a corporate meeting. The meeting will end with a decision being democratically reached using a vote. The manipulator tends to be an interested member of the corporate management but can also be a union representative, a group of corporate creditors, managers or directors etc.

Interpersonal: In human relationships, agenda control is used to curtail an adversary's options. Typically a manipulator will seize control of the agenda, create a credible set of options (tailored to a particular outcome) and present this as a complete, honest agenda ending in an objective and representative vote.

The perpetrator must be responsible for establishing the agenda of the discussion. The agenda setter, in a manipulative sense, protects and advances their own interests or prevents others from protecting theirs, simply by virtue of their position.

Examples of such individuals are government ministers, party-leaders, company chairmen, labour leaders, team leaders, dispute arbitrators etc. These are the type of people who are seen as competent to oversee the writing of a meeting agenda.

In an interpersonal context, the agenda setter needs to be an "alpha dog" who takes control of the agenda, appealing to the common sense and weakness of a victim or group and presenting themselves as strong, honest brokers.

8.5 Methodology/Refinements/Sub-species: There are four important ways to successfully set an agenda to manipulate a voting body to produce a favourable decision:

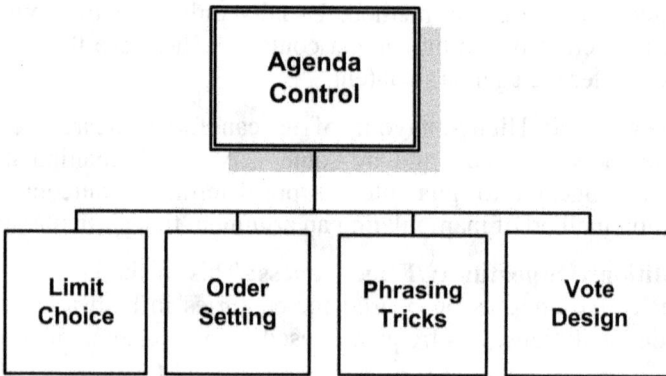

```
                    ┌──────────────┐
                    │   Agenda     │
                    │   Control    │
                    └──────────────┘
       ┌───────────┬──────┴──────┬───────────┐
  ┌─────────┐ ┌─────────┐ ┌─────────┐ ┌─────────┐
  │  Limit  │ │  Order  │ │Phrasing │ │  Vote   │
  │ Choice  │ │ Setting │ │ Tricks  │ │ Design  │
  └─────────┘ └─────────┘ └─────────┘ └─────────┘
```

8.5.1 Choice limitation. Here a manipulator restricts the range of discussion and subject matter to a series of choices which they have designed in advance. The purpose is to generate a result which embodies either their desired goals or minimizes the effect of not achieving the optimal result.

In the case of a restriction of choices, there is no alternative for the victim but to choose from what is on offer. When the choices cannot be restricted as the manipulator would prefer, they can add unattractive alternatives or contrive to make the real alternatives unattractive.

This is common practice in industrial disputes. A management seeking the redundancy of a number of employees will always start the negotiations by calling for perhaps three times the real number to be laid off. They will offer a very limited and unattractive set of choices, such as closure of the company, relocation, employee demotion etc., whilst there will be one attractive option such as a large severance payment to those affected. The union negotiator will demand zero redundancies or strike action, but the voting workers will inevitably opt for the least damaging and most available alternative when called upon to choose. Many alternative possibilities are excluded by both sides of the dispute, because the management is controlling the agenda and the union and workforce are forced to operate within the deliberately limited agenda.

8.5.2 Order setting. In this case the manipulator controls the order of discussion and voting. There are two ways in which this might be done:

- **Distracting attention:** Firstly, the sequence of an entire agenda can be set so as to dissipate the importance of an issue which the manipulator wishes to receive less than normal attention. The contentious issue is partly concealed from the rest of the voting body.

  One option for doing this would be to put such an issue at the end of an agenda for a very long meeting. Another possibility is to use the cover of a very important item of breaking news to divert attention, or hide something contentious or controversial. A disaster may represent a good opportunity or to put it another way, "a good day to hide bad news".

  In the famous example of 11 September 2001, after both World Trade Centre towers had been hit in terrorist attacks, but before either tower had collapsed, Jo Moore, special advisor to the Blair government sent an email to the press office of her department which read: "It's now a very good day to get out anything we want to bury, i.e. councillors' expenses?" The intention was to hide some relatively bad news whilst the press and public were distracted by the enormity of the 9/11 attacks.

- **Stage management:** Secondly, if an agenda setter wants to get a vote in favour of a particular option, they can do so by setting the sequence of business so that "the scene is set" for a vote in their favour.

  They do this by preceding the target agenda item with other items upon which they are sure to obtain pre-determined majority decisions. These decisions subsequently oblige the victims to vote in favour of a manipulator's issue because the voters have already set a precedent in their earlier decisions, and their attitudes towards the issue have already been modified by their responses to the preceding business.

  For example, if a manager presiding over a budgetary meeting is seeking additional financial allocations for his manufacturing department he may wait to make his play for funding until the issue of say, purchasing new company cars has been discussed. He can then, in advance, place an agenda item after the "company car vote". The precedent of buying luxury fringe benefits is made nice and clear in everybody's mind. Then, if he meets any opposition to the motion for a budget allocation for real operational costs for his department, the manager has a very persuasive precedent available. Very few could argue with a straight face for new cars but against new production equipment.

8.5.3 Phrasing tricks. An agenda setter is responsible for writing and circulating the agenda. Normally they have a great deal of personal discretion in terms of the phrasing of agenda items. The manipulator may turn this to their advantage by wording issues for discussion with emphasis placed according to personal preferences. Thus the victims of this trick are forced to answer in a particular, predetermined way.

A manipulator may precede a contentious question with another harmless one. The expected answer to the first question may then be used to exclude an undesirable response to the second.

Another trick is to pose a question with alternative answers both of which are beneficial to the manipulator but of no value to the victims.

A useful biblical example of this technique is the story of Jesus being asked whether the Jews should pay their taxes to the occupying Romans. If he answered "yes", he offended the powerful Jewish nationalist faction. If he said "no" he was inciting civil disobedience against the Romans. Both responses were therefore fatally damaging to him. Fortunately he had a coin in his pocket which helped him out of this squeeze by attributing both arguments equally.

8.5.4 Vote design. In most democratic or pseudo-democratic institutions the voting methods used are embodied in some kind of constitution. However, constitutions usually deal only with matters such as the minimum majority required for the passage of a motion, quorum size etc., and not with the order in which votes are taken.

The objective of vote design is to select a system of voting which will guarantee that a desired alternative is endorsed or that an undesirable result is avoided. In less rigorously organized votes, such as those found in labour disputes and informal meetings, there are no restrictions on the agenda setter or promoter of a motion in using this method.

Take the classical example described by Pliny the Younger in the Roman senate. A number of slaves had been accused of murdering their lord. There was some possibility of his suicide or of the slaves having been asked to kill the old man because he was terminally sick. They were to be tried by a jury. After their hearing the jury was split in its opinion. The alternatives were acquittal, banishment, or death.

The jury was split as follows:

> Acquitters 45%
>
> Banishers 35%
>
> Executioners 20%

In other words, a majority of the jury felt the slaves to be guilty of either murder or assisting in the suicide of their master. However, more of the jury believed in acquittal than in either other choice.

Pliny personally believed that the slaves were completely innocent and he was thus in favour of their acquittal. He also happened to be the court's presiding officer. He recognized that the "Banishers" were more in favour of acquittal than death, that the "Executioners" were more in favour of banishment than acquittal and that the "Acquitters" were more in favour of banishment than death. He also realized that he couldn't bring about acquittal using the normal voting method because the majority was saying "guilty".

What Pliny decided was to adopt a tripartite approach to the problem, in which he assumed that each of the jury's options was exclusive to the others. In order to do this he had to avoid the question of "innocent or guilty" and so he employed a so-called ternary voting method instead of the more usual binary voting order.

In the binary scenario, the jury would be asked first, "guilty or innocent?" followed in this case, by "Death or Banishment?" The majority believed the prisoners guilty, but the majority were also against the death penalty and so the prisoners would certainly be banished.

But using the ternary method, Pliny simply asked "death, banishment or acquittal?", and required those in favour of each option to go and seat themselves together in separate places. The group with the largest number of supporters was to represent the decision of the court. In this case of course, the largest numbers sat with the "acquitters" with 45% and Pliny had his own way.

He got himself into a certain amount of bother for this trickery, although he claims that he knew of no precedent for not using this method of voting.

Naturally the method relies upon the victims voting myopically but since this is what most people do, the technique is successful in either achieving the desired result or some next best alternative for the manipulator.

8.6 Avoidance and Counteraction: For the manipulator, there are virtually no drawbacks to this procedure because it is the prerogative of the Agenda setter to establish the rules of the agenda. The way in which the manipulator constructs the agenda is entirely at his discretion.

The choice to manipulate is moral rather than constitutional. He only risks the disapproval of the voting population who may attempt to make changes in the constitution at a later date. In the short term, the only counteraction is the removal of the agenda setter or the resignation of the voting group.

---oOo---

9. Strategic voting

9.1 Definition: In a constitutional structure within a democratic institution it is possible for a manipulator to achieve all or some of his goals by the strategic use of his and other people's voting-rights and habits.

Apart from the democratic use of strategic voting, there is also the tactical use of voting fraud or as Joe Stalin observed: "It's not the votes that matter... it's who counts the votes that matters". All of these types fall within the manipulative method we call "Strategic Voting".

9.2 Persistence: Short - it can only be used during periods when votes are being used in the decision making process. The effects of swinging a vote may be long but the availability of the method is confined to the period of an election.

9.3 Accessibility: High - anyone with a vote can vote strategically in some way by voting tactically, abstaining, or optimising their votes. More sophisticated strategic voting manipulation involving fraud is less accessible to ordinary people and fraud is usually much more difficult to carry out.

9.4 Conditions/Opportunity/Effectiveness: The use of these techniques relies upon the fact that democratic constitutions expect an electorate to vote simply and myopically in favour of their considered choice or ranked preferences and that voting is carried out without any external fraudulent interference.

Normally this is true, most of us do vote in this way with consideration only to our preferred outcome. We know what we want and we vote for it.

However, when voting populations are small or majorities are very tight then conditions may exist for strategic voting to be effective in getting a particular result.

The tactical voter: The basic strategic-tactical voter realizes that voting myopically is not always in their best interests. This is especially true when they are confronted by a so-called no-win situation, where they may decide on a "pyrrhic strategy" - some type of scorched earth strategy. They realise that they cannot succeed, so they use their vote to ensure that the opponents cannot succeed either. A typical example would be to force a "hung vote", where no-one wins outright.

The prime objective of the tactical voter or vote manipulator must be to obtain the "optimal result in the circumstances", but the technique is also used to minimize the damage done to the manipulator's own interests, even though it may not achieve their optimal goal.

Election size: The relevance of strategic voting to the individual is inversely proportional to the size of the voting population. In a general election the voting strategies of a citizen are much more insignificant, but at boardroom, party-election, or committee level, the individual strategic voter can really have dramatic effects.

Therefore, in larger electoral environments, the use of strategic voting techniques often need some help from vote fraud as well.

9.5 Methodology/Refinements/Sub-species: There are five basic types of strategic voting technique possible. Tactical voting also provides an additional 4 sub-types:

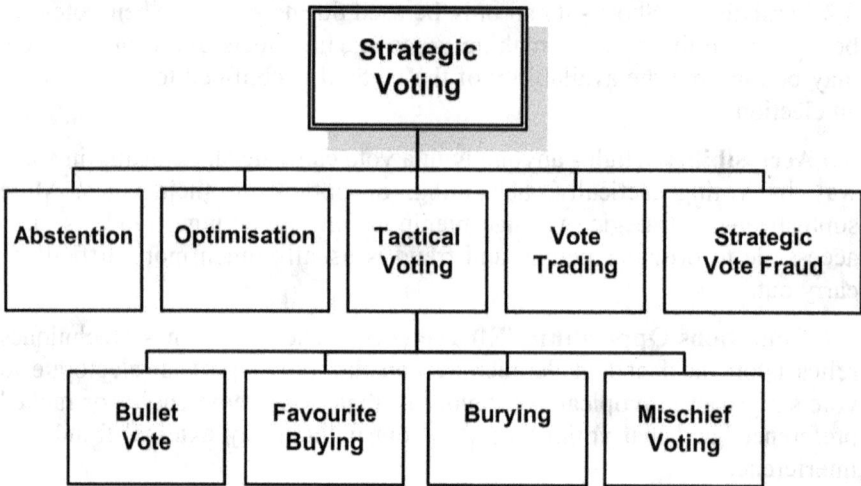

9.5.1 Abstention. Most democratic and pseudo-democratic institutions have constitutions which set out certain rules concerning the taking of a vote, such as the minimum majority required to carry a motion, quorum size, e.g. "two thirds of members must be present", etc.

It is these rules which the strategic voter exploits when he decides to abstain. For instance, in a committee of ten where there is a split of 7:3 against the manipulator and a clause in the voting constitution which demands a 100% vote, the manipulator cannot win by voting, but he can abstain and thus have the motion dismissed. This at least buys him time until the motion is raised again. The advantage of abstention depends entirely on which voting rules apply in a given situation.

Example: Abstention or None of the above: [9.1] Abstention has many possible effects depending on the circumstances and the particular rules of how abstentions are managed. A sizable abstention may cause a vote to fail completely when a minimum percentage of electors or quorum is not reached. In other cases, abstention may politically invalidate the outcome of an election. If only 20% of the electorate turn out to vote, few politicians can really claim a resounding vote of confidence.

In small votes, abstention can also be useful. Members of the UN Security Council often abstain rather than using their veto. It has the effect of allowing a popular move to proceed but without giving it the moral consent of their nation.

In elections in 1991 in the Soviet Union the use of the "none of the above" forced new elections in over 200 cases and led to the defeat of over 100 incumbents. Boris Yeltsin later claimed that the use of the "none of the above" had been pivotal in convincing the Soviet population that, despite the rigged elections, they could still exercise some power by using this form of abstention.

9.5.2 Optimisation. The most common use of strategic voting is not necessarily the achievement of a manipulator's objective, but may be some damage limitation or "next best" objective.

This entails the strategist recognising that their cause is hopeless and therefore voting for another cause. This alternative choice is the best, or the least damaging the manipulator can hope to achieve in the absence of their original option. For this strategy to work, the alternate choice must have a good chance of winning.

For example, in a three cornered fight, such as a disciplinary action against an employee for some misdemeanour, a manager may believe that the employee should be dismissed. But realizing that the cause is hopeless, he will vote for suspension rather than allow those who advocate only a written warning to form the majority. He may recognize that he has a greater chance of bringing about some punitive action in this way than by voting for his first choice, which is doomed.

9.5.3 Tactical Voting: In a voting system, tactical voting happens when a voter misrepresents their sincere preferences in order to gain a more favourable outcome.

Every voting system attracts some form of tactical voting. However, the type of tactical voting and the extent to which it affects the tone of the campaign and the results of the election vary significantly from one voting system to another.

There are several sub-types of tactical voting. Here we describe the four most commonly used techniques:

- **Bullet Vote:** Bullet voting happens when a voter votes for just one candidate, even though they have the right to vote for more than one candidate in their particular voting system. In this way, a voter helps their preferred candidate by not giving any votes to their rivals.

- **Favourite Buying:** This is a type of tactical voting in which a voter insincerely ranks an alternative choice higher in the hope of getting it elected. In a "first-past-the-post" system a voter may vote for an option they perceive as having a greater chance of winning over an option they prefer.

  For example a tactical left-wing voter may vote for a popular moderate left-wing candidate over the unpopular hard left candidate he prefers. This tendency is one of the reasons that the "first-past-the-post" system tends to lead to 2 party states, like Britain and the USA.

- **Burying:** Burying is a type of tactical voting in which the voter insincerely ranks an alternative lower in the hopes of defeating it. For example, a voter may insincerely rank a perceived strong alternative last in order to help their preferred alternative beat it. A real-world analogy would be US voters of one party voting in the other party's primary elections against the candidate that they think might beat the candidate of their own party.

- **Mischief Vote:** This is a type of tactical voting in which a voter ranks a perceived weak alternative higher, but not in the hopes of getting it elected. This usually occurs in runoff voting where a voter already believes that their favoured candidate will make it to the next round.

  The voter then ranks an unwanted, but easily beatable, candidate higher so that their preferred candidate can win later. It may involve a voter ranking an alternative lower in the hope of getting it elected, or ranking an alternative higher in the hope of defeating it. This is also called paradoxical voting.

Tactical voting example: In the 1997 UK general election, the Democratic Left helped activist Bruce Kent set up "GROT - Get Rid of Them". This was a tactical voter campaign designed to help prevent the Conservative party from gaining another term in office. This voting coalition was made up of individuals in all opposition parties plus some who were un-aligned with any other party. This diverse group was united in a wish to stop the re-election of the Conservatives and indeed the Conservatives were roundly defeated. While it is impossible to prove that GROT swung the election, it did attract significant media attention and brought tactical voting into the mainstream for the first time in UK politics.

9.5.4 Vote-trading. All voters have a greater or lesser interest in different issues. What is vitally important for one voter may be irrelevant to another person. It is upon this fact that vote trading relies.

The manipulative vote trader must understand in some detail what the preferences are and have the strength of opinion in the voting population within which they are operating. Having established this, they can then set about trading their votes with their colleagues on any number of issues.

A manipulator uses this by first deciding on which issues he requires additional support. He then determines which issues are of no particular interest to him, but in which other voters have a particular interest. The manipulator then simply has to approach the right voters and offer his support on their priority issues, in return for their votes for his.

It's not fraudulent, but it's not morally honest either because it persuades voters who have higher and lower priorities to sacrifice their voting rights on lower priority issues.

9.5.5 Strategic Vote Fraud: Vote fraud on a large scale is easy to detect and hard to cover up. However, vote fraud can be effective on a small scale where the fraud is strategically executed and where its effect is disproportionately effective to the small scale of the fraud.

A small voting fraud, like small scale ballot stuffing or buying the votes of ambivalent voters is quite hard to detect in a large scale election. But by targeting key swing constituencies where the fraud is unlikely to be noticed, a vote fraud can be very effective and low risk. It is particularly effective where margins are extremely tight.

Strategic fraud example: The election of George W. Bush as president of the U.S.A. in 2000 hung in the balance for 36 days because of the voting returns from the state of Florida, where Bush's brother was governor.

Because the margin was so very tight, a recount was called. As a result of this, a large number of voting irregularities emerged which disqualified many voters. Despite legal attempts by Bush to stop the recounts, the manual recounts continued.

On December 8, Florida's high court upheld the manual recount. However, the next day, Bush successfully appealed for a stay from the U.S. Supreme Court to stop the recount. Bush's team argued that the Constitution's guarantee of equal protection for all citizens disqualified a manual recount because Florida's counties had followed differing vote-counting procedures. The Gore team demanded that every vote be counted.

On December 12, the Republican dominated U.S. Supreme Court, in a 5-to-4 vote, stopped the Florida recount. Though Gore received more popular votes than Bush, he conceded the next day. This was a case where strategic vote fraud took place at the count, with the collusion of the US Supreme Court. And the rest, as they say, is history.

9.6 Avoidance and Counteraction: Apart from strategic vote fraud, there isn't a lot that anyone can do to avoid and counteract these manipulative methods. Abstention, optimisation, tactical voting and vote trading are generally not illegal or in breach of most state or corporate rules.

The only counteraction possibilities are to pre-warn the rest of the electorate that the manipulator is acting in a certain way to swing the vote. This may make possible partners more reluctant to assist the manipulator for fear of being seen as having lost their independence. But, ultimately, the manipulator has the right to vote in any way he wishes and to persuade others to vote with him. Another alternative is to encourage large numbers of otherwise apathetic voters to participate in order to dilute the effects of the manipulator.

However, it gets a bit trickier if strategic vote fraud is involved. In such cases the risk of being uncovered as a fraud must be avoided by the manipulator, at least until power is transferred and the fraud can be hidden or blamed on someone else or just "sour grapes" by the losers. In terms of avoidance and counteraction, a victim can only warn of the risks of fraud and demand vigilance.

---oOo---

10. Moving the goalposts - Manipulate dimensions

10.1 Definition: Manipulation of dimensions is the technique wherein a manipulator introduces completely new issues or a new set of rules into a discussion or decision making process.

This is done to alter the balance of existing opinions of the voting or decision-making group. The fixing of dimensions, the antithesis of this, is also included here.

10.2 Persistence: Medium to long - the new rules or "facts" that are introduced by a manipulator may become a highly credible part of the story accepted by a gullible general public.

10.3 Accessibility: High. Almost anyone can introduce a rumour or lie which could have the effect of altering the "facts" of a discussion or decision. As a result, a victim's opposition is deflected into a completely new direction which promotes the interests of the manipulator.

"Moving the goalposts" can be something as trivial as someone introducing a little lie about some previous event, thus setting a precedent, or it could be some rumour which is difficult to disprove but which has strong emotive undercurrents.

One contemporary instance is often heard in discussions between evolutionists and creationists in the United States. Evolutionists repeatedly argue that the theory of evolution only seeks to explain the evolution of species and they say it makes no statement on the theological concept of creation at all.

However, creationists object to the principle of evolution because they say it seeks to explain the creation of life. They manipulatively transform the argument about evolution into an argument about theological concepts of creation, so as to rally support from fundamentalist Christians.

10.4 Conditions/Opportunity/Effectiveness: The technique is also referred to colloquially as "moving the goalposts" [in the middle of the game].

This is a very appropriate title, because the whole idea of the method is to change the rules or issues involved in a discussion, decision or vote by interfering with the original available alternatives or by introducing strong, new influences into the discussion.

It can be a highly effective form of manipulation when used against inexperienced subjects. Many opportunities exist for its use, even in interpersonal contacts where a conversation or argument can be completely side-tracked into a totally new direction by a clever manipulator.

10.5 Methodology/Refinements/Sub-species: There are five common ways in which the method can be manifested by a manipulator:

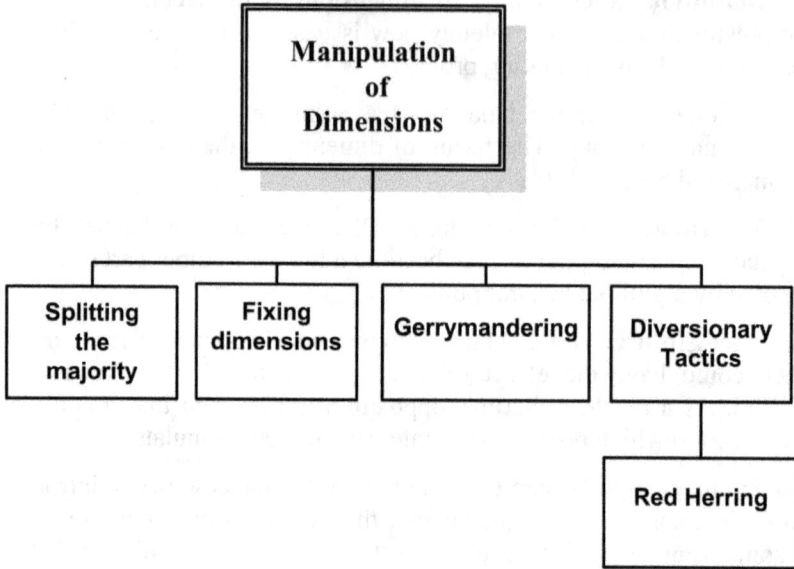

```
                    ┌─────────────────────┐
                    │    Manipulation     │
                    │         of          │
                    │     Dimensions      │
                    └─────────────────────┘
                               │
   ┌───────────┬───────────────┼───────────────┬──────────────┐
┌──────────┐ ┌───────────┐ ┌───────────────┐ ┌──────────────┐
│ Splitting│ │  Fixing   │ │ Gerrymandering│ │ Diversionary │
│   the    │ │dimensions │ │               │ │   Tactics    │
│ majority │ │           │ │               │ │              │
└──────────┘ └───────────┘ └───────────────┘ └──────────────┘
                                                      │
                                              ┌──────────────┐
                                              │ Red Herring  │
                                              └──────────────┘
```

10.5.1 Splitting the majority: In the event that a manipulator encounters a majority in favour of or against a motion with which he does not agree, he may introduce a new dimension into a previously simple decision. The objective here is to splinter the majority into parts, one or more of which the manipulator can then use to form a new allegiance and a new majority.

The manipulator must be certain that there is sufficiently strong support amongst elements of the original majority for his "new dimension". Once assured, the next stage is the formation of a new majority from the newly segmented parts and the manipulator's original minority.

For instance, in a labour dispute concerning a management's limitation on overtime, the management can diffuse the majority demanding the status quo by offering productivity bonuses for the normal working week.

Whilst most of the workers may have been initially in favour of keeping the amount of overtime as it was, the introduction of the dimension of additional productivity payments for normal working hours will split this majority. Some of the workers will undoubtedly prefer to earn more for their standard working week than to hold out for overtime payments.

The effect is a split majority: the workers' overtime demand is no longer unanimous and the new proposal wins the day. The net effect is that employees are paid a little more for higher productivity during standard working hours with no net cost to the company.

10.5.2 Fixing dimensions: An experienced manipulator will quickly recognize when a new dimension is being added to split his majority or deflate support for his particular issue and he will undoubtedly take steps to fix the parameters as he intends. He will endeavour to suspend the range of discussion and choice as they were originally arranged so that he can be sure of getting his own preferred decision.

A common method of specifying the dimensions is to first allow outside interference with the imposition of another dimension and then to intervene with some rapid stage management to separate off or neutralize the offending interloper.

In the example just mentioned concerning an overtime dispute, an astute union-leader would readily overcome the addition of a new dimension (i.e. productivity payments) and the management's attempts to split his majority. He would do this by firstly allowing management to offer productivity payments to the employees and then secondly suggesting to his members that their demands be extended to include productivity payments on overtime hours as well. Needless to say this would be unacceptable to the management as the "overtime dimension" would then be fixed, whilst the "productivity dimension" would be invalidated for use by the management because the new dimension would be now seen as an even higher cost outcome.

10.5.3 Gerrymandering: This involves the redrawing of districts to benefit politicians or political parties. The term derives from Governor Eldridge Gerry whose redistricting of Massachusetts resulted in one district that resembled a salamander. The practice no longer just applies to the configuring of district boundaries to the benefit of one party at the expense of another, but also refers to the rigging of electoral maps to favour incumbents.

In the sense of a manipulative method, gerrymandering is an artificial restriction or extension of voting or decision making rights within an area or group, so as to minimize opposition from or maximize support for the manipulator.

In national and local elections this is done by moving physical boundaries around to ensure that the maximum numbers of seats are won by the minimum number of the manipulator's candidates. It's such an old and obvious trick that it's amazing governments still get away with it, but they always have and still do.

In Britain there is no doubt that the Northern Irish constituencies were gerrymandered. Until the recent past this happened in order to ensure that the Protestant land-owning population held a disproportionately large majority in any Parliament and could block attempts towards representation of Irish nationalists.

More fundamentally in Britain, the "first past the post" electoral system certainly doesn't permit a truly democratic election. The only parties which express any desire to change the electoral system to allow proportional representation are those parties which are unlikely ever to gain power under the present electoral regime. Their votes are effectively wasted and this is despite a very sizeable proportion of the population wishing to see the system reformed into something more representative than the present system.

In commerce a management can gerrymander a vote on some issue of working conditions by excluding part-time and contract personnel from a canvas of opinion. A union can do the same by recognizing only its member's opinions and ignoring non-union workers. There are numerous opportunities to artificially redraw boundaries in ways which seems perfectly reasonable but which are really just manipulative gerrymandering.

10.5.4 Diversionary tactics: This is the introduction of tangential or irrelevant issues in order to preoccupy the public whilst more important events are taking place.

We suffer from this manipulation daily these days as our "drive-by media" inundates us with endless sensationalistic stories of crisis and doom, but then shows no follow-up on these stories. The doom is more important than the story because it is designed simply to deflect us from the central news story line which is often completely unconnected.

When stories expose a scandal in a particular political party or show another party too favourably, incidental news stories suddenly emerge to distract attention away from the really important newsworthy events. Pop culture occurrences, like the death of a celebrity, may be hyped to the extreme in order to divert the public's attention away from more important matters like political corruption.

10.5.5 Red Herring: This is a form of diversionary tactic where completely irrelevant information is added to a discussion or decision making process in an attempt to derail debate or opposition by causing confusion on the issues involved. To distinguish from "diversionary tactics", a "Red Herring" is not about new issues, it's just new irrelevant data about the same issues.

The concept of red herrings is also discussed later in the context of rhetorical manipulation.

10.6 Avoidance and Counteraction: A manipulator must ensure that he has watertight reasons for introducing a new dimension, fixing the old dimensions, or changing the rules of a discussion or conflict, otherwise his motives will become obvious and the victims will employ the same strategies against him.

Avoiding goalpost moving: Identifying a manipulation of dimensions is pretty straightforward to an experienced negotiator. After it has been detected it's only a matter of deciding how to stop the "goalposts being moved". The standard way to avoid and counteract this manipulation is to fix the dimensions back to where they started.

To do this, the victim must stop the manipulator introducing alternative options, other rules and boundaries, different issues or irrelevant information into the discussion. The victim can demand that the manipulator provide much more detail of any alternative options and issues. This will certainly slow down the process of altering the dimensions.

Avoiding diversions: To manage the introduction of tangential or misleading issues or irrelevant data, a victim can use repetition to constantly restate the original issues in simple, clear mantras and can reinforce the clear definition of all language or data used in the discussion.

This sort of pedantry can be very disconcerting for the "drive-by" operator or seller of red herrings. They rely on the rapid uptake of their false issues and irrelevant data. Anything which delays this process will make the public less likely to fall into their diversionary traps.

---o0o---

11. Lying (Deceit)

11.1 Definition: Deceit is the deliberate exploitation of a victim's rational ignorance. In the case of manipulative untruth, it is done with a view to promoting an exploiter's interests or damaging the interests of a victim.

11.2 Persistence: Short to long, depending on the deceit.

11.3 Accessibility: High - Deceit is available to everyone.

11.4 Conditions/Opportunity/Effectiveness: Apart from the fact that a victim must be ignorant of the knowledge possessed by the manipulator, deceit works when the cost of discovering and assessing the truth is too great for the victim.

The cost of truth: The ratio of the cost of truth versus the value of establishing the facts by an alternative method must be high for deceit to work, the higher the better for the manipulator.

When we discuss the cost of truth here, we are referring to the time and resources which must be expended by a victim to research an issue in sufficient depth for both a complete range of alternatives to be formulated and to prove deception.

Except in very simple cases of deceit, the cost of establishing the truth tends to be very significant and prohibitive. The benefits are measurable only in terms of how much accepting a manipulator's assertion will damage the victim's interests.

Generally speaking, when a victim is presented with some fact which is difficult to verify or disclaim, he will simply accept it or wait for someone else to challenge it. Naturally everyone waits for someone else to check out the facts, and, of course, in the end usually no one does anything. The manipulator relies upon this phenomenon.

From a "normal", cautious deceiver's point of view, a lie should generally be kept small and simple if it is not to be discovered.

Information being communicated to a victim must be difficult to verify. This, therefore, limits the use of deceit as a method of manipulation in its simplest form.

Small lies and proxies: An obvious way to avoid being caught telling a lie is for the manipulator to use a proxy to carry out the deceit. This is a very economical policy for the deceiver because they must only lie to one individual, who is then charged with the dissemination of the lie to others.

Thus, if the deceit is discovered, the manipulator can disclaim any involvement and only has to deal with the proxy, who is now publicly recognized and discredited as a deceiver.

11.5 Methodology/Refinements/Sub-species: There are seven basic "refinements" used in deceit as a manipulative method.

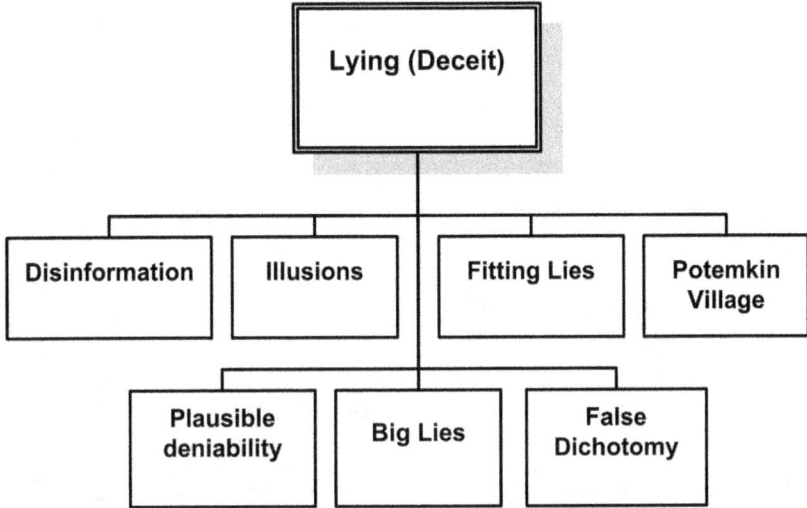

11.5.1 Disinformation: Disinformation is a broad category of political manipulation whose origins can be traced back to techniques of intelligence and spying operations over centuries of history.

The KGB was the unquestioned master of "Dezinformatsia" and a great deal of insight on this subject can be gained by reading about the Soviet agency's tactics. Since the Cold war ended, Western intelligence agencies have adopted STASI and KGB techniques in similar campaigns of disinformation, for use both internally and externally.

The goal of disinformation is not merely to misinform, but rather to condition the victim to respond to information in a predictable way. The responses of victims may range from knee-jerk revulsion, anger, sympathy, to fits of rage and other types of irrational behaviour.

Disinformation can be a one-off operation or part of a coordinated campaign working in tandem with an educational system.

War-time disinformation: According to the old adage, the first casualty of war is truth. Modern proxy wars manipulated by the super-powers are no exception to this. One of the most manipulated facts in most modern wars is the casualty rate and who is responsible for what. Take the case of the so-called Syrian civil war, still raging in January 2013, when suddenly the number of deaths according to the UN jumped by 15,000 on the 1st of

January without any explanation. Why was this sudden adjustment necessary? The answer lies in changes in policy. The numbers are entirely invented just to support these political imperatives. In the case of Syria, the UN was providing political cover for the arming and supply of the "rebels" by the Western powers and the Arab League so it was felt that the number of deaths needed to be higher to provide sufficient political justification.

It's not just a question of lies, damned lies and statistics in a war. Each side produces its own rules for the dead. And none of them tell the truth. Figuring out just how many souls die in a civil war and whose "side" they were on when they died is a dangerous game. News desks must beware.

History suggests that the "bad guys" must always be held responsible in the media for the greatest number of deaths of innocent civilians. In the Middle Eastern wars of recent years, civilians who became "freedom fighters" for the West often ended up in civilian death lists. However, men and women killed by the "good guys" (the West) often don't get onto lists of the dead at all. This was witnessed in Iraq and Afghanistan where the US military made no secret of the fact that they did not keep statistics on civilian deaths (collateral damage).

11.5.2 Plausible deniability: This form of deceit relies on the ability to persuasively argue that a manipulator is not connected to a person, group, or event responsible for some particular action - even when this assertion is not true.

It may include other tactics such as hedging one's lie with some truth (a "half-truth"), or making surprisingly candid statements to gain credibility so that a future lie is more effectively and credibly received.

11.5.3 Illusions: The creation and maintenance of an illusion can be a powerful method of control. A topical case in point is the bank executive who argues to the bitter end that his bank is solvent.

Similarly, the Minister of Finance who maintains that the economy is in good shape even while his civil servants prepare for sovereign default. The technique could be described as a form of "latent deceit" because it can often be disguised as incompetence rather than malice.

Instances abound, such as the case where Irish beef burgers were found to contain up to 29% horse meat. Despite the hard reality that Irish meat factories were adulterating food, various officials made almost immediate public statements to the effect that Ireland had the "best food production and oversight systems in the world" - an amazing contradiction between fact and illusion.

Another contemporary case occurred when in 2012 the Spanish government's Minister of Finance repeatedly proclaimed for almost 9 months that his government required no IMF bailout. Towards the end of that year the government finally admitted that it was effectively insolvent and had to obtain a record 100 billion Euros in "bailout" funding and the loss of its economic sovereignty. The illusion of solvency was held up for 9 months before finally collapsing under the weight of reality. The victims of the Spanish government's temporary manipulation were the international capital markets and credit rating agencies. For a while they were convinced of the liquidity of Spain's banking system. But once the illusion collapsed, the cost of Spanish debt increased dramatically to unsustainable levels. The country's debt was downgraded to "junk", and rating agencies viciously downgraded the credit worthiness of Spain. The manipulators' victims took a merciless economic revenge.

11.5.4 Big Lies: "Shit sticks": A possible method of improving the effectiveness of deceit and overcoming its potential drawbacks, is for a manipulator to tell "big lies".

A "big lie" may be either complex or have wide ranging implications. As we explain later in this chapter, the more complex a lie, the more likely it is to be exposed.

So why tell "big lies" if there is more risk of the manipulator being discovered?

When large scale deceit is employed, the manipulator may be willing to accept exposure. This is because they may still achieve or partially achieve their goals before the lie is uncovered. Even when discovered, a large deceit may have already had the necessary effect, dramatic impact or initiated certain important events before it is exposed. This is the concept of "shit sticks", where if a manipulator throws enough dirt at least some of it will stick to the victim.

Corporate deceit of this kind is very common when a company wishes to discredit its competitors, for instance, by suggesting that the victim has acute financial problems or that there is some technical problem with its product.

The "Big Lie" concept was made famous by Joseph Goebbels (and Adolf Hitler). The strategy often works because big lies are so preposterous that many people do not suspect that anyone would dare tell such a big lie.

As Goebbels put it, "If you tell a lie big enough and keep repeating it, people will eventually come to believe it."

Let us take a modern example of the Big Lie: "ISAF (NATO) and the Afghanistan army are cooperating well and the whole country is under ISAF control". With the benefit of hindsight we can now say how absurd this huge deception was. How could anyone have believed it? [11.1]

One weakness of "the Big Lie" is that it can only be maintained for as long as the state can shield the people from the political, economic and/or military consequences and realities behind the lie.

It thus becomes vitally important for the state to use all of its powers to repress dissent. Truth is the mortal enemy of the lie, and thus by extension, truth is the greatest enemy of a deceitful state.

11.5.5 Fitting Lies: Another very effective and sinister method of using deceit is when a manipulator knows in advance what the public wishes to hear. In this case the manipulator can tell unsophisticated lies which are hard to contradict and which assist in his overall strategy.

Since a manipulator's statements gratify or are at least expected by the public (victims), they are rarely challenged.

11.5.6 False dichotomies: This method creates a deception which also includes a moral or emotional dichotomy. This dichotomy makes the basic deception harder to deny.

For instance, there is duplicity in the statement "genetically manipulated crops can feed the world".

Who would stand against the aspiration of feeding the world and the technological possibility that GM could do this?

And so an entirely false dichotomy is established, both completely incorrect and also totally improvable - but it's also very hard to contradict the assertion because it is so emotive and attractive.

11.5.7 Potemkin village: "Suitcase by the Door": This concept was made famous by the idyllic villages constructed to please the Tsarina Catherine the Great on her river-tours of Russia. A Potemkin village is a specially constructed or designed program or policy intended to sell to the public or to policymakers.

At the core, these Potemkin Villages are hollow and false like the hired men and women and the facades erected to please Catherine on her voyages. They create a strong impression on the victim which is based on an entirely empty image.

It is akin to leaving a suitcase next to the front door. Any passing observer will conclude that you are about to leave even though the suitcase is totally empty and you are actually going nowhere.

11.6 Avoidance and Counteraction: Deceit is a very flexible manipulative technique and it comes in an infinite number of forms. It can be difficult to detect.

A manipulator's greatest fear is that his deceits will be exposed, leading to loss of credibility.

Once detected, deceit can be avoided by proving that the manipulator's assertions are lies. Counteracting a deceit comes when a majority of victims stop believing in a particular set of lies and challenge their owner in public.

---oOo---

12. Secrecy

12.1 Definition: Secrecy, as a manipulative tool, involves the withholding of information from an individual or group in the interests of another party which has privileged access to it.

12.2 Persistence: Short to Long. Most secrets emerge eventually but it can take a long time before they are fully revealed, especially if they are actively maintained by the manipulator.

As an example, many atrocities were committed by the British Army and Colonial Service in various British colonies both before and during the break up of the empire in the 1960s[12.1]. However, these cases are only now being discovered because decades of British governments (of all political parties) have deliberately covered up or destroyed evidence of the crimes of previous governments and used legal restrictions like the 30 year rule to hide Cabinet documents from the public.

In June 2009, a small group of elderly Kenyan men and women lodged a claim for compensation against the government in the British High Court. They claim that they had been beaten, raped and castrated by British forces and military of the colonial administration, during the Kenyan "emergency" between 1952 and 1960. The five are veterans of the Mau Mau movement, which rose up against the British colonial administration. This was the first time that the British government had been held to account in a court of law for its terrible deeds in Kenya. A number of male victims suffered from castration, women suffered from horrendous sexual abuse, many thousands of Mau Mau members were beaten, tortured and killed. The Mau Mau movement remained proscribed as a terrorist movement in Kenya until 2003. This was part of a "quiet conspiracy" between the Kenyan and British governments to cover up the appalling atrocities committed at that time by the British colonial services.

Only now, after 50 years of secrecy and conspiracy to hide the truth, are these crimes finally getting a hearing in a court of law.

Secrecy can be very, very persistent.

12.3 Accessibility: High. Everyone has access to the use of secrecy in a manipulative sense. We all have secrets; and many secrets have a value of some kind to someone. In the case of the crimes committed by Britain's governments in its colonies, the value of keeping these atrocities secret lies in the fact that Britain can avoid legal responsibility and demands for reparation and financial compensation.

However not all secrets are valuable and some are almost completely worthless. For example, many people are sensitive about discussing money or politics with others. They therefore keep their own financial and political positions closely guarded secrets. This is despite the fact that such information has almost no value at all to anyone and even if it did have a value, the information could probably be easily found anyway. Such secrets are the result of other social preoccupations and irrelevant in the context of real manipulation.

12.4 Conditions/Opportunity/Effectiveness:

12.4.1 Secrecy is different: The use of secrecy is a form of "super-manipulation" for several reasons and this sets secrecy aside from other manipulative techniques. Why is this? Secrecy is different from other manipulative methods simply because it is also intrinsic in all other manipulative processes discussed here.

All manipulation is partly covert and therefore all manipulative methods rely on part of the action being kept secret from the victim. So, in this sense, secrecy is both a manipulative technique in its own right and is also a property common to every other manipulative method as well.

12.4.2 Advantages of secrecy in manipulation: The major advantage of secrecy in a manipulation is that it is very unlikely to be discovered by those against whom it is directed. Unlike deceit, a secret properly kept, cannot damage the manipulator because it is intended to never be revealed or to be revealed only when it doesn't matter anymore.

12.4.3 Secrecy. How does it manipulate? Secrecy brings about its desired manipulative results because it reduces the victim's base of information and thus restricts the ability of the victim to make properly informed decisions or come to reliable conclusions. This is why we so often hear the phrase "knowledge is power" because an absence of knowledge definitely can be a major cause of weakness.

So, withholding information (keeping a secret) also withholds a victim's right and ability to act according to their will and in their own best interests.

In the case of the crimes of the British Empire we have used above, this translates into denying access to justice for the victims of British government sponsored atrocities. This denies the victims any form of recognition and economic reparation. The secrets are maintained long enough for the victims to have died of old age and therefore there is no legal basis for any economic claims against the government.

Similar secrecy games continue to be played out, in cases like Bloody Sunday, the illegal invasion of Iraq and Afghanistan, the attack on the World Trade Centre in New York, Guantanamo, Secret rendition(aka.

extraordinary rendition in "CIA speak"), the recent Libyan invasion etc. Wherever there is a "nest" of conspiracy theories, there is also a cluster of secrets somewhere close by.

12.4.4 Potency of effect: The use of secrecy rarely exists in isolation. We have mentioned how the high "cost" of information can be used to deter a victim from uncovering the truth. This high cost stops a victim from making informed decisions.

Secrecy is an even more aggressive means of imposing this kind of "information drought" against a victim. Secrecy leaves no opportunity for the victim to uncover the truth. This total depravation of knowledge (secrecy) is even more effective than a simple lie which might be possible to unravel. With secrecy a victim doesn't even know that they are being deprived of some information. They know nothing at all. This makes secrecy the most potent manipulative weapon.

12.4.5 Evolution of Secrecy: Secrecy, as a method of manipulation, is a very ancient phenomenon. Some primitive societies used it as a method of identifying members of their ruling elites. When inaugurating new leaders, they revealed part of a secret myth known only to a small group of tribal elders. The repetition of a part of this myth to the tribal elders was the only means by which a new leader could affirm his divine right to govern.

The proliferation of Secrecy: Today, maintaining secrets is much more widespread and institutionalized throughout our society. One of the reasons is that the amount of information generated in sophisticated societies such as Western capitalist states, is necessarily much greater than in more primitive, less contrived communities of human beings.

- **By government:** The United States had, for instance, some 460 million secret documents in its archives in 1985, and this has certainly increased enormously since then. However, we don't have an estimate for the current level because this fact is also a secret.

- **By religions:** The Vatican Secret Archives have been estimated to contain 84km of shelving. Customarily, documents are made available to the public after a period of 75 years when survivors of church atrocities are most likely to be dead and unable to make civil claims against the Catholic Church.

- **By capitalists:** Non-governmental secrecy is a widely used method of exploitation. The whole edifice of global capital markets relies on the secrecy of investment choices and timing. After all, if we all knew that the value of a particular investment was about to rise, there wouldn't be a competitive market any longer because the concept of risk would be eliminated. Profit and loss would become highly predictable.

12.4.6 Availability of secrecy: Secrecy is employed by all of us at some time or other. Obviously a manipulator's political or social position determines how important their secrets really are in a manipulative sense.

Many private and domestic secrets have no relevance to anyone else apart from us and our immediate families. At a group or political level, secrets tend to become more relevant to the broader community.

Bureaucrats, managers, labour leaders, politicians and many others keep secrets from each other for internal political reasons, such as rendering their colleagues unable to do their job or undercutting their competitors. Secrecy can also be used in an inert way against a subordinate to maintain the elite status of a superior in the work situation. One way or another, there is always a use and an opportunity for secrecy in a manipulative ploy.

12.4.7 The future of secrecy: Secrecy is big business now. A whole industry which existed to maintain the integrity of data confidentiality has blossomed beyond recognition since the advent of the internet and the use of very large databases.

Increased volumes and risks: The sheer volume of data now available electronically has altered the landscape of secrecy in the last 2 decades. Once, databases were stored on paper in locked files behind many layers of physical and administrative security. Today data is stored in several places in electronic format (original and a backup as a minimum). The electronic formats are components of complex networked systems which are almost always connected to many users or even, indirectly, to the general public. Secrecy has become a big issue.

Democratic rights: The risks to democratic principles of governments storing and being able to search such large volumes of personal and other data is now very great indeed. However, the risk to the keeper of secrets and to the actual secrecy of the data being held is also very high. The more data you have, the likelier it is that some of it will be revealed. Ask Wikileaks and the Pentagon.

There appears to be a natural relationship limiting the effectiveness of secrecy in inverse proportion to the amount of secrets being held. As the US found to its great embarrassment, it only takes an unhappy or morally principled low ranking soldier a few minutes to blow away the entire global diplomatic secret communications of the world's most powerful and paranoid nation.

The cost of revelation: The US punishment and persecution of those who blew these secrets can in no sense repair the enormous damage caused to confidential foreign relations and US diplomatic credibility.

This rapidly increasing risk of revelation is the single biggest political reason why secrecy should be curtailed and why governments should be more transparent. However, the opposite is actually happening, with governments becoming more obscure and hording more and more secrets.

It is only a matter of time before large scale unauthorised revelations begin to have really important geo-political impacts. We are rapidly entering a new era of data wars.

12.4.8 Types of secrecy: The following general types of secrecy exist:

- **Personal Secrecy:** Personal secrets held to maintain image, hide unpleasant personal facts or family histories out of fear, shame, risk of rejection, harassment or loss of honour.

- **Government secrecy:** So called state secrets include military and diplomatic information and plans, intelligence gathered regarding foreign powers. Domestic state secrets include intelligence gathered to control citizens, institutions of the state and private businesses.

- **Corporate secrecy:** Corporate institutions keep secret data on products, markets and employees. Increasingly, commercial organisations are also contracted to gather and store data for government agencies, such as the national census in the UK. Non commercial organisations like so-called "Think-tanks" also gather data, ostensibly for research purposes but often to pass on to their political or commercial clients.

- **Technological secrecy:** This has become big business since the advent of the internet. Technological security is used to defend the public from fraud, governments from loss of secrecy and commercial organisations from loss of intellectual ownership. Despite the rapid improvement in technology there are still many security flaws in most software systems including the main operating systems used by the world's largest organisations, as witnessed by the apparent ease with which amateur hackers enter and roam around the central servers of the Pentagon at will.

- **Military secrecy:** A military secret is secret information that is purposely not made available to the general public and hence to an enemy. This is done in order to gain an advantage or to not reveal a weakness, avoid embarrassment or to help in propaganda efforts. Most of these secrets are strictly military in nature, such as the strengths and weaknesses of weapons systems, tactics, training methods, number and location of specific weapons and plans.

12.4.9 The use of secrecy and the rise of conspiracy theories: The ever widening use of secrecy in the name of security by both government and commerce institutions has a number of side-effects in contemporary society. One of these is the rapid rise in the popularity of conspiracy theories.

Filling gaps in knowledge: As governments become less transparent, the general public begins to see larger and more obvious gaps in the information that they are being shown by their governments. This is because as governments' paranoia increases more and more information becomes classified as secret. This knowledge drought leads the public to look for alternatives to the actual truth and their invention of plausible explanations for unexplained events now being kept secret from them.

The 9/11 attacks are a case in point. Many theories exist about what really happened, some are completely wild and some are very plausible and credible. What can be said for sure is that the official version is far from the whole truth and that many important facts and pieces of evidence have been withheld from the public. With the absence of real evidence or facts, the public simply speculates on what actually happened in a myriad of conspiracy theories.

Nonetheless, because state secrecy and conspiracy theories are now so popular, the phenomena can also be used to deliver credible but incorrect messages, so conspiracy theories have become, in their own right, a manipulative technique.

12.5 Methodology/Refinements/Sub-species: There are several sub-species of secrecy which are used to manipulate:

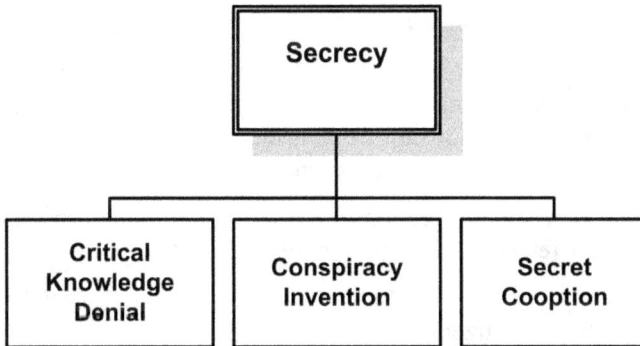

12.5.1 Critical knowledge denial: This is the obvious use of secrecy: denial of critically important knowledge puts an adversary at a disadvantage. Lack of knowledge reduces the ability of a victim to make good decisions or gain a full understanding. Not all secrets are damaging and some are quite trivial but all secrets deny a victim access to the facts to the advantage of the manipulator.

Some secrets can have a truly awful physical effect on the victims, such as the use of unwitting East German victims who were tricked into taking part in drug trials by several Western drug companies in the 1970s. In these trials some patients with serious heart diseases were secretly given placebos instead of the appropriate medical treatment and many then subsequently died from lack of treatment. They were the so-called "control group" required by the Western drugs companies to prove that their new anti-hypertensive drugs actually worked - dispensable victims of murder and greed coupled with secrecy. These victims of secrecy are doubly hurt because secrecy can be very hard to uncover and avoid, as was the case for these victims of Western medical and corporate malpractice.

Again, the economics of the manipulation put the victim at a great disadvantage because the cost of discovery is simply too great for most victims. On the other hand the risk of secret revelation can be a highly "tradable" threat to the manipulator and secrets can command very great economic value.

12.5.2 Conspiracy invention: A manipulator can use the existence of one or more secrets about a particular issue to create and communicate credible alternative scripts to a victim or group. These alternative stories deliver a deceptive and manipulative payload. However, they rely entirely on the existence of an environment of secrecy to be effective.

When some agency or institution is being secretive on an issue of topical interest, it is relatively easy for a manipulator to "sell" a properly fabricated conspiracy theory to the victim or public, provided that the theory is both credible and contains some real facts.

Even if a conspiracy theory is incomplete, a manipulator can still deliver powerful innuendos about "the secrets they are not telling us". The innuendos may or may not be true, but they can be designed to serve the interests of the manipulator at the expense of gullible victims.

Here is just a very small selection of currently popular conspiracy theories, some plainly far fetched, some quite plausible:

- The US government is collaborating with extra-terrestrials to abduct and indoctrinate citizens

- The British royal family and Bush family, amongst others, are actually alien reptiles who require periodic supplies of human blood to exist.

- Fluoridation was pioneered by a German chemical company to make people submissive to those in power

- HIV was created by the CIA. It is thought to have been created as a tool of genocide and/or population control

- Pharmaceutical companies are in league with some medical

practitioners to "invent" new diseases, such as HSV, HPV and even HIV to maintain their income stream

- Venezuelan state-run TV station has claimed that the 2010 Haiti earthquake was caused by US government weapons testing, and a government cover-up took place

- Electric car technology has been largely suppressed by big oil and gas firms.

- A global community of agricultural and biological scientists has conspired to fabricate scientific evidence supporting the safety and benefit of genetically modified food crops, whilst suppressing evidence suggesting the dangers of these crops.

All of the above conspiracy theories, however whacko, do point at some real facts, despite their often extreme conclusions. Some conspiracy theories are totally nonsense, some are more fact than fantasy and some are actually almost certainly completely true but have not yet been accepted as such.

12.5.3 Secret Cooption (aka Secret Cooptation): Apart from the simple withholding of information, there is an interesting hybrid of the use of secrecy which is available to a manipulator. It is referred to as Secret Cooption.

In this method a secret is used as a means of co-opting an individual into bearing part of the responsibility for keeping a secret. Most people will acquiesce in maintaining a secret if the consequences of failing to do so are made clear to them, because they are gratified to be entrusted with it in the first place.

This strategy actually involves the manipulator showing his hand whilst revealing a threat. It can be most useful in forming a captive relationship with an individual or group from an opposing faction.

It compromises the victim and the longer it goes on the more compromised the victim becomes. The manipulator is, in effect, trading access to his secrets in return for the co-operation of the victim. Of course, the manipulator sets the limits on how much of a secret is revealed or how many secrets are shared with the victim.

Criminal gangs and insurgent organisations use this technique to lock in their members. They do this by revealing some part of their secret operations to members. Any attempt by a member to leave is then blocked because the member "knows too much".

12.6 Avoidance and Counteraction: Secrecy is hard to avoid in general. Conspiracy theories and co-option can be avoided by simply refusing to listen to them, but the simple withholding of information is very pernicious for a victim.

In the event that a secret is somehow revealed, a manipulator can escape the consequences much more easily than if they had been found to have been deliberately deceitful. There are plenty of ways of explaining secrecy to most people. One can talk about security, the great complexity of the information, or simply plead that the victim had no need to know.

Consider the case of a company which knowingly and secretly continues to sell a product which is unfit or unsafe whilst a better alternative is being developed. The purpose of the strategy is to maintain the sales of its existing stocks until the alternative product is ready for release. If this secret is inadvertently revealed, then there are myriad plausible explanations for the facts not yet having been published, such as the avoidance of panic, an alternative product not being fully tested yet etc. The drugs industry has a vast repertoire of such excuses for use in such an eventuality.

However, there are 3 basic strategies which can be used to force a manipulator to reveal potentially damaging information to the victim:

Investigation: A victim can start investigating and gathering information about the activities of the manipulator. Often secrets can be detected not by what is said or written on a particular subject but by what is NOT said, by what is deliberately omitted. Asking leading questions can reveal a lot about what might be being withheld.

Intimidation: A victim can threaten a manipulator with the revelation of other secrets in retaliation for the information on a specific secret not being revealed. Other forms of intimidation of the manipulator can force a secret to be revealed. This will work only if the "cost" to the manipulator of keeping the secret can be increased to a level where it is cheaper to tell the victim the facts.

Invention: If all else fails, a victim can create expensive and destructive "secrets" about the manipulator which in time can be corrosive to the point that the manipulator is obliged to reveal the truth because the insinuations are actually worse than the original secret truth. This uses that ancient principle that if you throw enough shit, some of it will stick.

---oOo---

13. Propaganda

13.1 Definition: Propaganda is defined as the dissemination of information which is favourable to the objectives of the manipulator but which omits information which is unfavourable. The information distributed in propaganda is normally accurate as far as it goes, but the reports issued by a manipulator are incomplete, and whatever facts considered contrary to the manipulator's interests are filtered out before transmission to the victim.

13.2 Persistence: Medium to Long: Well delivered and credible propaganda can be very long lasting and very difficult to budge.

Take for example the concept that, until quite recently, every UK schoolchild learned: Britain won the 2nd World War with a little help from the USA. Similar historical delusions exist in many countries disseminated over the years by well organised propaganda machines. So let us take a closer look at this particular type of propaganda-based delusion.

The dominant role of the US as the "saviours" of Europe and Asia in WWII is a common perception in the minds of many in the developed world. Many Americans and their allies really do believe in the absolute global military supremacy of the USA. This is despite a history of strategic military embarrassments for the US in the last 50 years. We could include military humiliations in North Korea, Cuba, Vietnam, Iraq and Afghanistan. We could also add to this list the decline of American military and political influence in the global arena. Even quite close to home, despite decades of CIA interference, most of Central and South America is now governed by left-wing regimes, generally quite antagonistic to the US and to its policies.

Despite all of this, every American citizen and many non-Americans will repeat the mantra that the USA is the most (militarily) powerful country in the world. It is surprising then that this popular belief in US military prowess still exists despite the rather catastrophic military and diplomatic history. The reason for this apparent contradiction is the extraordinary use of propaganda in the domestic US media since WWII. If the US military were even 10% as effective as its propaganda apparatus says it is, the world would be covered in stars and stripes by now, but it is not. Certainly their propaganda isn't based on the US military's ability to gain and hold territory or their diplomats' ability to gain and exert political influence in foreign countries, because in all these respects the USA has failed and continues to fail.

Wartime propaganda: What was the real role of the US and Britain in

WWII? A cursory reading of any rational history of the war demonstrates that if there were any victors in the Second World War, it was actually the Soviet Union. They not only unintentionally gained some substantial real-estate and influence in Eastern Europe, but they altered the global balance of power away from the old imperial European nations.

The USSR in just a few years moved from being a lumbering backward post-feudal society into a modern industrial state. At the end of WWII, the USSR had a newly mechanised army (partly financed by the USA), a modern industrial infrastructure and it shortly afterwards became a nuclear-armed member of the Security Council of the new United Nations. As a result of WWII, The USSR became a super-power at the same time as France and Britain became post-imperial "have-beens" and contracted back to their own small European territories.

This is not however the storyline that the Western Allies (Britain and the USA) wanted the public to believe at the end of the war, as the Cold War between the West and the USSR began in earnest. So, let us look at the facts:

The role of the US and USSR in WWII: Neither the USSR nor the USA wanted any part in WWII. It was 2 years after the start of the war with Germany before either country became involved. The Nazi invasion of the USSR in June 1941 finally triggered Soviet involvement, and the Japanese attack on Pearl Harbour in December 1941 forced a reluctant US government to participate on the side of the Western Allies.

As a result of WWII, on the Western front, the Allies managed to recover the territories of France, Holland, Austria, Italy and Belgium from Nazi occupation. However, amazingly, Britain and the USA were unable or unwilling to liberate Spain, which remained a fascist state until 1975 under the control of Hitler's Axis ally Francisco Franco.

By contrast, on the Eastern front, the largest military confrontation in human history was taking place between Germany and the USSR. The final result of this huge conflict was that Germany lost 30% of its territory to the Soviet armies as they swept westwards. Meanwhile, the Soviet Union added a dozen Eastern and Central European countries to its already huge territory, including most of the old Habsburg Empire. More importantly, the Soviet's successful defence of its homeland and the conquest of Nazi occupied Central and Eastern Europe finally cost the Nazis the war.

In terms of hardware and infrastructure losses, the Soviet intervention was overwhelmingly damaging to the Nazi military regime, much more so than the limited war on the Western front or in North Africa, being fought by Britain and the USA. On the Eastern front Germany alone lost 4.3 million troops (with another 3.3 million German troops being taken prisoner by the Soviet army). This compares with 1.2 million deaths of German and other Axis troops on the Western front and in North Africa. The Soviet "human waves" of attacks against Nazi forces caused a huge and tragic loss of life to ordinary soldiers and citizens of the Soviet Union, but it effectively annihilated the Nazi military.

The cost of Soviet involvement in WWII was staggering in comparison with that of any other nation involved, including the USA and Britain: The USSR lost 23.4 million soldiers and civilians (14% of its total population) and the USA and Britain together had 890,000 war dead. These are horrendous numbers in either case, but of different orders of magnitude.

A similar story can be told about the participation of China in the war. Huge numbers of Chinese military and civilian casualties resulted from their 11 year struggle against Japanese occupying forces, including the deaths of an estimated 20 million Chinese civilians. Despite this, the role of China in defeating the Japanese empire is hardly mentioned in our Western historical narrative.

Propaganda sticks: Despite all these stark historical realities, ask any Englishman and he will proudly announce that "we (Great Britain) won the war (WWII)". The average American citizen will proclaim the same "truth" about the USA. Neither person will have the slightest idea of the scale of the contribution of the USSR and China in the war. It simply isn't part of the Western propagandists' narrative.

The reason for this is that almost immediately when WWII ended, the West entered into the Cold War with the Soviet Union, which continued until the early 1990s. Obviously it would have been entirely contrary to the US and UK anti-communist position to say anything positive about the USSR and the immense role of the Red Army in the Second World War.

Since the end of the Cold War, the facts of what really happened are very gradually beginning to emerge and be understood by a broader public, However, until very recently even respectable Western historians have tended to ignore the pivotal role of the USSR or China in WWII because it was considered unpatriotic to play down the Allied contribution by making any comparison with the Soviet intervention.

Propaganda sticks for a long time, even in the face of some very hard historical facts.

13.3 Accessibility: Low. This is not for amateurs. Propaganda needs well-resourced, professional management of information to deliver subtle, persistent manipulative payloads. It needs access to and a good understanding of media techniques and some exceptional talent in delivery and a credible story line. It is therefore an expensive business.

13.4 Conditions/Opportunity/Effectiveness: Propaganda is very effective at altering mass public opinion. In the absence of alternative information sources, the average individual will rely on what has been communicated to them as propaganda, even when they may know that it is not entirely true.

For instance, most people will still confidently quote from the most retrograde tabloid newspaper or the company notice board, if there is no other source of information available. When it comes to knowledge it seems that anything is better than nothing.

Propaganda also works well because it creates a group dynamic in which most participants are convinced of the truth contained in the propaganda. It becomes self-reinforcing because anyone who steps out of line is considered a pariah. Thus the propaganda is maintained by the threat of exclusion from the group for any dissident that refuses to believe it.

Propaganda has a long history as a successful manipulative mechanism. It has certainly been used since the Roman Empire and probably long before.

Propaganda is yet another method which relies on the ignorance of the victim and the victim's problems of cost to obtain and interpret quality information. Propaganda works because the cost of the information provided by the manipulator is "subsidised" in effect. It is therefore cheaper and easier for the victim to acquire than from any other source. The interpretation of propaganda is also made easier because the information has been "pre-digested" at source. It is therefore much more palatable and credible to the victim.

Most of us are basically lazy. If propaganda is well constructed without any obvious signs of interference, (and professional propaganda is very credible indeed), we don't know that the information has been tampered with at all, and it can be made to appear like a completely detached and believable report.

13.5 Methodology/Refinements/Sub-species: Some well-used sub-species of propaganda exist. Here we will examine some of them:

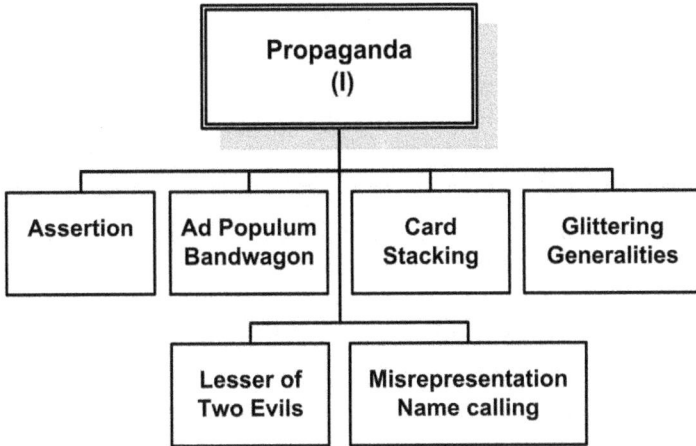

```
                    ┌─────────────────┐
                    │   Propaganda    │
                    │      (I)        │
                    └─────────────────┘
    ┌──────────┬──────────────┬──────────────┬──────────────┐
┌─────────┐ ┌──────────┐ ┌──────────┐ ┌──────────────┐
│Assertion│ │Ad Populum│ │  Card    │ │  Glittering  │
│         │ │Bandwagon │ │ Stacking │ │ Generalities │
└─────────┘ └──────────┘ └──────────┘ └──────────────┘
              ┌──────────┬──────────────────┐
        ┌──────────┐ ┌──────────────────┐
        │Lesser of │ │ Misrepresentation│
        │Two Evils │ │   Name calling   │
        └──────────┘ └──────────────────┘
```

13.5.1 Assertion: Assertion is a propaganda technique often used in advertising and modern propaganda. An assertion is an enthusiastic statement presented as a fact, although it is not necessarily true.

The manipulator implies that the statement requires no explanation but that it should merely be accepted without question. Examples of the assertion technique can often be found in modern advertising propaganda. Any time an advertiser states that their product is the best without providing evidence for this, they are using assertive propaganda.

The subject, ideally, should simply agree to their statement without searching for additional information or reasoning. Assertions, although usually simple to spot, are often dangerous forms of propaganda because they may include several falsehoods.

13.5.2 Ad populum fallacy - Bandwagon: The ad populum fallacy is an appeal by a manipulator to the popularity of a claim as a reason for accepting it.

In truth, the number of people who believe a claim is irrelevant to its truth. Fifty million people can be wrong. In fact, millions of people have been wrong about many things many times, for instance: the concept that the Earth is flat and motionless, or that the stars are lights shining through holes in the sky. Total nonsense, we now know, but widely believed for millennia.

The ad populum fallacy is also sometimes referred to as "mob appeal", the "bandwagon fallacy", or the "democratic fallacy". The ad populum fallacy is very attractive because it appeals to our desire to belong to the group and to conform to the larger "group-think". It satisfies our desire for security and safety in numbers. It is widely used in advertising, politics and in time of war.

Generally as beliefs spread among people, as fashions and trends often do, the probability of any individual adopting it increases in direct proportion to the number of people that that have already done so. So, as more people come to believe in something, others also "hop on the bandwagon" regardless of the underlying evidence.

A clever manipulator of the masses will try to seduce those who assume that the majority is always right. Also seduced by this appeal are the insecure who may be made to feel guilty if they oppose the majority or conversely may feel stronger by agreeing with a group.

The method uses statements like "Some kind of God must exist. Every culture has had some sort of belief in a higher being."

13.5.3 Card stacking - Selective Omission: Card stacking, also called selective omission, is a classic propagandist technique. It involves only presenting information that is positive to an idea or proposal and omitting information contrary to it.

Although the majority of information presented by the card stacking approach is true, it is unreliable because it also omits important information. Card stacking is used in all forms of propaganda and is extremely effective in convincing the public. The best way to deal with card stacking is to get more information.

An instance of card stacking would be for a company director to deliver a glowing report about past performance to a group of potential shareholders, without mentioning that several of the company's most important patents are about to expire.

13.5.4 Glittering Generalities: Glittering generalities are another classical propaganda technique identified by the Institute for Propaganda Analysis in 1938. It also occurs very often in politics and political propaganda.

Glittering generalities are words that have different positive meanings for individual subjects, but are linked to highly valued concepts. When these words are used, they demand approval without consideration, simply because such an important concept is involved. Words often used as glittering generalities are "honour", "glory", "love of country", and especially in the United States, "freedom".

For instance, when a person is asked to do something in "defence of democracy" they are more likely to agree. The concept of democracy has a positive connotation to them because it is linked to a concept that they value.

13.5.5 Lesser of Two Evils: The "lesser of two evils" technique which is also a form of "manipulation of dimensions", tries to convince us of an idea or proposal by presenting it as the least offensive option. It is also a form of the technique called "Rigging the obvious" because it manipulatively emasculates rational decision into a simple "obvious" choice.

This technique is often used in times of war to convince people of the need for sacrifices or to justify difficult decisions. It is often accompanied by adding blame to an enemy country or political group. One idea or proposal is often depicted as one of the only options or paths available to us because of their actions.

13.5.6 Misrepresentation / Name Calling: This is the portrayal of an event, group, policy, or politician in a disproportionate or distorted manner. This can be done with selective editing, showing unsavoury images while discussing a person or party, or framing a discussion of an event or issue by showing something disturbing or alarming just prior to the discussion. Name calling occurs often in politics and wartime scenarios, but very seldom in advertising. It is another classical technique of the propagandist.

It uses derogatory language, words or symbolism that carries negative connotations when describing an adversary. The propagandist attempts to arouse prejudice among the public by labelling the target as something that the public dislikes.

Often name calling is employed using sarcasm and ridicule and it frequently shows up in political cartoons or writings.

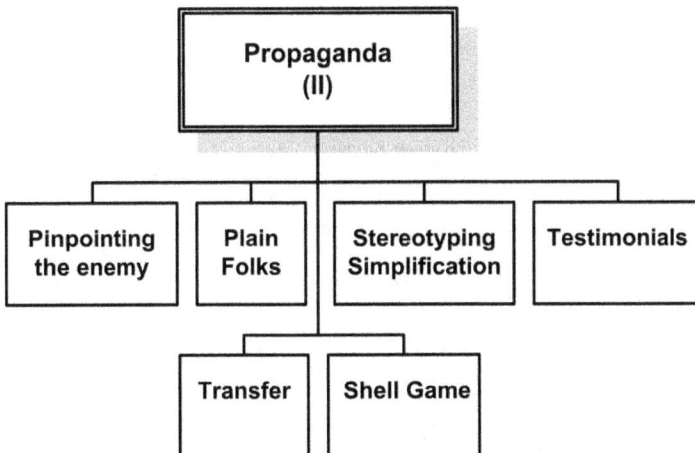

13.5.7 Pinpointing the Enemy: Pinpointing the enemy is commonly used during war-time and in political campaigns and debates. This propaganda technique is an attempt to simplify a complex situation by presenting one specific group or person as the enemy. Although there may be many other complex factors involved, the subject is urged to view the situation in simple terms of clear-cut right and wrong.

13.5.8 Plain Folks: The "plain folks" device is an attempt by a propagandist to convince the public that his views reflect those of the "common" person (Mr. Average), and that they are also working for the benefit of the common person.

The propagandist often attempts to use the accent of a specific audience as well as using specific idioms, colloquialisms or jokes. Also, the propagandist, especially during speeches, may attempt to increase the illusion through imperfect pronunciation, stuttering, and a deliberately limited vocabulary. Errors such as these help add to the impression of sincerity and spontaneity for "Mr. Average".

This technique is usually most effective when used with glittering generalities, in an attempt to convince the public that the propagandist's views about highly valued ideas are similar to their own and therefore more valid.

13.5.9 Simplification (Stereotyping): Simplification is similar to the technique of "pinpointing the enemy". It tends to reduce a complex situation to a clear-cut choice between good and evil. The technique is often useful in swaying uneducated audiences.

13.5.10 Testimonials: Testimonials are quotations or endorsements, in or out of context, which attempt to connect famous and/or respectable people with an idea, philosophy, product or item.

Testimonials are very closely connected to the transfer technique, in that an attempt is made to connect an agreeable concept (in this case a respectable person) to another idea or product etc. Testimonials are often used in advertising and political campaigns.

13.5.11 Transfer: Transfer is another classical propagandist technique first documented by the Institute for Propaganda Analysis in 1938.

Transfer is often used in politics and during wartime. It is an attempt to make the subject view a certain item in the same way as they view another item, to link the two in the subject's mind. Although this technique is often used to transfer negative feelings for one object to another, it can also be used in positive ways.

By linking an item to something the subject respects or enjoys, positive feelings can be generated for it. However, in politics, transfer is most often used to transfer blame or bad feelings from one politician to another of his friends or party members, or even to the party itself.

13.5.12 Shell game: Named after the popular street game in which a hustler engages in sleight-of-hand to hide an object under one of three shells, he manipulates the shells quickly to conceal the one the object is hidden under, and asks one of the onlookers to tell him which shell is the winner. Analogously, the term describes a game where one piece of information hides another piece of information.

In a "shell game" politicians can play with the public whereby they hide information by switching the terms of a policy or debate.

One recent example is the contention that the unemployment situation is actually better than the official rate suggests. When certain classes of unemployed workers (like married women) start to re-enter the job market again because they think there is finally a real chance they may be able to find a job, so the argument goes, it pushes up the unemployment rate. This is because previously uncounted, unemployed people have now started to seek work. The manipulator says that this really means that the job market is actually getting better, even though the unemployment rate is going up.

This argument is a type of shell game where the "true information" on the employment situation is hidden within other indicators. It is not deceit; it is a simple manipulation of truths to hide one fact behind another.

13.6 Avoidance and Counteraction: The use of propaganda in industry and government is so widespread, that one might almost believe that it is being taught at business school. The problem for a victim is that the last three generations have experienced two world wars and a revolution in mass-communication. Along with the proliferation of both positive and negative advertising, these factors have gone a long way towards inoculating the general public against any feeling of outrage at the use of propaganda. We're just used to it. We know a lot of the information we get is, at best, only half the truth, but we've come to expect this behaviour from our leaders, both in government and in industry and we're stoical about it. This does not however affect the potency of the method.

A major hazard for the propagandist is the use of counter- propaganda by an organized group of victims or an opposing faction. Apart from this there is very little else that can go wrong. If he is accused of telling half-truths, he always has the defence that he didn't know the rest of the facts.

Propaganda is a method of mass manipulation. Even if it doesn't work on everyone, it will work on most subjects. In this case, the propagandist feels safe that he has the majority on his side and only needs to deal with a small number of "dissenters".

But, each of these propagandist methods has its own opportunity for avoidance and counteraction, however limited they may be:

13.6.1 Assertion: This can be detected by anyone really and can be overwhelmed by simply asking and repeating a lot of questions about the underlying basis of the assertion. Eventually the manipulation will dry up and the manipulator will be unable to provide rational-sounding answers to defend the assertion.

13.6.2 Ad-populum: The ad populum manipulation can be rapidly unravelled by a victim citing more and more absurd cases where large numbers of ignorant human beings have believed the most absurd propositions for years and years. By making the parallel concept totally absurd, a vocal victim can make the manipulative proposition backfire on the manipulator.

13.6.3 Card stacking - Selective Omission: This is a dangerous means of propaganda and can be very convincing for poorly informed members of the public. The only guard against card stacking is to be well informed and to carefully check the completeness and truth of the information being presented.

13.6.4 Glittering Generalities: When faced with glittering generalities, we should consider the merits of the idea itself devoid of the glittering abstract nouns such as 'glory'. In other words: examine the concept plainly with the emotive language stripped out. If it still looks valid then one can proceed further.

13.6.5 Lesser of Two Evils: When confronted with this technique, the victim should consider the value of any proposal independent of those it is being compared with. This will quickly reveal that choice is being deliberately limited.

13.6.6 Misrepresentation / Name calling: When examining name calling propaganda, we should attempt to separate our feelings about the names and our feelings about the actual idea or proposal.

13.6.7 Pinpointing the enemy: When coming into contact with this type of propaganda, the subject should attempt to consider all factors related to the situation. The victim should not apply the manipulator's pre-designed simplification.

As with almost all propaganda techniques, the subject should attempt to obtain more information on the topic. An informed person is much less susceptible to this sort of propaganda.

13.6.8 Plain Folks: When confronted by this type of propaganda, the subject should consider the proposals and ideas separately from the personality of the presenter and the method of delivery.

13.6.9 Simplification: When faced with simplification, it is often useful to examine other factors and pieces of the proposal or idea, and, as with all other forms of propaganda, it is essential to get more information. Lack of knowledge or nuance is the main weapon of the manipulator here.

13.6.10 Testimonials: When coming across testimonials, the subject should consider the merits of the item or proposal independently of the person of organization giving the testimonial.

13.6.11 Transfer: When confronted with propaganda using the transfer technique, we should question the merits or problems of the proposal or idea independently of convictions about other objects or proposals.

13.6.12 Shell games: Shell games rely on audiences being poorly informed and easily confused by apparently conflicting or coinciding data. It's hard for most people to avoid or counteract because most people have such a poor understanding of the logic or relationships between sets of data.

---o0o---

14. Overload

14.1 Definition: Overload is the delivery of a massive surplus of true and genuine raw data and information by a manipulator to a victim. The manipulation undermines an individual's ability to fully understand or make rational decisions on a particular issue in any of the following three ways:

- By taking advantage of a victim's inability to process the large volume of data and information (also known as "cognitive overload").

- By slowing down a victim's interpretative process overall.

- An associated form of this manipulative method overloads the victim's ability to conform to a fixed set of rules and simultaneously make high quality, high-speed decisions, whilst also placed in a stressful or dangerous situation (Ego depletion).

14.2 Persistence: Short, Medium or Long. Depending on the issue, the use of overload can be a short process or can last for many years. If a victim has only a few seconds to make a decision based on too much data, the effect of failing to evaluate the data is over very quickly. However, when a huge volume of historical data is provided to a victim it may take years for a proper evaluation to be conducted and accurate conclusions reached.

14.3 Accessibility: Medium to High: It's not a technique everyone can use easily because it requires large volumes of data. But nonetheless it is reasonably easy to deliver for someone in a government or business institution with access to large databases.

Governments routinely present vast amounts of data to the public on issues like environment, health, water quality etc. They usually deliver these data with a set of pre-digested conclusions, with the idea that we read and accept the conclusions and skip the other 1000 pages of data.

Most of us can't afford the time or don't have the facilities to evaluate millions of drinking water quality test results for instance, and so we tend to simply accept the government's (politically driven) conclusions. In this way the manipulator (a government) has successfully overloaded the victim (the public).

At a more personal level, a manipulator can overwhelm a victim with a surfeit of data in a work environment. A malicious colleague could dump vast amounts of historical marketing data on a colleague and then complain when the colleague was unable to interpret the data in a reasonable time.

14.4 Conditions/Opportunity/Effectiveness: This is a highly effective technique from a manipulator's point of view because it employs a strategy entirely opposite to those of deceit and secrecy. It also doesn't carry the same moral stigma as deceit or secrecy, since there is, on the surface at any rate, no deceit and no manipulation.

This method may also be applied when a victim does not command the necessary skills, such as statistical or linguistic training, to make a considered interpretation.

Secondly, the method can be used where there is a time constraint upon a victim's response.

The technique relies entirely on the fact that most people are used to having decisions and interpretations made for them by politicians, bureaucrats, professionals and managers. It relies therefore on the "cost" of interpretation of the data being too great for the victim.

Whereas secrecy and deceit rely on a manipulated subject being unable to afford to research or verify certain facts because of the cost of the exercise, the technique of overload brings about the same result by "jamming" a victim's ability to interpret the information with which they are presented.

14.5 Methodology/Refinements/Sub-species: There are several hybrids to this method:

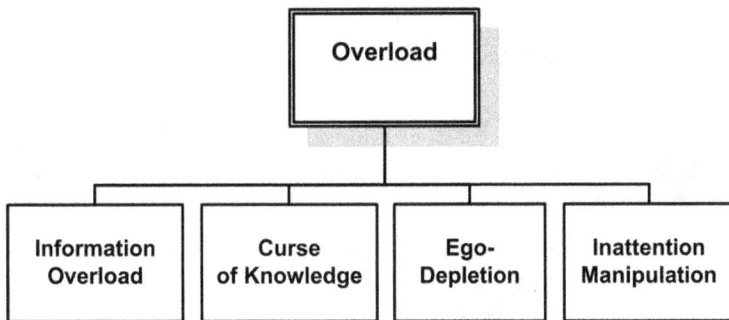

14.5.1 Information overload: First mentioned in the 1970 book "Future Shock" by Alvin Tofler, the concept of information overload is not new to us. However, the incidence of the problem and its use in manipulation has grown dramatically since the invention of modern media like cinema, radio and television and even more so with the advent of the internet and global media.

In industry and government it is quite easy to confuse people by overloading them with too much data, information or new concepts. Of course, the manipulator has the benefit of being able to prepare in advance, whereas the victim has the disadvantage of having to try and wade through what is presented to him in a reasonable amount of time.

It is not unknown for certain consulting companies to use this technique with their clients. Their reports usually take a considerable time to read, digest and implement. By the time any adverse reaction occurs, the advisers are often long gone and far away from any repercussions, having ensured first, of course, to pick up their cheque.

14.5.1.1 What are the general causes and methods of information overload: The world is producing more and more data every year, both in kind and quality. This is the result of the obvious innovations in data processing, but also because of the new global media and global market in data:

- **Internet** communications allow data and information to be rapidly disseminated and replicated over vast numbers of recipients, without geographical limit.

- **More communications channels** allow more communications. Just look at the history of the Western world in the last 100 years in terms of communications:

  o 100 years ago we had newspapers and elite groups had some crude telephonic and/or radio equipment.

  o 50 years ago, we had many more newspapers, most of us had radio, most had access to a telephone and television, and cinemas were common.

  o 20 years ago, the internet was arriving, telephone, television and radio use was universal. Mobile telephony was just beginning. Email was used in business.

  o Today, the internet has spread across the globe and has become entirely mobile. Email, short-messaging is in constant use for business and social contact. Few people do not possess a mobile phone. Communication by voice and exchange of data, sounds or images is universal and virtually continuous.

- **Inability to process:** The victim's poor ability and lack of methods for interpreting a large volume of data and separating quality data from junk.

- **Background noise:** The volume of data interference (background noise) versus the volume of quality data means that we have much more work to do to filter the quality data out.

- **Data diversity:** The lack of relationship between data we receive. We may receive emails, SMS messages, tweets or other social network messages from family members, employers, subordinates, marketing organisations, friends or just perfect strangers on a whole range of topics, some important, some urgent, some totally irrelevant, all often unconnected.

- **Email:** Email is still considered to be the single biggest source of information overload in most corporate environments. The term "email wars" was cited to describe the use of CC and BCC to cause vast numbers of emails to proliferate with a basic purpose to damage or cause embarrassment to another colleague, department or company. The perpetrator claims he is just keeping everyone informed whereas there is obviously a more mischievous motive.

  Email has become the tool of choice for "hedging bets" by copying in anyone remotely connected with a particular topic or issue. By doing this a manipulator (or victim) can insure against peer accusations of withholding information.

14.5.2 The Curse of knowledge: This effect occurs when knowledge of a topic diminishes one's ability to think about it from a less-informed perspective. It implies that better-informed persons or groups find it extremely difficult to think about problems from the perspective of less-informed people. The implication is that in some cases, the addition of knowledge may actually become a disadvantage.

It is a phenomenon that many of us will have noticed at school or college where an obviously very talented specialist makes an appalling teacher. The individual is unable to relate to the ignorance of his students and makes assumptions about knowledge his students simply don't have.

This effect is similar to "Information Overload" but deals with more than a simple overload of data or information; rather it concerns an overload of knowledge. It is commonplace in the academic world where a specialist may propose the most complex and convoluted motives to explain a problem whereas the reality is much simpler.

For instance, a sociologist could extrapolate all kinds of motives for the behaviour of a petty thief found shoplifting, when in reality the primary motive of the thief could simply be hunger or maybe being just too lazy to work.

This is a frequently used manipulative technique in the legal and political fields where a specialist witness can be easily confused or manipulated in trying to explain a rather simple crime or politically embarrassing event. A manipulator can take advantage of this propensity in a specialist witness to influence the conclusions that are drawn about a particular subject.

14.5.3 Ego-depletion: This unpleasant manipulative technique can be applied to an individual victim or a small group of victims. Current psychological thinking states that we do not have an infinite font of willpower, and that in fact our willpower is a finite commodity which can be overstretched by events in our environment. This is referred to as ego-depletion and can have some unfortunate and destructive side effects for the victim.

The causes of ego-depletion are all connected with the need and obligation of an individual to conform to a set of rules of behaviour or performance which are external to the victim.

This can be something as simple as abiding by rules of business protocol, such as addressing customers properly or applying professional trading practices. It can also apply to being able to rapidly make large numbers of high quality decisions (like a futures trader), or being able to work in an antagonistic or dangerous environment where you are apparently ostracised or threatened (like a policeman), etc.

The range of causes of ego-depletion is huge. Challenging jobs such as a stock market trader, a prison warder, a military combatant are just a few cases where a victim is at risk of ego-depletion.

Normally we manage our "Ego-fuel" situation by regulating our intake of ego-depleting events, with rest, recreation, breaks, distractions, food, sleep etc. We need to do this because there is plenty of evidence to suggest that over-use of our willpower, i.e. ego-depletion, can lead to behavioural and psychological problems. These may be manifested as mild reductions in efficiency, exhaustion, right through to extreme psychological issues like so-called "burn-out", irrational and uncontrolled behaviour or even some form of criminality by a victim. These effects are believed to occur because a victim is suffering from a breakdown in their will to control their current behaviour.

A manipulator in the right circumstances can use an understanding of this phenomenon to crush a victim under a weight of willpower taxing work or responsibilities and bring about the apparent "self-destruction" of a victim. It is often used as a way of forcing an employee to resign without compensation.

14.5.4 Inattention Manipulation: This technique takes advantage of a victim's rational inattention, i.e. the inherent difficulty that all human beings have in processing information. When a victim's attention is limited by their processing of a lot of data, their decisions depend on what is currently being focused upon rather than on other data that is arriving at that moment.

This gives interested parties an opportunity to manipulate not only the substance of communication but also the decision-maker's attention allocation. This actually creates a competition for data processing time which can reduce the decision-maker's knowledge by causing temporary information overload.

Furthermore, a single manipulative information provider may deliberately induce information overload to conceal some manipulative "payload" information, such as "if you use my toothpaste you will have a lovely happy family and gorgeous children".

This technique of inattention manipulation as a means of delivering information is constantly in use by marketing organisations with their customers. For instance, in a TV ad a toothpaste manufacturer extols the barely understandable technical qualities of their product. The images show invigorating scenes of facial beauty, happy families and cute loveliness in a scene of idyllic natural freshness tinged with pseudo sexual innuendos. Meanwhile the latest pop song massages the victim's aspirations to like what the rest of the group also likes.

Finally the message is delivered to the victim to buy the product because it is good for them. The amount of information delivered or implied in the 30 second advert is much more than can be carefully evaluated by the subject and so the overload is complete and summarised in the easily digestible punch line.

If anyone bothered to analyse the contents of the advert in terms of the product, the advert images, words and sounds, we would all rapidly come to the conclusion that the product is at best mediocre and that we are being tricked.

But most of us never bother to analyse the data, we simply allow it and dozens of other ads to wash over us, subliminally conditioning our buying habits.

14.6 Avoidance and Counteraction: The means of detection, avoidance and counteraction depend on the sub-type used.

14.6.1 Information overload: There are a number of techniques for recognising, avoiding and counteracting Information Overload:

- **Out of office:** This really comes down to prioritising communications. Avoid being pushed by external agendas. An email pulls your attention away from the plan you had for today's work. Don't allow an external agency to distract you from your plan. This may mean not being home, not being on MSN or Skype, not answering the phone, not answering emails etc. When you have completed your agenda, you can look at the incoming requests calmly and decide which you will attend to. One simple system uses the criteria of NEVER responding to or commenting on anything which is not addressed directly to you and never informally accepting responsibility for anything which is outside your strict area of responsibility.

- **Dump the inbox:** One extreme method is simply to delete your entire in-tray when it becomes overly full with unanswered emails or other requests. This has the effect of filtering the junk from the important and of automatically prioritising the communications. You will be amazed at how few of the emails are ever followed up by a reminder, meaning basically that they were just junk mail.

- **It's urgent for you but not for me:** People with "urgent requests" are altering your agenda for their own reasons and for their own benefit, not for yours. Requests become "urgent" because someone else (not you) has messed up. Never accept the urgency of a request from an outside source. Always schedule the request as normal and make sure the external source knows this. Don't budge on it. The manipulator will either ignore you in future or start to behave properly.

- **Prioritise data:** Not all data is equally important in all circumstances. During working time, a tweet from an acquaintance is not as important as a marketing report from your boss. And vice versa - your free time is your time and not your bosses.

- **Demand time to evaluate:** When confronted with a deliberate data overload, refuse to accept time limits. First establish what is necessary to evaluate the data, document these steps and then document the time and other resources you need. Send this "reasonable" schedule to the manipulator and other related agencies and ask them to provide you with an explanation of their time limits and schedule. If the time and resources are not made available then refuse to participate in the evaluation of the data.

- **Undo the Overload Payload:** When it's obvious that a manipulator is trying to force a victim to accept their summary or their set of conclusions rather than allowing the victim to evaluate the data, the victim can neutralise the manipulative strategy by "playing it back" to the manipulator. The victim can simply pick any single conclusion or random set of conclusions from the manipulator's "payload summary" and question its veracity.

If a conclusion is based on a large and complex dataset, the manipulator will be faced with the task of explaining in detail how the conclusion was calculated or reached and all the associated assumptions involved. The explanation will take longer than the original calculation and will effectively increase the cost of the manipulation. If this strategy can be extended the manipulator will soon come to see that there is too much to lose a/ in terms of time and b/ in terms of credibility.

14.6.2 Curse of Knowledge: If as an expert you find your listeners drifting off or you believe you are being deliberately manipulated to make an expert statement that confuses another victim group, then you need to act to overcome the curse of knowledge.

The solution generally comes down to issues of how to communicate with non-experts. As Einstein said, "If you can't explain it simply, you don't understand it well enough." So if an expert is having difficulty communicating with a novice group, obviously some preparatory work is missing. Experts can be trained to work effectively with novice groups and specialist training companies carry out such training.

Firstly the concepts need to be isolated and reduced into deliverable bits of information as if they were being explained to teenage kids - intelligent but with no prior knowledge.

Then this information needs to be delivered calmly and the knowledge needs to be consolidated at each step, with an eye to the slowest member of the audience. It's not a race.

Things to avoid: All jargon should be avoided even if it is explained. Jargon takes more than a few minutes to sink in so it just remains meaningless and confusing to a listener.

Things which help: Analogies, examples, diagrams, comparisons, empathy with the listener and time - enough time for the listener to absorb the packages of knowledge.

14.6.3 Ego-depletion: It's not always a deliberate manipulation but the use of ego-depletion to change the behaviour of a victim is quite common. Professional trainers in the army or police use ego-depleting exercises to induce their trainees with fast or conditioned reactions in hostile conditions such as search and rescue, combat etc.

Such training is obviously aimed at helping the trainee to survive or perform correctly in difficult conditions. Its use by trainers is carefully controlled so as not to overwhelm the subjects.

However, employers and governments have been known to use ego-depletion to break down a victim or victim group by overwhelming them with a battery of urgent or impossible tasks, new and urgent responsibilities, and insoluble problems whilst creating a hostile atmosphere. Employers generally do this to remove someone they no longer want without paying any compensation for terminating them.

Politicians do it to their colleagues or civil servants to force them to withdraw, diplomats of powerful countries do it to small, weak countries to make it impossible for them to conform. For instance, if you don't actually have nuclear weapons it's very hard for you to declare or dismantle them.

Ego depletion relies on the victim's inability to recover. This can be managed somewhat by a victim. The primary means by which a potential victim can manage this (once it is recognised) is to channel ego-depleting demands away by refusing or sharing certain tasks and responsibilities with colleagues. Alternatively, the victim can break the cycle of ego over-usage by altering working times, or working from home, demanding shorter working days etc.

This preventative behaviour may carry some career risks but none as radical as the risk of the complete mental breakdown of the victim.

An individual victim can interfere with the agenda and timescale of the manipulator by absenting themselves (as an employee by being sick, on holiday or some other form of leave). At a political level, a victim can cause or take advantage of a distraction which reduces the manipulator's urgency (for a nation this might be called multi-lateral talks with a huge agenda in a logistically difficult place).

Once the manipulator has lost control of the timing, the urgency is gone, work is rescheduled, and the victim has an opportunity to recover - to refuel- before continuing. These delaying tactics can be used almost without limit.

14.6.4 Inattention Manipulation: There is only one way to avoid being manipulated whilst you are being overloaded - don't allow the overload in the first place. Insist on all data being properly evaluated in a calm way and allow no assumptions to pass without them being tested.

Education and the pooling of resources by educated members in the victim group are the real enemies of this manipulative technique. If an individual or group has the necessary skills to quickly draw relevant conclusions from the data which are used to bring about an overload, then the effect is negated.

Organised pressure groups exist to fight the manipulative use of overload in commercial and consumer contacts. But it is in the manipulator's best interests if his victims are a/ not appropriately educated or b/ are badly informed or c/ if they are just lazy about accepting information as fact.

Sadly most of us fall into at least one of these classes.

---oOo---

15. Linguistic manipulation

15.1 Definition: Language is not a neutral medium as most of us prefer to believe. It is actually a potent method for delivering concepts and values which are not expressly mentioned in the main text but are communicated by means of a linguistic "sub-text". This sub-text uses language itself to deliver subtle manipulative messages to a victim.

These linguistic tricks present an opportunity for a manipulator to influence a victim whilst actually delivering what seem to be neutral facts. More potently, a manipulator can use language to demonstrate a point or deliver a long-lasting impression which is actually untrue, irrational or in some other way manipulative to the victim.

Linguistic manipulation may be defined as the exploitation of a victim by means of one of the following techniques:

- **Biased vocabulary**. Deliberately influential vocabulary is used by the manipulator. So, a conversation with a conservative manipulator will see phrases like "free market", "market driven", "law and order", "defence forces" being banded about whilst, talking to a socialist or liberal we may hear terms such as "free will", "liberation", "human and civil rights", "redistribution of wealth", "social justice", etc.

  This group of techniques includes journalistic, lexico-semantic, metaphoric manipulation and linguistic invention.

- **Restrictive vocabulary:** The linguistic rules are defined by the manipulator with their limitations on language, including the use of context manipulation, context dropping and vocabulary restriction.

- **Topical deprivation:** The subject matter, the topic in hand, is restricted by the manipulator by fixing linguistic rules. This deprives a victim of the opportunity to verbalize on certain topics.

- **Syntactic manipulation:** Various syntactic tricks can alter the meaning or implications of a statement.

15.2 Persistence: Short - Medium - Long. Depending on the type of linguistic manipulation, the effect can last between a few seconds to several generations.

15.3 Accessibility: High - We are all capable of using linguistic tricks. Some of us are better at it than others. Some do it unconsciously whilst others consciously use language to manipulate.

15.4 Conditions/Opportunity/Effectiveness: The following is an analysis of linguistic manipulation:

15.4.1 The Pen is mightier than the Sword: However much we may ridicule or cast aspersions upon the words of mistrusted politicians and leaders the fact is that words do mediate between the underlying motives of a politician or party or company and the actions they advocate. We ignore their effect at our peril.

So, language should not, on any account, be dismissed as immaterial in the overall manipulative landscape. Many millions of people have died in the last century alone, because powerful individuals have stirred ordinary people into a frenzy of blind hatred and bloody revenge through the medium of rhetoric and linguistic manipulation of the spoken and written word. Indeed, the use of language in contemporary politics is one of the most potent weapons in the armoury of the manipulator, both in government and commerce.

15.4.2 History, incidence and spread of linguistic manipulation: Playing games with language and laying linguistic traps are popular pastimes of politicians and politically motivated media outlets. The use of linguistic manipulation has been around for a very long time, but tends to proliferate at times of conflict, or severe political polarisation or radicalisation.

The increased use of linguistic manipulation is quite noticeable in recent years, ever since the United States declared its so-called "war on terror", and started on a round of foreign military adventures. The global political polarisation this triggered off led to very obvious attempts at linguistic manipulation by both politicians and the press, leading to hostile reactions from the public at times. When France refused to enter the Iraq war, Bush and his GOP political operators attempted to discredit French people by inventing and releasing racially laden slurs, as with the word "French fries" substituted by "freedom fries", and French people being referred to as "Cheese-eating surrender monkeys" in parts of the US press.

In hindsight it was a ludicrous reaction from a supposedly serious government, but it did give vent to the anger felt by extreme right-wing groups and the GOP in the United States, and indeed it did appear to endorse Bush's bellicose behaviour in Iraq and Afghanistan when contrasted with France's apparent indecision and more reticent approach to the invasion.

Oddly, the US right-wing did not apply the same linguistic insults against Germany, another NATO ally which refused to join the attack on Iraq. Could this be because France has no US air-bases in contrast to Germany? It would appear so.

15.4.3 How does it work? Most people regard language as a sort of neutral conduit, through which ideas flow - pure and uncorrupted from the mind of the speaker or writer to the listener and reader.

But this is a grave and naive mistake. Language is actually the means by which concepts and impressions are stored in the "information bins" of our memory and then retransmitted and many personal interpretations take place between the hearing and the repetition of a piece of information. These interpretations cannot be treated as neutral or independent of our own moral concepts, emotional and cognitive and social biases.

We all use language to persuade others, from the market stall holder urging the public to buy his wares to the speeches of US presidential candidates vying for the job as the world's "most powerful person".

Because language is finite and personal, it is a very effective constraining factor in human thought and behaviour. It is commonly used either to restrict the moral views of other individuals or groups, or to spur them into action by inducing them with new moral imperatives.

15.4.4 Why is language important to how we think? We can understand this easily when we recognize that our own language embodies words reflecting the social regime or environment in which we live. Eskimos, for instance, have ten different words to describe snow. Indians in Calcutta are said to have forty-one ways of describing a policeman and even more ways of describing a bomb. The Russians have three hundred ways of expressing or implying kinship.

Thus linguistic conditions may either help or restrict our ability to translate concepts into suitable language. In addition, linguistic restrictions may also reduce our ability to easily conceptualize certain ideas. We may just have no easy way to describe something in our own particular language.

This is not a recent theory by any means. Alexander the Great reported that he had found some indigenous African languages unsuited to the discussion of "modern" institutional politics. It's not surprising really because the concepts he wanted to discuss were totally alien to the peoples he was describing.

Some scholars would go as far as to ask us to believe that Marxism didn't become popular in English-speaking countries because the English language isn't cut out for Marx's brand of Teutonic metaphysics. This may be going a bit too far, but at any rate language can be restrictive, or as Wittgenstein puts it: "The limits of my language are the limits of my world".

15.4.5 How is language used to manipulate? The question which we must really address in the context of manipulation is: to what extent does our language exist because of our environment (like the Eskimo's many words for snow)? Or conversely, does a certain social regime exist partly because of limitations in our language and thinking? Or are both of these concepts true?

Certainly linguistic distinctions bolster certain social regimes and are specially used to maintain social differentiation, like social and class roles. Take the words "nurse" and "patient". As soon as an individual enters a hospital with some medical condition, they become a "patient" and are thus assumed to be virtually helpless in all things. They are stripped of much of his personal freedom and choice and become the responsibility of "the nurse". On the street the two persons may previously have regarded each other as having an equal social status, but once the words "patient" and "nurse" have been introduced, a differential in status is determined by both parties. The nurse is charged with the patient's well-being. The patient is effectively no longer in control of their physical health and consigns themselves to the care of the nurse.

Even outside the hospital, and well after the patient's treatment, the nurse will still regard and describe the individual to others as an "old patient". The nurse does this not merely as a matter of historical fact, but also because their concept of the individual has changed as a result of a new linguistic label being applied in new circumstances. Ask any nurse or patient.

15.5 Methodology/Refinements/Sub-species: There are many techniques of linguistic manipulation as demonstrated in this simple hierarchy:

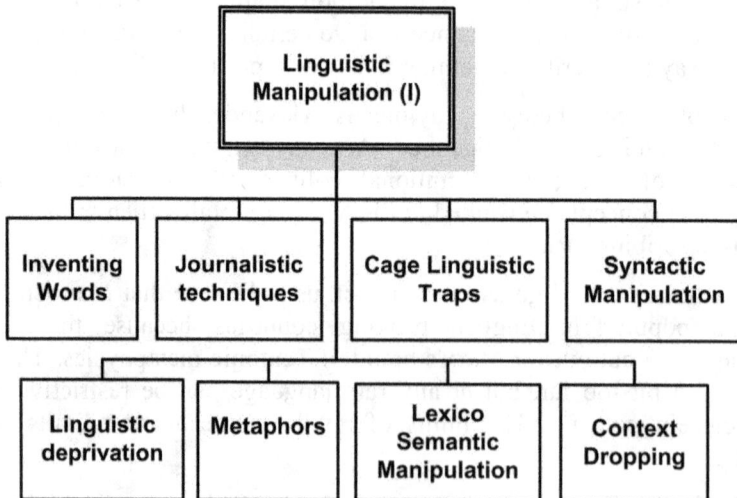

Within Syntactic Manipulation:

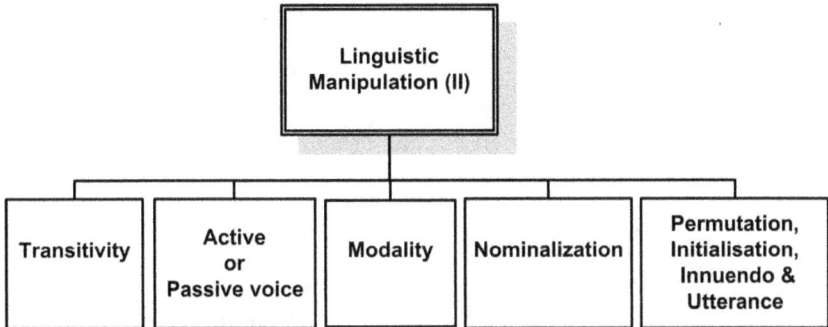

```
                    ┌─────────────────────┐
                    │     Linguistic      │
                    │  Manipulation (II)  │
                    └─────────────────────┘
                               │
    ┌────────────┬─────────────┼─────────────┬──────────────────┐
┌─────────┐ ┌───────────┐ ┌─────────┐ ┌──────────────┐ ┌────────────────┐
│Transit- │ │  Active   │ │Modality │ │Nominalization│ │  Permutation,  │
│ ivity   │ │    or     │ │         │ │              │ │ Initialisation,│
│         │ │Passive    │ │         │ │              │ │   Innuendo &   │
│         │ │ voice     │ │         │ │              │ │   Utterance    │
└─────────┘ └───────────┘ └─────────┘ └──────────────┘ └────────────────┘
```

15.5.1 Inventing Words: It's easy in this techno age to add new words to describe concepts that are entirely new to the world. However, this ease of linguistic invention also opens opportunities for the manipulator to alter both language and perception for reasons other than a simple desire to communicate clearly. Here are 2 examples:

Inventing Words - Example 1: "Anomalous cognition" is a new term coined by "Science Applications International Corporation" (SAIC) to refer to Extra Sensory Perception, including telepathy, clairvoyance, precognition and remote viewing. SAIC also refers to "psycho kinesis" as "anomalous perturbation". SAIC claim their terminology is "neutral" but it is actually entirely invented. It does sound more scientific and therefore looks better on grant applications and in fund raising brochures.

Inventing Words - Example 2: "Cisgenics": The capacity of new language to confuse and manipulate comes into sharp focus in the GM crops debate. In this contentious world concerning the vital issues of the control of food crops, powerful interests are at play. On one side a cadre of very powerful companies appear hell-bent on patenting any living organism. This is a commercial attempt to control agricultural production by patenting GM seeds, farm animals, fish, birds etc. On the other side is arraigned a vast alliance of environmental organisations equally determined to stop the GM companies from achieving these ambitions.

Both sides try to show that their arguments are scientific and fact based. However the illusion slips sometimes when the frustrations of the GM industry show through their calm façade. When this happens, the GM companies and their agents start to play some fairly overt linguistic games with the general public.

A case in point concerned the origins and use of the invented word

"Cisgenic" which appeared recently. It is an entirely invented word. The word is used by the GM industry to indicate a form of genetic manipulation which is somehow less dramatic that "Transgenic" manipulation.

The word "Cisgenic" was coined to describe the use of genetic material from closely related organisms in genetic manipulation. The word "Transgenic" was then limited to the use of material from completely unrelated organisms in genetic manipulation.

It appears that the word Cisgenic was invented by the GM industry to weaken opposition to GM crops. It is a kind of linguistic "foot in the door" ploy because the GM industry implies that Cisgenic is some kind of "GM Light". The implication is that using DNA from more closely related organisms is somehow more acceptable than crossing a cabbage with botulism bacteria using the DNA taken from cells of a fruit bat!

GM technology is not a simple subject and the issues are complex even for the best informed members of the general public. This ignorance allows a manipulator to play lots of games with pseudo-scientific linguistics.

The facts: The defining feature of a GM crop species is that it contains a gene transferred from another species by means of genetic engineering. A "Species" can be usefully defined as a group of organisms all of whose members are capable of interbreeding and producing fertile offspring. So the kind of "Transgenic" jump involved in the production of GM crops is not something that could ever happen in nature. It is only in the past 20 years or so that we have seen the emergence of GM/transgenic crops. European public opinion remains stubbornly nervous of and opposed to GM food products.

In addition, the EU regulatory door to GM/transgenic crops has been very difficult to open for the GM industry. In the face of such opposition, promoters of the GM industry seized upon the concept of "Cisgenic", a word that was literally invented in the course of a PhD thesis submitted to Wageningen University in the Netherlands in 2004.

"Cisgenic" is said to describe close relative breeding. It is a clever word in this context with its scientific connotations of opposites or mirror images, one labelled with the prefix "cis-" and its mirror image, "trans-".

From this usage in science, "Cisgenic" suggests itself to be the opposite of "transgenic". And once the "c-word" appeared in referred journals, despite challenges by fellow scientists it gained currency and began to be seen as a potential key to open the door the EU had virtually closed to GM crops.

"Cisgenic", however, is a classification subset of transgenic. "Cisgenic" clearly involves genetically engineered transferral of a gene from a different species and is unequivocally transgenic. It is this transformation process, not the source of the transferred gene that gives rise to the unpredictable effects of GM crops and foods.

However such critical subtleties are lost on the general public and here we now have a case where some very risky science is being air-brushed out by the use of some fast linguistic manipulation. The use of the name of the prestigious Wageningen University in the context of this imaginary word adds to the manipulative plot.

15.5.2 Journalistic techniques: Newspapers (or any other reporting media) are never neutral reporters of news. Media organisations are owned by people or controlled by governments. All media are selectively consumed by a critical public and all of these groups have interests, opinions and private political agendas which impact on the attitudes and language used by the media.

Because of this, no media article exists which does not carry some of the baggage of its journalist, the media owners, its producer or its consumers. These influences on content may use a number of journalistic methods to manipulatively alter a message:

-   **Sharpening**: The summarisation of a story based on the selection of the "angle" to be used.
-   **Abstract avoidance:** The journalist refuses to generalise a story and focuses only on a particular event.
-   **Simplification:** A complex subject is deliberately simplified.
-   **Polarisation**: The journalist calls attention to opposites.
-   **Intensification:** The journalist focuses on conflict rather than consensus.
-   **Personification:** Events are personalised from an individual's point of view.
-   **Stereotyping**: The journalist links a character in a report to a strong stereotype - Saint or Sinner.
-   **Concealment**: The journalist withholds relevant information.
-   **Distortion:** The journalist manipulates facts by exaggeration, equivocation or minimisation of the truth.
-   **Falsification:** The use of deceit in a story.

15.5.3 The cage-type linguistic trap involves the manipulator establishing linguistic barriers or limits within which his victim finds he must operate, in effect restricting any alternative perspective or response by the victim other than the one which uses the predetermined nomenclature of the manipulator.

This is used in the framing of statements or questions where a manipulator formulates the desired reactions and responses in advance. The beauty of the technique is that it is almost transparent to the victim. In fact, from within "the cage" the barriers and restrictions imposed on his language are quite welcome for most people. They provide a means by which the victim doesn't have to conceive a mode of response because it has already been prepared by the manipulator.

The linguistically caged individual confines himself to the use of the language with which he has been provided.

A simple case is the use of analogy. When an analogy is used to demonstrate some concept or principle, a victim naturally assumes that, in the first instance anyway, they must verbalize their reactions in the same vein. They are thus constrained to the narrow rules of the analogy used by the manipulator. The victim thereafter commits themselves to reactions which may be totally irrelevant, inappropriate, out of character or just incorrect. For instance, a manipulative financial advisor might try to sell us an investment and use the train analogy by saying, "you know, if you miss this train, you will have to wait a long time till the next one comes along". In reality, there are worthy investments arriving constantly and the train analogy is totally invalid. However, if we accept the analogy we will feel pressured to "jump aboard".

To be effective, a cage-type linguistic trap must be simple. If the manipulator operates in too complex an idiom or extends an idiom too far, the victim will be provided with conceptual methods of exploring the language. He will soon find fault with it and realise what is going on. As with all systems of deceit, the more complex they are, the more unstable they become. The same is true with linguistic manipulation.

In addition, the method only works for short periods of time. Most people eventually recognize the restrictions under which they are being made to respond and will challenge the manipulator by breaking out of the linguistic trap, using a completely different, broader vocabulary.

15.5.4 Syntactic manipulation: Syntax opens up a world of possibilities to alter the meaning of a text by evoking different reactions in a reader or hearer. Some syntactic techniques are:

-   **Transitivity**: Transitive verbs are verbs which refer to an action by one person to another person, like "Peter hits Paul". The linguistic technique transitivity involves the use of verbs to transform a story from one involving an actor and a recipient equally into a story which focuses attention on the actor or recipient. For example, "Peter hits

Paul" can become "Paul was hit by Peter". This often involves the use of the passive voice.

- **Active or passive voice**: Switching between the active and passive voice can alter the apparent role of a participant by moving the actor between the background and foreground of a sentence. For instance the following two sentences convey different senses:

    1. Police shot blacks dead as meeting turned to riot.

    2. Blacks shot dead by police as meeting turned to riot.

    Obviously the first of the two phrases is more direct, blaming the police for the deaths, whereas the second mentions the police as a matter of secondary importance.

- **Modality**: This refers to different ways of referring to a person, event or situation and how it is judged to be true or desirable.

    It uses modal auxiliary verbs (like "can", "could", "may", "might", "must", "ought", "shall", "should" etc.) to convey opinions and speculation rather than facts.

    For example "The theatre was 50% full for the play" or "The play might have barely half-filled the theatre". The first statement is factual, the second conveys an opinion.

- **Nominalization:** This is similar to using the passive voice in that it removes specific details from the script of a story by neutralising specifics of an event, such as the participants, timing or modality. This is done by exchanging a verb phrase describing an unpleasant action for a single noun phrase describing an event.

    For example, "The demonstrator was taken to hospital after being beaten by several policemen" or "The demonstrator received hospital treatment after a beating by several policemen". The latter is more neutral about the action of the policemen than the former.

- **Permutations, initialisation, innuendo and utterance context:** These are primitive methods of linguistic manipulation:

- **Permutation** refers to the fact that the first word of a sentence captures the reader's attention and is therefore decisive in how the rest of the sentence is viewed:

    For instance, compare these two sentences: "Employers always quarrel with unions" and "Unions always quarrel with employers". Where is blame implied in these two sentences?

    The classical case are the phrases "The glass is half-full" or "The glass is half empty", which are factually identical but convey a very different sense to the reader.

- **Initialisation**: Adjusting word order alters perception of events:

    1. Police shot blacks dead as meeting turned into riot.

    2. Blacks shot dead by police as meeting turned into riot.

    3. Blacks shot dead as meeting turned into riot.

    And going a bit further this can become:

    4. Rioting blacks shot dead by police.

    5. Rioting blacks shot dead.

So the structure of the sentence alters the sense of the events from the original where police killed black people at a meeting which turned into a riot to the last structure which implies that black rioters had only themselves to blame.

- **Innuendo:** This is a statement which contains a qualifier (denial or question). An example would be "Fred is not a criminal" versus "Is Fred a criminal?"

- **Utterance Context:** Here a manipulator takes advantage of complex reports to alter the references between sentences. For instance, "Black youths attacked police whilst white youths looted shops" can become "Black and white youths attacked police and looted shops". The references back to the subjects are being deliberately confused in the second version of this report.

15.5.5 Linguistic deprivation is basically an extreme extension of the cage-trap method. It doesn't provide a linguistic framework for a victim's response, but goes even further by depriving them of any linguistic structure or method to respond or to adequately verbalize their response. It aims to make certain predetermined topics impossible to discuss.

There are many cases of linguistic deprivation based on social taboos and prejudices. For instance, in some societies discussion of sexuality or personal emotions is taboo. In other countries it is socially forbidden to discuss personal medical problems, or money matters or even personal political attitudes. These are all forms of linguistic deprivation because they limit both subject matter and the language that can be used.

History of education: This is by no means a new trick. For centuries the ruling classes of many societies have refused an adequate education to the peasantry reasoning that once the working classes are educated and capable of fluency and verbalisation, they can more easily conceptualize their feelings and communicate to others. An organised bunch of hungry, angry and articulate peasants would spell the end of a feudal system very quickly. It's long been understood that restricting the ability of the "working classes" to express themselves either verbally or in writing, is a sure method of keeping them docile and powerless.

A poignant example of this principle is the treatment which some white southerners of pre-abolition America meted out to their slaves. Many plantation owners forbade their slaves to learn to read and write or even speak English "properly". When caught trying to learn or actually converse in non-pigeon English, an offending slave was summarily flogged for his efforts.

Education was and is frequently seen by those in power as the precursor to conspiracy. Paradoxically, a similar barbarism was used to linguistically deprive many Irish schoolchildren in the nineteenth century of their mother tongue. Anglophile teachers forbade the use of the native Irish language because they themselves did not understand its complex dialects and they naturally suspected that it was being used to spread sedition. To combat this, (and they nearly succeeded in making the language extinct), these "educators" hung a small blackboard around their pupils' necks. When a linguistic "offence" was committed by a child, a mark was put on this blackboard and at the end of the day the marks on a child's chest were converted into harsh beatings[15.1].

Jargons and elitism: In the context of manipulation on a day-to-day basis, modern linguistic deprivation manifests itself in a more mundane way. All elite groups practise the technique, either consciously or unconsciously, by inventing and using jargon to hide their real meaning from "the masses", to protect their privileged position and to curtail discussion.

Scientists, civil servants, legislators, and capitalists all use their own peculiar form of "gobbledegook" in communicating amongst themselves to the exclusion of other groups and most of the population. An example of this would be the so-called "small print" in a contract or "terms and conditions". These tend to be phrased in a language completely alien to most of us. The objective is that we won't even bother trying to read and understand the "small print".

15.5.6 Metaphors: This is the use of a word or phrase that invokes a comparison with another idea. The most commonly used metaphors come from war and sport. For instance, "taking flak", or "being on the offensive" are two common metaphors used to convey aggression and toughness. Other metaphors have different connotations - the possibilities are almost limitless. They are very useful in conveying an opinion or personal feeling in a story and bear no relationship to the facts.

15.5.7 Lexico-semantic manipulation: This is the use of language which incorporates emotionally or culturally loaded words. The phrase "Fred is a bastard" has emotional and cultural consequences in some societies and none in others. In some societies this sentence would merely be a statement of fact; in others it contains a harsh moral condemnation of Fred.

15.5.8 Context-dropping: This is the distortion of something a person says, writes or does by extricating it from its context so as to render a completely different meaning. One easy way is to use a sound bite or line from a satirical piece without mentioning that it is satire and to represent it as being said in all seriousness. This could involve the use of edited audio and video media to showcase just one particular statement.

Another context altering technique is to refer to the target person in conjunction with a now maligned institution, even though the person has long ago broken all contacts with that institution.

For instance, a respectable, democratic politician who was once a member of the communist party as a student in the 1940s, long ago repudiated the Stalinist views of that party, but it's easy to link him again with that old, unfortunate association. All it needs is for a few contextual details to be left out by the reporter and we suddenly have the statement, "Mr Brown, whose formative years were spent as an active supporter of Stalin ......" etc.

15.6 Avoidance and Counteraction: Whilst these techniques are in common usage and often achieve their desired effects, linguistic manipulation is something of a blunt instrument.

A manipulator tries to put the victim in unknown linguistic territory by either depriving them of a valid "linguistic roadmap" or by providing them with a manipulated version of it. Once this is detected it can be quite rapidly overturned. Eventually most victims discover they are being tricked and can discredit the perpetrator's intentions, but this can take a long time during which the objectives of the manipulator may well be achieved. We all know now that Goebbels was a linguistically manipulative psychopath. But his linguistic tricks cost millions of lives in war and the death camps before his linguistic manipulations were finally revealed.

So what can we do to detect, avoid and counteract linguistic manipulation now?

15.6.1 Check multiple versions: The cost of detection may deter us, but the only way linguistic manipulation can be absolutely discovered is when information is available from multiple independent sources about the same event. By reading different reports of the same event it should be possible to detect a deliberate linguistic manipulation.

15.6.2 Look for symptoms of linguistic tricks: All of the linguistic games above leave telltale signs and with some practice it is possible to spot them: look for the use of passive voice, unreasonable abbreviation of critical details, emotive language, the use of metaphors, over-simplification etc. All will indicate that there is a manipulative payload hidden somewhere in the report.

15.6.3 Linguistic traps and restrictions: Don't allow restrictions to be placed on the use of language or the subject matter of a discussion. Any attempt to limit the language or terms of reference of a conversation is an attempt to manipulate. Refuse to participate unless such linguistic pre-conditions are removed. Refuse to discuss or consider issues or reports which use analogies - just ignore them. At best analogies are invalid and more than likely they are manipulative. Challenge the language being used directly and denounce it if it is manipulative. It's much better to walk away than to be dragged into a linguistic trap. If linguistic manipulation is detected in the public press, we should do what we can to expose it to the rest of the public, although there is little chance that we will ever be able to stamp out linguistic manipulation. It is now completely embedded in the popular media.

15.6.4 Detection is half the battle: Once linguistic manipulation has been detected, avoidance and counteraction can soon follow. Generally it should be easy enough to find the payload in a linguistic trick. Once this has been isolated, the victim can either confront the manipulator or play the trick back to the manipulator by demanding clarification of the intentions of the manipulator's statements and reasons for their phraseology, line by line.

By suggesting more rational alternatives to the manipulator, the linguistic trick can be painstakingly dismantled. A manipulator will always claim lack of time or resources to re-write a text and so it is wise for a victim to have one or two alternative versions ready to go in advance so that this tactic is also neutralised. If a manipulator accepts an alternative storyline, then the case is won. If a manipulator refuses the alternatives, then the victim can legitimately demand the reasons for this refusal using the same arguments as the manipulator did when they were discovered.

---oOo---

16. Rigging the obvious

16.1 Definition: The artificial creation of a favourable alternative amongst a group of unfavourable possibilities. The favourable alternative must be an "obvious" one in terms of the target group or individual. It must appear to be a self-evident and common-sense option, conclusion or solution.

The gap between a victim's perception of the obvious and reality is the scope for the manipulator's use of this technique.

16.2 Persistence: Brief to Medium. Some concepts which have been embedded as "obvious" will be hard to dislodge. The victim needs to undergo a radical review of a strongly founded view for them to question the obvious.

16.3 Accessibility: High. We can all manipulate the obvious. So, if you want your neighbours to think you have gone away, just stay indoors, leave the milk bottles on the doorstep and don't empty the letterbox. Very soon, everyone will be convinced that you are not there. This is just an example of how very simple stage management can be used easily by anyone in many different personal scenarios to manipulate "the obvious".

16.4 Conditions/Opportunity/Effectiveness: This manipulative technique is best illustrated by comparing it to a piece of cheese on a mousetrap seen through the eyes of the mouse. The mouse perceives a piece of food resting on a strange wooden contraption. It is obvious that he should eat it. The alternative is hunger. The reality is the trap.

A manipulator can choose to make the preferred alternative obvious by making it more attractive than the other possibilities. Alternatively a choice can be made "obvious" by making the other options appear totally unattractive. A manipulator also needn't necessarily provide obvious positive choices. Using the same technique, a manipulator may wish to create obvious barriers to options they do not favour.

To persuade a victim that his choice is "obvious", a manipulator must orchestrate his plan so that the victim sees the choice as a natural unfolding of events plainly leading to this choice, rather than some sudden revelation. To do this, the "obvious fact" must not appear too blatant or else the victim may suspect that it is being contrived for their benefit.

16.5 Methodology/Refinements/Sub-species: There are four hybrid techniques in this method of manipulation:

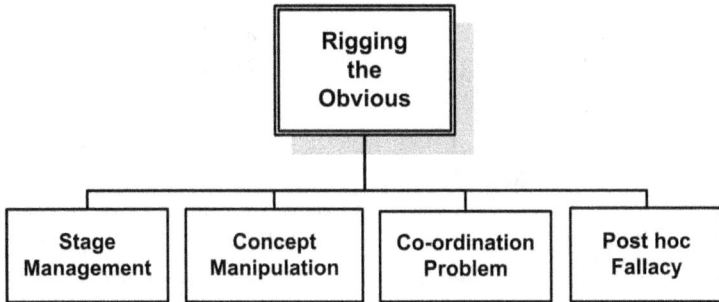

```
              ┌─────────────┐
              │   Rigging   │
              │     the     │
              │   Obvious   │
              └─────────────┘
        ┌──────────┬──────┴──────┬──────────┐
┌─────────────┐┌─────────────┐┌──────────────┐┌──────────┐
│    Stage    ││   Concept   ││ Co-ordination││ Post hoc │
│ Management  ││ Manipulation││   Problem    ││  Fallacy │
└─────────────┘└─────────────┘└──────────────┘└──────────┘
```

16.5.1 Stage Management: Stage management is the preparation required for the arrival of an apparently obvious conclusion or choice.

Pre-conditions: For the stage management of choices to work there are two important issues that a manipulator must address when delivering their "obvious" choice:

- **Credible evidence:** The manipulator must ensure that there is sufficiently strong supporting evidence available to the victim to endorse the "obvious decision".

- **In your face evidence:** The manipulator must ensure this information is clearly in front of his victim without arousing any suspicion.

Steps in Stage Management: With the use of stage management to rig obvious choices there are several possible steps for the manipulator:

- Firstly, a manipulator can rig the facts concerning the "obvious" choices which are presented to a victim, or interfere with a victim's ability to interpret them. For instance, we could highlight a decline in sales in a particular area whilst simultaneously complaining about the frequent absenteeism and poor time keeping of a colleague responsible for that sales area.

- Secondly, the manipulator interferes with the way a victim perceives the other alternatives by discrediting them. In our example, we could consolidate our stage management by casually implying to the boss that we often see our colleague carousing at night during the working week with his drinking friends.

- Thirdly (in the case of social manipulation of a group's choice), a manipulator can set up a situation where, providing that more than one victim is involved, he can modify the opinions and actions of all the parties by making a pre-determined joint action the "obvious" alternative to their acting independently. In this case he wishes to force the victims to act in unison. In our example, we could spread these malign rumours about our colleague amongst other staff members by implying that he is "not a team player", not "pulling his weight" etc., thus gradually alienating an entire group against him.

With this method, the objective is to convince the victims that certain facts are true and obvious, when in fact they are not. The manipulator relies on the victim's rational ignorance. Most people quite happily and routinely make decisions on the validity of facts, without anything like full information or any independent means of validation. They do this because of the high cost of verifying the "obvious facts" they see around them. Because of this, the victim when faced with an obvious and easily acceptable option will always select this in preference to other less comfortable or expensive to prove alternatives.

Providing the "audience" with a plethora of unfavourable data regarding the alternatives, whilst leaving the information on the obvious alternative simple and uncluttered, also has the effect of jamming the interpretative ability of the victim. In desperation, the audience will select the simplest and most "obvious" solution.

Use in social/aspiration manipulation: We all fall victim to this method of manipulation because of the high cost of information on alternative possibilities. For instance, when one stops to think about the reasons why most people in a given social group have such similar social and personal goals, one realizes that they could not possibly all have made the same informed choice by coincidence. In reality, part of the reason that many individuals behave in a similar way, is that they have all made the same "obvious" choices and they all think that they have made the same informed choice voluntarily.

We could sum up western middle-class, male aspirations as follows: marriage, two kids in a local school, steady job, 25 year mortgage on a house in suburbia, 2 holidays a year, pension, little car for the wife etc. These aspirations are identical and "obvious" for huge groups of men. The alternatives are obviously much less desirable and even dangerous, such as working as a high-earning freelancer making more money than an American president, living where you want, taking 60% of your working year off on holiday, sending your kids to private schools of your choice, having several residences, private capital reserves, and no debt. Of course, on the other hand, you could run a business that fails, lose your home and possibly your wife and kids. Skid row could beckon, so it's far better to opt for the "obvious" safe, suburban choice.

These forms of social manipulation of choice exclude many real options by emphasising the risks of stepping outside the path of conformity. We are encouraged to stay close to home and step into the shoes of our parents. Capitalism relies on a steady stream of cooperative workers willing to conform and deliver reasonable productivity. The system simply cannot tolerate too many ambitious or demanding individuals in society. There just wouldn't be enough workers left to provide wealth for them all.

16.5.2 Concept manipulation: In concept manipulation, the manipulator sets out to "fit" their preferred choice into the victim's moral or philosophical concept of order. The victim must feel that the "obvious choice" is part of a "greater truth", which he already has a "gut-feeling" about. It has to seem self-evident.

If a victim's concept of what is philosophically obvious is not suitable, then the manipulator must impose a new interpretative framework onto the victim, with the "obvious" policy at its centre. This latter involves discrediting those aspects of all those alternative scripts which reject the manipulator's "obvious" choice and substituting them with "respectable" standards which favour the manipulator's option.

The ultimate objective of this manipulative technique is that the victim will actually make the decision entirely alone, apparently unaffected by external influences. For instance, the technique is in continuous use when trying to reconcile concepts like racism and gun-ownership with fundamentalist white Christian beliefs in the United States.

16.5.3 Co-ordination problem: In the third method, the so-called co-ordination problem technique, the manipulator relies on the fact, or originates the circumstances, wherein two or more victims see the alternative of working together to achieve a mutually profitable result as the obvious choice. The result must appear to reward them more than if they worked independently.

A well-known analogy to this method is that of two parachutists. They have been dropped into unknown territory and are required to meet in order to escape together. However, they have made no previous arrangements about meeting at any predetermined location and are forced therefore to rely upon a map and knowledge of each other's behaviour. Whilst they have the same map, it is also slightly out of date and it doesn't show all the new features in the area. Each will assume that the other will go to the largest landmark in the region, a certain bridge marked on the map. Whatever they see that is not on their map, such as a large new church or another large bridge, they will not consider relevant. This is because it is not on their mutual map or part of the "obvious" course of action. The manipulator is the cartographer of this analogy. The victim's likely behaviour is obvious to the cartographer.

This is a method of social manipulation where groups of victims can be obliged to take particular, mutually beneficial choices which are pre-defined by the manipulator. The manipulator is taking advantage of situations in which all parties can realise mutual gains, but only by making mutually consistent decisions

16.5.4 Post hoc fallacy: A manipulator can alter the victim's understanding of cause and effect in demonstrating that something happened as an obvious result of a previous event. The post hoc ergo propter hoc (after this therefore because of this) fallacy is based upon the mistaken notion that simply because one thing happens after another, the first event was a cause of the second event. Post hoc reasoning is the basis for many superstitions and erroneous beliefs. It is also used as a manipulative means of delivering an apparently "obvious" conclusion to an unsuspecting victim.

Many events follow sequential patterns without being causally related. Perhaps you have a cold. So you drink lots of fluids and two weeks later your cold goes away. Was that because of your fluid intake? A solar eclipse occurs so you beat your drums to make the gods give back the sun. The sun returns, proving to you the efficacy of your priest's religious power, or does it? You use a water diviner and start drilling where he points and then you find water. The water diviner is truly a semi-magician or was it just coincidence? You imagine heads coming up on a coin toss and heads comes up, you muse on your powers of prediction. Or was it just luck?

But such sequences of events don't establish the causality any more than simple correlations do. Coincidences happen. An occurrence after an event is not sufficient to establish that the prior event caused the later one. To establish the probability of a causal connection between two events, controls must be established to rule out other factors such as chance or some unknown causal factor. Anecdotes aren't sufficient because they rely on intuition and subjective interpretation. A controlled study is necessary to reduce the chance of error from self-deception or deliberate external manipulation.

The tendency of the general public to believe in the "obvious" causal links between events is very useful to the manipulator, because it provides a fertile, gullible audience to sell a hidden agenda. For instance, in economics, it is truly amazing how often employment figures suddenly rise prior to budget announcements or elections.

The improved employment figures are implied to be the result of the good economic stewardship of the ruling party. Employment figures may (or may not) be better but the relationship between the timing of the budget / election and the publication of the figures is a deliberate decision made by a manipulator knowing that the public will readily accept the relationship between the improved economy and the actions of the government. It's self evident, obvious!

16.6 Avoidance and Counteraction: Rigging of the obvious is a difficult and maybe impossible technique to detect because victims are normally convinced that they are making a rational considered decision or an obvious choice. Indeed trying to persuade a victim that they have been duped into making a bad choice can lead to some real opposition from the victim.

16.6.1 An example - "Obvious" investments: The relative ease with which anyone could get credit in the decade up to 2008, made borrowing money an obvious choice for many.

Few of the millions of people in Western Europe who borrowed money to buy over-priced housing in these years could foresee the economic crash. None of them would take kindly to being told that they were duped into making the choices they made. These victims of negative equity will offer all kinds of excuses for their behaviour, like: their acute need to own a house, that there was no alternative to borrowing, that there were no signs of a market bubble, or that the banks were at fault, or that they were told they couldn't lose, or that everyone takes credit etc., etc. Their defence will be vehement.

Nonetheless, a rational examination of their defence of the financial decisions they made will reveal that they were driven like sheep into choosing from a restricted range of "obvious choices" which had been manipulated for them by the banks and the speculative building industry. An honest evaluation will reveal that consumers did not really need to borrow on this scale. It will reveal that the complexities of credit and risk are alien to most consumers, that they were actually driven by greed to make a killing on their property, that banks are not honest brokers, and that anyone who believes that an investment "can never lose" is a fool. These victims (known by certain banks as "muppets" because of the ease with which they could be manipulated) borrowed well beyond their means for capital items (houses) they could not afford, with the full support and encouragement of the banks.

The banks had little to fear because their debts were "socialised" by the governments anyway, i.e. the banks' debts were state guaranteed. For the banks it was a no-loss gamble. However, for the victims, it was a no-win choice. And so millions of "muppets" borrowed to buy property with the hope of personal gain, thus starting and maintaining a property price bubble. More investors piled into the market, inflating the bubble and imperilling real home buyers further. The banks threw petrol on the speculative fire by pouring more easy and cheap credit onto the markets.

Few ordinary people could resist the temptation of easy credit, personal profit and the possibility of even paying off their mortgages just out of profit on the profits of rapidly rising house prices. No-one paused for thought about issues like "fundamental value" or "capital risk" or "should a home be considered an investment?" So, like lambs to the slaughter, millions were given credit to buy at the top of a hugely inflated market. It all seemed so absolutely "obvious" as a way of making money.

It was all too good to be true of course. The bubble burst and the depth of economic decline is now a modern legend in its own time. Recriminations are still flying about regarding lack of bank regulation, etc. On the other hand, without gullible house buyers and borrowers, this could not have happened. So, to some extent, the victims were at least partly culpable for their own demise and have themselves to blame to a large extent - caveat emptor.

Lessons will not be learned from this and certainly in a few years time when this episode is long forgotten, it will probably all happen again. After all, the first "internet bubble" catastrophe didn't stop the recent world record IPO capitalisation of Facebook Corporation when billions were invested in a company that doesn't generate one cent in productive value. It just seemed to be such an "obvious" investment.

I guess we will have to listen to the crying and gnashing of teeth from more failed investors when Facebook is finally flushed down the toilet of the capital markets in a year or two.

16.6.2 Avoidance of the "obvious": So is there any way to avoid falling into the trap of a deliberately rigged "obvious choice"? Well, there are a few golden rules in making decisions which can help:

- **Think outside the box**. Try to take a long view when making decisions and don't be pushed into a parochial view of the world.

- **Don't be rushed into a decision.** Anything which demands an instant decision is almost certainly a manipulation.

- **Don't assume you are being rational.** Get independent advice from someone who is not involved at all.

- **No free dinners:** Generally obvious choices are wrong choices. If in doubt do nothing.

- **Nothing is that simple:** The world tends to operate with highly nuanced issues, so decisions based on simplistic mantras like "You can't lose on property" are almost certain to be wrong or manipulated.

- **Assume nothing:** Never assume the veracity of anything you are told. Check and double check the truth of every assumption. If an assumption cannot be verified, then abandon the choice and decision until it can.

- **Avoid emotional decisions:** Don't become emotional about a decision OR the lack of a decision. If a decision doesn't work out, don't worry - there will be more and better opportunities in the future.

- **Stay independent:** Don't enter into allegiances unless you can see an obvious mutual advantage and where the value of an allegiance is greater than the cost.

- **Too good to be true:** Follow the old adage that says "If something looks too good to be true, then it probably is".

16.6.3 A Warning to the victim: The manipulation of the obvious is quite a safe technique for the manipulator. The obvious is usually seen as unbiased and apolitical because a victim feels that they are making their own decision for what they consider to be the self-evident choice.

A manipulator ensures that the response "obvious" originates from the victim, and for this reason the opinion once voiced is rarely shaken by any interfering third party.

An assertion can in fact only be degraded from its status as "obvious" by an extraordinary or abnormal event which casts a completely new light on the range or quality of the alternatives. Ask the general public in Western Europe now suffering from austerity measures and negative equity if new light has finally been cast on their view of the "obvious" investments they made in the property market.

---o0o---

17. Symbolic reward

17.1 Definition: Symbolic reward is the manipulative process used to gratify a victim by giving or promising to give them some low-cost or intangible reward in return for co-operation with the manipulator.

Symbolic reward is employed in either a negative sense such as to prevent alienation and enmity or in a positive way to reaffirm loyalties and membership. It may strengthen group attachments or be in return for a material service or effort of some kind.

A symbolic gesture replaces a real reward which has a real value. A symbolic reward always has a value less than the real award that it replaces.

17.2 Persistence: Brief to Medium. A victim can continue to believe in an ultimate reward for a long time (years), if the reward is sufficiently attractive.

17.3 Accessibility: Low to Medium. To use this method of manipulation you need to have a reward to offer or at least be able to convince a victim that you have something that they want.

17.4 Conditions/Opportunity/Effectiveness: Symbolic reward is a useful technique for a manipulator, especially when he must deal with individuals or groups making excessive demands on him.

It is very difficult for a victim not to be disarmed by the giving or the promise of a gift or favour, however small. It is almost always possible for a manipulator to find a suitable small reward for a particular victim in any circumstance.

When used with a group, the technique of symbolic reward can be very effective in placating dissatisfaction, especially amongst those less likely to suspect the insincerity of a manipulator and those who may be impressed by the prestige of such a reward.

The only important considerations for a manipulator when deciding on the giving of symbolic rewards, are its symbolic value versus its real cost. The symbolic reward must be less costly than the tangible reward that it replaces; otherwise there would be no need to use a symbolic gesture. A symbolic reward replaces a tangible reward for precisely this reason.

The symbolic value to a victim depends entirely on two criteria:

-   **Future promise**: A symbolic reward is often accompanied by some physical item or privilege, and it often points towards or implies a future tangible reward of some kind. For example, calling a salesman a

166

"sales executive" and giving him a BMW car in which to carry his samples gratifies him, and the gesture points towards a bright future with all kinds of implied promises like a directorship. This is important to the victim's valuation of a symbolic reward.

- **Rarity/Prestige value:** The frequency with which a particular symbolic reward is given will determine the value it commands to the receiver. If it is commonly awarded then it is debased, if it is rarely given then it commands more value in exactly the same way as rare commodities command greater value than everyday products. A "Best Employee of the Week" award would soon fail to raise any enthusiasm but "Best Employee of the Year" with a handsome prize might be something to go for.

17.5 Methodology/Refinements/Sub-species: There are 4 basic sub-species of the technique:

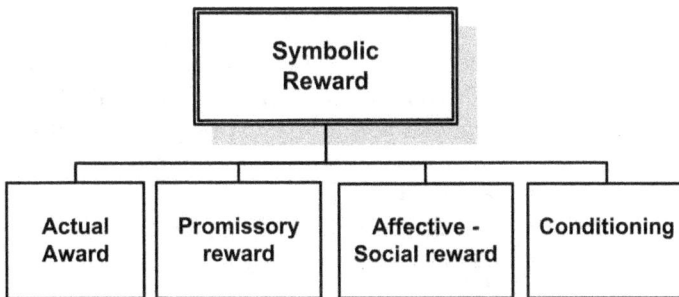

```
                    ┌─────────────────┐
                    │    Symbolic     │
                    │     Reward      │
                    └─────────────────┘
        ┌──────────────┬──────────┴──────────┬──────────────┐
  ┌──────────┐  ┌──────────────┐  ┌────────────────┐  ┌──────────────┐
  │  Actual  │  │  Promissory  │  │  Affective -   │  │ Conditioning │
  │  Award   │  │    reward    │  │ Social reward  │  │              │
  └──────────┘  └──────────────┘  └────────────────┘  └──────────────┘
```

17.5.1 Actual reward: An actual reward is a physical reward given to a victim in return for certain behaviour or services rendered. Of course the actual reward has only a fraction of the value of the service rendered, but it carries prestige and promise of future advancement.

For instance, in industry there are the so called "Suggestion plans". These are widely used in American and Japanese companies. Employees are given a one-off reward for making a suggestion which improves profitability. The reward is just a token amount. The real value is in its symbolic and prestige impact, i.e. the recognition of a worker's commitment to his employer's increased profits. It replaces a real share in the company's profits.

Companies may receive a short-term grant or allowance from the government to employ someone who has been unemployed long-term. The amount granted to the company is tiny in comparison to the cost of maintaining the unemployed person with social security benefits over years of unemployment, but it is a sort of symbolic "thank you" to the company for cooperating with the state.

17.5.2 Promissory reward: This is the use of a promise or implication of future rewards ahead. It substitutes any real rewards now. Politicians and managers often use promissory rewards because they are short of tangible rewards but in need of favours now.

Cases abound in the world of management where promissory rewards are termed "positive reinforcement". This term really refers to publicly slapping an employee on the back for work well done. The teaching of "positive reinforcement" is much favoured in contemporary man-management training.

In fact it is just a form of symbolic / promissory reward. A real financial reward is being replaced by this symbolic gesture. Such rewards are held in low esteem by many employees who are aware of their hollowness, but they can work in some circumstances with young or naïve victims.

17.5.3 Affective reward: This is the emotional reward which plays on individuals and groups when objectives are successfully achieved. It is also known as "getting a buzz" from completing some difficult or long task. It may knit social groups together and provide strong sources of motivation, but it in no way implies the delivery of any material reward to the subjects. Such symbolic rewards are felt to be far less objectionable than those with promissory overtones because the subjects are rewarded simply by being part of a group that successfully achieved its goal.

Nonetheless, the existence of affective rewards is used as a form of indirect reward and again, it substitutes for real tangible rewards such as a share in the goal success or any economic or social spin offs of the success.

17.5.4 Conditioning: Also known as classical conditioning or Pavlovian conditioning, it's a form of learning and expectation based on the experience of association between a stimulus and a response. The Russian scientist Ivan Pavlov is credited with the discovery of this conditioning mechanism. Pavlov found that dogs can be conditioned to salivate in the presence of a non-food stimulus that they have learned to associate with food. If Pavlov brings the food and claps before feeding the dog, the dog will eventually salivate when Ivan (or any other human being) walks into the room or when the dog hears a clap.

A response to conditioning can be involuntary, as in the case of salivation, and it can be unconscious as in the case of expecting to get relief from an ailment by following a doctor's orders. Human beings are also capable of being conditioned to respond in ways not directly connected with a particular real event.

Negative conditioning example: In contrast, this refers to victims reacting negatively to mistreatment. For instance, members of continuously persecuted groups may react defensively when confronted by the presence of police or other uniformed officials. The symbolism of the uniforms is enough to trigger a conditioned response.

Such were the conclusions of some sociologists regarding the rapid escalation of violence in the 2011 riots in England[17.1]. Many researchers documented that rioters were reporting that even the presence of the police made them feel and behave violently. A long standing antagonism to the police had become entrenched in minority populations. This was attributed by researchers to decades of racial prejudice in the British police force, the racially biased use of stop and search by English police and similar long-term conditioning behaviours against black or Asian British citizens.

Thus the effect of decades of discrimination and oppression of minority groups has been enough to create a negative conditioned reaction in a sizable part of the nation's youth towards the country's main institution of law and order - the police.

17.6 Avoidance and Counteraction: If a victim recognizes a symbolic reward in its real light it becomes valueless to him and the manipulator.

The technique can also backfire if a victim calls for the tangible reward which the symbolic gesture is designed to substitute. A salesman who performs very well may well after a couple of years demand his promised promotion. If this should happen, the original symbolic reward becomes irrelevant because there is no saving made by the manipulator.

The success of a symbolic reward relies therefore on its implementation, good timing and selection of the right type of victim. Victims prone to falling for prestige-related rewards will always be good candidates for symbolic reward manipulation. Subjects who are more sceptical and more interested in tangible rewards are better placed to recognise and avoid the use of symbolic rewards.

Conditioned behaviour can generally be avoided by refusing to participate in organised group events like "team building", "scrum meetings", "casual Fridays" and other similarly fashionable nonsense designed to create the impression of "community" by doling out valueless symbolic rewards, like not having to wear a tie in the office on Fridays.

---o0o---

18. Institutional inertia

18.1 Definition: Institutional inertia is deliberate inactivity or delay by an institution or group with the objective of causing damage to a victim or to his interests, or to render a victim impotent.

18.2 Persistence: Short to Long: Institutional inertia describes all delays resulting from involvement with any institution. All institutions are inefficient and certain types of institutional involvement can cause short hold-ups measured in hours whilst others (i.e. legal actions) can trigger delays measured in years.

18.3 Accessibility: High. You don't need to be an institution to use this technique. Anyone who has access to certain institutions can use them to manipulate a victim.

For instance, any citizen may have the right to object to planning permission for a building. The complaint is made to an institution like a local council or municipality and the victim (the builder) suffers the institutional delay. The manipulator, in this case, is the complainant.

This example suggests that the institution is being used as a proxy for the manipulator. In some cases, the institution itself may well act on its own behalf, driven by its own political interests and/or agenda.

18.4 Conditions/Opportunity/Effectiveness: All of us have been troubled by institutional delays at some time in our lives. This most frustrating phenomenon generally occurs at the hands of central and local government agencies.

Not all institutional delays are manipulative of course. Institutional incompetence is often "blind" to its victims. Incompetence knows no boundaries. But, it can and is used as part of a manipulative method to delay a victim or bias a victim's behaviour.

Deliberate inertia: Deliberate institutional inertia is as common in corporate management as it is in a government bureaucracy. Like many other methods of manipulation, it relies on the fact that a manipulator has some useful information which the victim does not. In this case the victim may be subject to a time constraint. Knowing about this time constraint provides the manipulator with power over their victim. Perhaps a victim needs to appeal a decision by a certain date. This time-constraint locks the victim into an externally imposed schedule. This fact could be used by a manipulator to fatally frustrate or block a victim's efforts by impeding their appeal so that it is delivered too late and disqualified.

Cooling effect of inertia: Inertia can have the effect of cooling off or dispersing support for a victim's cause. For instance, waiting a little longer to call an arbitrator into an industrial dispute or letting a company's creditors cool down can dissipate the emotions of aggrieved participants.

Cost of discovery: As with other manipulative techniques, the cost to a victim of avoiding or uncovering a deliberate plot to use institutional inertia is high. It is measurable in terms of the personal energy required by a victim in trying to understand and unravel the intricacies of the institutional procedures which are being used to delay or dissipate the victim's efforts.

18.4.1 Use by managements: In management, institutional inertia can be applied in a number of directions. A manager can use it against fellow managers, directors or the workforce. A director can stall subordinate managers or fob off a workforce.

18.4.2 Use by workforce: An organised workforce can cause delays to management by not processing the decisions of its union's membership or by holding up changes in working practices. All that this technique requires to be effective is an organisation or institution of some kind which can be used to hide the real source and mechanism of the inertia.

18.4.3 Use by campaigning groups: In campaigning organisations such as environmental pressure groups, the use of institutional inertia is a really useful tool for causing delays in contested developments.

The use of lengthy procedural appeals or requests for information can effectively jam up or derail a planning or development process with little cost to the campaigning group, but with potentially great cost to the developer. The technique is not, of course, confined to environmental pressure groups. It is equally usable for human rights, consumer rights, minority rights and other pressure groups.

18.4.4 Use by the individual: From the point of view of the ordinary individual, the use of institutional inertia is very attractive. It is a widely available means of "jamming- up" a much more powerful organisation's decisions and actions. It is thus not a method of manipulation exclusively in the control of any elite group.

An individual is inherently more flexible than any organization and this potential for flexibility makes institutional inertia a very democratically available and two-way manipulative method.

Knowledge of institutional systems: All that a manipulator needs is a reasonable knowledge of the roles and basic procedures of various large proxy institutions. Once these are understood, a manipulator can set up an institutional giant against a victim, and then cause a delay, derail the action of a victim, or force a stalemate.

And all of this can be done by the manipulator from the safety of great distance and under the cover of using normal institutional process.

18.5 Methodology/Refinements/Sub-species: There is only one manipulative method involved here. For this manipulative method to work, the following components are necessary:

- Ability to force a delay: The reasons for the delay or suspension could be a/ to cause the victim to miss a critical deadline or b/ to cause a delay which weakens the victim's support base

- A victim with deadlines: A victim that is a/ subject to a time-based constraint such as a legal deadline or a start date or b/ whose support base is weak and prone to collapse if subjected to delays.

- A delaying Institution: An institution that can be used to cause an appropriate delay to the victim

- Schedule the delay: A choreographed schedule of how and when delays will be triggered off by the manipulator. Several delays may be planned using different institutions and/or different types of delay. A manipulator may want the manipulated delays to run consecutively or concurrently, depending on the overall effect required (i.e. a long delay causing attrition or a more rapid demoralisation of a victim having to deal with multiple institutional delays).

18.5.1 Which institution? The institutions, in which the inertia is centred, need not necessarily be a manipulator's own organization or even connected to the manipulator. This realisation leads us to an important refinement because it means that a "proxy institution" can be used and then blamed by the manipulator for causing delays contrary to the interests of a victim. This is useful in terms of deniability.

18.5.2 Using a Proxy: The most effective proxy organizations that can cause institutional delays are, of course, government or international agencies. Despite this, there are also many opportunities for using the technique within a corporation, by appointing a bureaucratic internal department, a consulting organisation or a company auditor or similar as the "proxy".

18.5.3 An example of how institutional inertia can be used: A fictional case could be an industrial dispute involving a health and safety issue. The management requires more time to make improvements or wishes to ignore and dissipate the issue entirely. They have several opportunities to employ institutional inertia.

Step 1: Take as much time as allowed: In the first instance, the company itself can delay addressing the issue for as long as possible by putting off its consideration until the next board-meeting and so on. This buys some time, but eventually they will be forced by union pressure to act.

Step 2: Involve an external institution: At this point, the company can request independent advice or even the assistance and advice of the state on the relevant regulations.

Step 3: Request information, clarification, collaboration: When a government agency has finally submitted their report, the management can dispute and question its findings and ask the union to conduct its own evaluation.

After this is complete, the workforce finally believes that the management is about to act and make practical improvements.

Step 4: Invoke the "special case": The management can now request further information from various local and international organisations and solution providers claiming there are specific problems, i.e. it's a "special case".

For instance, the International Labour Office, the European Commission and many other organisations will be only too pleased to offer advice on various topics relevant to the workplace. Advice from suppliers (solution providers) can be sought almost indefinitely.

Step 5: Start "churning" the paperwork for consultation: Of course, this all takes a lot of time and generates a very great deal of paper, including reports, alternative proposals etc. And, naturally, all of this paperwork must be duly submitted to the local union representative office, the Health and Safety executive office and the board of directors for their opinions which must also be circulated, in writing, to everyone else. This "churning" of paperwork also creates huge additional external delays - plus it also adds a little "bonus" manipulative information overload to the victims.

Step 6: Commercial delays: When all this has been circulated, consulted upon and agreed, commercial contractor tenders for the improvement works can be sought and evaluated by the company. After the selection of a contractor, the schedule of work must be agreed and all parties must agree the specifics of the proposed solution, costing, contract and specifications.

Step 7: Economic delays: Finally when all is specified, discussed, agreed, and signed off, the company can finally apply for grant assistance for the capital works required. Oh! Did we forget to mention the capital grant applications? "Well yes, of course, we have to get approval for all capital works for the purpose of obtaining capital grant assistance....."

And so it can go on, for years if necessary, or basically as long as the manipulator wants to maintain the delay. From the moment when such an issue is initiated, a hold-up of several years can be "won" by using postponements caused by employing proxies to generate delays.

In this case neither the union nor the local state authorities have any cause to complain or deny the right of the management to act in this way. The delays are all caused by consulting with relevant authorities and they are outside of the control of the company.

From the manipulator's point of view, with a bit of luck the natural turnover of labour will have swept away the original antagonists by the time conclusions are finally reached. In the end, the company may never need to act at all.

18.5.4 A real example from the recent past: It has long been proved that Nazi war criminals were smuggled to certain South American countries to escape justice. Walther Rauff's case was typical. This notorious SS-colonel developed and used a mobile gas chamber and was responsible for the murder of 100,000 people during the Second World War. After he escaped to Chile, his address in Santiago was known to post-war West Germany's foreign ministry. Hans Strack, the German ambassador to Chile, was ordered to request his extradition. But Strack sympathised with war criminals in exile and delayed applying for Rauff's extradition for 14 months. When he finally did so in 1962, Chile was able to refuse the extradition request because his murderous crimes had by then occurred too long ago under the country's statute of limitations.

Here institutional inertia is used to maintain the liberty of a war criminal, simply by allowing the slippage of time to pass the Statute of Limitations limit. In this case, Hans Strack, the Ambassador deliberately allowed a delay so that a war criminal could escape justice in Germany.

18.6 Avoidance and Counteraction:

18.6.1 Effectiveness: For a manipulator, institutional inertia is a fairly safe method of manipulation because an institution comprises just too many individuals and complex rules for anyone to notice that it is being used to cause delays.

Most victims find it quite difficult to isolate the exact cause of a delay. Because a victim is not privy to the workings of the manipulator's organisation or the proxy organisation they are using, it is often virtually impossible for a victim to have access to the paper trail they need to demonstrate a deliberate delay.

18.6.2 Detection: Knowing that you are suffering institutional inertia is fairly obvious: Progress on the main "project" will halt and the traffic of paperwork will increase.

18.6.3 Avoidance and Counteraction: The only possible avoidance technique is to have pre-prepared responses to institutional demands in advance of the delaying action being taken. But in the absence of these, here are the two basic counter-measures:

- Drop out and restart: One response may well be to withdraw from the original plan of action and disengage from the delaying institution. In this scenario, a victim can simultaneously restart the original action under a different name or guise and hope that the manipulator doesn't notice.

This is a popular trick in building planning processes where a developer just drops his plans, walks away, and then a couple of months later a new company comes with a new set of (very) similar plans. The hope is that the "new plans" are not noticed by the group that is trying to derail the development.

- Undermine the institution: This strategy requires that the victim plays the manipulative game back to the manipulator or the proxy institution.

This is done by undermining the authority of the institution by either denying the quality of their information, their legal right to act or their mode of action. In some jurisdictions this can be done using the concept of a "judicial review" - a legal concept which challenges the legal basis of the modus operandi of an institution of government.

Of course, this won't work in a corporate environment where a proxy such as a lawyer or auditor is being used. In these circumstances the victim needs to undermine the proxy's authority by threatening and taking legal action for breaches of professional codes of conduct. This "plays back" the manipulative inertia to the proxy and the manipulator by locking them into an alternative struggle with the victim.

---o0o---

19. Timing games

19.1 Definition: Human perceptions of time are quite unreliable; most of us tend to underestimate the time we take to complete common daily tasks. Our inability to estimate time creates a weakness which can be exploited by a manipulator. The basis of "timing games" is an agenda-setting manipulation, forcing a victim to accept an externally imposed timescale for some activity or effort.

Once committed to an external time-scale the victim is at the mercy of the manipulator if they fail to deliver on time. The manipulator then uses the "time-box" to force the victim to deliver other benefits to the manipulator, contrary to the interests of the victim.

19.2 Persistence: Short to Medium. This depends entirely on the length of time estimated by the victim for the task but can last from minutes to months.

19.3 Accessibility: High. Anyone can force a victim to conform to their own time estimates and penalise them if they do not. This technique can be used to penalise a tradesman for taking too long to complete a task or it can be used to derail a multi-billion dollar project which is off schedule.

19.4 Conditions/Opportunity/Effectiveness: Timing games take advantage of an inherent human weakness in making rational time estimates. We all tend to make estimates based on various kinds of psychological biases. Most of us have no idea how long some tasks take to complete. We are often shocked when we are confronted by the actual time taken to complete ordinary, routine tasks. Most of us, when it comes to time, are optimists.

Our weakness in estimating the relationship between time and effort puts us at risk of becoming victims of a particular form of manipulation involving the use of time constraints by an external manipulator.

19.5 Methodology/Refinements/Sub-species: There are two basic sub-types of timing games:

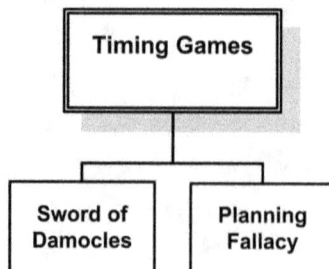

19.5.1 Sword of Damocles: Here, the manipulator uses the threat of deadlines to pressure victims into making decisions. A victim becomes obliged to make "time-boxed" decisions which are often not in their best interests.

A typical example could be, "if you don't buy these shares now, then by next week the price will have doubled". The pressure to act alters the victim's rational view of the relationship between stock prices and time. We all know that stock prices hardly ever double in a week and that when they do, they often collapse even more rapidly soon afterwards. Nonetheless, the sword of Damocles starts to swing above our heads and the fear of missing a good deal often eclipses common sense. A manipulator may even infer that not only will we miss an opportunity but that doing nothing may also be dangerous to our current investments.

19.5.2 The Planning Fallacy: This is the tendency of people and organizations to underestimate how long they will need to complete a task, even when they have experience of similar tasks overrunning their schedule in previous projects. We can even say that there is a general tendency to deliberately underestimate the time, costs, and risks of future actions whilst at the same time overestimating the benefits of the same actions.

According to this definition, the planning fallacy results in not only time overruns, but also cost overruns and benefit shortfalls. These represent possible rewards for a manipulator.

For instance, a commercial contract can be so tightly priced that competitors may chase each other down an ever less profitable rabbit hole in bidding for the project. This can lead to the unfortunate situation where the hapless winning bidder can actually find himself losing money. The real winner is the company receiving the bids.

19.6 Avoidance and Counteraction: There are 2 issues at stake here:

- Should you allow an external manipulating agent to determine or force you to determine a timescale for a task?

- How can a manipulator be defeated using rational methods of determining the timing of effort and events?

Firstly we have to ask whether we can avoid the setting of timescales for an unknown task. If we can then we should. However, if we are absolutely obliged to set timescales, then we must be extremely careful to be realistic and to allow for contingencies in our planning. Here are three basic strategies for avoidance of this manipulative game:

- **Set your own timescale:** Never accept a timetable imposed from outside. A statement that proposes a very tight time limit on a decision is a manipulative statement. Anything which forces urgency of decision is, by definition, manipulative. Missing an opportunity is not the end of the world; it is just one of many billions of missed opportunities that occur every minute on our planet.

- **Plan well and be reasonable:** Always estimate your own timetables and propose them as "reasonable alternatives". This means estimating timescales based on experience, reflection, allowing for reasonable contingencies and delays, external influences and human frailty. Document your timescales exactly with high quality, stated assumptions. A manipulator will always be forced to climb down in the face of superior planning.

- **If it can't be estimated, it can't be done:** Never engage in a complex, risky activity without a reasonable plan. Regardless of how a plan may change (and it will and should) during implementation, starting a complex task without a plan is like going to sea without charts or navigational instruments.

To avoid timing manipulation, you must be a better planner than the manipulator.

---oOo---

20. Baiting and switching

20.1 Definition: Named after the marketing technique, this manipulative method consists of "baiting" the customer by advertising a discount or rebate on one product and then "switching" the customer to another costlier product once in the shop.

It comes down to a type of "soft fraud" where the victim is offered one option but is given another (lesser) option.

It is used in politics to entice the electorate to an attractive idea, and then deliver a much less inviting reality. For instance, it may be a call for lowering taxes but then delivering a tough budget containing a massive new "tax and spend" program or vice versa.

More generally, it is the idea of a victim going in thinking that they are going to get one thing and then winding up getting something completely different and less desirable.

20.2 Persistence: Short. Generally this doesn't take very long to be exposed and the manipulative ploy to fail.

20.3 Accessibility: High. The technique is widely used in the airline and hotel industry where a "low-cost" airline such as Ryanair, offers low headline ticket prices. When the customer tries to avail of these prices, the reality is a bunch of price hiking supplements, like extra charges to reserve a seat, bring hold luggage, and pay by credit card, etc., so that in the end the ticket becomes rather expensive. There was even talk of Ryanair charging to use the toilets on their planes.[20.1] This would certainly bring customer exploitation to a new and cynical highpoint.

20.4 Conditions/Opportunity/Effectiveness: An example of baiting in US legislation are the so-called "caption bills" which propose minor changes in law using simplistic titles. These are the bait. They are introduced with the ultimate objective of substantially changing the wording of the bill in a so-called "switch" at a later date.

The objective is to try to smooth the passage of a controversial or major change in the law by using a non-controversial title to initiate the process in parliament. Whilst all this is legal, the political objective is to get legislation or regulations passed without attracting the expected negative reactions.

20.5 Methodology/Refinements/Sub-species: None

20.6 Avoidance and Counteraction: Avoidance of this trick will depend upon the level at which this manipulation is occurring:

- **Document and denounce:** If it is a simple semi-fraud, such as the Ryanair case, then just make sure that the transaction steps are carefully documented and report the fraud to the regulatory authorities in the country where it occurred. Most countries have laws in place to prosecute misrepresentation of consumer products and prices. Ryanair has been singled out for its devious practices over air fares.

- **Acceptance:** If the manipulation is taking place at a political level, it may be impossible to avoid because it may lie within the legal framework.

- **Be aware:** The minimum a victim can do is to be aware of the manipulation and warn others that it exists.

---oOo---

21. Sensory and symbolic manipulation

21.1 Definition: Sensory and symbolic manipulation is concerned with conveying biased messages, impressions and emotional triggers to a victim by means of sensory imagery, emotive symbolism and the use of stage management to create and manage a victim's impressions. It may or may not involve deceit or fraudulent imagery.

This type of manipulation is often used in the projection of so-called "soft-power" by national interests or other institutions like religions.

21.2 Persistence: Short to Long. The impressions caused by sensory manipulation can last for as little as a few moments or, when repeated and reinforced, can be embedded in a victim's long-term perspective.

Visual imagery linked with political or social perceptions can be very hard to shift. In some cases, we will deny the veracity of new images which seem to contradict the image-perception we already have of a person or event.

For instance, the discovery of Hitler's lover's movies showed hours of intimate scenes of domestic life with Der Führer and Eva Braun. These colourful and revelatory home movies conveyed a scene of routine domestic life which could be described in the words of political theorist Hannah Arendt as "the banality of evil".

The impact of the release of edited versions of these movies (in the documentary "Swastika") when shown in the Cannes film festival of 1973 was marked. The audience was outraged; they booed and whistled at the screen shouting 'murderers!' The presentation of the Führer as a friendly uncle, a petit bourgeois figure in a suit and tie, popping in and out of a family gathering, was intolerable. The iron-clad image of Hitler that had been so carefully shaped by Heinrich Hoffman still exerted a fierce grip on the public imagination.

Becker, the documentary producer, was tormented by the first reactions to Eva Braun's home movies. "I was punished for puncturing a negative myth. People saw something that was banal in action and banal in its colour". He believes that many had become comfortable with the carefully composed, black-and-white propaganda images of the Nazis built by propagandist Hoffman. "People hate it when you tinker with their mythologies," he says.

There are many instances of public outrage or distress caused when a commonly held perception is punctured by visual revelations such as when celebrities or respected politicians are caught on camera in compromising disturbing or absurd positions.

21.3 Accessibility: High. Almost everyone has some access to sensory and symbolic manipulation. For instance, ordinary members of the public can induce their children to attend highly symbolic religious services or military pageants. At a very personal level, individuals may attempt to mould their appearance and accent to appear to belong to a different socio-economic group.

Local politicians, business and non-secular leaders can take advantage of a wide range of sensory and symbolic manipulative options to deliver messages to the general public in their village and town. These manipulative actions can be about how a politician appears or what they represent, for instance. It could be the local church leader, or an imam leading impressive religious ceremonies or a local mayor and council, displaying their pomp, ceremony, respectability and wealth to the public. Businessmen may demonstrate their wealth and power with expensive cars, elegant tailor made suits and a large entourage in tow.

Beyond this level, the large institutions of "church" and state in the Western world have an almost limitless capacity for the stage management of large and highly impressive ceremonial examples of sensory manipulation.

21.4 Conditions/Opportunity/Effectiveness: Sensory manipulation is extremely widespread and ancient. It ranges from the first human cave images, some as primitive as the shadow of a human hand on a cave wall. It developed through to the grandeur of medieval religious and fortress architecture, art and music. Today it has become the modern means of demonstrating national and institutional prowess in grand spectaculars of nationalistic, technological, religious and military power.

21.4.1 Common factors: All of theses demonstrations of sensory manipulation have the same common factors:

- **Sensory:** They rely on purely sensory communication.

- **Non intellectual:** They communicate at an emotional level, rather than an intellectual level

- **Emotional:** They are laden with emotive symbolism, a mixture of culturally biased and cross-cultural traits fundamental to all human beings.

- **Potency:** They rely on the fact that sensory stimulus is the most potent means of human communication (A picture is worth a thousand words).

- **Extreme:** They rely on the fact that more is generally better when it comes to sensory impression. A very large mosque or church says a great deal more about the might and glory of God than a very small one.

- **Sub-conscious:** Sensory manipulation always attempts to communicate a message or create an impression on the victim at a level below the cognitive.

- **Ritualistic:** Sensory manipulation is most frequently employed in ritualistic behaviour where belief systems are created and reinforced using sensory and symbolic manipulation rather than rational knowledge.

- **Irrational:** Sensory manipulation works best on less informed, more impressionable, less educated victim audiences who rely much more on their physical senses and emotion than on rational analysis and intellectual evaluation.

- **Group use:** Sensory manipulation works best in groups of victims where it can trigger self-reinforcing reactions within a group.... the so-called "wow" factor.

21.4.2 Effectiveness: Sensory stimulus, especially visual stimulus, is extremely effective in communication and therefore in manipulation. Verbal and written communication is less trustworthy than a first hand visual encounter. "Believe nothing you hear and only half of what you see" so goes the adage.

In the right conditions and with the right victim types, sensory manipulation is very effective. The ideal victim tends to be ill-informed, poorly educated, and politically naive. These victims will also be part of that social group which is more prone to preferring simple to understand monosyllabic mantras rather than nuanced intellectual arguments.

Within this large group we know that sensory and symbolic manipulation works. Simply witness the millions of neatly cut lawns with their stars and stripes hanging out in the United States. Why do so many US citizens respond so stereotypically to calls for patriotism from the US government? Are they more patriotic than citizens of other Western countries? Or is it something to do with their educational status, their insularity and their level of awareness of the world around them?

Again, look at the attitudes of the majority of the UK population regarding their role in the European Union. The parochial nationalism of many British citizens has been manipulated by the British establishment since the entry of the UK in the 1970s. The current popular opposition demonstrates the discomfort that many British citizens feel as a result of decades of symbolic manipulation by the politicians and British media to mistrust "Europe". It's totally irrational, but the symbolism being used (Agincourt,

Crecy, WWII etc) is totally "clear" to the victims. This manipulation works especially well with those citizens who have had less education, a limited experience of the world outside their suburban lives and a poor understanding of politics and economics.

Such signals of patriotism are evidence of self-reinforcing symbolic manipulation within largely isolated, naïve, poorly educated, politically ill-informed groups which share a parochial, simplified view of the world and their role in it.

21.4.3 Is imagery too effective sometimes? The potency of physical imagery is the most influential of sensory media and sometimes a manipulator may wish to restrict access to sights for manipulative reasons.

George W. Bush, during the Iraq war, ordered the continued suppression of media images of the flag covered coffins of the thousands of dead American soldiers returning for burial in the USA[21.1]. He (or his political masters) rightly calculated that the effect of these repeated images would have a strong negative effect on the opinions of the US public.

At the time the US public wasn't that sure whether it should have its young men and women slaughtered in large numbers in a far-away country that no-one had heard of and that the USA had just invaded. Therefore Bush ordered that the imagery of the dead bodies arriving home should not be broadcast.

It didn't alter the casualty rates at all, but it kept the population of the USA oblivious of the poignant reality and the powerful sensory symbols that these dead represent to a politically unstable population in the U.S.A.

21.4.4 Is there a political bias? No, there isn't any particular political or cultural leaning in the use of sensory or symbolic manipulation. Furthermore, sensory manipulation may even be used apparently in the interests of the victim, for instance with the labelling of cigarettes using imagery designed to deter the purchase of these products on health grounds.

Both left and right of the political divide engage in sensory manipulation and it knows no cultural boundaries. The only political bias which we can see is that right-wing governments tend to use deceit more often than an appeal to public solidarity. Therefore the use of manipulative imagery tends to come more naturally to the right-wing.

The Nazis in pre-war Germany were masters of the use of visual media to convey anti-Semitic messages to the public. Ironically, the current Israeli government has also made a point of depriving the Palestinian people of access to production methods for the international media for similar reasons. One of the Israeli's first targets in the short war against Gaza in

2012 was the media centre of the Hamas government of Gaza [21.2] This attack by Israel allowed the promotion of the Israeli view of the conflict whilst suppressing (destroying completely) the contrary Palestinian view of the situation.

But then of course, Israel learned its manipulative trade (albeit unwillingly) under the heel of Goebbels and Nazi Germany[21.3]. The logic of abusive behaviour being continued by the victim of the abuse is tragically evident in this particular case. Here we can see the complementary relationship between a "Dictator" and a "Victim" being played out in an historical sense.

21.4.5 Right-wing displays: In the UK, the right-wing regularly uses spectacular events to bolster the status quo of the Conservative establishment. These spectacles range from royal events where the queen and royal family are taken out and displayed to their public in gilded carriages with ostentatious displays of wealth and power, often associated with military might, (just in case anyone gets any bright ideas about deposing the monarchy).

At a more middle class level, the Church of England (aka. the Tory party at prayer) has institutionalised the use of visual and symbolic manipulation to demonstrate the supremacy of Christianity in Britain, backed by the head of the Church (the Queen) who in turn is commander in chief of the armed forces. It's all very neat and well integrated. The use of large, spectacular buildings during the feudal period must have sent waves of fear into the peasants of the time. Even today, displays of the huge accumulated wealth of Church, Monarchy and Aristocracy still impress us all somewhat.

21.4.6 Uses by the Left-wing: Whilst the left-wing is unlikely to have the most impressive buildings, it very often has the best songs and imagery. Images of Che Guevara, the voices of Joan Baez, Bob Dylan, Billy Bragg and countless other protest singers still echo around the world.

The left-wing in the Western world is not averse to using sensory stimuli to influence its members, although not quite on the same scale and without the benefit of the vast feudal resources of the right-wing political bloc.

The use of tragic imagery of starving children in developing nations has long been used by many NGOs to morally oblige richer members of Western society to be charitable and contribute economically to a charity.

21.4.7 Cultural neutrality: The use of sensory manipulation crosses cultures, the King of Saudi Arabia is also referred to as "the custodian of the two holy mosques of Mecca and Medina", whilst Queen Elisabeth of England is referred to as the "Head of the Church of England and Defender of the Faith".

The Saudi family are masters of huge visual and architectural demonstrations of their wealth and "God-given" power. They put on some of the world's most impressive shows to demonstrate that their power is not only great, but also absolute and is theirs by direct authority from above. Their current reconstruction of Mecca to include the world's largest mosque is testimony to their desire and ability to impress the masses.

Similar visual exhibitions of might and majesty are found in all societies and religions

21.4.8 Uses by the individual: This is not just a manipulative method limited to an institution. At a personal level, individuals often attempt to mould their appearance and accent to appear to belong to a different socio-economic group. Some of us believe that this in some ways creates a better impression to those around us and grants some additional privileges. Its nonsense and insincere but, nonetheless, many people in our own societies are busy trying to alter the way in which they are physically perceived by those around them.

21.4.9 Conditions: Sensory manipulation and the use of symbolism rely on the victim being prepared to some extent. Religious art or patriotic imagery only works if the victim can fit it into an existing scheme of belief. So, a child being taken to a church or cathedral for the first time must know how this fits into a general social and religious scheme of things. The value of sensory or symbolic manipulation is mostly that of reinforcing existing manipulated concepts and impressions.

21.5 Methodology/Refinements/Sub-species: There are four main sub-types of this manipulative method:

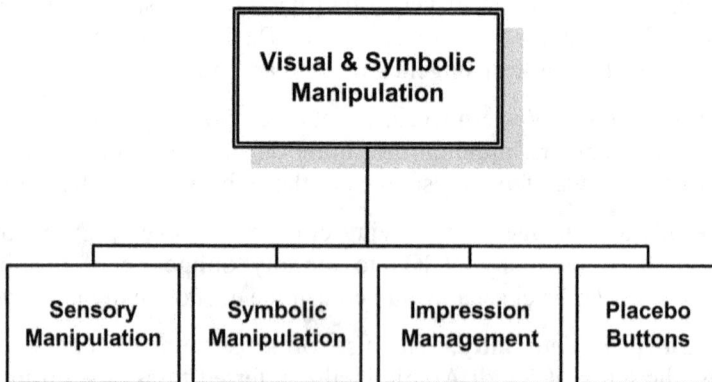

21.5.1 Sensory manipulation: Sensory manipulation employs visual and auditory stimuli to transmit messages to a victim which work in favour of

the manipulator. It also includes the filtering or deprivation of sensory information to a victim.

In both cases, the victim is influenced by either displaying or hiding emotive images without any reference to rational considerations of truth. Visual manipulation is the most potent method of sensory manipulation.

Traditional instances of sensory manipulation include large architectural and artistic works designed to convince gullible groups of victims of the correctness or supremacy of the manipulative group - the church, the government, the party, the military etc.

21.5.2 Symbolic manipulation: This is the placement of signs or symbols in such a manner as to evoke a desired or undesired response. For example, the flag of Malta is very obviously a Christian symbol and a statement about that country's ultra conservative, violent and post-crusader history of which it appears to be still proud.

And the symbolism becomes more subtle if one looks at the icons used by organisations which are obviously biased towards particular cultural origins, like NATO, for instance, which has an unashamedly cruciform symbol and is openly dedicated to the defence of the Western "Christian" world.

Another case is the use of the medieval hoods worn by penitents in thousands of Spanish liturgical processions at Easter time every year and by members of the shadowy, racist Ku Klux Klan in the USA at their secret meetings. Similar costumes were used during the European Inquisition to identify heretics at various points in their torture, conversion or execution. Sometimes the pointed hats were filled with burning tar which brought about a slow and excruciating death to the Muslim, Jewish or other heretic victims of the papal inquisitions in Spain and elsewhere.

The use and repetition of religious symbols occurs across all cultures and religions. The use of the crescent by the Muslim branch of the International Red Cross is a potent symbol in Islamic countries, where the crescent has been used for centuries as a sign of Islamic civil and religious power.

Symbolism is one of the most powerful forms of manipulation because it is often resistant to analysis, and therefore people can "read into" the symbol what they want to see. So, for the modern Spanish liberal the pointed hat is a reminder of the penitence of the bad old days of Inquisition, whereas for the caricature "red-neck" American, it is the symbol of blind racial hatred of the black population of the USA and their white "supremacy".

21.5.3 Impression management: In social psychology, impression management is a conscious or unconscious process by which people attempt to influence the perceptions of other people about a person, object or event, including themselves. They do this by regulating and controlling information in social interactions. It is often used to mean "self-presentation", in which a person tries to influence the perception of their own image. The notion of impression management also refers to the efforts of professional communication and public relations departments to mould a company or organisation's public image.

Such behaviour is in the credo of the conman who spends considerable energy creating a false impression in the eyes of his potential victims. For the same reasons, impression management is high on the list of priorities for any politician or community leader attempting to appeal to the public. The process is ripe for manipulation because it invites the alteration of an impression of personal or corporate image in order to deliver an alternative impression.

21.5.4 Placebo buttons: This is a small but important sub-type of symbolic manipulation, where a victim is presented with symbol labelled options which actually don't do anything. They exist to act as placebos to the victim.

An example is a customer service department. It only exists to create the impression that someone is listening, that the company cares and values its customers even if the voice at the company's end is pre-recorded.

The symbolism is important because it creates the impression of honesty and respectability. When you ring the much vaunted customer service number you get to hear a friendly robotic voice telling you to press 1 for Accounts, 2 for Complaints etc. The impression created is at least comforting.

21.6 Avoidance and Counteraction: It's a difficult manipulative influence for any of us to avoid, because it uses very primal routes to influence our behaviour: i.e. our own physical senses and associations with existing strong emotional conditioning.

We also find it difficult to avoid such powerful manipulative influences, because we very often find ourselves pleasantly awed and comforted by many of these ancient, evocative sensory and symbolic reminders of our cultural, social or religious origins. Some of this is very deeply embedded in our personalities.

In reality, the best way to deal with potential manipulative sensory content is to enjoy the cultural and aesthetic aspects of the stimuli, but to just remember that it is not necessarily real - that the emotions it evokes may be entirely artificial - and that big buildings, big parades, big concerts, big emotions and big wealth do not necessarily make big truths.

---oOo---

22. Reputation control

22.1 Definition: This is a group of manipulative techniques used to control the public reputation of a person, group, or institution.

The reputation of an individual or an institution is important, because it may determine whether or not they are trusted or accepted by the public or a peer group. Reputation as a criterion deals basically with the trustworthiness of an individual or institution when measured against a particular set of cultural standards of respectability, reliability, and other standards of honour. Damage to one's reputation has long been held to be a grave issue. As Shakespeare put it in Othello:

> "Good name in man and woman, dear my lord,
> Is the immediate jewel of their souls.
> Who steals my purse steals trash; 'tis something, nothing;
> 'Twas mine, 'tis his, and has been slave to thousands;
> But he that filches from me my good name
> Robs me of that which not enriches him,
> And makes me poor indeed.

Reputation is an issue of public rather than private perception; therefore the consequences of a "poor reputation" can be very damaging publicly. Reputation control is known to be a ubiquitous, spontaneous and highly efficient mechanism of social control in society. It is a subject of study in social and management sciences. Having a "good" reputation amongst peers is considered important to the success of members of a group.

Reputation control acts on different levels, both individual and "supra-individual". At the supra-individual level, it concerns groups, communities, collectives and abstract social entities (such as firms, corporations, organizations, countries, cultures and even civilizations). It affects phenomena of hugely different scales, from interpersonal relationships in everyday life to diplomatic relationships between nations.

Reputation control is a very obvious opportunity for manipulative agencies because a manipulator has many possibilities to negatively alter the reputation of a victim, quite safely, at long distance if necessary, with a very low risk. Similarly, reputation control provides many opportunities for the manipulator to positively adjust the reputation of an individual.

Conversely, the ease of access and relatively low risk of reputation control also provides opportunities for both avoidance and counteraction.

22.2 Persistence: Short to Long. A damaged reputation can survive through centuries.

Let's take the case of Richard III, Britain's most reviled king. History belongs to the victors and this is aptly demonstrated in the case of Richard III, the hunchbacked king demonised by Shakespeare as a man so "rudely stamp'd" that "dogs bark at me as I halt by them". The last Plantagenet monarch fell at the Battle of Bosworth in 1485, after which his body was said to have been stripped and publicly displayed for several days. Some accounts reported that his corpse was tipped into the local river; others said he was given a Christian burial at Grey friars monastery.

Richard's name became synonymous with evil deeds, epitomised by later accounts that he ordered the murder of his boy nephews, the two "Princes in the tower". The hatchet job on Richard was perfected by Shakespeare, who preserved the dead king's image as a "bottled spider" with a twisted body – a pantomime villain.

Historians do not know what happened to the two princes, except that they disappeared from the Tower in 1483. Some historians also point out that during Richard's reign he oversaw some important and progressive changes, such as the command to all judges that they administer the law impartially.

Nonetheless Richard III's reputation remains shot to pieces. Strangely, the recent discovery of the bones of Richard, have elicited some resistance from the present Queen of England and the Anglican Church for DNA testing of the corpses of the two princes in Westminster Abbey. Is the British royal establishment worried that some "unfortunate" fact may be revealed? For instance, could the bodies of the children buried in the marble vessel in Westminster not actually be Richard's nephews at all, in which case, we have all been the victim of an enormous manipulation lasting almost 600 years - and someone knows it.

22.3 Accessibility: Low to High

22.4 Conditions/Opportunity/Effectiveness: There are two possible objectives in manipulative reputation control:

- To damage the reputation of a subject.

- To enhance the reputation of a subject.

There are many ways to alter a subject's reputation, creating and/or propagating a good or bad personal history of the subject, spreading rumours etc. We will deal with the methodology in more detail later in the chapter.

However, it's important to understand that interference with a subject's reputation is very effective because it is very hard to reverse in the public perception. So even after a character assassination attempt on a subject is totally disproved, it often continues to linger and taint the victim's reputation. The same is also true of reputation-enhancing manipulations. Once a subject is considered to have a good reputation, it is often hard to dislodge the idea in the mind of the public

22.4.1 Conditions: Both objectives of reputation enhancement or reputation damage rely on altering the information available to the public about the subject. Therefore it is essential to have access to the information sources used by the public. In the past these sources were confined to word of mouth, books and the conventional media.

Today, we have the internet and generalised direct access to potentially vast parts of the global general public, without having to use 3rd party media. The spread of social networking has also automated the concept of "word of mouth" communication so that reputation control is now well and truly in the technological forefront of manipulative techniques. We can idolise someone or rip them to pieces in the space of a few minutes in this virtual world.

22.4.2 Opportunity: The opportunities for managing (or damaging) reputations have never been greater. The corollary of this is also true: the quality of information used in determining a subject's reputation has never been less reliable.

The internet is constantly used by interested parties to massage consumer impressions and it is a perfect conduit for manipulating a reputation. The democratic nature of the internet also ensures that it can be used by both manipulator and victim. But it also means that we can defend our reputations and launch counterattacks quite easily using just the same medium. So the internet and strength of media fire-power may be key factors in reputation control and not just a source of fundamental facts about someone.

22.4.3 Traditional methods of reputation control: Originally reputation was based on word of mouth descriptions of an individual's behaviour. In Western societies it centred on whether the individual behaved in an honourable way when judged against some Christian ethical standards.

Later, reputations were made and broken by those who controlled the printing presses. Thus, wealthy individuals found it important to have control of parts of the press or at least have very reliable contacts in the media. This control of the media allowed these elites to control their own and others' reputations in the eyes of the general public.

And so this allowed for a person or company to be perceived as "decent", "highly trustworthy", "efficient", "well-financed", "dynamic", "generous" or whatever adjective was appropriate to the reputation controller.

Pandora's Box of manipulative opportunities had been opened.

A very cosy "closed shop" of wealth, influence, corporate power and media control began to prevail in modern industrial society, basically replacing the system of functional dissemination of information used in the middle ages.

Since the conquest of the media by establishment capitalism, only rarely has the link between establishment power and the media been interrupted by the occasional scurrilous press attacking a reputation here or there.

In some countries, such as the United Kingdom, draconian libel laws favouring the libel victim rather than public interest or the rights of the journalist to investigate, have hampered investigative journalism and our knowledge of the backgrounds of our leaders.

22.4.4 Revolutionary changes in reputation control: However, all that changed after the arrival of the internet. Almost overnight, we moved from a moribund system of establishment and capital controlled media to a completely open, anarchic, cheap and totally democratic system of open communication. Anyone can open a newspaper now, or a radio or TV station. Anyone can make and publish a movie, a book, a documentary or a bunch of photographs. We can publish our suspicions at will on an internet that is essentially without any form of censorship.

And this "revolution" continues to open access to ordinary people to this new media. News now travels straight from the smart phone on the street to the internet and via social networks to potentially millions of viewers.

A policeman beating up a demonstrator in Delhi is now transmitted instantaneously across the globe. There is no time and no opportunity for any kind of censorship. News is "out there" without even being replayed, without editing. It is truly "live news".

The torturers of the streets, police or criminal, are not only revealed but are exposed in real time and witnessed by millions, their acts frozen forever in YouTube or endless other repositories of daily life. We live in a world where the oppressed are making documentaries about their oppressors and broadcasting them real-time and globally.

These huge changes in accessibility to a global media do provide opportunities for manipulative reputation control. But they also provide a means of redress as well, never before possible unless you happened to belong to one of the powerful elites or own a newspaper.

Internet technology and reputation control: Here are some examples of how a reputation can now be controlled using these new technologies:

- **Corporate slander:** A corporation may be given a poor review in order to damage its share price (or vice versa). The use of tip sheets is totally uncontrolled on the internet. Similar systems of reputation control can be used to discredit a book, a hotel, a movie, a restaurant or an album using bad internet reviews.

- **Exclude employment:** Employers can search for potential employees on the internet, looking for undesirable material and build up profiles of candidates which may disqualify them from possible positions. Employees thus excluded from a job should count themselves lucky not to have been employed by such a paranoid organisation.

- **Mud-slinging:** Manipulators may use social media or blogs to malign or compliment an individual, a company, an institution, or a government.

- **Rumour mongering:** Carefully coordinated attacks can cause the rapid spread of rumours or "facts" across vast numbers of internet users.

- **Unfortunate connections:** The manipulation of SEO (search engine optimisation) techniques can force associations to occur between certain data, like a victim and a criminal activity.

- **Innuendos:** The bending of truth and the use of innuendo in static articles on websites and blogs can alter public perceptions of a subject over long periods of time.

- **Anonymous Libel:** A manipulator can easily sidestep legal considerations by using anonymous methods of delivery of potentially libellous material to a blog, social networking site or website using techniques like "Tor", which provides anonymous access to the internet.

- **Counterattack is possible:** Individuals can also now openly defend themselves on the internet against any libellous attacks

22.5 Methodology/Refinements/Sub-species: There are five basic methods of reputation control:

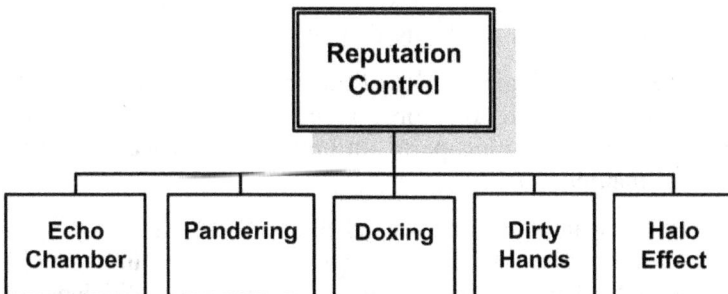

193

22.5.1 Echo Chamber: This is the repetition of a rumour, scandal, news story or issue by several ostensibly different sources in order to present a false impression of "reasonable" consensus, and to alter the reputation of a subject, either positively or negatively.

Several media outlets can use the same language, images, and catchphrases in an attempt to reinforce the agreed-upon narrative. The key is to create a false impression of consensus among apparently credible sources from differing media outlets.

It is a method of the "Old Media" and was used to gain "control of the narrative", thus achieving a monopoly of information. The method has now been extended to the internet, but it is also being threatened by the internet because of the loss of monopoly of information. There is no limit to the type of information which can be reiterated using this method.

22.5.2 Pandering: This method of reputation control uses misrepresentation of a person or group to cater to the tastes of a prospective constituency or benefactor.

The manipulator first determines the biases of the victim and then panders to these biases.

Politicians do this constantly; they turn up in jeans and jumper and discuss football at a social function in a working man's club, they arrive in a dinner jacket and discuss business issues when invited to the Rotary club annual ball.

They pander to their audiences by altering the perception that their victims have of them. The working men will say that the politician is very much a man of the people and the local businessmen will count him as one of their own.

22.5.3 Doxing: This is a deliberate attack on someone's political reputation. A common technique, it involves building a case against an opponent by gathering damaging evidence about their ideology or lifestyle. The term is often used among hackers to describe the process of obtaining incriminating "docs" that can be used against the target - hence the name.

Another method of digging up "dirt" on one's opponents is to drag the targeted party into court and force them to divulge information to the public or to the prosecuting party, information which can be politically useful to the manipulator.

The corruption scandals which rocked the political system of Spain after 2008 was largely based on a pile of hand-written accounting documents from the Popular Party, showing illegal donations to politicians in return for contracts to property developers etc. Not only did these "docs" damn many of the party's grandees as corrupt, they also forced the issue into the courts where more evidence of even greater corruption emerged.

22.5.4 Dirty hands argument: In a similar way, a political enemy can seek to damage an opponent's reputation by using a fallacious argument that implies that the target person, social group, or party cannot do or mean well because of some past offence, association or mistake.

Sometimes this is used to smear opponents using a tactic of "guilt by association", where the reputation of a political adversary is damaged by implying that they are associates of some criminal or morally undesirable person, group or institution.

Dirty hands arguments are often unbalanced, historically inaccurate, or paint a picture based on speculation. A good example is how a perfectly liberal politician can be dishonestly maligned as being an extreme nationalist or racist, simply because some extreme right-wing political group has expressed approval for some of the victim's manifesto.

22.5.5 The Halo effect: This is the tendency for a person's positive or negative traits to "spill over" from one area of their personality to another in others' perceptions of them. The phenomenon was first studied in 1977, by social psychologists Richard Nisbett and Timothy Wilson

This is highly relevant in the arena of reputation management, where perception is everything. The effect is equally applicable to groups, companies, institutions, governments and even product brands.

The halo effect refers to a bias whereby the perception of a positive trait in a subject positively influences further judgments about traits of that subject.

One of the more common halo effects is the judgment that a good looking person is also intelligent and amiable. In reality, there is actually no evidence of a correlation between ugliness and a tendency to violent psychopathic behaviour. Murderers and saints come in all shapes and sizes but very often the ugly ones get the longest jail sentences.[22.1]

22.5.5.1 The Reverse Halo effect: There is also a reverse halo effect whereby perceptions of a negative or undesirable trait in the subject negatively influences judgments about the traits of that individual.

For instance, if a person "looks evil" or "looks guilty" you may judge everything they say or do with suspicion. Eventually you may feel confident that you have confirmed your first impression with solid evidence when, in fact, your evidence is completely tainted - conditioned by your first irrational impression.

22.5.5.2 Uses and Origins of the Halo effect: The hope that the halo effect will influence a judge or jury is one reason some criminal lawyers like their clients to be clean-shaven and dressed neatly when they appear at trial. "How could such a nice looking boy have committed a murder?"

The original phrase "Halo Effect" was coined by psychologist Edward Thorndike in 1920 to describe the way commanding officers rated their soldiers. He found that officers usually judged their men as being either good or bad "right across the board. There was little mixing of traits; few people were said to be good in one respect but bad in another."

The old saying that first impressions make lasting impressions is at the heart of the halo effect. If a soldier made a good (or bad) first impression on his commanding officer, that impression would influence the officer's judgment of future behaviour.

It is very unlikely that in a particular group of soldiers every one of them would be totally good or totally bad at everything, but the evaluations seemed to indicate that this was the case. More likely however, the earlier perceptions either positively or negatively influenced those later perceptions and judgments.

22.5.5.3 Psychological origin: The halo effect seems to be closely connected with confirmation bias: this implies that once we've made a judgment about positive or negative traits, that judgment influences all future perceptions so that they confirm our initial judgment.

Some researchers have found evidence that student's evaluations of their lecturers are formed and remain stable after only a few minutes or hours into a lecture. If a student evaluated a teacher highly early on in the course, he or she was likely to rank the teacher highly at the end of the course.

Unfortunately for those teachers who made bad first impressions on the students, their performance over the course of the term would be largely irrelevant as to how they would be perceived by their students.

Some might think this shows how wonderful intuition is: students can perceive how good a teacher is within minutes or hours of meeting. On the other hand, the halo effect may be at work here. Also, the fact that the evaluations are similar at the beginning and end of term might indicate that there is something seriously wrong with the typical evaluation. It may be measuring little more than "likeability" and the halo effect.

22.5.5.4 Implication in the corporate arena: Much of our thinking about company performance is shaped by the halo effect. When a company is growing and profitable, we tend to infer that it has a brilliant strategy, a good product, a visionary CEO, motivated people, and a vibrant culture.

When performance drops a little, we are quick to say the strategy was misguided, the CEO became arrogant, and the people were complacent, product quality poor and the culture stodgy.

22.5.5.5 Phenomena caused by the Halo Effect: At first glance the halo effect seems to be fairly harmless, but it does have a contaminating effect on perception and it is therefore used in a manipulative sense. Here are some of the best known effects (there are more):

- **Good, Bad and Ugly:** Personnel are often judged on criteria other than their real performance. This can give rise to pervasive and unpleasant effects. Pretty people tend to be rewarded for performance even when it is the less attractive people who are really doing the work. This creates prejudices and injustices and is often used to injure less attractive victims.

- **Never admit a mistake:** The halo effect tends to benefit the reputation of the successful. This is also known as the principle that "Nothing succeeds like success".

  Thus the halo effect from a continued success (or from a series of failures) affects the reputation of an individual or institution. But this can also cause some problems when it comes to dealing with or admitting problems or failures. A subject who is reliant on the halo effect cannot admit to being wrong or having made a mistake. This restriction can apply to an individual or even an entire society. We often see reluctance by certain social groups in some countries to admit that they messed up, because that would undermine their halo effect. This is especially true in countries which are preoccupied by performance: Germany and the United States spring to mind.

- **Never mind the quality, feel the glow:** Ronald Reagan must have been one of the most stupid and incompetent presidents in global history. He was educationally deficient, poorly informed and fantastically parochial. And yet he was extremely popular and credible, both nationally and internationally. This is generally attributed to the fact that at a personal level, Reagan was an extremely affable, amiable person, quite charming, generous, self-effacing and amusing. His personal characteristics outshone his huge professional weaknesses as a president and got him out of numerous political scrapes, including the Iran-Contra affair, hence his nickname "Teflon-Ron".

  When people express their desire for another leader like Ronald Reagan to lead America what they are really longing for is a Hollywood actor who could put people at ease with his perceived authority, honesty, confident manner, wry smile, his great sense of humour and his superb speech writers.

197

- **The Halo effect in advertising**: the halo effect is at work when we buy a product because it was made by a company that makes something else that we believe is a good product. We seem to assume that if a company made a good product in the past it means that the company always makes good products because it is obviously a "good company". Many of us know from experience that this isn't true.

  Advertisers take advantage of the halo effect when they hire famous people or beautiful people to sell their products. The advertisers are banking on the consumer's tendency to judge the product positively because they judge the handsome actor or beautiful actress favourably.

- **Health halos (I):** A health halo effect also applies to certain foods considered by many to be especially healthy, such as organic products. Specifically, some people mistakenly assume that these foods are more nutritious just because they carry an "organic" label - an area of longstanding active debate among food and nutrition scientists.

  One study was conducted where the subjects were all given organic food, although some was labelled non-organic. The participants found the "organic" food tastier, less fatty, and believed they were lower in calories, higher in fibre, and more nutritious than the "non-organic" food.

  The truth of the matter is that most organic food probably tastes fairly similar to non-organic food. The real difference between these types of food is the damage they do to the environment in their production, or the potentially dangerous chemical residues they may contain - NOT their flavour or nutritional value.[22.2]

- **Health halos (II):** Research has shown that people tend to consume more calories at fast-food restaurants claiming to serve "healthier" foods, than at a typical burger joint.

  The reasoning is that when people perceive a food to be more nutritious, they tend to let their guard down when it comes to being careful about counting calories - ultimately leading them to overeat or feel entitled to over-indulge.

22.6 Avoidance and Counteraction: The first issue of course is recognising that someone is manipulating a reputation. When this has been confirmed, the next question is, does this matter to you? If it does impact on you, the next step is to find out how the effects of this can be avoided and counteracted.

22.6.1 Detection: Deliberate interference with the information which builds up a reputation is difficult to detect. However, by carrying out a lot of research it is usually possible to build up an extensive picture of all the contributory information which constitutes a reputation. If this body of information is consistent and coming from reliable sources, then one can assume that a reputation is reliable. If, however, the research reveals large inconsistencies or a bias towards overtly negative or positive information coming from unreliable sources, then it would be fair to assume that someone (the manipulator) is interfering with the source information which constitutes the reputation. It's not a precise science but strong correlations will tend to show up when someone is trying to deliberately damage or elevate a reputation.

22.6.2 Avoidance: Controlling external reputation control: For most of us these days, our personal reputations are embedded in the public domain via the internet. Most of what is there is inaccurate, incomplete, biased and misleading but there it sits, representing us to the outside world: to employers, friends, and professional colleagues, family, everyone in fact, until we contradict it or knock it off the top place of a search engine listing.

A whole industry has grown up now in helping people clean up their internet image. Even if we have no real internet presence, we still show up as people with the same name or via credit check agencies using our names to fish for customers.

The only sure way to guard against internet misrepresentation is not to use the internet at all. But, for most of us this is tantamount to sealing up the letter-box at home to avoid receiving unpleasant mail. It is not the solution.

The alternative solution is to stay on top of your interactions with the internet:

- Don't publish more about yourself than is absolutely necessary

- Make your identity ambiguous by altering personal information so that a viewer can never be sure of the validity of the data.

- Don't use social networks - or at least not as someone identifiable. Use abstract or corporate identities if absolutely essential.

- In the event of an attack on your own reputation via the internet, then use the internet to respond and make sure the responses are fully search engine optimised so that any future search engine queries arrive at your rebuttal page before they arrive at the original accusations.

- Use anonymous domain registrations so as to avoid detection as a domain owner.

22.6.3 Counteraction: If a manipulator is acting to damage your reputation in some way, firstly you must make sure that your rebuttal is readily available via conventional and internet media. Then the simple solution is to attack the manipulator in exactly the same way, if possible attacking their good name and reputation.

The cost of the manipulator's actions against you, the victim, must begin to exceed the benefits that they are getting or expect to gain from damaging you.

---o0o---

23. Media-Techno manipulation

23.1 Definition: Media manipulation is a series of related manipulative techniques in which partisan media operators create an image or argument that favours their particular interests rather than their victims.

The tactics may include the use of logical fallacies and propaganda techniques, and involve the suppression of information or points of view by crowding them out, by inducing other people or groups of people to stop listening to certain arguments, or by simply diverting attention elsewhere.

Techno manipulation is similar but it uses technological knowledge gaps to include or exclude information from the public domain. It may also be used to grant or refuse access to technological capacities to the general public or particular victim groups.

23.2 Persistence: Short to Medium. Media manipulation moves very quickly and can be rapidly superseded by new material. Techno manipulative techniques may have longer lasting effects because they are renewed less frequently than media presentations.

23.3 Accessibility: Low. For these techniques, you will need access to and influence on the conventional media, a lot of expertise and a lot of time.

23.4 Conditions/Opportunity/Effectiveness: Media manipulative techniques are generally not available to ordinary people - they require access to mass media outlets generally, although the advent of the internet has opened up the possibilities of access to a wider group of manipulators. There is an enormous amount of manipulative material on the internet; it is hard to see how these media-centric techniques can really work in a fairly cynical environment like the internet. These techniques need large, simultaneous audiences like a TV show or newspaper edition to be effective, rather than the drip feeding of the internet. However the careful use of social media has been shown to work with these conventional media control methods.

23.4.1 An Example: Currently North Korea is under siege from South Korean soap operas. These are hugely popular in North Korea and they are also totally banned by the government under pain of imprisonment or worse, because they are considered to undermine the frugal policies of the North Korean regime.

Despite this however, smugglers from South Korea via China and Russia are managing to get digital copies of pirated soap operas into North Korea. Millions of foreign TV and movie recordings are thought to be circulating around North Korea, though they are most easily available in cities near the Chinese border. With a recent North Korean crackdown, analysts say smugglers have shifted to new techniques, at least for videos: carrying recordings on tiny thumb drives, and then transferring the programs to DVDs for distribution inside North Korea.

Although there is some evidence that the South Korean government have encouraged this trade, the hunger for information about and entertainment from South Korea is so great, that once the information starts to flow, it just cannot be turned off like a tap. At most it can be slowed down and this is all that North Korea's Kim Jong-un can now do, despite the draconian punishments.

In many ways, Kim is now facing an authoritarian contradiction, not dissimilar to that faced by Western governments when attacked in the social media or Middle Eastern regimes torn down via Twitter and Facebook. In the case of North Korea it is revolution by soap operas on thumb drives.

23.5 Methodology/Refinements/Sub-species: There are 9 well known methods of media and technological manipulation:

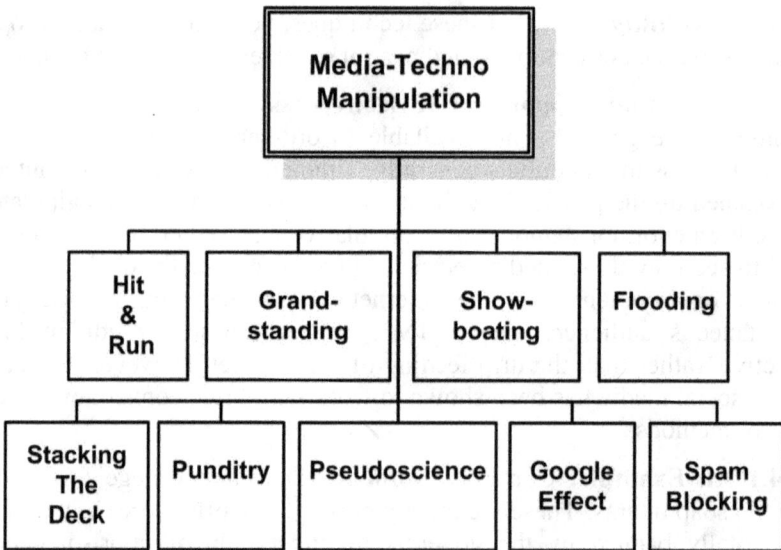

23.5.1 Hit-and-run: This is the delivery of sensationalistic news stories without context or follow-up. It can also be applied to politicians who switch agendas so rapidly that the average citizen does not know what to expect next or cannot keep up.

202

It can be used to create a sensation of omnipresent, continuous "crisis," and is often used by fascistic and pseudo-fascistic regimes to keep us on the edge of our seats.

23.5.2 Grandstanding: This occurs when an individual, usually a politician or party abuses public office to make an ostentatious display to an audience, usually via the conventional mass-media.

Typically, this is done for public relations purposes, such as to shore up the manipulator's image, communicate values to the political "base" or to create a veneer under which to covertly work at cross-purposes to the official public message of the political party.

23.5.3 Showboating: This technique was named after the touring riverboat theatres. It describes the behaviour of an individual, often a politician, or political party that engages in self-serving attention-seeking. This may describe a politician who shows off a skill or talent, when such exhibitionism is unwarranted, repetitive, and/or staged. The manipulative politician uses the ostentatious show to attract attention and gain acclaim or acceptance from a target audience.

23.5.4 Flooding: This technique involves the creation of a virtual flood of reinforcing or complementary messages, signs and symbolic media aimed at an audience, with the objective of indoctrinating a victim into believing some false representation of reality.

Nowadays, western citizens are virtually swimming in an ocean of cultural consumerism, largely due to the "flooding" of our mainstream media by Hollywood, the broadcasting of 24 hour news, and, of course, the omnipresence of commercials on most mainstream media. We are constantly confronted with symbols and messages that overtly or covertly reinforce capitalist and consumerist messages.

For a case in point, look at the overwrought emphasis on "achievement", "ambition", and "image" as the primary subliminal lessons being promoted by the media to our children from their earliest years. As opposed to our children learning and understanding the meaning of basic humanist morality or how the world really works, our educational system, with the support of the conventional media, pushes them to achieve material success. Instead of using the language of true education, like "knowledge", "curiosity", "understanding", etc., our media constantly use the language of career and material success, like "getting a good job", "ambition", "career development", "paying your way" etc. This indoctrinates our young people to believe that the only raison d'être for education is as a means to achieve material security. This degrades education as a liberating pursuit but nonetheless it is the popular view of education and we are flooded by such views in the media.

23.5.5 Stacking the deck: This is the tactic of arranging more supporters (or opponents) of a particular person, party, or position on one side of a debate than are on the other side of a debate. This may be done simply by biasing the numbers of commentators supporting one side of an argument.

The technique can also be used to bias an argument by using repetition, overstatement or even misrepresentation. The manipulator sets up the situation in advance of media presence and then allows the game to unfold in front of the rolling cameras.

23.5.6 Punditry: This is a type of "Confirmation bias", which occurs when a victim is given information which they accept because it confirms what they already believe. Much of the media operates by taking advantage of this phenomenon. The media provide fuel for certain beliefs, because they pre-filter the world to match existing world-views.

If their particular filter is like your filter, then you like and agree with that particular media outlet. If it isn't, then you will dislike and disagree with that media outlet. This form of manipulation requires a combination of self-delusion by the victim in combination with an orchestrated strategy by a particular media organ.

As a method of political manipulation it is so pervasive and obvious that one wonders why it still works, but ask anyone who reads a newspaper if they have a particular preference and also suggest alternative titles. Generally the reader will have strong, fixed ideas on the subject of their newspaper or TV channel preferences and will be loath to change their reading or viewing habits.

23.5.7 Pseudoscience: A pseudoscience is a set of ideas put forth as scientific when they are not scientific.

The media has never been more replete with pseudoscience than it is these days. Real science itself has retreated into a very small group of professional periodicals which are normally unheard of and unread by the general public.

It's a dangerous phenomenon because it allows a perpetrator to wrap up any number of hidden messages in a scientific sounding package which seems eminently credible but may be entirely fallacious. There is a good chance that the listener has no idea either way.

23.5.7.1 Pseudoscience - Uninformed victims: The proliferation of pseudoscience has happened because the teaching of real science in schools has been progressively "dumbed down". Also, fewer and fewer children pursue science subjects at school because these subjects are perceived to be "too hard". The effect of these trends is that we have a society which has a very poor grasp on any of the core science subjects.

This knowledge vacuum provides an opportunity for the media to peddle their pseudoscience stories to us. We know so little about real science that we are incapable of challenging a lot of junk science we are being fed.

23.5.7.2 Pseudoscience - Contemporary Examples:

Anti-abortion: The anti abortion lobby are masters at selling all kinds of absurd contentions wrapped up in a sufficiently impressive sounding language. The unsuspecting victim is unable to check the facts - because they have no scientific training - so they simply accept the conclusions as truths:

For instance, the anti-abortion lobby has long claimed that having an abortion may increase the risks of breast cancer. They surround the assertion will much pseudoscience but no studies to back it up. In fact, in 1997, the New England Journal of Medicine published the largest-scale study ever on this subject--with 1.5 million participants--which concluded that there is no independent link between abortion and breast cancer. Clearly if abortion does increase the risk of breast cancer, it does so by an undetectable margin.

GM Pseudoscience: The GM industry in its war with the anti-GM lobby reverts to pseudoscience constantly to demonstrate the value and safety of GM crops. For example, until recently the GM industry, via its lobbyists, was claiming that GM crops were the sole method by which we could feed the world's population in 2020. This "fact" was disputed and then roundly disproved by some large international organisations like the United Nations' FAO and many academic specialists in agro-economics.[23.1]

In a similar way, the GM industry carries out short feeding trials on laboratory animals to prove the safety of a new GM crop. When the animals survive the trials, the product is declared safe. This is despite the very limited range of tests and very short duration of the trials. When longer feeding trials of GM corn were conducted by the researcher Seralini, during which the laboratory rats developed tumours, the GM industry cried "foul" because Seralini's trials were apparently "too long" (Monsanto trials being only 90 days). Such a statement of statistical nonsense is another example of pseudoscience. How can a safety trial conducted on live laboratory animals be considered "too long" when surely more data is better than less data. In fact, the reaction from the GM industry was more of an emotional than a scientific reaction but it had to be wrapped up in appropriate pseudoscientific language. Seralini later roundly rebuffed the GM industry sound bites in a detailed 300 page scientific defence of his trials and the original paper.[23.2]

23.5.7.3 Pseudoscience tactics: Here is a list of the different tactics used in pseudoscience:

- **Use of Referenced Text:** Some pseudoscientific claims are based on an authoritative text rather than observation or empirical investigation.

   Creationists, for example, make observations only to confirm their dogmas, not to discover the truth of the natural world. Their dogmas are static and their observation can lead to no new scientific discoveries of the natural world. The main purpose of research in creationism and "intelligent design" is to defend a set of religious beliefs not to promote scientific knowledge.

- **Vague and unspecific:** Some pseudoscientific ideas can't be tested because they are so vague and conceptually malleable that anything relevant can be shoehorned to fit their claims, like the ideas behind many New Age psychotherapies, and reflexology etc. Protagonists make statements like "these stones will help increase your 'life' energy and dispel negative energies". Such statements are so vague and fluffy that they cannot even be evaluated.

- **Tautology:** Pseudoscience manipulators, like the "creationists", often mistake the fact that discoveries in real science continue to confirm evolutionary hypotheses as evidence that evolutionists just won't give up their theory, no matter what.

   This outrageous idea puts the tautology of the manipulators into clear perspective. The arguments of the creationists work something like this "What we believe (Genesis) is true, anything which contradicts this is a deceit, whether it is scientifically demonstrable or not, whether it is repeatable or not. Our beliefs are based on something higher than science and cannot therefore be challenged by science". This type of circular argument is completely contrary to all norms of logical, scientific method, which requires that a hypothesis be demonstrated by experiment, correlation and repeatability not just by repeating a personal or religious belief again and again.

   The unconscious tautology makes creationism more of a psychological disorder than an alternative scientific explanation for our existence or evolution.

- **Anecdotes and intuition as "science":** Some pseudoscientific ideas are supported mainly by selective use of anecdotes, intuition, and cases of confirming instances, e.g. in aromatherapy, graphology, personology, and physiognomy etc. These anecdotal origins give pseudoscience manipulation a stronghold in the popular mind because, even if the victim doesn't understand "the scientific stuff", they can at least confirm the anecdotal or intuitive content.

   For instance, aromatherapy adherents will tell you that lavender will help you sleep, basil can clear headaches and lemon can be an antidepressant and such ideas have now become widely accepted. However, researchers at Ohio State University have recently found that lemon and lavender oil had no physiological effect on study subjects, despite lemon's reputation as a stimulant and lavender's as a sleep aid.

But, despite the absence of any real scientific studies to prove the claims of aromatherapy, the unsubstantiated pseudoscience continues to be believed by large parts of the general public and the cash keeps flowing.

- **Metaphysical-Empirical conflation:** Some pseudoscientific ideas deliberately confuse metaphysical claims with empirical claims, e.g., acupuncture, alchemy, etc.

By definition, a supernatural claim is non-empirical unless it also delivers evidence, which it doesn't. Science maintains that all hypotheses about the causes it studies refer to natural causes that have empirical manifestations and may be supported or refuted by empirical facts.

For example, coming back to creationism again, it is essentially a metaphysical notion about the origins of the universe and of life. This is because it asserts the cause of life on Earth to be supernatural. Creationism asserts that no empirical fact could ever refute it because it is known a priori to be absolutely true.

- **The theory of pseudo-proofs:** Many pseudo-scientists relish being able to point out the consistency of their ideas with known facts or with predicted consequences. However, they do not recognize that consistency does not prove anything. It is a necessary but not a sufficient condition that a good scientific theory be consistent with the facts. A theory which is contradicted by the facts is obviously not a very good scientific theory, but a theory or hypothesis that is consistent with the facts is not necessarily a good theory.

For example, the truth of the hypothesis that "plague is due to evil spirits" is not established by the correctness of the deduction that "you can avoid the plague by keeping out of the reach of the evil spirits". Real science demands a bit more external proof.

- **Everyone makes mistakes:** Pseudoscience manipulators often point to errors made in real science, to defend their own notions arguing that their scientist gainsayers are also capable of error and fallibility and that they "don't know it all".

This is a fairly cheap attempt to undermine the (normally) rational behaviour of the scientific community because occasionally they also make mistakes. But comparing occasional errors in scientific method with some of the more bizarre claims of the pseudoscience manipulators is just another demonstration of the underlying denial of reality from which many pseudoscience victims and manipulators suffer.

After all what rational person would either suggest or actually accept that the Grand Canyon was formed by the "Great Flood" which caused Noah's ark to finally land in Turkey?! It is self-evident isn't it?

23.5.8 Google effect: This is the tendency to forget information that can be easily found online. The phenomenon was described and named by Sparrow, Liu and Wegner [23.3] in July 2011. Having easy access to the Internet, the study showed, makes people less likely to remember certain details they believe will be accessible online.

People can still remember, because they will remember what they cannot find online. They also remember how to find what they need on the Internet. Sparrow said this made the Internet a type of transactive memory. One result of this phenomenon is dependence on the Internet; if an online connection is lost, the researchers said, it may give rise to a similar feeling as when losing a friend.

This phenomenon has been used in a manipulative way, where a victim is challenged to defend a position without having access to the internet. Traditionally, a position or opinion would be defended by recourse to first principles in combination with personal memories, anecdotes and examples. In the case of a Google dependent victim, the inability to research an issue via the internet leaves the victim feeling vulnerable and defenceless, and unable to defend a position.

Many professions now have their Google pseudo-specialists - like "Google farmers", "Google doctors", "Google lawyers" etc. These "specialists" know little or nothing about a subject but are very adept in using a search engine like Google and can create a credible argument by plagiarising what they find on the internet.

23.5.9 Spam and Troll blocking: Spam is junk or unwanted email. Trolling is the act of pursuing and attacking someone real-time in a blog, or in the social media. Neither practice is welcome. Many mechanisms now exist to stop both Spam mail and to report Trolls. Mail can be filtered at the mail server to block certain subjects like "Rolex watch" or "Viagra" etc. Trolling behaviour can be reported to a moderator and the person blocked.

However, these "safety" techniques can also be used to manipulate a victim or group of victims by suppressing their ability to communicate. For instance, a manipulator can report a victim's email addresses for inclusion on a so-called grey or blacklist of Spam originators. The effect of this is that the victim's emails are effectively frozen and will be refused by any mail servers using these grey or black lists (there are many).

In a similar way, a real "troll" can effectively silence a blog contributor who seems to be attracting too much support from other contributors. To do this the manipulator simply sends multiple reports to the blog or social network moderator, until the victim is suspended or has membership cancelled. Some newspapers basically forbid any negative commentary on the behaviour of Israel. Any attempt to make even mild criticisms of Israel's conduct of its various wars will quickly lead to a suspension and eventually complete expulsion in certain right-wing publications.

The latter is a popular ploy. Many high-profile blogs are patrolled by paid representatives of various politically biased lobby groups and think tanks. So, for example, a newspaper blog about America's invasion of Afghanistan will certainly be attended by some hard-line rightwing US supporters acting on behalf of one or more of the lobby groups. If a normal contributor appears to be getting too popular and is expressing views which are not in line with those of the lobbyist trolls, these contributors will almost certainly be attacked by the trolls in an attempt to suppress their writings.

This is a particularly popular trick for trolls with right-wing views. Incapable of defending an argument in a normal way, they tend to use this method to remove their opposition. It is the cyber equivalent of the assassination of our political opponents. In effect the technique comes down to emasculation of opinions which don't match the manipulator. Newspaper blogs often participate in the game and tend to "block first and ask questions later", simply for legal reasons.

23.6 Avoidance and Counteraction: Here are some strategies for detection, avoidance and counteraction:

23.6.1 Hit-and-run: Any news item that isn't followed up or cannot be verified from an independent source is probably rubbish and should be ignored; or better still, publicly challenged. Responsible media doesn't work like this and we can be pretty sure that such a "drive by" report is manipulative.

23.6.2 Grandstanding: The use of ostentatious behaviour or language is not the action of someone who feels confident that they can persuade you by means of a calm, rational presentation of facts and an accompanying argument. Grandstanding, and the politicians that do it, cannot be taken seriously and should be ignored.

23.6.3 Showboating: As for grandstanding, the user of this manipulative technique relies on a low-IQ audience. They need to be ignored.

23.6.4 Flooding: It's difficult to manage this phenomenon, especially when a victim is being totally overwhelmed with media of a particular bias. The only solution is to find alternative sources of information and simply refuse to be the manipulated audience. It is always possible somehow, even if that means increased isolation.

23.6.5 Stacking the deck: This kind of media manipulation needs to be exposed and probably social media or news blogs are the best way to do this. Describe how the "deck was stacked" and keep publishing it on the internet. You won't stop it happening, but at least the manipulator knows they are being watched.

23.6.6 Punditry: Again, there is little to be done about this, apart from ignoring such low quality media tricks. Although this won't change much, you can also write on the newspaper's blogs or maybe on other newspaper blogs to discredit their manipulative behaviour.

23.6.7 Pseudoscience: There is really only one sure way to recognise and avoid manipulation using pseudoscience, and that is to get a decent understanding of real scientific methodologies.

The problem with pseudoscientific assertions is that even researching them may give rise to a lot of material which seems to support the assertions, especially on the internet. Therefore, you really just need to understand how well-designed scientific tests are developed and executed, how basic statistical analysis works etc. You can start by looking at "Scientific Method" in Wikipedia.

23.6.8 Google effect: Don't rely too much on the internet. Firstly it is, after all, a completely unverified source of data. Secondly, it's important to carry some information around with you and have a real, rather than superficial, understanding because one day you may well be stuck without an internet connection and have to think for yourself.

23.6.9 Spam and Troll blocking: If you have been manipulatively grey or blacklisted you can have this undone by applying to the list owners for delisting or by requesting white listing. It takes a couple of days, but it's not a big issue to organise it. To find out how to do this, visit the websites of the companies which hold and distribute these lists. These companies are aware that people maliciously block email addresses in this way and are happy to oblige you to have this undone.

Troll blocking can be a little more complicated. When a user is blocked from a newspaper blog by a manipulative troll, the blog will generally not allow the user to register again, even with a different email address.

Usually the blog will block all users coming from your IP address (even if it is dynamic). To overcome this problem you can use "Tor" or a similar technology to connect to the blog again and register a lot of users under various email addresses. You can then start using the blog again. Generally, the best strategy is to find the trolls and report them as soon as you can and have them blocked. They will also fall back to other user identities, so the process may take time. Eventually, the best way to deal with this is to have a group of users working together to "hunt trolls down". Eventually they will run out of user ids and have to get some new ones. In the meantime, you should contact the moderator and discuss the problem with them.

---o0o---

24. Cultural manipulation

24.1 Definition: This is a form of manipulation which takes advantage of cultural differences to either attract or repel victims and to deliver manipulative payloads to a victim based on cultural bias. The victims can also be the subject of cultural vilification by the manipulator.

24.2 Persistence: High - racial and cultural perceptions, once established are hard to shift.

24.3 Accessibility: High - anyone can deliver racially or culturally manipulative messages.

24.4 Conditions/Opportunity/Effectiveness: There are 3 parties in this form of manipulation with different roles:

- **The manipulator** who wishes to create and capitalise on cultural, racial, or ethnic differences between two target groups of people, the majority and the minority group.

- **The cultural majority** group. This is the group that represents the cultural majority. They are manipulated in order to adopt attitudes which are irrational towards the cultural minority group.

- **The cultural minority** group. This is the second victim group. They will be vilified or demeaned by the manipulator in the eyes of the majority group.

The manipulator's objective is to maintain both groups in a threatened state by creating fear in the majority group about the intentions of the minority group. Simultaneously, the minority group is kept in a state of fear by the aggressive behaviour of the majority.

The social and political reasons for the manipulator's actions can vary from a desire to control the capital of the minority group, a real fear of political ascendancy by the minority group or a host of other motivations, including simple irrational racism and xenophobia. However, the usual motivation is the division of a population along cultural grounds in order to eliminate any form of solidarity and any risk of rebellion by a united group of citizens.

24.5 Methodology/Refinements/Sub-species: There are two basic methods by which cultural manipulation is manifested:

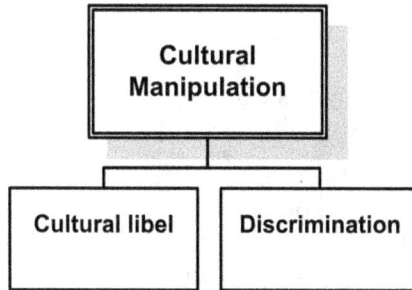

24.5.1 Cultural libel: This is the invention and dissemination of derogatory myths about another race or culture. It is used to build up a negative image of the target minority group in the minds of the majority group. The veracity or content of the myths are entirely irrelevant - the most outrageous claims can be made. The only criterion for these libels are that they are very negative and extreme - the more unpleasant the better, from the perpetrators' point of view.

Examples of Cultural Manipulation:

Racism in the USA: The most virulently racist nation in the Western world is the United States of America [24.1]. It has a very recent history of overt racism (including slavery) which has persisted right up to the present day. The nation was founded on a savage act of genocide against the original native inhabitants. Its early history is one of appalling slavery based on racial origin - there were only black slaves. The USA is still actively culturally imperialistic and has a history of trying to "civilise" the rest of the world. It is currently engaged in several foreign wars, which have been justified on the basis of cultural biases against Muslims. In the past, the USA has also attacked several other sovereign states such as the Koreans ("gooks"), Vietnamese ("zits" or "charlies"), etc. The derogatory terms in brackets serve to illustrate the underlying racist attitudes of the US military personnel that used these terms.

Traditionally, culturally elitist and supremacist groups in the USA have come from the Anglo-Saxon political dynasties, with the majority populations of the US being white citizens of European extraction.

There are many minority groups in the USA and each has its own set of cultural libel to deal with. The "Latinos" are from South of the Rio Grande. The "native Americans" are the original occupants of North America, once referred to as "Red Indians" because of the Anglo-Saxon and Spanish ignorance of geography. Then there are Irish and other Europeans including Italians, and people of Jewish origins. Then of course we have black Americans (now called African Americans), mostly descendents of the slaves brought from Africa to work the plantations of the first Anglo-Saxon settlers. This latter group have traditionally been the target of most discrimination in the United States. The fear of the white Anglo-Saxon population for this minority has caused some of the most tragic and violent confrontations in the history of the country.

In addition, there are Asian groups of different origins, which have traditionally avoided confrontation with the majority population by keeping out of politics and using their own astute economic principles to stay "below the radar" of the main racist manipulators in the US establishment.

In recent years, the ethnic group that has rapidly come to the fore is the Muslim American group. They have attracted the attention of racist manipulators and are currently the single most persecuted group [47.9]. A concerted anti-Islamic campaign of discrimination has been engineered, which has successfully caused alienation, most especially in the eyes of America's most ignorant and politically naïve white, republican voting, population.

Some of the acts of cultural libel used against the Muslim population include accusations of mistreatment against women in Muslim society, implications that Islam is a religion of war and violence, subliminal accusations of the most sinister type against the founders of Islam, and the implication that Islam is at war with Christendom. The latter libel was entirely unfounded, like the rest of the libels, until America finally provoked a real conflict with ordinary Muslims as a result of their bellicose behaviour in Iraq, Afghanistan, Pakistan, their threats against Iran, their interference in Libya, and their continued support of Israel in its genocide of the Palestinian people.

European racism: Simultaneous with the use of cultural libel in the USA against Muslim populations, several European countries joined in the pogrom against civilian Muslims, including France and Italy. Under the neo-fascist President Sarkozy, the government banned the wearing of some traditional Muslim women's clothing in public (except for rich Saudi princesses on shopping trips to Paris, of course). They also launched a witch-hunt against Roma gypsy migrants, and expelled over 1000 in one month.[24.2]

The hypocrisy of banning the headscarf of ordinary Muslim women in France (and other countries in Europe) whilst Christian nuns and monks are walking the streets of Europe, wearing the most overtly religious, face-

214

covering medieval costumes, was not lost on the general public, who still can't enter most Catholic cathedrals without wearing a headscarf. Nor, for a theoretically secular state was the presence of crucifixes in German classrooms consistent with the separation of church and state and their religiously neutral constitution. The racist, cultural and religious bias is obvious and quite repugnant.

In more recent times, France, Italy and Germany have all taken actions to harass and intimidate their Romany populations in a chilling reminder of the actions of the fascist regimes of the 1930s.[24.3]

24.5.2 Discrimination: At some point in the process of cultural alienation, the majority group is encouraged to actively discriminate against the minority group; socially, politically, administratively and economically.

In this scenario, the minority group is forced to live in ghettos, has little access to good jobs, proper social services, or decent education. The group is often disenfranchised politically.

The physical and economic isolation of the group causes a reinforcing poverty and deepening depravity, with attendant problems of social disorder and crime amongst the unemployed youth. This, in turn, provides the manipulator with more material for cultural libel and so the spiral of separation continues without the manipulator's active intervention.

The manipulation of discrimination is self-sustaining until it is actively switched off by the political power which initiated it.

Discrimination relies on ignorance and having enough poorly educated, dysfunctional citizens in the majority population. Sadly, the victims of such discrimination can be literally anyone: In late December 2012, a 31 year old woman pushed a man under a subway train in New York because "she has always hated Muslims and Hindus since the 9/11 attacks, and since the attacks I have been beating them up". Firstly, there is no evidence at all that any Hindu was involved in the 9/11 attacks. Secondly, the man she murdered was, in fact, an Indian, and was not a Muslim. In any event, he was completely innocent of anything even remotely connected with 9/11. The murderer had never met her victim before.

This kind of psychopathic and racist behaviour is typical of the reactions often generated amongst the poorly educated, uninformed, gullible, deprived white populations of the USA, looking for someone to blame for their own awful life. In fact, they really need to go and talk to the politicians that manipulated their racist attitudes in order to find answers as to why so many poor white people have no education, no opportunities but plenty of racist attitudes.

24.6 Avoidance and Counteraction: Sadly, the phenomenon of racism is very hard to avoid if you happen to belong to a minority in a country where discrimination is permitted or encouraged like the USA or many parts of Europe.

It is a pervasive disease that knows no borders. Nonetheless, thankfully, the disease of racism does not afflict everyone. There are large parts of the population of all the countries mentioned that do not participate in this. As a member of the majority population, the case is quite clear: the obviously evil and manipulative use of cultural discrimination is clearly immoral from a humanist perspective.

24.6.1 Racism-Baiting: One method of counteraction is sometimes referred to as "race-baiting". In this case, politicians who have racist contacts, tendencies or backgrounds are monitored and exposed in the conventional press as racists. This is similar exercise to the exposé of politicians that have been engaged in child abuse (a politically similar activity to racism since both rely on the abuse of the weak).

The same surveillance methods can be applied to members of the police forces, the military, state institutions, schools, universities etc. A small group of committed individuals like the European Anti-Fascist leagues can do wonders to keep these manipulators under control.

The enforcement of laws to control racism and demands for stronger laws to protect against racism is the subject of constant political lobbying in the "civilised world".

---o0o---

25. Political / organisational tricks

25.1 Definition: There are a range of manipulative techniques that are particular to politics, and rarely used outside this environment. Politics in this case isn't restricted to conventional party politics; it also refers to corporate politics.

One common aspect of these manipulative methods is that the victim is nearly always a large group, i.e. the general public or a group of the public or a group of employees.

25.2 Persistence: Low to High, depending on the political trick being used.

25.3 Accessibility: Medium: Generally these methods are only available to manipulators with existing political influence or positions in management.

25.4 Conditions/Opportunity/Effectiveness: These methods are highly specific in use and effectiveness. Refer to the individual method for more details.

25.5 Methodology/Refinements/Sub-species: There are many manipulative tricks used specifically in political circles and in management. Here is a description of the most common sub-types:

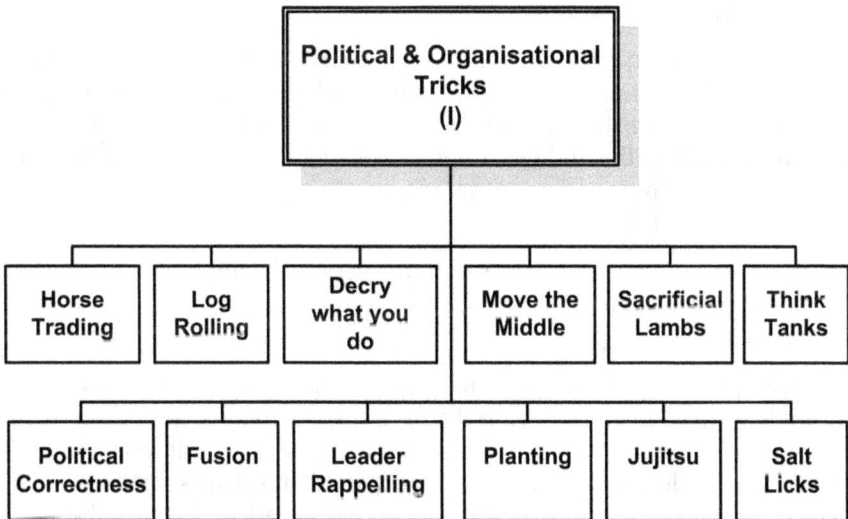

```
                    ┌──────────────────────────┐
                    │ Political & Organisational│
                    │          Tricks           │
                    │           (I)             │
                    └──────────────────────────┘
                                 │
  ┌─────────┬─────────┬─────────┼─────────┬─────────┬─────────┐
┌───────┐┌───────┐┌───────┐ ┌────────┐┌──────────┐┌───────┐
│ Horse ││  Log  ││ Decry │ │Move the││Sacrificial││ Think │
│Trading││Rolling││what you│ │ Middle ││  Lambs   ││ Tanks │
│       ││       ││  do   │ │        ││          ││       │
└───────┘└───────┘└───────┘ └────────┘└──────────┘└───────┘
  ┌──────────┬─────────┬─────────┬─────────┬─────────┐
┌──────────┐┌───────┐┌──────────┐┌────────┐┌────────┐┌───────┐
│ Political ││Fusion ││  Leader  ││Planting││Jujitsu ││  Salt │
│Correctness││       ││Rappelling││        ││        ││ Licks │
└──────────┘└───────┘└──────────┘└────────┘└────────┘└───────┘
```

25.5.1 Horse-trading: This method is named after the very subjective business of trading horses. It applies to shrewd bargaining by politicians, usually with wink-and-nod agreements as to the true import of legislation.

Certain regulations, for example, harm particular business interests more than others. Businesses that benefit from a regulation, may donate more to a politician who indirectly assists them in opposing damaging legislation or promoting helpful legislation.

25.5.2 Logrolling: This refers to the practice of trading favours by politicians. Legislation that might not be passed because it favours one group at the expense of another can be passed in exchange for the quid pro quo support on other such legislation by fellow "logrolling" parliamentarians. It happens continuously but only when free-voting is permitted.

25.5.3 Decry what you do: This is a technique where politicians criticise behaviour in which they themselves are engaged, hoping to portray themselves as the victim. For example when a party accuses another political group of harassment it may well be that the denouncing party is in fact guiltier of bullying and persecution. It is a form of distraction, often used by small children when caught with their hand in the biscuit tin: "I definitely have not stolen any biscuits. But I know who has!"

25.5.4 Moving the Middle: These techniques aim to alter the perception of a policy, politician, person, or party by manipulating the perceived middle ground or mean position. Moving the middle tends to be used in times of economic difficulty when populations may become either more conservative or more radical.

The centre may be misrepresented to alter the perception of what is considered "mainstream". It may involve excluding moderate views so as to politically move the "mainstream" position in a polarising way. It can also mean shifting the middle, which may be an incremental process taking place over the course of years to move a group, party, or nation to the political right or left.

Shifting the middle may be the result of a series of compromises benefiting one particular group or ideology, or it may occur due to systematic propaganda.

For example, the Labour Party in the UK under Tony Blair subtly moved its middle somewhere to the right of the Conservative party[25.1]. In this planned process, the party, based as it was on traditional socialist principles, gradually compromised and purged itself of socialists until it became a fairly reactionary right-wing party called "New Labour". It retained very little connection with the ethical basis of "Old Labour".

Finally, when his ruse was revealed Tony Blair and his cronies were virtually expelled from the party but the underhand manipulative dishonesty caused catastrophic political damage to the reputation and workings of an old and respected political party. The party will require years of recuperation to regain its place in the political consciousness of Britain. Worse still, the actions of Blair severely undermined public interest in party politics since political parties are, at the time of writing, perceived by much of the general public to be "all the same", with nothing to distinguish between Labour, Liberal-Democratic and Conservative parties- except their names.

25.5.5 Sacrificial lambs: This refers to the tactic wherein radical politicians sell themselves as "moderates" and then sacrifice themselves over an important issue once elected. This tactic is most effective when utilized at a predetermined time in coordination with other like-minded politicians.

A case in point was the massive vote by Democrat party members for universal healthcare in the USA, knowing that it meant certain doom for them come the next election. The cause was deemed worthy of the sacrifice.

25.5.6 Think Tanks: A think tank is a notionally independent organisation which claims to carry out "research" on behalf of corporations, political parties and sometimes governments. They are also sometimes referred to as policy institutes.

Their primary role is to perform research and advocacy on topics such as economics, social policy, technology, political strategy, military issues, and culture. Most think tanks are non-profit organizations. Other think tanks are funded by governments, advocacy groups, or businesses. Many derive revenue from consulting or research work related to their projects.

There is much justifiable suspicion of the actions of think tanks. In the last 40 years, they have been central to some fairly undemocratic behaviour both in the Western world and outside on behalf of Western nations.[25.2]

Characteristics: To understand the climate of suspicion surrounding think tanks", it is useful to appreciate some of their common characteristics:

- **Donor anonymity:** The source of their funding is often kept secret.[25.3]

- **Client anonymity:** They are not required to reveal their clients.

- **Immunity from retribution:** They are protected because they simply present the results of their "research". They have no legal liability for its rectitude.

- **Proxy action:** They often act as proxy agencies for the dirty work of their corporate sponsors because of their "untouchable" legal status.

- **Press support:** Most think tanks are also heavily supported by their co-opted (pet) journalists, so that think tank agendas move seamlessly to leader columns.

- **Secretive and unaccountable:** Mostly NGOs and "Not for profit", these think tanks" are accountable to no-one.

- **Openly deceitful:** Commonly these organisations claim to campaign on apparently worthy issues such as "freedom", "democracy", "open society" etc., whereas they have strict political agendas paid for by their secretive sponsors.

- **Used to influence lawmakers, no holds barred:** Frequently act as unofficial drafters of preferential laws for their sponsors as a service to lawmakers.

- **Corporate biases:** Think tanks exist on both sides of the political spectrum, but they are most concentrated on the right-wing. They are often active as implementers and propagandists of corporate policies for which they are handsomely financed.

Central to their behaviour is the status of think tanks as "not for profit" or charitable status organisations. This status gives them advantages of confidentiality that corporate or governmental institutions cannot enjoy. Their use of this status is somewhat fraudulent, but there is little that can be done to change this, at present.

Think tanks take money for "services rendered" from their anonymous clients and then use that money to deliver "other services" for their clients. Thus, they never show a profit and they act as largely anonymous agents of their clients, doing and saying things that the clients would otherwise be forbidden to do or say. Think tanks are most frequently found as the proxies of big capital.

Moral position: In recent years, the ascendance of corporate power has started to alarm the general public and with some justification. The most recent economic meltdowns caused by a global, greedy, unregulated and irresponsible banking sector have diminished the trust of the ordinary man in the street for corporate governance. It is now the common perception that voluntary regulation simply does not function in a capitalist environment. It is rapidly becoming obvious that one of the greatest risks to the democratic state and its functions comes not from mob rule or leftwing insurrection, but from the very rich and the corporations they run.

Corporations are viewed by much of the public as bandits roaming a global marketplace, paying no taxes and with little or no regulation. They admit to almost no corporate responsibility when things go wrong as they inevitably do. These forces of big capital have now redefined their assault on democratic governance. But there is no need for them to discuss the possibility of launching a military coup against democratic governments: the plutocrats of big capital have other means of turning the system, and one of their greatest tools is the neo-liberal think tank.

Often think tanks use the language of insurrection: "Smashing things", "creative destruction", the "breaking of chains" and the "slipping of leashes". But in general their main objective is to free the rich from the constraints of democracy and law.

Examples: Here are a couple of cases of manipulative behaviour from several conservative Think Tanks. There are many more:

- **Smoking:** Think tanks have been used to influence legislation for and against smoking: For instance, the think tank called "The Advancement of Sound Science Coalition" was formed during the mid 1990s to dispute research findings which demonstrated an association between second-hand smoke and cancer.

- **GM Food Labelling:** In late 2012, the attempt in California to have GM foods labelled as "GM" was defeated with the assistance of several think tanks and their public interventions:

  The Washington Legal Foundation, a free-market think tank, claimed that California's proposition 37 on GM labelling had "gone too far". The proposition 37 would have forced food producers to come clean about whether their products used GM products. As one proponent put it, "If Kellogg had been obliged to put a label on their packaging which stated that Corn Flakes were "Genetically modified", it would have been the kiss of death to their flagship product. Big Food Corp and their think tanks had to stop this at any price." And they did..... at least for now.

- **Climate Change:** In May 2012, the conservative Heartland Institute used electronic billboards on highways into Chicago with various manipulative signs messages: One, using a quote, and an image of Ted Kaczynski, the "Unabomber" was displayed on the electronic billboard, saying "I still believe in global warming. Do you?" The sign was the first in a campaign that was supposed to include Osama bin Laden, Fidel Castro and Charles Manson. It was quickly removed after a storm of public protest. This think tank had overstepped the line on this occasion.

25.5.7 Political Correctness: This is the technique of silencing opposition to an idea, party, politician, policy, race, religion, ethnicity, or sexual preference by stating or implying that such an opinion is inappropriate, insensitive, racist, discriminatory, biased, or judgmental. (It is similar to the "race-baiting" of a politician already described).

Political correctness often preys on the desire of most people to fit in or to be non-controversial and non-judgemental. It draws on the assumption of a civil society that each is entitled to his or her opinion, but by extension one cannot understand another person's or group's perspective, and therefore criticism of that person or group is somehow invalid. Political correctness is routinely used to attack progressive or leftist positions, although it can work in either political direction.

25.5.8 Fusion: This is a manipulative tactic (reputedly designed by Trotsky) whereby a party or group is deliberately radicalized by groups who affiliate with them with a view to gaining control. One example is the formation of a radical environmentalist group which then latches itself onto a left-wing or right-wing party and then steers the agenda of that party in favour of the infiltrators' real environmentalist agenda.

25.5.9 Leader-rappelling: This is the technique of dropping a relatively unknown politician into the role as new leader. Often new leaders are populist politicians who are taking advantage of a weak opposition. The idea is to present a completely new, clean, popular image to a disgruntled electorate. To some extent, President Obama was such a candidate.

25.5.10 Planting: This is the use of apparent sympathizers or "plants" to infiltrate, spy on, influence, and/or potentially sabotage a group or political party. They are also sometimes called "moles".

25.5.11 Jujitsu: In martial arts, the use of an opponent's weight or force against him is also referred to as judo. It is a strategy which leads to the self-destruction of an opponent.

In politics, this is the encouragement of a foe to continue to act in an imprudent way to the point where their behaviour is untenable. This often requires perverse incentives and false rewards and is complicated to achieve. Nagging an opponent on sensitive topics in order to cause an emotional or violent outburst is a good example of political Judo in action.

25.5.12 Salt Licks: This is the creation of a group, movement, program or cause in order to scout the population (especially its fringe elements) and to steer cooperate parts of the electorate toward a desired objective. It is similar to gathering farm animals at a pre-defined point where they can find the salt lick.

```
                    ┌─────────────────┐
                    │   Political &   │
                    │  Organisational │
                    │     Tricks      │
                    │      (II)       │
                    └─────────────────┘
```

Puppets	Pawns	Responsibility Avoidance	Fall Guys	Protection Racket	System Overload

Kabuki Theater	Front Group	Kickbacks	Plantation Farming	Pork Barrelling

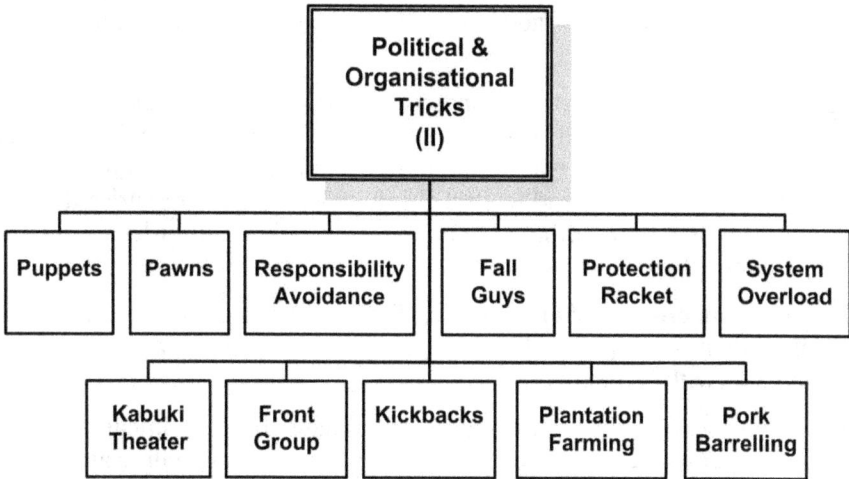

25.5.13 Puppets: This is where a politician appears to be independent, but he or she is actually a puppet of some special interest group or hidden parties. Almost all politicians suffer some lack of independence, either from their electorate or their patrons.

25.5.14 Pawns: A pawn is an unsuspecting and unaware person, manipulated by politicians for their own ends. A pawn may be another politician, a community leader, civil servant, a businessman or just an individual citizen. Politicians constantly use pawns to do their dirty work and sometimes take the blame as well. Pawns hardly ever get the credit for services rendered, though.

25.5.15 Responsibility avoidance: This is the political strategy of making sure that responsibility for a particular action doesn't fall on you or your group or party. There are several nuances to this strategy. Responsibility can be directed towards any of the following:

- **It was the Opposition's fault:** Another party or group unconnected with the action - i.e. the opposition

- **It was terrorists:** An outside agency with a generally malicious intent (e.g. "terrorists")

- **It was him/me:** A predetermined "fall guy" who has agreed to take the blame for a particular action. See "Fall guys".

- **Public is to blame:** The general public is always a good target for blame, because generally there is no-one to speak up for them.

Politicians are masters in the use of responsibility avoidance. A clever politician personalises successes and socialises failures. In other words, if all goes well it was his good idea, but if anything goes badly it was someone else's fault.

25.5.16 Fall guys: These are disposable personalities who take the blame for the illicit activities of a politician. A good example would be a huge scandal that runs all the way to the top of an organization or government. The reaction is for the head to start firing underlings or pressurise them to resign. This is a way to throw people to the "wolves" in order to sate the public's appetite to blame someone.

25.5.17 Protection racket: This is a form of manipulative coercion that occurs when one party threatens unpleasant consequences for non-compliance with its policy.

When businesses donate money to politicians or a political party to persuade them to regulate their particular industry in a certain way there is an implicit threat involved which states that there will be consequences if the politicians fail to deliver.

25.5.18 Kabuki Theatre: This tactic was named after a form of Japanese puppet show. It is a type of political debate, where political opponents (tacitly) agree to put on a show for the respective target audiences.

This may reduce public tension and apprehension by airing grievances, and bolster the images of the political participants by making them appear more principled and civilised than they actually are. It is also known as a dog and pony show in US political circles.

25.5.18 Front groups: This is the strategy where a political party or movement controls proxy groups who are not formally affiliated with the party or movement.

These may include "non-partisan" groups like think tanks, which may include radical left or right-wing groups, such as feminist, environmentalist, pro-choice or pro-minority groups. There could be conservative equivalents like the National Rifle Association or in Britain the Countryside alliance etc. Think tanks are such an important and specific influential phenomenon that they are considered as a separate topic.

25.5.19 Kickbacks: This is the political practice of returning a portion of funding, particularly public funding, to a politician who helped make the funding possible. It may also refer to a secret payment for an explicit or implicit service rendered, which may include "looking the other way", ignoring corruption or corrupt and illegal actions.

The effect of such corruption is that political events occur for reasons unknown to the public. This is a way of recognising that something is not quite right. When a political action seems too secretive or out of character, or contrary to party policy, there is a good chance that some form of kickback is being engineered.

25.5.20 Plantation farming: This is the creation of a relationship of dependency to cultivate a political client group. It may include minorities or even civil servants. The politician or party makes the client group dependent on them by the granting of favours. This locks the client group into supporting the politician or party.

25.5.21 Pork-barrelling: This tactic involves the allocation of public funds for dubious special interests. The origin of the term comes from the American Civil War era, when having pork indicated a family's general well-being. The term has come to have connotations with piggish behaviour, excess, inefficiency and bending to special interest groups, sometimes corruptly.

25.5.22 System overload: This strategy seeks to deliberately overload the budgets of various state-controlled departments in order to precipitate a crisis and force a change in policy. Social welfare or universal medical insurance are the oft-mentioned examples where this has been mooted as a possible strategy.

Although the strategy has never knowingly been successfully implemented in full, it is used to deliberately pressurize government budgets for political reasons.

It was originally an idea of a pair of US sociologists and political activists (Cloward and Fox) in 1966, who suggested that the social welfare system needed to be deliberately overloaded in order to force the US government to implement a fairer system of guaranteed annual income. The idea was that this would bring a final end to poverty, a goal which the social welfare system could never achieve.

25.6 Avoidance and Counteraction: It is difficult to generalise about how to detect, avoid and counteract political manipulation. Generally, the victim of political manipulation is the general public. However, with political manipulation, the action is generally taking place somewhere else, and the public are just delivered the fait accompli. As a rule, one can make a few generalisations about political events and the statements coming from politicians:

- Politicians eat and breathe manipulation of some kind. It is their stock in trade. Therefore always be cautious of statements by all politicians. Some may be honest, but for certain: most are not, most of the time.

- Never accept pre-digested summaries of political events. These are almost certainly tainted by political influences in the press. Everyone has an agenda and if you want the truth you have to do the research.

Sadly, most people are not that bothered and allow themselves to be manipulated (until there is a crisis, of course).

For ordinary citizens, counteracting political manipulation is almost impossible; unless you choose to become a politician as well.

---o0o---

26. Judicial manipulation

26.1 Definition: This is the manipulation of a judicial process, in order to give the impression of justice being done, whilst in fact it is being manipulated for other reasons. The method is often used to provide judicial and political "cover" to those who need to claim publicly that they have followed due legal processes.

26.2 Persistence: Short to Long

26.3 Accessibility: Low. Only those with access to management of judicial processes can engage in this.

26.4 Conditions/Opportunity/Effectiveness: The technique is in widespread use throughout the world, including in the "liberal" Western world. It isn't generally available to members of the public, apart from in the use or threat of libel actions.

It is most commonly used in cases of national interference with the judicial process, where a government executive uses his influence to either:

-   Alter legislation in a draconian way,

-   Trump up charges against a victim,

-   Use the power of government to pin down a victim in continuous legal actions and appeals

It is effective because its victims are generally locked up and voiceless and therefore have little opportunity to get a proper hearing. Governments and rich manipulators generally have the upper hand in this arena, because they can afford the best teams of lawyers, whereas a victim rarely can.

26.4.1 Types of judicial manipulation:

-   Suspension of legal process (internment etc)

-   Kangaroo courts / "Diplock" courts

-   Show trials

-   Libel laws

26.5 Methodology/Refinements/Sub-species: There are four known forms of judicial manipulation:

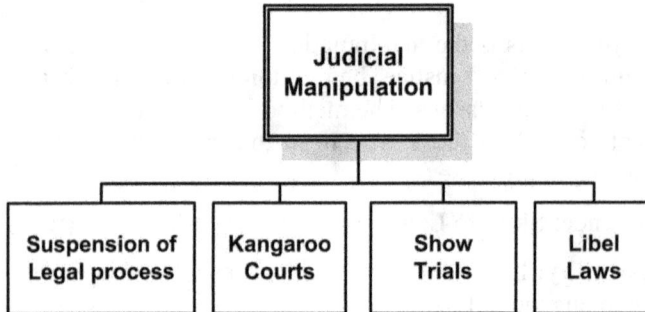

```
            ┌─────────────────┐
            │    Judicial     │
            │  Manipulation   │
            └─────────────────┘
                     │
   ┌─────────────┬───┴───────┬─────────────┐
┌──────────┐ ┌──────────┐ ┌────────┐ ┌────────┐
│Suspension│ │ Kangaroo │ │  Show  │ │ Libel  │
│of        │ │ Courts   │ │ Trials │ │ Laws   │
│Legal     │ │          │ │        │ │        │
│process   │ │          │ │        │ │        │
└──────────┘ └──────────┘ └────────┘ └────────┘
```

26.5.1 Suspension of legal process (internment etc.): The suspension of legal process generally occurs when a government has lost control of a situation and, in a desperate attempt to regain civil power, resorts to the suspension of normal judicial process. The "logic" is that by arresting everyone remotely connected, they are bound to get the real perpetrators. It's an absurd and ineffective strategy, but it is common amongst desperate governments.

During the "troubles" in Northern Ireland, the British government suspended normal legal process for several years and implemented an illegal process of internment without trial[26.1]. We use the term "illegal" advisedly, because the United Kingdom's treatment of those detained was later considered to be "illegal" in terms of the British constitution (as far as it exists). But it was also described by the European Court of Human Rights as "inhuman and degrading", and by the European Commission of Human Rights as "torture". The effect of this decision was to bolster republican antagonism, which gave rise to a generation of armed unrest in Ireland.

Guantanamo provides an even more contemporary example of the manipulative folly of suspending due process of law. Eleven years after the establishment of this illegal process and institution, the United States is still, internationally, considered a pariah state because of its use of kidnapping, torture and illegal detention without trial[26.2]. The consequences of this strategy continue to cost the USA both "blood and gold", as it did the United Kingdom in Northern Ireland for more than two generations.

26.5.2 Kangaroo Courts: Following the same historical theme, a kangaroo court is a mock court in which the principles of law and justice are disregarded or perverted.

In response to the harsh criticism of internment without trial in Northern

Ireland, the British government was obliged to re-introduce something that resembled a normal judicial process. So, they created an entirely artificial system of courts, which became known as the "Diplock courts".

In these mock military courts, trial by jury was suspended and hand-picked judges were used to send suspects into detention. This manipulative strategy was designed to deflect criticism of the British government coming from the UN, the USA and many European neighbours. However, the strategy caused even greater outrage in Ireland.

Again, a more contemporary example is the use of "military tribunals" by the USA against Muslim political prisoners. Many were tortured by the CIA and US troops whilst in detention in Guantanamo, and thus it is now impossible to try them using the normal criminal justice system in the USA.

The only remaining option for the US administration was the establishment of completely ex-constitutional and (internationally) illegal military tribunals to deal with the remaining Guantanamo inmates, some of whom were arrested whilst still children. The historical consequences of these judicial manipulations are yet to be fully realised, but it seems inevitable that the Muslim world sees these injustices as a blank cheque to seek revenge against the USA and UK.[26.3]

26.5.3 Show Trials: This is a manipulative technique where politicians make a public display of an opponent in a trial whose results are pre-determined. Show trials can have willing, bribed or coerced defendants.

One example is the recent show trial of certain Goldman Sachs executives[26.4]. Show trials may prop up a regime by sending implicit messages or threats to similar groups, chilling the economic, social, or political environment as a whole, and may be used to mobilise populist sentiment. In return, a willing show trial defendant may receive reduced penalties or hidden rewards. Conversely, an unwilling defendant may be used as an example of government "resolve" and be very harshly punished.

26.5.4 Libel laws: In some countries (like Britain), draconian libel laws have been developed to give extraordinary protection to individuals. These laws are more protective than those that protect the general public's right to free speech. The concept of libel also extends to organisations such as companies. The fact that libel laws are mostly used by rich and famous people tends to suggest that their existence was contrived to protect the privileged from the prying eyes of "commoners".

26.6 Avoidance and Counteraction: It is difficult to stay clear of a government whose executive is willing to use its judiciary to persecute its political opponents or discontented minorities. If you happen to be a member of either of these groups, the ideal strategy is to avoid countries that have governments with such little real respect for the rule of law. The United Kingdom and the USA, for example, have demonstrated some extraordinary disregard for due legal process in the last 40 years.

---o0o---

27. Rhetorical manipulation

27.1 Definition: The objective of rhetorical manipulation is to persuade victims to believe in various assertions without necessarily delivering proof of their validity. The assertions may concern an idea, a person, a group or a political case.

Elegant, eloquent, artificial or ostentatious expressions are often employed, and various aggressive tactics and manipulative tricks may attempt to block the victim's ability to access the arguments rationally. There are 4 basic types of rhetorical manipulation:

- Cognitive appeal
- Emotional appeal
- Attacking approach
- Content manipulation

27.2 Persistence: Low to High, depending on technique and type of victim.

27.3 Accessibility: High, almost all of us can use rhetorical manipulation, at times without even being aware of it.

27.4 Conditions/Opportunity/Effectiveness: Rhetorical manipulation works because most people accept certain premises. These assumptions are used by a manipulator to appeal to the emotions of a victim and take advantage of certain cognitive biases (weaknesses of rationalisation), to which most of us are prone to some extent.

The general method has a potential similar to the irrational power of flattery. The manipulator knows in advance how his victims will react to various assertions. Once he is familiar with his victims, he is then in a position to play upon their prejudices to gain their acceptance of the various hidden presuppositions.

Rhetorical tricks are traditionally thought to be the exclusive domain of politicians, but they are far more commonly used than that. They are applied almost constantly by most of us to achieve even the most trivial of our daily goals.

27.5 Methodology/Refinements/Sub species: Rhetoric which is manipulative, seeks to make a set of assertions and a course of action acceptable to a victim by means of deliberately contrived language and the clever ordering of statements, so that a victim reaches a preordained "personal" conclusion, apparently without pressure from the manipulator.

This manipulated conclusion would not normally be considered either acceptable or logical when communicated explicitly and considered rationally by the victim. For rhetorical manipulation to be successful, the victim must not be aware that they are being manipulated.

The most important aspect of rhetorical manipulation is, that the assertions being made are less important than the manipulated presuppositions from which they derive. They are constructed by making a number of suppositions which are reasonably acceptable or distracting to a victim. These assertions endorse the acceptance by the victim of the payload presupposition which the manipulator really wishes to deliver.

For instance, when a pressure group shouts "Freedom Now", the general reaction is "OK. These people have a right to be free", but underlying this reaction we have already ratified the presupposition that "these people are oppressed".

In recent British politics we have a continuous dialogue about "Job training schemes". The average listener reflects to himself, "Training for employment is good". The underlying presupposition which one has accepted here, is that "there are jobs available for the trained but unemployed people", but this is not necessary true, as millions of unemployed and underemployed citizens may well testify.

Methods of delivery and free will: Rhetorical manipulation may be written or spoken in its delivery. It is, and has been used to pacify, excite, or shock an audience, but more often it is used to whip its victims into actions which they would ordinarily not consider, and which may be contrary to their putative will.

The use of rhetoric is not, however, always manipulative. There are some circumstances in which an audience knows it is being roused into action and is gratified by what is happening to it. This is the case in most patriotic rallies, for instance, where an audience can easily determine that it is being emotionally manipulated, but chooses to allow it to carry on, and in fact endorses it.

Four Types of Manipulative Rhetoric: The following are the main sub-types of rhetorical manipulation:

- Cognitive appeals
- Emotional appeals
- Attacking approach
- Content manipulation

All of which will now be described in detail.

27.5.1 Cognitive Appeal: There are ten main rhetorical manipulative methods which have a cognitive appeal.

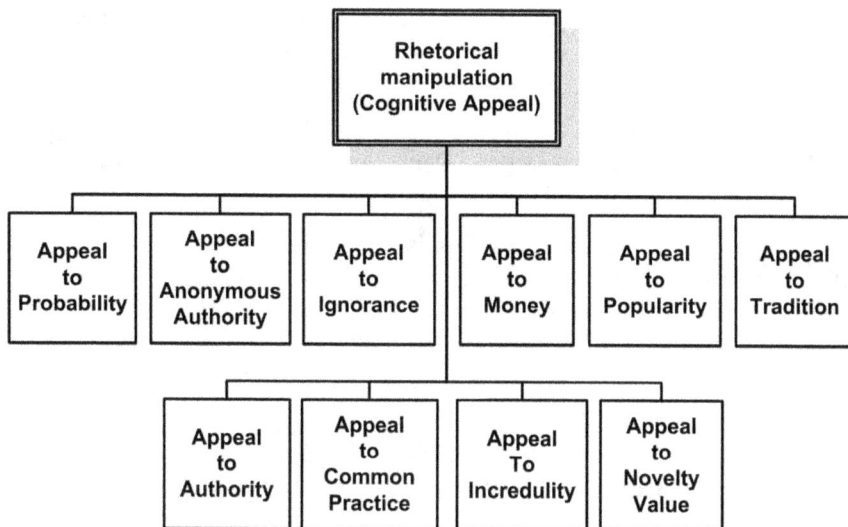

27.5.1.2 Appeal to Probability: This is the assumption that because something could possibly happen, then it probably will happen.

27.5.1.3 Appeal to Anonymous Authority: Appealing to unnamed "experts" to prove something is true or false.

The appeal to authority is a fallacy of irrelevance when the authority being cited is not really an authority or is not cited at all, e.g. to appeal to Einstein to support a point in religion, would be to make an irrelevant appeal to authority. Einstein was an expert in physics, not religion. An appeal to unspecified "experts" is even less valid.

Also appealing to non-experts as if they were experts is fraudulent. Appealing to experts in controversial fields, such as religion, is equally invalid in establishing the correctness of the belief.

27.5.1.4 Appeal to Ignorance: Claiming that something is true because it hasn't been proven false (or vice versa).

Examples abound in discussions of the supernatural. Normally we have no way of proving that a supernatural phenomenon is not real and so we are obliged to accept that it could be. The glass seems to move on the Ouija board and no-one has proven that it is not the result of a supernatural event, therefore it is true.

27.5.1.5 Appeal to Money: This is the assumption that if something is expensive then it must be good, or if someone is rich then their wealth makes their words and deeds more trustworthy.

27.5.1.6 Appeal to Popular Belief: This is the assertion that something is true simply because a lot of people believe it.

This is a constant trick, where the manipulator asserts "50 million people can't be wrong, can they?." In fact, yes, 50 million people can be wrong. History is full of cases were they were: the Flat Earth, the Sun revolving around the Earth etc. These were all popular beliefs and all were wrong.[27.1]

27.5.1.7 Appeal to Tradition: This is the claim that something could be true simply because it has always been that way. The use of cliché, allegory and metaphor can be used to refer to traditional associations with an assertion being foisted on the victim.

27.5.1.8 Appeal to Authority: A favourite of elitists is an appeal to authority making a claim based on the reputation of a person, group, or other source. It is often used to diminish an argument made by an intellectual opponent by referring to the supposed prestige of one's own source.

The irrelevant appeal to authority is a type of genetic fallacy, i.e. attempting to judge a belief by its origin rather than by the arguments for and against the belief. If the belief originated with an authoritative person, then the belief is held to be true. However, even authoritative persons can hold false beliefs.

Appeals to authority do not become more relevant when, instead of a single source one cites several experts who believe something is true. If the authorities are speaking outside of their range of expertise or the subject is controversial, piling up long lists of supporters does not make the appeal any more relevant. On any given controversial matter there are likely to be equally competent experts on different sides of the issue. The truth or falsity, reasonableness or unreasonableness of a belief must stand independently of those who accept or reject the belief.

Finally, it should be noted that it is not irrelevant to cite an authority to support a claim that one is not competent to judge. However, in such cases the authority must be speaking in their own field of expertise and the claim should be one that other experts in the field do not generally consider to be controversial.

In a subject, such as physics, it is reasonable to believe a claim made by a physicist that most other physicists also consider to be true. Presumably, they believe it because there is strong evidence to support it. Such beliefs could turn out to be false, of course, but it is obvious that no belief becomes true simply on the basis of who believes it and how much authority they wield.

27.5.1.9 Appeal to Common Practice: Claiming something is true because it's in common practice: "These politicians are corrupt but so what - all politicians are corrupt aren't they?"

27.5.1.10 Appeal to Incredulity: Claiming that because something sounds incredible, it cannot be true

For example: "I cannot believe the CIA was involved in the 9/11 attacks therefore it cannot be true."

27.5.1.11 Appeal to Novelty: This is the supposition that because something is new or newer, it must therefore be better.

27.5.2 Emotional appeal: There are nine basic emotional appeals made in manipulative rhetorical technique:

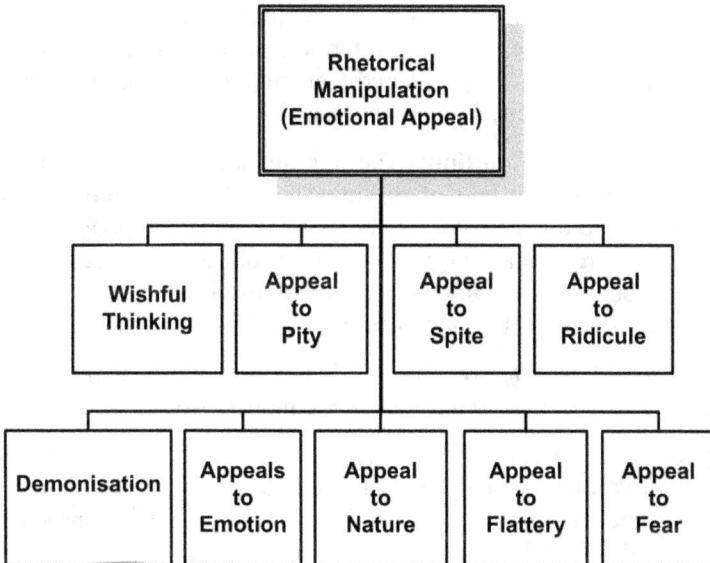

27.5.2.1 Appeal to Wishful Thinking: This is the expression that an assertion is true because you or your opponent strongly hope that it is.

Example: "But wouldn't the world be wonderful if everyone had enough to eat and a decent standard of living".

27.5.2.2 Appeal to Pity: The use of pity as a means of influencing an argument.

For example: "Ladies and gentlemen of the jury: look at this miserable man, in a wheelchair, unable to use his legs. Could such a man really be guilty of fraud?"

27.5.2.3 Appeal to Spite: This is an attempt to win favour for an argument by exploiting feelings of bitterness, spite in the opposing party. It is an attempt to sway the audience emotionally by associating a hate-figure with opposition to the speaker's argument.

27.5.2.4 Appeal to Ridicule: A favourite tactic of modern politicians, which presents an opponent's argument as absurd, ridiculous, or in any way humorous. It is difficult to defend against, because it triggers emotional reactions and not rational ones, leading to overreaction, anger, or withdrawal.

To be effective, ridicule requires an audience because it is based on instilling contempt for the victim or their cause. The best defence is to laugh it off, while ridiculing the attacker back, as if you were his friend.

27.5.2.5 Demonisation: A broad term that includes overt or subtle defamation of someone, with the intention of making them seem evil or insidious. It can be used to discredit an opponent or a supporter of an opponent or an expert cited by an opponent.

27.5.2.6 Appeal to Emotion: The argumentum ad misericordium, or "appeal to emotion", is one of the most prevalent manipulative political techniques. It is the general use of emotion to persuade people to support, or conversely, reject an argument based on emotion rather than on evidence, reason, or self-interest. It attempts to make an argument truer or more valid by imbuing it with emotional force.

27.5.2.7 Appeal to Nature: Attempting to validate a claim by making comparisons with events or realities in the natural world.

For example: The appeal to nature can be found on labels and advertisements for food, clothing, and alternative herbal remedies. Labels may use the phrase "all-natural", to imply that products are environmentally friendly and safe.

27.5.2.8 Appeal to Flattery: Using complimentary language in order to deliver an unfounded claim, which, along with the compliment, is accepted by the victim.

Example: "Surely an audience as intelligent and perceptive as you can see that this is a superb proposal." The implication is that if you don't find it superb, then you aren't that intelligent and perceptive.

27.5.2.9 Appeal to Fear: Also called "argumentum ad metum" An argument is made by trying to induce fear towards the opposing side.

Example: "Voting for him is the same as voting for the terrorists."

27.5.3 Attacking Approach: There are eleven types of attack using rhetoric. These are used as criticisms of the opponent or their associates rather than the claims they make:

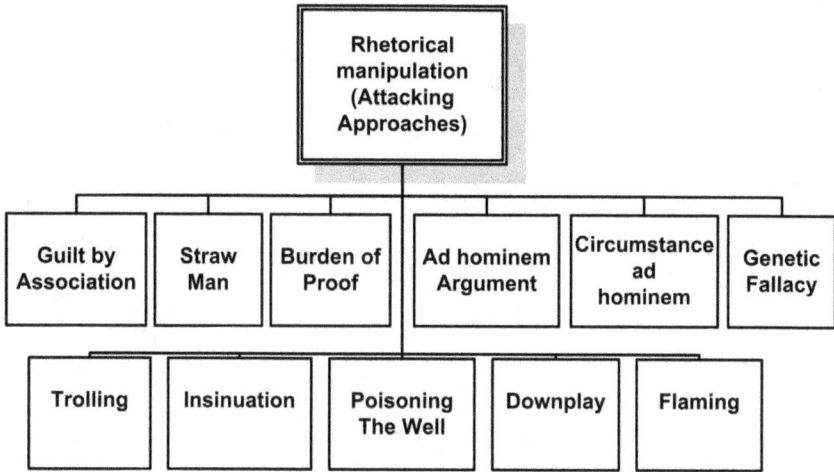

27.5.3.1 Guilt by Association: This is the discrediting of a claim or idea by associating it with an undesirable person or group.

Example: "Jane appears good at mathematics. Jane cheated in her exams. Therefore, all exam cheats appear good at mathematics."

27.5.3.2 Straw Man arguments: This is the restating of an argument in such an extreme form that it provides an easy target (or "straw man") to tear apart. For instance, one could argue that "Israel should stop building on West Bank sites". The straw man attack would be "So, you are saying that Israel has no right to be a nation."[47.7] The two statements are unconnected, but the second is easier to defend than the real statement.

27.5.3.3 Burden of Proof: This is where the manipulator claims that his argument doesn't require him to provide proof and that it is up to the opponent (victim) to disprove the manipulator's assertions.

Example: "This GM vaccine is safe as far as we are concerned, unless anyone has proof to the contrary?"

27.5.3.4 Ad hominem argument: This is the discrediting of an argument by making unfounded or irrelevant charges against a party, rather than by rationally addressing what is being argued.

This is also known popularly as "attacking the messenger" or "character assassination"; it is a way of diminishing the merit of an argument by spuriously attacking the moral authority of its advocate.

27.5.3.5 Circumstance Ad hominem: This is discrediting an argument only because of the advocate's interest in the claim. For example, a study of health risks of mobile phones could not be valid because the study involved research by the telephone companies.

27.5.3.6 Genetic Fallacy: This is an attack on the origin of an idea rather than the substance of the claim.

Example "America will never settle down; look at the rabble-rousers who founded it."

27.5.3.7 Trolling: In Internet jargon, the subversion or harassment of an online community by a troll or cooperating trolls, for purposes of disruption, attention-seeking, publicity, advertising, espionage, or propaganda. Some trolls simply seek attention, others stir up trouble for their own personal amusement, and some are even dedicated and malicious. If not checked, effective trolling can drive a wedge in an online community. A good rule of thumb is to evaluate if people are benign by determining if they are intellectually honest. If not, there are various ways to ban a persistent or nagging troll.[27.2]

27.5.3.8 Insinuation: The implanting of an idea in the minds of an audience by asserting the opposite of the intended message. For example, in a political debate, a candidate may say: "Now, I would never suggest that my opponent believes himself to be above the law." But of course the candidate does mean exactly that and now he has put the idea in the minds of the audience, while leaving open the possibility for "plausible deniability". This can be effective, because psychologically, most people remember the accusation better than they do the denial.

One can thereby taint the image of one's opponents without ever making a direct charge or accusation.

The use of euphemisms and ambiguity are related methods of rhetorical insinuation. Phrases like "collateral damage" convert the reality of horrendous civilian casualties in war into an apparently innocuous and emotionless phrase.

27.5.3.9 Poisoning the well: In debate, the tactic of pre-emptively using unseemly and usually personal information to discredit what an opponent has to say. Typically done as an ad hominem or personal attack, intended "to freeze, personalize, and polarise" a target.

Example: "Everything I say is correct, no matter what you say". The well is poisoned and nothing a person says (be it true or false) will matter by the initiator's definition.

27.5.3.10 Laugh it off / Downplay: Similar to, and perhaps a subcategory of, ridicule. This is when one meets an accusation head on and laughs it off. This can be done in combination with straw man arguments. One illustration might be when President Obama of the USA laughed off the Neo-con idea that he was "engaging in some sort of Bolshevik plot."

27.5.3.11 Inflammation "Flaming": The agitation of a group through incendiary tactics in order to expose the radical elements and to discredit the group to the broader public. A provocateur may send a "troll" into a group to flame its members, meanwhile grabbing screenshots to be broadcast to a select audience later.

27.5.4 Content manipulation: This deals with alterations in the content and delivery of a statement as part of a rhetorical manipulation. Here are the diagrammatic representations of the manipulative methods in use in content manipulation (divided into 2 parts for clarity):

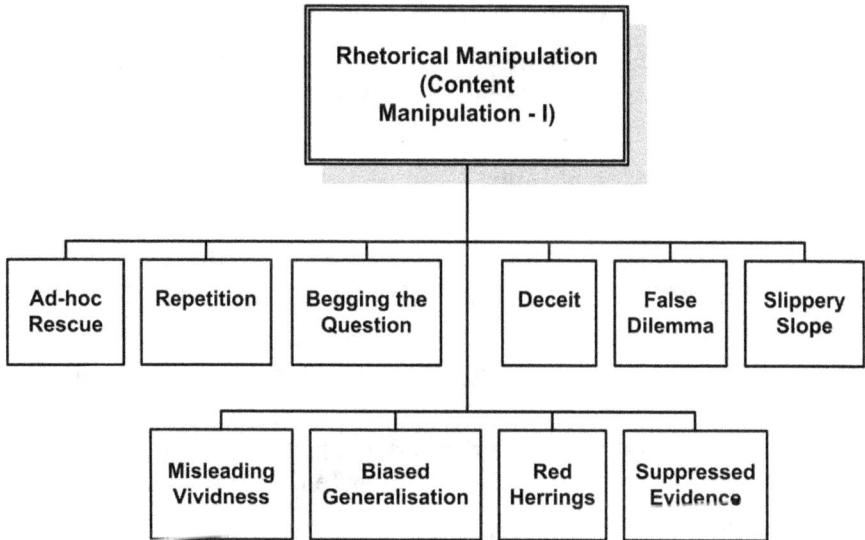

27.5.4.1 Ad Hoc Rescue: Trying to save a claim by repeating and revising the argument, in an attempt to explain problems with the original claim.

27.5.4.2 Repetition: Generally speaking, a tactic to ingrain an idea or image into the minds of the victim audience by using repetition. This includes chanting at rallies to reinforce branding, loyalty, and group cohesion. More broadly, repetition defuses critical thinking and systematically desensitizes a subject to certain stimuli. In terms of mass culture, repetition achieves the effect of demystifying a cultural object, in essence, commoditizing it for popular consumption.

27.5.4.3 Begging the question: This is claiming something to be a support for a statement, without any actual supporting facts, e.g. "Illegal drugs are harmful, and that is why they are illegal".

27.5.4.4 Deceit: This is the deliberate use of an untruth presented as a fact, in order to sway an argument.

27.5.4.5 False Dilemma: This is the manipulative presentation of only two options whilst hiding all other alternatives.

For instance, "we have to cut the social welfare budget or go further into debt. We can't go further into debt, so we will have to cut the social welfare budget."

27.5.4.6 Slippery Slope: This is the idea that a relatively small initial step will inevitably lead to a series of serious negative consequences.

Example: "Once same sex unions are allowed, that will undermine the sanctity of heterosexual marriage between man and woman."

27.5.4.7 Misleading Vividness: This is the exaggerated use of vivid descriptions of an object or event to make it appear as if it is a problem, even though the event may be a one-off.

27.5.4.8 Biased Generalisation: This is a generalisation based on an unrepresentative sample in order to support a claim.

Example: "I sampled 3 of the 1000 boxes and 1 of them was bad, so I estimate that there are 300 bad ones there".

27.5.4.9 Red herrings: Issues, phrases, or words meant to derail debate or opposition (also called a "manipulation of dimensions") and alter the outcome of an argument.

Example: "There is no evidence that torture elicits usable intelligence, but lives are on the line, so we can't use other proven measures".

27.5.4.10 Suppressed Evidence: This is the deliberate failure to present relevant and important information in the presentation of an argument. This type of manipulation was used by Tony Blair to convince the British parliament to allow the invasion of Iraq when he asserted that "Iraq possesses Chemical and Biological Weapons and is seeking to produce Nuclear weapons", but Blair suppressed the negative military intelligence that Saddam's stockpiles were ancient and unusable.

Rhetorical Manipulation (Content Manipulation-II)

- Unfalsifiability
- Hidden co-option
- Shadow Boxing
- Mainstreaming
- Pragmatic Fallacy
- Hidden Implication
- Framing
- Anecdotal Evidence
- Cherry Picking

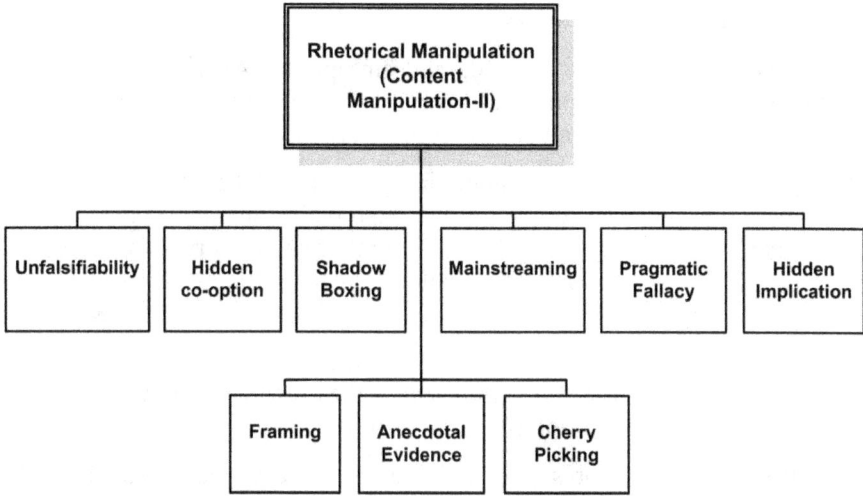

27.5.4.11 Unfalsifiability: This is the technique of using data which cannot be proved or disproved.

27.5.4.12 Hidden co-option: This is another powerful hybrid of rhetorical manipulation. Here the manipulator relies on their knowledge of the victim's personality. The manipulator claims to share their perspective and demonstrates this by vocalizing the victim's views and prejudices which are phrased as "mutual aspirations". The manipulator speaks in terms of "we" rather than "I".

The Japanese actually have a word for this process of "consensus-building". "Nemawashi" is a method used by Japanese executives to lay the groundwork amongst their employees for new initiatives. The word is borrowed from bonsai-tree cultivation meaning "binding of roots".

27.5.4.13 Shadow-boxing: This refers to debating an issue that is irrelevant or effectively moot, in order to stall the discussion or to pander to the manipulator's supporters.

27.5.4.14 Mainstreaming: This is the discussion of a controversial topic in an offhand way, in order to make it appear acceptable. The idea is to move a sensitive subject into the mainstream.

27.5.4.15 Pragmatic fallacy: This is the rhetorical manipulative technique which argues that an assertion is true because it "works". In this sense "works" means something like "I'm satisfied with it," "I feel better," "I find it beneficial, meaningful, or significant," or "It explains things for me."

For instance, many people claim that astrology works, acupuncture works, chiropractic works, homeopathy works, numerology works, palmistry works, therapeutic touch works.

What 'works' means here is vague and ambiguous. At the least, it means that one perceives some practical benefit in believing that it is true, despite the fact that the utility of a belief is completely independent of its truth.

The pragmatic fallacy is common in "alternative" health claims and is often based on post hoc reasoning. For example, someone has a sore back; they wear the new magnetic belt and find relief soon afterwards. They then declare that the magic belt caused the pain to go away. How does one know this? Because it works.

27.5.4.16 Hidden implication: This is the use of oblique hints and traditional associations. A manipulator makes an assertion with obvious reference to a presupposition (the "payload").

Both the assertion and presupposition may be quite respectable as far as the victim is concerned, but the obvious presupposition has strong traditional and emotional associations with other premises, one of which is the real subject of the manipulator's delivery.

For instance, a politician can discuss his country's financial contribution in aid to ex-colonies, and its strain on the financial resources of the "fatherland", which already has a huge unemployment and poverty problem. If he immediately afterwards discusses immigration policy, the scene is set for him to gain positive responses from his audience, if he asserts tougher restrictions on ex-colonial subjects entering the country.

27.5.4.17 Framing: This is a more sophisticated technique that "primes" a victim for their reception of subsequent information. It operates by providing a theme and then associating information with that theme. An example may be mentioning a Vietnamese restaurant before discussing the Iraq War. The term "quagmire" is sure to come up at some point.

27.5.4.18 Anecdotal evidence: Testimonials and vivid anecdotes are one of the most popular and convincing forms of evidence, and very popular in manipulative rhetoric. Nevertheless, testimonials and anecdotes in such matters are often valueless.

Anecdotes tend to be unreliable, because they are prone to contamination by beliefs, later experiences, feedback, selective attention to details, and so on. Most stories get distorted in the telling and the retelling. Events get exaggerated. Time sequences get confused. Details get muddled. Memories are imperfect and selective; gaps are often filled in after the fact. People misinterpret their experiences. Experiences are conditioned by biases, memories and beliefs, so people's perceptions might not be accurate.

Anecdotal evidence is in common use in political, religious and commercial manipulation when it suits the manipulator.

27.5.4.19 Cherry picking: This is the selection of evidence that supports the manipulator's claim, but ignores all other evidence which does not support it.

27.6 Avoidance and Counteraction: The manipulative rhetorician is most threatened by a strong-willed, clear-thinking dogmatic adversary. A victim, who rises above the emotional considerations and demands clear, documented, authenticated, logical links between premises and conclusions, is very dangerous to a manipulator. A listener, who wishes to explore all the implications of these premises in total detail, is unbeatable. If the demands for more information are perceived as reasonable, the victim will be unassailable.

Co-option or exclusion of such individual victims may be possible for the manipulator. However, there are no precautions a manipulator can take against a victim that keeps asking: What? Why? Who? How? At some point the rhetorical manipulator will run out of answers and the game is over.

---o0o---

28. Historical manipulation

28.1 Definition: This is a form of manipulation in which a victim's understanding of history is altered by a manipulator. It generally involves altering the importance of certain events, the order of events, responsibility for events and the implantation of new events into the historical perception of the victim. It may be related to the techniques used in "manipulation of memory", if the history is within the living memory of the victim.

28.1.1 Why is it important? Controlling a victim's view of history is an important concept in political manipulation, because it alters the historical context of present actions.

For instance, the US attempted immediately after 9/11 to show that Bin Laden was based in Afghanistan. These assertions were used to justify the invasion of that country. This was despite the fact that Bin Laden was not particularly interested in Afghanistan after the Taliban had taken control. In fact, the presence of Bin Laden in Afghanistan was almost certainly fictional and the reasoning for the US invasion was totally disingenuous. We now know that Bin Laden was much more likely to be with his US financed ISI handlers in Pakistan (the ISI being the main conduit for the billion dollar CIA budget for Afghan - Soviet resistance, of which Bin Laden was an important part).[28.2]

In a similar way, history was altered in the case of Iraq, where previous US ally Saddam Hussein was toppled and the country invaded, because he had "weapons of mass destruction". In reality, most of the weapons that Saddam Hussein possessed had been financed by the United States, so that he could fight a proxy war with Iran on behalf of the USA.

Thus, historical manipulation is important in justifying current actions: Iraq must be invaded because it used chemical weapons against its own people, etc., and Afghanistan must be invaded because Bin Laden had travelled there during the Russian occupation and had assisted in the training of mujahideen, who were also financed by the USA and Saudi Arabia. The historical realities are quite different and would never have supported these invasions, so it was necessary for the manipulators to simply "change history". The realities were actually that the USA felt it needed to try to control Iraq's huge oil reserves and Afghanistan as the most important central Asian transit point an also an energy and resource centric zone.

But in the rewritten history, Saddam Hussein becomes an out of control monstrous dictator killing his own people and threatening the West with weapons of mass destruction. Afghanistan becomes the headquarters of

Bin Laden's international terrorist organisation which was seeking to invade the Christian world.[28.2]

28.2 Persistence: Long. It can take decades or even centuries for history to be fully revealed and then properly understood. Sometimes, it is never fully understood.

28.3 Accessibility: At a national political level, accessibility is low - only the victors get to write the history. However, at a personal level almost everyone can attempt to rewrite their own or their victim's history.

28.4 Conditions/Opportunity/Effectiveness: The manipulation of historical "fact" is very effective in altering public perceptions. History can generate extreme emotions of anger, humiliation, nationalism, desire for revenge, hatred. It can, in other circumstances, create sentiments of warmth, dependency, friendship and trust.

28.4.1 Uses: Historical manipulation can be used at a very personal level between individuals or groups, but it can also be used to influence whole nations. It can have cataclysmic effects and has often been held responsible for the starting of extremist movements, leading eventually to wars and bloodshed.

For instance, the Nazi party's manipulation of the German public perception of the Treaty of Versailles laid the foundation for WW II. Romanticised views of our own national histories may be based entirely on pure historical fantasy, but the imagery they contain can generate strong emotional feelings.

28.4.2 Personal History: At a personal level, an individual can rewrite their own history to explain away or airbrush out some unpleasant aspects of their lives. This re-written version of events then becomes the official version used in all future social interactions.

To some extent we all indulge in personal historical manipulation. The dangers of this depend on the extent to which we fail to face the reality of our own lives. Small adjustments in our personal history may be required to survive bad memories or traumas, but complete "rewrites" should probably be a subject for a psychiatrist.

28.5 Methodology/Refinements/Sub-species: There are three basic sub-species of historical manipulation:

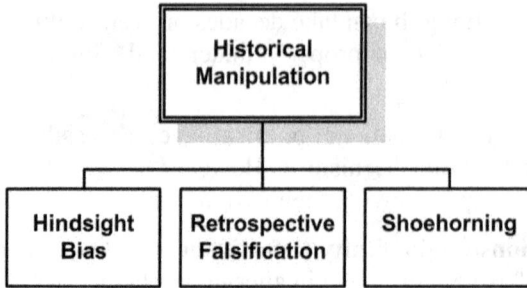

```
              ┌─────────────────┐
              │   Historical    │
              │  Manipulation   │
              └─────────────────┘
         ┌────────────┼────────────┐
   ┌──────────┐ ┌──────────────┐ ┌────────────┐
   │Hindsight │ │Retrospective │ │Shoehorning │
   │  Bias    │ │Falsification │ │            │
   └──────────┘ └──────────────┘ └────────────┘
```

28.5.1 Hindsight bias: This is also known as the "I knew-it-all-along" effect or "creeping determinism". It has been redefined in recent years as the theory of black swan events, a metaphor that describes an event that is a surprise (to the observer), has a major effect, and after the fact is often inappropriately rationalized with the benefit of hindsight.

It is the technique of manipulation which attempts to show events that have already occurred as being more predictable than they were before they took place. It has a lot of potential applications for the manipulator and works at all levels: from personal manipulation right up to international politics.

In the individual, hindsight bias is the tendency to construct one's memory after the fact (or interpret the meaning of something said in the past), according to currently known facts and one's current beliefs. It is also a form of self-delusion. In this way, one appears to make the past consistent with the present, and more predictable than it actually was.

When it is used by a manipulator towards a victim or group, it is highly disorientating because it causes memory distortion, even in large groups where the recollection and reconstruction of an event, or the content of what actually happened, can lead to false conclusions.

As a manipulative technique, "hindsight bias" is most potent because it creates serious practical and methodological problems to anyone trying to gainsay a statement where hindsight is quoted.

There are plenty of cases where historians describe the outcomes of battles; physicians recall clinical trials and judicial systems very astutely attribute responsibility and the predictability of accidents, after the event.

It is a potent tool when used by religious sects to demonstrate the validity of their propositions after the event, like the sexual revolution and the rate of divorce: "We warned you that this (the sexual revolution) would lead to chaos, evil and unhappiness (and divorce)."

28.5.2 Retrospective falsification: This term was first coined to refer to the process of telling a story that is factual to some extent, but which gets distorted and falsified over time by re-telling it with embellishments.

The embellishments may include conflating events, speculation, using different times and places, and the incorporation of historical material without checking accuracy or plausibility.

The term is used in psychology to describe the process of creating false memories by selecting and reshaping incidents from the past to fit present needs. Retrospective falsification occurs in most, if not all, people and is generally an unconscious process.

The overriding force that drives the story is to find or invent details that fit with a desired outcome. The process can be conscious or unconscious. The original story gets remodelled with favourable points being emphasized and unfavourable ones being dropped. The distorted and false version becomes a memory and record of a remarkable tale.

A manipulator uses this tendency to alter historical recollection. For instance, all "battles were glorious", simply because all defeats have been removed from the public record. "All generals are courageous", because all the cowards were shot and forgotten about. "All soldiers were honourable and brave", because all the others have been disregarded, silenced and forgotten.

Examples of this process include stories of miraculous events, the glamorisation of failed or costly military actions, the covering-up of war-crimes, and the rewriting of biographies of politicians with poor reputations to make them seem more virtuous than they really were.

When this process occurs consciously, as it often does in manipulative politics, it may be called by other names, such as "political historical revisionism." Historical revisionism is a central pillar of the political manipulator's art and is widely used by all colours of politicians.

The technique is also used in the corporate world where some companies work hard to rewrite their own corporate histories. There are many cases of global corporations that have (and are) engaged in the process of retrospective falsification. They all have some serious skeletons in their corporate wardrobes that they would prefer us to forget about, many dating back to Vietnam and even WWII.[28.1]

Governments constantly employ retrospective falsification in education constantly to alter the next generation's view of history in order to fit their current political agenda. For instance, the use of a history textbook sceptical about Britain's entry into the EU was published in 2008 and immediately employed in the British A level curriculum after the

Conservative party came into power.[28.3]

28.5.3 Shoehorning: Shoehorning is the process of force-fitting some current affairs into a personal, political, or religious agenda.

So-called "psychics" frequently shoehorn events to fit vague statements they made in the past. This is an extremely safe procedure, since they can't be proven wrong, and many people aren't aware of how easy it is to make something look like confirmation of a claim after the fact, especially if you give them wide latitude in making the shoe fit.

It is common, for instance, for the famous "prophecies" of Nostradamus to be "shoehorned" with events which match his vague texts rather than his texts actually truly predicting anything at all.

Shoehorning is also extremely popular in political manipulation where the manipulator uses events to demonstrate the validity of their political standpoint and justify their position.

28.5.3.1 Example: After the attacks on the World Trade Centre and the Pentagon on September 11, 2001, fundamentalist Christian evangelists Jerry Falwell and Pat Robertson shoehorned the events to fit their agenda. They claimed that "liberal civil liberties groups, feminists, homosexuals and abortion rights supporters bear partial responsibility... because their actions have turned God's anger against America." According to Falwell, his God allowed "the enemies of America...to give us probably what we deserve." Robertson agreed. The American Civil Liberties Union has "got to take a lot of blame for this," said Falwell and Robertson. Federal courts bear part of the blame, too, said Falwell, because they've been "throwing God out of the public square". Also "abortionists have got to bear some burden for this because God will not be mocked," said Falwell, with Robertson agreeing.

Neither Falwell nor Robertson has any way of proving any of their claims, as they are by their nature unprovable. But such claims can't be disproved, either. Their purpose is simply to call attention to their agenda and to get free publicity in the news media.

28.6 Avoidance and Counteraction: There is only one way to recognise and avoid historical manipulation, and that is to have a better and more rounded knowledge of human history than the manipulator.

Accept only properly tested historical facts and refuse all assumptions.

---oOo---

29. "We, the people" fallacy

29.1 Definition: This is a method of gaining popularity in which politicians pretend to have the same origins and motivations as the "common folk". The manipulative politician implies that they have a proper understanding of and sympathy for the daily strife of "ordinary" working people.

Politicians almost always talk about "what the people feel", but really, there is no such thing as "the people". It is just a discursive device for summoning "the people" that the politicians want to or pretend to represent.

The use of this fallacy in political manipulation is similar in form to the "plain folk" technique discussed earlier in this book.

29.2 Persistence: Short to Long. Winston Churchill is still perceived as a politician of "the people" despite his family relationship with the Royal family and the higher echelons of the British aristocracy. And that myth was created more than 70 years ago.

29.3 Accessibility: Low to Medium: This is really only available to existing members of the political classes.

29.4 Conditions/Opportunity/Effectiveness: This is a predominantly political technique used to try and alter the perception of a politician. It is therefore really only available to active politicians.

It can be very effective in creating a long term impression that a politician, political party or other leader has sympathy with "ordinary people". It can be hard and time-consuming to dismantle an impression of empathy with the electorate. Attempts to undermine the manipulator in this case may lead to accusations of sour grapes and dirty tricks by the manipulator.

29.5 Methodology/Refinements/Sub-species: There are five basic sub-types of this manipulative method:

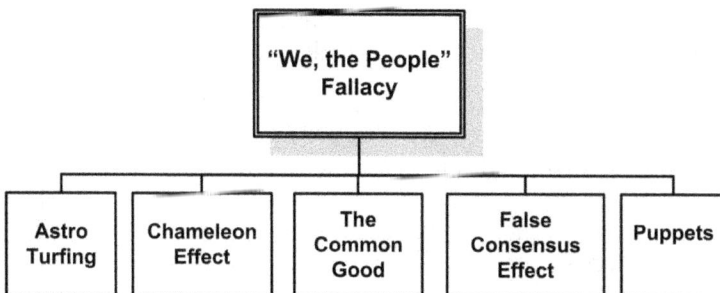

29.5.1 Astro-turfing: This is the manipulative technique of paying or employing people or groups to appear to be part of a "grass roots" movement. This is really a fraudulent rent-a-crowd technique that is often used in undemocratic or poorly regulated democratic regimes, including the USA, where the use of money in politics is not properly regulated or policed. However, this technique can also be found in more regulated societies where payment is not made in money but by means of influence.

29.5.2 Chameleon effect: This is the ability of a politician to adapt to their surroundings, or to portray what his audience wants to see. This effect is reinforced by a lack of details about a candidate. Generally, the more unknown or mysterious the "real" politician is, the more effective he can be at imitation and misrepresentation.

All successful politicians seem to be proficient at this tactic, but some figures are so shadowy and disingenuous, that this ability can take on a comical effect for observant members of the public. One of the funniest cases is when Hillary Clinton pretended to sound like she was from a southern US state while giving a speech on civil rights.

29.5.3 The Common Good: This is the technique where politicians make political justifications for good causes or the common good, which may be insincere.

These appeals to the "common good" are used by almost all politicians. The only question which separates their use is the honesty of intention. For some politicians it is a sincere intention, whilst for some manipulative politicians it is just a cynical appeal for support from the "common folk".

29.5.4 False-consensus effect: This is the tendency of a person or group to overestimate how much other people agree with them. This can be a deliberate attitude or it can be the result of a failure to properly understand the range of views of the general population. There is a tendency for people to assume that their own opinions, beliefs, preferences, values and habits are "normal" and shared by everyone in society.

This attitude tends to lead to the idea of a consensus that does not actually exist, a 'false consensus'. This false consensus is significant because it increases the self-esteem of the individual.

In organised groups, such as political parties, government and corporate organisations, the effect is often promoted internally to maintain group morale and self-esteem. It is also protected externally to bolster the illusion of an organisation having wide-ranging public support. This "fake consensus" is seen to have a positive impact in creating and maintaining real support and real consensus.

29.5.5 Puppets: This is a phenomenon where a politician appears to be independent but is actually a puppet of special interests or hidden parties. The phrase is often used when a local election is fought by "a puppet".

In the context of the "We the People" fallacy, puppet politicians who really are popular with the electorate are often used to front an unpopular political party. The puppet may appear to be a true representative of the people but really he is just a tool of a cynical and manipulative political party.

29.6 Avoidance and Counteraction: As with other forms of manipulation, it is important to maintain a healthy suspicion of those who are seeking us out as "friends".

Generally, no politician looks for friends or allies unless they have something to gain.. Beware anyone claiming to be a "man of the people", it is something that shouldn't need to be said if the person genuinely is one of the "common folk".

---o0o---

30. Ritualism

30.1 Definition: Ritualism can be best described as a solemn or formal activity or procedure which refers to or reaffirms an important premise, like the existence of God or the power of the sovereign.

All ritualism is manipulative. It has no intrinsic reasons for being, except to alter the perceptions of its victims in a way which benefits a manipulator.

Ritualism is used to confer an importance on an individual, a group or an event. It is used in religion and politics, in group and social contexts and in interpersonal manipulation.

30.2 Persistence: Short to Long, depending on whether its associated premise remains believable.

30.3 Accessibility: Low - This form of manipulation is really only available to institutions like governments, monarchies, religions etc.

30.4 Conditions/Opportunity/Effectiveness: At first sight, it wouldn't appear that ritualism is very relevant in a discussion of manipulation in a modern context. Most of us consider ritualism in terms of some kind of religious activity of our distant past, with little place in the life of modern industrial man. This is not the case, though. Ritualism is alive and well in modern society.

30.4.1 Ritualism is not just part of a religion: A narrow religious view of ritualism gives only part of the picture. Ritualism extends far beyond religion. When we understand ritualism in the broader sense of attempting the affirmation or reaffirmation of a premise, concept or philosophy, then the manipulative uses of ritualism suddenly become much more extensive.

In the case of, say, "Holy Communion", the church is reaffirming certain theological assumptions. In the case of the ubiquitous monthly stock take, a management may be saying to its workers: "We're in control and we're watching you in case you steal from us".

We tend to believe that political rituals are irrational and irrelevant, but they are also demonstrations of power by powerful institutions. If nothing else, they lend an impression of continuity and respectability to the proceedings of which they are a part.

Governments and managements still prefer the use of all kinds of taboos and rituals to that of force, when they are trying to establish a code of behaviour, or gain a victim's respect for and fear of their institutions.

There are several pre-conditions required for ritualism to work as a manipulative method:

- Everyone must share in it.

- Everyone must be convinced by it.

- The perceptions created by the ritual must not appear to stem from or be promoted by any manipulative elite group or individual.

- A ritual must incorporate potent and unverifiable premises, such as - in the case of a religious ritual - the existence of a deity.

30.5 Methodology/Refinements/Sub-species: There are four basic types of ritual available to the manipulator: Magico-religious, status or constitutive, schematizing and representational. The following illustrates the differences between them:

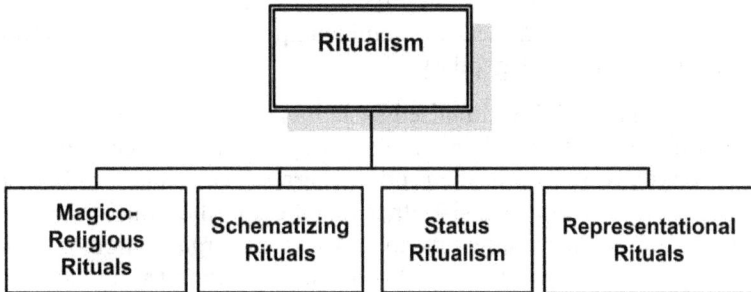

30.5.1 Magico-religious rituals: These are often assumed to be limited to primitive societies and the religious community. They certainly appear to have no place in modern government or management.

The use of magico-religious rituals in the manipulation of the masses has it's origins in prehistoric times. The Romans knew all about the potency of the technique, as demonstrated in the widespread building of temples in every imperial outpost. There's no doubt religion has underpinned civil jurisdiction, excused or participated in the widespread oppression of the masses in western society. In Europe, the church was omnipresent in daily life until very recently.

Machiavelli, that great theorist of manipulative government, although an anti-cleric, believed that the citizen should be encouraged to "occupy himself enthusiastically with religion". Machiavelli knew quite well that the tenets of Christianity would certainly contribute to keeping the masses pliable, because a civil government could always appeal to the divinity of their right to rule, or to the moral codes underlying civil law.[30.1]

Marx and others demolished the myth of religion's role and it's rituals a century ago, but we still, have Kings and Queens who are heads of the state religion, some Western civil states still swear-in their presidents and prime ministers on the bible, and so we cannot dismiss the role of these rituals completely.

In Business Management? In the context of the modern commercial world, respect for the magico-religious ritual has to some extend been replaced by a kind of "civil" religion, which surfaces as an underlying respect for a broad code of social order, based on conventional religious morality. You shouldn't steal from your employer, you should be honourable to your employer, and you should cooperate with your colleagues, etc. So, religious morality is definitely not entirely irrelevant in modern commercial management. It is not beyond reason that someone wishing to manipulate a victim may make reference to the tenets of Christian or other religious beliefs held by a victim, in a rhetorical way. The role of organisations like the Free Masons or Scientology in business is well known. The usefulness of membership of other secret societies like Opus Dei in business is legendary.

These groups have highly ritualised systems for initiation of new members and identifying each other in public. They use some very strange and antique-looking ritualism in the routine operations of their "brotherhoods". They use their network to assist other members in their business interests, and use their business interests to assist their organisation. A lot has already been written on the subject of these organisations, but suffice it to say that when considering manipulation in commerce, religion often turns up to be the joker in the pack of an astute manipulative manager or chief executive.

30.5.2 Status-ritualism: This technique involves the playing out by a subject of a procedure or structured activity under a set of artificial rules imposed by a manipulator.

The individual participating in the ritual may be either a victim or the manipulator himself, with the audience as his victims. It makes reference to a strict convention. Status ritualism first confers upon an individual a role, an authority or a responsibility, and then is used to invoke that position.

This invocation is central to the acceptance of the validity of the subject's role by others.

Examples of status-ritualism are to be found in corporate personnel recruitment. For example, the formal interview and an employee's induction process embody all kinds of ritualistic protocols designed to subjugate the candidate to the will of the employer. A new employee arriving for his first day of work is formally introduced to his superiors and colleagues. His status and their future mutual relationships are set. The process is a solemn and structured affair. He is then formally trained before commencing his duties. The visibility of his training is the necessary invocation of his new role.

This formal ceremony must be played out for the victim to be properly initiated, for him to be accepted into his particular group by the other members, and for him to really feel and become part of his new "club".

There are many forms of status-ritual: Graduation from university, first communion, medal giving, knighthoods etc., awards like the Oscars, the Nobel prizes etc

30.5.2 Schematizing rituals: Here the concept of "truth" and the manipulation of natural power are the primary considerations of the participants. The scientific, technical, legal community are all ideal cases of groups which indulge in this type of ritual, but it is by no means exclusive to them.

This method of ritualistic manipulation tends to be associated with the use of strange coded language, which only the elite ritual participants can understand, and with a preoccupation with certain forms of logical methodology which are totally alien to most of the human population.

Along with being generally lazy, most of us are naturally fairly sloppy when it comes to being objective. "Objectivity" is the high altar of many of these rituals and the participants develop methods of working, communicating, innovating, and gaining insight, which are quite outside the understanding of non-participants. The use of abbreviation in language is a typical trait in schematizing ritualism.

Apart from their core objective of "seeking truth", one of the main priorities of these elite groups is the exclusion of non-initiates from access to information and methodologies held or understood only by the elite group itself. Science must be left to the scientists, law to the lawyers and technology to the technologists.

30.5.3 Representational rituals: These occur at certain moments in everyone's life. They are designed to mark, memorialize, and demonstrate to others a milestone in an individual or group's history, such as graduation or retirement.

For instance, when a doctor finally takes the Hippocratic Oath, he is affirming his new status. They are also used to demonstrate or reaffirm a status, and in this sense, victims can have their status set for them by a manipulator. Such is the case in making inferior seating arrangements for a black audience in comparison with that of a white audience attending a South African cricket match during the apartheid years.[30.2]

Another common manipulative use of this type of ritual is the demonstration of an external threat which really doesn't exist - by marking out certain events as historically significant. Such was the case in the political witch hunt for non-existent communists by the FBI under McCarthy et al in the USA.[30.3] We were all led to believe that communism had "come of age", it had achieved nuclear potential and it was about to take over the free world. US-led paranoia drove us all in the Western world into a ritualistic hatred of "the Soviets".

30.6 Avoidance and Counteraction: The most obvious hazard in using ritualistic manipulation of any kind from a manipulator's point of view, is the possibility of it's no longer being adhered to or taken seriously by a potential victim. Once the ethos surrounding a ritual has been discredited, its existence becomes irrelevant. To protect against this eventuality, a manipulator designing a ritual must incorporate unverifiable "facts" in the ritual. In addition to this, the elites which participate in rituals (either knowingly or otherwise) must be effectively motivated to perpetuate the practice of the ritual by a wide range of tangible rewards, favours and personal gratification.

To avoid the power of ritualism, a victim must never accept any premises which cannot be rationally proven, demonstrable and repeatable. A victim must insist on a proper explanation of all potentially manipulative rituals, their contents and their reasons. Generally, the basis of ritualistic acts becomes rather absurd when questioned.

This "test everything" strategy can very quickly result in a manipulator running short of rational explanations or justifications for their rituals. After all, it's hard to sell the idea of rolling up one's trouser leg as a necessary and rational action to any sane human being, or the concept that we are all reincarnations of creatures from other planets as a likely explanation for the origin of our species. As some point the validity of the manipulator's premises start wearing very thin.

---oOo---

31. Sport and manipulation

31.1 Definition: This section describes the use of sport as a means to manipulate diplomatic, social, and political relations.

If ever there was a perfect marriage, one would be hard pressed to find a more compatible couple than sport and politics. The use of sport in social control is truly ancient and it has had both positive and negative implications over the years. Both the ancient Greeks and Romans used sport to entertain, placate and distract their populations, whilst simultaneously demonstrating their physical prowess to the world.

Sport is also used to manipulate domestic populations and to distract their attention from more pressing issues, like poverty, war or political controversy, and to absorb the time and energy of the masses. The Roman poet Juvenal in 100AD described the shallowness and ignorance of the people in being more interested in "bread and games". The phrase is still used today to imply the erosion and ignorance of civic duty amongst the concerns of the "common man".

In more recent times, sporting events have been and are used as an excellent adjunct to propaganda campaign. Jingoistic sentiments are often linked to victories or losses on the sports field. Grand sporting events like the Olympics are used as a means of projecting state power, nationalist sentiments and unifying populations in nationalist fervour.

Sometimes sport is used to build diplomatic bridges between groups or nations that are antagonistic towards each other. Sports competitions or activities have had the intention to bring about change (improvements) in relationships.

31.2 Persistence: Short - Medium. Sport can be influential in altering national attitudes, changing social behaviour and in uniting or dividing whole populations.

31.3 Accessibility: High. Almost anyone can organise a sporting event which may have some hidden agenda, such as engendering antipathy or unity, or demonstrating prowess. However, the use of sport in manipulation is generally restricted to government or managements of larger companies.

Sport in the 21st century is about huge amounts of money; the days of a small local club with a few men running around a field on a Saturday afternoon chasing a football are long gone. Sport is now big, global business.

31.4 Conditions/Opportunity/Effectiveness: Enthusiasm for sport tends to be at its height in poorer and/or less well-educated groups of the population. Those parts of our society with the least opportunities and the greatest social and economic problems tend to exhibit the strongest interest in sport, because it provides a release from their often mundane existence.

This group also tends to represent the majority of the population in many Western industrial societies. Governments and other potential manipulators know all this. They therefore focus their manipulative efforts on using sport as a means of social control. They target these population groups with government produced, sports related propaganda and subliminal nationalist agendas etc.

In the Western world, right-wing governments tend to be more enthusiastic about sport than left-wing governments. This is because right-wing governments tend to be more connected to, and sponsored by, the big business interests which drive large-scale consumer sport. However, as a manipulative tool, sport has used been by all parts of the political spectrum.

As a political and diplomatic tool in international relations, sport can be useful, positive and effective. It is easy and cheap to use and has had some successes in the past in defusing dangerous diplomatic situations. In a negative diplomatic sense, sport can also be effective at alienating and vilifying an adversary.

31.5 Methodology/Refinements/Sub-species: There are several sub-types for the manipulative use of sport:

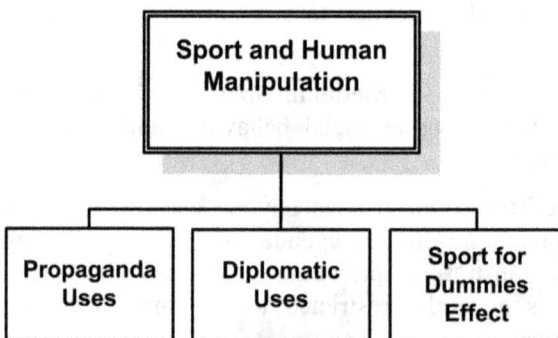

31.5.1 Propaganda Uses: There are several ways in which sport can be manipulated to fit into a larger program of propaganda. This propaganda can be designed for national or external consumption:

National supremacy: All international sporting events carry with them some attempt to demonstrate the (sporting) supremacy of a particular nation - that is their purpose after all. It is harmless enough when it isn't meant to be taken seriously. However, there have been cases where sport has been used to seriously attempt to demonstrate racial supremacy.

The obvious example would be the use of the Olympic Games in Berlin, Germany in 1936 by the Nazi party. Hitler saw the Games as an opportunity to promote his government and ideals of racial supremacy. The official Nazi party paper, the "Völkischer Beobachter" wrote in the strongest terms that Jews and Black people should not be allowed to participate in the Games.

Under threat of a boycott of the games, the Nazis were obliged to relent and allow Jewish and Black people to participate, although (with one exception) all German Jewish and Roma participants were forbidden to participate. In the event, the Nazis used the games to showcase the strength of the Nazi party to the world.

National projection: The vast budgets available for the major international sporting events like the World Cup, the Olympics or Formula I racing provide a way for national governments to project their power and the wealth of their nations on visiting audiences and to the global television teams that attend these events.

In ancient Greece, huge organised games were often staged in order to encourage health and exercise, military sporting prowess (like javelin throwing), but also to demonstrate to the world that Greece was a potent military force.

In the recent London Olympics, the British government brought this militaristic sub-plot to a new level by placing anti-aircraft missile batteries on top of apartment blocks in central London[31.1] and having a large armed naval presence in the Thames in addition to several layers of police and military security. The entire event was more akin to an international arms fair than a civilian games event for the pleasure of sporting participants and the public. At the same event, the British government also took the opportunity to make strong cultural statements about the United Kingdom's history, its "freedom and democracy" in an enormous Hollywood style extravaganza, which was shown around the world and cost an absolute fortune. The entire exercise took place against a back drop of Britain and the rest of the western world entering its longest period of economic recession in 80 years, massive government cuts, unemployment, poverty and seething social unrest.

Jingoistic manipulation: International sporting events are second only to a war in terms of their ability to generate strong nationalist sentiments and jingoism. Indeed George Orwell referred to large international sporting events as "vicarious war" meaning "a war minus the shooting".

These nationalistic manifestations are, of course, encouraged by governments for several reasons:

- Nationalism unites people in a common cause against an external "enemy".

- Nationalism puts the government in a good light as the leaders of the nation.

- Nationalism uses time and energy which might otherwise be directed against the government by the people.

- Nationalism encourages the use of negative stereotypes against other nations, which may well fit the political philosophy and agenda of a government.

Internal propaganda and social control: Sport has a long history in supporting a wider domestic political narrative as part of a propaganda campaign. Sometimes, the manipulative use of sport is applied to domestic and foreign affairs at the same time - as in Cuba since the revolution.

During the Cold War we see that sport was considered to be highly important in many "Eastern Bloc" countries. In Cuba, for instance, sport is still seen as being bound up with vital domestic and international issues because:

a. Sport is used as an ideological support to the Cuban version of socialism,

b. Sport has been used in Cuba to contribute to the creation of a post-revolutionary spirit of national identity and collective solidarity,

c. Through sport, in very different ways, Cuba has been able to define and develop its relationship with two of the world's super powers.

In Cuba, since 1959, sport has been deliberately and unashamedly manipulated as a vehicle for the inculcation of the ideals of the revolution and the development of socialist and communist values. After the revolution, many people fled to the United States and sport was used in the service of nationalism, for uniting the population and establishing a shared national identity by Castro's fledgling regime.

In much the same way as the West Indies once celebrated world superiority in cricket as a symbolic victory over their former colonial oppressor - England-, so too do Cubans see their prowess at certain sports as a means of equalizing their relationship with the United States, particularly if they can do well in American sports and/or beat the US in world competitions. More on this subject anon.

31.5.2 Diplomatic Uses: Sporting events have often been used to "break the ice" in diplomatic impasses. But sport can be used to send either negative or positive signals to another nation. Sports diplomacy is attractive to governments, partly because international sport adds to the pursuit of foreign policy goals, but also because of the subtlety and malleability of sports diplomacy. Leaders can meet on the periphery of a sporting event and develop some kind of camaraderie as a pre-cursor to more serious diplomatic discussions. Here are just a few of the many examples of how sport is used and affected by political and diplomatic initiatives:

Cuba versus U.S.A. baseball: Despite the frosty relations between the USA and Cuba, baseball matches between the countries continued until 1996 - when relations between the two countries became especially frosty following the Cuban shooting down of two small planes entering Cuban airspace to drop anti-Castro pamphlets. In 2012 the baseball matches resumed as relations began to warm somewhat under the auspices of Barack Obama and Raul Castro. Both Cubans and Americans share a passion for this particular sport.

China and the USA: One of the best known cases of the political use of sport is the one from the early 1970s, when attempts were being made to improve relations between the US and China. Following an invitation from the Chinese in 1971, the United States sent a table tennis team to the PRC, followed, a year later, by a basketball team. The sports were carefully chosen for their diplomatic value; it was expected that the Chinese would win at table tennis and the Americans at basketball with no loss of face on either side.

Other examples: Sport was used in a similar fashion during a period of great tension between the United States and the former Soviet Union. In the late 1950s, US troops were in the Lebanon and British forces were in Jordan ostensibly to forestall Soviet expansion, and Khrushchev talked of the world being on the brink of catastrophe. At the same time the US and the former USSR initiated an annual track and field competition which, while at times reflecting the tensions of the Cold War, generally provided opportunities for diplomatic bridge-building.

31.5.3 Sport for Dummies - Sport as social control: In many societies, sport has largely replaced religion as the great "opiate of the people" and very often this has happened with the continued enthusiasm of a manipulative government.

However, sport is also a force for social integration, and it has often provided powerful opportunities for the creation of political oppositions. Thus there are several reasons why sport can be useful as a manipulative method in social control and why politicians find it so important to keep an eye on it:

- **Social integration:** Social integration is one of the important aspects of social control. It is a loose term which covers a wide range of policy objectives, including combating juvenile delinquency, establishing a sense of community during periods of rapid urbanization and the integration of diverse ethnic groups. One motive for state involvement in sport (and one of the most common) is the belief that sport imbues the populace with the right type of values and norms: of obedience, self-discipline, team-work, and therefore: participation in sport will facilitate social integration and thus further achieve social control.

  For instance, in Northern Ireland there was an extensive program of investment in public sport and recreational facilities aimed at bridging the gap between the Catholic/Nationalist and Protestant/Unionist communities. In a similar fashion, in Great Britain during the 1970s, the role of sport in preventing youth delinquency and vandalism was clearly expressed in various White Papers. The UK Government publication, 'Sport and Recreation', which was published by the Department of the Environment in 1975, emphasized the importance of the role of sport and physical recreation as follows: "For many people physical activity makes an important contribution to physical and mental well-being…by reducing boredom and urban frustration, participation in active recreation contributes to the reduction of hooliganism and delinquency among young people".

  We can also extend this social integration idea into the work routines of a capitalist / industrial economy through an acceptance of the language, reasoning and governing structures of modern sports. In addition, sport is also used as a means to promote traditional values and social arrangements, such as gender roles and sexuality in society. For instance, in the US, sport is used to transmit the values of success in competition, hard work, perseverance, discipline, teamwork and obedience to authority, to participants and observers. This is the explicit reason given for the existence of children's sports programs such as "Little League" baseball and the tremendous emphasis on sports in US schools.

  The use of golf in business management in some cultures, as a means of social integration between members of the same socio-economic group is another instance of how sport is used to form alliances and exert influence - in the case of golf, often between capitalists with shared interests.

- **Political opposition:** Sport has often provided an opportunity for political opposition, especially in repressive regimes. For example, in Korea, during the Japanese colonial period, the formation of sports groups was among the ways in which Koreans could organize against Japanese cultural and political hegemony and encourage independence from the Japanese.

In South Africa, during the apartheid period, visits by foreign teams provided black South Africans with the opportunity to voice their support for the anti-apartheid movement.

In Ireland, in the decades leading up to the uprising against the British crown forces in 1916, the nationalist movement had formed a complex alter-culture of Gaelic sporting organisations which covered the entire country with an ostensibly harmless network of sporting groups, organising teams, Gaelic sports training and regular games. This organisation was later used as a means of organising opposition to British rule and as a means of arming and organising the Irish population prior to the uprising. It is still in existence (GAA) and very popular, and continues to have a strong Irish nationalist political outlook.[31.2]

In many European countries, football has sadly become a rallying point for extreme right-wing groups like the British National Party. Racist insults are screamed at non-white players and pitches are often awash with dangerous objects thrown at players and officials. The stereotypical shaven-headed racist-fascist thug has unfortunately turned much ordinary football into an unwatchable fiasco.

- **The Opiate Effect:** Apart from the use of sport as a force for both positive and negative affiliation, many popular sports have had a very negative effect on a large segment of Western society, (and this is) because strong sporting affiliations tend to distract populations away from real-life political issues in which they should take an active interest.

Many sporting enthusiasts find the camaraderie and "group-think" of a sporting event comforting and they loose themselves in an enthusiasm for something which is, after all, completely unreal. Sport offers an alternative agenda to many suffering from the very real cognitive dissonance between their real lives and their aspirations. Through sport they can escape the inevitable reality of their often miserable existence. Religion and narcotics have the same effect.

This effect is very useful to both governments and managements, because it "keeps the lid on the pot" of an often discontented population, and relax a situation which could otherwise rapidly make both management and government very difficult in many capitalist economies.

To this end, most western governments and many capitalist companies are very enthusiastic about sport. It is somewhat akin to sending the kids out to play football with their pals so that when they come home again they will be tired, easy to control and go off to bed without any fuss. That is the main role of sport in modern capitalist society - as a tiring distraction for the masses to keep their mind off any real radical political action.

31.6 Avoidance and Counteraction: Sport as a means of having physical exercise is absurd. It produces nothing in terms of value. If the objective was simply to have some healthy exercise, would it not be more beneficial to tackle some socially or personally useful physical work? After all there is an endless supply of things which need to be done in the world and which could provide any of us with physical exercise.

But it isn't about exercise, is it? Sport is actually about something much more primitive and manipulative than simply having enough healthy physical exertion. Sport has a lot to do with maintaining a sense of communal union, solidarity, and it has a lot to do with escapism.

Sport provides a sort of tribal alternative to the depressing grind of daily life at a personal and social level. It opens opportunities for the expression of some very primordial instincts of violence, but without the blood. Ultimately, it is soothing and secure, whilst remaining sociable, exciting and predictable.

As a manipulative method, sport is one of the best there is. The victim is almost always willing; the manipulator meets no resistance and needs no encouragement to participate, either as a player or a spectator. Like lambs to the slaughter we waste our lives, our intellect, our energy and our enthusiasm watching endlessly futile and repetitive sporting events like heroin junkies. Meanwhile, outside of our sport-induced haze, the real world passes us by.

There is only one way to avoid manipulation by means of sport, and that is simply to ignore it in all its forms and rejoin the real world.

---oOo---

32. Complex manipulative techniques - Statistical manipulation

32.1 Definition: This is a group of manipulative methods used to convey incorrect or misleading messages to victims, using obscure and often very complex arguments.

The arguments used and messages being delivered derive from various methodologies, like statistical or other scientific or mathematical analyses. Most of these are incomprehensible to the average victim, and this makes any kind of defence very difficult or even impossible.

32.2 Origins and motivation: It is interesting to see how groups and individual manipulators tend to come up with a hypothesis and then work to prove it right, instead of working to prove it wrong. Once satisfied, the manipulator stops searching.

This works for the individual as well. We often seek safe havens for our ideology with friends and co-workers who are like minded and have similar attitudes. We use only those media outlets which are guaranteed to reinforce our existing views. We rarely deliberately allow or encourage our conclusions to be tested, or our preconceptions to be challenged.

Statistical manipulation is a mathematical and logical adjunct to this strategy of seeking confirmation, because it relies on most people not being able to challenge its conclusions and therefore not bothering to even try. If the manipulator's message fits the victim's philosophical expectations, then why bother to challenge it or understand the terribly complex statistical methodology?

32.3 Methodology: The methodologies used in statistical manipulation are an inscrutable cover to the manipulator, because they are effectively opaque to the vast majority of the victim population. Because of this, a victim is obliged to accept a seemingly credible message simply because they have no way of verifying or denying it.

These types of manipulation are considered "complex", because they employ carefully chosen methods which require that the manipulator has an advanced understanding of certain scientific methodologies, such as statistical analysis. They rely on the generally poor understanding of these subjects by the victim (often the public) and the fact that the cost to the victim of disproving an assertion is too high and maybe just too difficult.

These manipulative methods also rely on the fact that the underlying manipulative scandal, if it is ever revealed, is often too complex to communicate in a single sound bite. Thus, this type of manipulative act doesn't always get the instant attention or interest of the victims that it deserves.

These techniques are effective in obscuring a proper intellectual understanding by the victim of some central reality of the chosen subject.

All scientific methodologies can be used to cover some attempted manipulation. Science is now so specialised and generally so poorly understood by the general public, that a manipulator can deliver an important set of messages before anyone gets time to contradict them. These days we are constantly bombarded by seemingly credible study results about our health and our diet. Many of these studies are complex, many have seemingly contradictory results and all claim a certain degree of accuracy. However, we don't totally understand the study, the results or the degree of reliability. For this reason, none of the sciences are better suited to the purpose of widespread manipulation than the use of statistical analysis.

This is a subject so open to debate and so poorly understood that it is ripe for misuse by a manipulator. And so we have focused here on the misuse of statistics. The use of complex manipulative techniques should not be confused with the manipulation derived from the "politicization of science", which is related but different. We deal with this subject in a separate chapter.

32.4 Methodology/Refinements/Sub-species: Here are the most often employed methods of statistical manipulation:

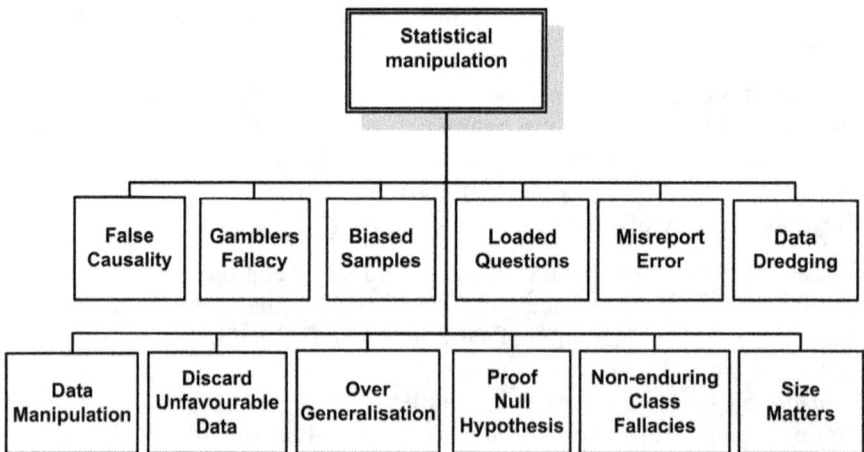

Being such a complex topic, the following chapters deal with each of these subjects separately.

32.5 Avoidance and Counteraction: The subject matter and methodologies used to deliver statistically manipulated messages is so difficult to understand for most of the general public that this form of manipulation is very hard to detect, avoid and contradict.

Again, this method relies on the very high cost to the victim of disproving the manipulator's assertions.

There are two possible avoidance and counteraction strategies for the victim:

- The first is to become personally familiar with statistical analysis and methodology. This may be a tall order for the average person.

- The second is to enlist a professional statistician to undermine the manipulator's arguments, if they are based on illicit statistical assumptions.

Fortunately for the victim, a properly phrased and credible denial of a statistical manipulator's assertions can deliver a knockout blow to the manipulator at a relatively low cost to the victim.

A victim needs to deliver this counterattack using highly credible and respectable expert sources in a properly argued case. A victim also needs to make their response more understandable and more reasonable than the manipulator's original assertion.

---oOo---

33. Statistical manipulation - False causality

33.1 Definition: The first thing to acknowledge is that "false causality" is not always manipulative. It can result from human error and the poor design of an experiment or the delivery of data. However, this is such a well known problem in scientific research that any excuse of human error doesn't really stand up to scrutiny unless an experiment has been designed and conducted in a totally unprofessional and unscientific way.

False Causality, (often just called the correlation fallacy or regression fallacy) seeks to make a victim conclude that there is a causal relationship between two events when in fact none exists. It takes advantage of the misconception that a correlation is the same as a causal relationship - which it most certainly is not.

A victim reaches this invalid conclusion based on the way the evidence is presented to him. The victim reaches the "self-evident" conclusion about an "obvious correlation" although any causal relationship between the data is ambiguous.

In political circles, this is an especially important technique. It allows political parties or individuals to demonstrate (disingenuously) that they are capable of making certain things happen. For instance, the technique is used to prove a politician's ability to bring about an increase in employment, GDP, personal income, whatever is on their political agenda. The technique is used to create an artificial perception which is beneficial to the manipulator's chances of (re-)election or acceptance.

In corporate circles, the technique is similarly employed to demonstrate the potency or safety of a product or service to a customer. It is also often used to demonstrate to shareholders, directors or employees that a corporate strategy is working, by "proving" correlations between improved business and a particular management strategy.

Similarly, this technique is used by government, corporate interests and individuals to demonstrate the safety or value of a behaviour based on previous historical precedence backed by copious amounts of obviously correlating, historical data.

33.2 Persistence: Short, Medium or Long.

33.3 Accessibility: Low. This is not generally for the layman, since it requires both a good understanding of statistics and the subject matter. It also requires access to some smart media presentation methods to deliver the manipulative message clearly and to a wide audience. Generally, this manipulative method is reserved for use by large corporations, political parties and governments.

33.4 Conditions/Opportunity/Effectiveness:

33.4.1 How does it work? False causality as a manipulative technique works, because most of us don't fully understand the relationships between cause and effect. There are several statistical techniques (like regression analysis) which can easily be used to demonstrate that a strong correlation exists between 2 or more sets of data.

For instance, when the temperature drops there is an increased incidence of the common cold. However, the correlation thus established, does not mean that we can jump to the conclusion that there is a causal relationship between the two data sets. It's not that simple.

33.4.2 Examples: The classic and absurd case used is a comparison between the number of people buying ice cream at the beach and the number of people who drown at the beach. A simple regression analysis will show that there is a strong correlation between these data. However, no-one would claim that ice cream causes drowning because it's obvious that this isn't so.

In this case, the drowning and the buying of ice cream are obviously related by a third factor, for instance the number of people at the beach, or the time of year etc.

A similar case compares the strong statistical correlation of the sales of blankets in London and the winter temperature in Toronto. Clearly the connecting variables are the latitude of both cities and the average night temperatures.

The list of cases of such "correlations without cause" is endless.

33.4.3 Correlation and Causality: So what are the real possibilities for cause and effect between data which appear to be very strongly correlated?

When a statistical test (like a regression analysis) shows a strong correlation between variables A and B, there are six possible scenarios in terms of causality:

- A causes B.
- B causes A.
- A and B both partly cause each other.
- A and B are both caused by a third factor, C.
- B is caused by C which is correlated to A.
- The observed correlation was due to chance alone.

This final possibility (just chance) can be established and quantified by various statistical tests that calculate the probability that the correlation observed would be as large as it is just by chance if, in fact, there is no relationship between the variables. So there is a way of eliminating this random correlation.

33.4.4 Manipulative applications: The false causality fallacy is used for all kinds of manipulative purposes.

Take, for example, a manipulator claims to prove that exposure to a particular chemical causes cancer. Using the simple ice-cream example above, we could make a similar and highly reasonable assertion for the incidence of cancer in a particular population and its exposure to a particular environmentally available chemical. In such a situation, there may be a statistical correlation even if there is no real causal effect. The existence of the chemical is actually just one of many potential causes, but by no means the only one.

For instance, in an industrial area, it may well be that there are higher cancer rates than in the more leafy suburbs or country areas far away from industrial sites. However, there is also a tendency for poorer people to live in or closer to industrial areas where real estate prices are lower. There is also a tendency for there to be more migrant workers of different ethnic origins in these communities, who have different medical profiles and propensities, and for these less-fortunate populations to have poorer diets, bad housing, higher levels of overcrowding etc. than those in more fortunate areas.

In other words, the high correlation between the environmental chemical concentration and the cancer incidence cannot, by itself, be taken to demonstrate causality.

However, such a correlation also demonstrates the possibility that there really is a causal relationship and that further investigation is required.

The discovery of nitro-glycerine as an important blood pressure reducing drug happened precisely because a number of workers in a large explosives factory suffering from angina (which included the boss), felt much better at work, where they ingested small amounts of nitro-glycerine, than they did at home. The correlation was noticed and investigated, resulting in the use, to this day, of nitro-glycerine as a life-saving drug.

33.5 Methodology/Refinements/Sub-species: There are two basic sub-types of the manipulative method of False Causality:

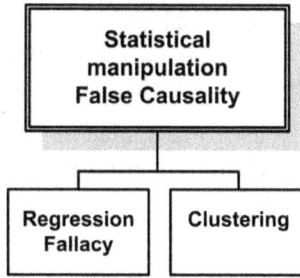

33.5.1 Regression fallacy: The regression fallacy is a failure to prove a causal relationship despite a strong correlation in a regression analysis.

The regression fallacy is a failure to take into account natural fluctuations in data when ascribing causes and it is also cause by overlooking other variables which may really have true causal links to otherwise unrelated data.

This phenomenon can be used to deliver a manipulative payload by attributing correlation between two sets of data, without proving any causal relationship. The world is full of obscure and irrelevant correlations, but to prove real cause and effect is a different matter.

33.5.1.1 Quack medical examples: Many people are led to believe in the causal effectiveness of worthless remedies, simply because of the regression fallacy. The intensity and duration of pain from arthritis, chronic backache, gout, etc., fluctuates. A remedy such as a chiropractic spinal treatment is usually sought when the pain is at its worst. The pain in most cases would begin to lessen after it has peaked. It is easy to deceive ourselves into thinking that the remedy we sought caused our reduction in pain. It is because of the ease with which we can deceive ourselves about causality in such matters, that scientists do controlled experiments to test these kinds of causal claims.

33.5.1.2 Big Pharma examples: A complex area of investigation at the moment is the use of drugs designed for one treatment and being used for an entirely different medical purpose. For the large pharmaceutical companies, this concept is a very attractive business opportunity because the costs of testing and licensing an existing drug for use in a different application are much, much lower than introducing a completely new drug.

A simple instance is the use of aspirin in the control of heart disease, but there are many more complex cases, like the use of Statin drugs in the possible control of various cancers. The practice of prescribing a drug normally used for one illness for a completely different ailment is called "Off Label Use", because its use not described in the drugs specification on the label.[33.1] For the pharmaceutical companies the practice of "off label use" is highly desirable because it opens up huge alternative markets for uses of their existing regulated drugs at very low cost.

The use of false causality as a manipulative method is very tempting in these circumstances. Correlations between a particular drug use and alternative medical benefits are being detected in patients that already have particular - pre-existing - conditions, such as high levels of cholesterol. The use of cholesterol-lowering drugs and a correlation with a lower incidence of colon cancer does not necessary prove a link between the drug and the benefit. It may well be that users of the Statin drugs are also receiving other related treatments which are actually the cause of the reduction in cancer incidence. It may well be that the lower levels of bad cholesterols is symptomatic of lower cancer propensities etc.

Extreme caution is required in responding to any correlative claims which cannot demonstrate causality.

33.5.2 Clustering illusion, aka the Texas sharpshooter fallacy, is a fallacy in which pieces of information that have no relationship to one another are highlighted because of their similarities, and that similarity is used to claim the existence of a pattern or correlation. The name comes from the joke about a Texan who fires some shots at the side of a barn, then paints a target centred on the biggest cluster of hits and claims to be a sharpshooter

33.5.2.1 Manipulative uses: In manipulation, a user claims that they take randomness into account when determining cause and effect, whereas in reality they do not. They may even deliberately choose a cluster to match their manipulative intent.

The manipulation works because, in reality, we all tend to ignore random chance when results seem meaningful, or when we (emotionally) want a random effect to have a meaningful cause. This irrational human tendency is known and used by the manipulator to prove a manipulative case to the victim.

33.5.2.2 Psychological origins and statistical explanations: In psychology, the effect is called "the clustering illusion". It describes the tendency in human cognition to interpret patterns in randomness where none actually exist. The clustering illusion is the intuition that random events which occur in clusters are not really random events.

The illusion is due to selective thinking, based on counterintuitive and false assumptions regarding statistical odds (see "The Gambler's Fallacy"). This is the idea that because, when tossing a coin, there is a 50% chance of getting heads or tails, that after 100 tosses of the coin giving heads, there is somehow a higher chance of getting tails. There isn't.

The clustering of a result like this in the short term is not at all unusual in nature, and this clustering phenomenon can be used to manipulatively imply or "demonstrate" some illicit conclusion to an unsuspecting victim.

For example, in epidemiological studies of cancer, finding a statistically unusual number of cancers in a given neighbourhood - such as six or seven times greater than the average - is not that rare or unexpected. Much depends on where you draw the boundaries of the neighbourhood and the demographics of a neighbourhood; these can radically affect the incidence. However, clusters of cancers that are seven thousand times higher than expected, such as the incidence of mesothelioma in Karian, Turkey, are very rare and unexpected. The incidence of thyroid cancer in children near Chernobyl was one hundred times higher after the disaster. Such clusters are the result of a real environmental cancer risk.

In epidemiology, Khaneman and Tversky called the clustering illusion the "belief in the Law of Small Numbers", because they identified the clustering illusion with the fallacy of assuming that the pattern of a large population will be replicated in all of its subsets.

Logically, this fallacy is known as the "fallacy of division", because it assumes that the parts must be exactly like the whole.

33.6 Avoidance and Counteraction: False Causality can be avoided by designing experiments to use so-called control groups, which are randomly selected to act as a "standard" against which to measure the results on an "affected group" or "treatment group".

But let us return to our example of the environmental chemical exposure and the incidence of cancer. In a statistically honest study, the effect of false causality can be eliminated by conducting tests using mammals similar to human beings. The researcher assigns some of the population to a treatment group and some to a so-called "control group". The assignment to each group is completely random. Then, in controlled tests the treatment group receives exposure to the suspected chemical agent and the control group receives no exposure. If the first group has higher cancer rates than the control group, the researcher knows that there is no "third factor" at play because he knows that he assigned subjects to the exposed and non-exposed groups completely at random. The causal relationship between the chemical exposure and the incidence of cancer is thus demonstrated.

If such tests of causality cannot be fully demonstrated, we can assume that a proposed causal relationship is just being manipulated

---o0o---

34. Statistical manipulation - the Gambler's fallacy

34.1 Definition: The gambler's fallacy is the mistaken notion that the odds for something with a fixed probability increase or decrease depending upon recent occurrences. This invalid concept is used in all kinds of ways by manipulators both in gambling and investment circles to persuade a victim to "stay at the table" because their "luck is bound to change".

The underlying notion of the gambler's fallacy works as follows: You might think that you can beat the odds by either selecting numbers that have not been chosen in recent draws, or by selecting numbers that have come up more frequently than expected in recent draws.

In either case, you are committing the gambler's fallacy. The fact of the matter is that the odds are always the same, no matter what numbers have been selected in the past and how frequently they were drawn.

This fallacy is commonly committed by gamblers who, for instance, bet on red at roulette when black has come up three times in a row. The odds of black coming up next are the same regardless of what colours have come up in previous turns.

The gambler's fallacy has led to some bizarre behaviour, like people blowing on the dice before throwing them or even talking to them in an attempt to influence the outcome. Obviously such rituals are based on some kind of misplaced, optimistic belief in the powers of magic, but they don't alter the rules of probability at all.

However, this basic and widespread misunderstanding means that gamblers are an easy target for the professional manipulator in both gambling and commercial circles.

The gambler's fallacy is not confined to gamblers: there is a general tendency to think that future probabilities are altered by past events, when in reality they are unchanged. For instance, an investor may argue, "I have made 10 bad investment decisions already; therefore my luck is bound to change soon".

It is a comforting idea, but it is absolute nonsense.

34.2 Persistence: Long. Potentially gamblers can be induced to continue playing indefinitely.

34.3 Accessibility: High. Most people will fall for this.

34.4 Conditions/Opportunity/Effectiveness: A general misunderstanding of statistical probability makes this a popular and easy- to- use vehicle for the manipulator. The fallacy is also very effective and self-reinforcing: when a victim fails to win again, they simply conclude that "next time they really just have to win" because their luck "just has to turn". If a victim does win, then that simply validates their belief in watching the table for a while before betting. The fallacy is so strongly felt by the victim, that regardless of the facts, everything that happens to the victim just validates their mistaken belief.

34.5 Methodology/Refinements/Sub-species: The phenomenon is also known as the "Monte Carlo fallacy", or the "Fallacy of the maturity of chances". There are no known sub-species.

34.6 Avoidance and Counteraction: The only way to avoid this manipulation is to read and understand a couple of chapters on probability before wasting money on gambling.

All gambling operations are designed to take money from the majority of players in order to pay out to a small number of big winners and of course the gambling operator. Lotteries, including government run lotteries, work on this basis as well. They are really no better than state-legalised pyramid schemes, designed for the benefit of a few big winners, using the total "investment" of the millions of losers.

As Kevin McKenna, the conservative journalist observed: "The most common dream of every "Bullingdon Tory" is the national lottery. And what a jolly wheeze it is: get the poor to fund our biggest capital projects in exchange for a cruel fairy story. (Sic)"

If one does happen to make a small gamble and also win - well then take your winnings, be happy, and never gamble again.

---oOo---

35. Statistical manipulation - Biased Sampling - Selective bias

35.1 Definition: This deals with manipulation based on "biased sampling". Biased sampling is also known as a form of "selective bias".

Many people may not realize that the randomness of a sample is very important. For instance, in practice, many opinion polls are conducted by phone, which already distorts the sample in several ways, i.e. the exclusion of people who do not have phones. It also favours the inclusion of people who have more than one phone, and, of course, those who are willing to participate in a phone survey over those who refuse, etc. Non-random sampling makes the estimated error associated with a particular sample size unreliable.

Selective bias also occurs when subjective choices of samples or study candidates are made based on some expectation, rather than being constructed by random. For example, in testing a drug, a laboratory may select candidates it thinks will be "good" trial subjects who will prove that the drug works very well. Sometimes, the bias is accidental - just sloppy test design - very often the bias is intentionally manipulative.

As a manipulative method, it attempts to control public opinion through the altering or filtering of results which promote the manipulator's chosen agenda, at the expense of the victim.

35.2 Persistence: Short to Long. The results of scientific studies based on a biased selection can have long term effects, unless they are quickly contradicted.

35.3 Accessibility: Low to Medium. Only people involved in experimental design or sampling can manipulate a sample selection. However, properly designed experiments are on the lookout for such interference and build in safeguards to avoid biased sampling. For instance, street surveyors will be required to have a properly balanced cross-section of samples, not just all men or women or all people of a certain age, etc.

News filtering as a form of sample bias is available only to those that have access to some form of media of news dissemination - this can be the internet of course, and therefore this manipulative technique is reasonably available to anyone. A website or blog can be made to select, filter and reproduce news items with a particular by-line; just news about human rights abuse, for instance.

35.4 Conditions/Opportunity/Effectiveness: This manipulative technique can be used in polling, product testing, sociological, medical, environmental and political studies, anywhere in fact where one or more sample groups are involved and where the sample groups should be selected without bias.

It is highly effective because it is obscured to the victim unless a manipulator chooses to reveal the detailed method of sample selection, which they obviously would not.

35.5 Methodology/Refinements/Sub-species: Selective bias comes in at least five flavours:

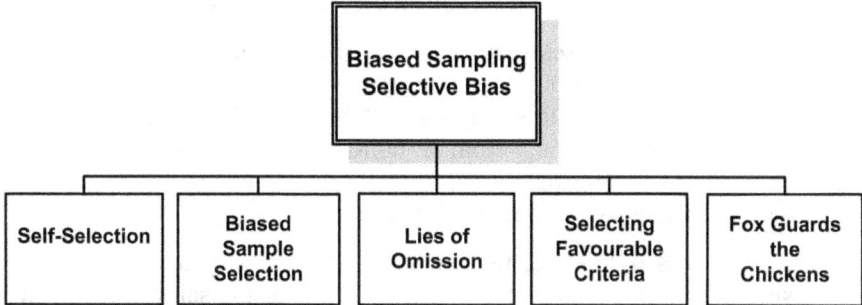

```
                    ┌─────────────────────┐
                    │  Biased Sampling    │
                    │  Selective Bias     │
                    └─────────────────────┘
   ┌────────────┬────────────┬──────────┬────────────┬────────────┐
┌──────────┐┌──────────┐┌──────────┐┌──────────┐┌──────────┐
│ Self-    ││ Biased   ││ Lies of  ││Selecting ││Fox Guards│
│Selection ││ Sample   ││ Omission ││Favourable││ the      │
│          ││Selection ││          ││ Criteria ││ Chickens │
└──────────┘└──────────┘└──────────┘└──────────┘└──────────┘
```

35.5.1 Self-selection. This is the accidental or deliberate selection of certain individuals to participate in a survey, or as a subject in an experimental study. This happens when individuals nominate themselves as participants in a study or survey or when a study designer or pollster nominates individuals using a limited selection process. The result is a biased sample.

"Self selection" is often used to describe a situation where the characteristics of the selected people in the survey create skewed figures.

For example, a right-wing newspaper survey of its readers will inevitably give rise to results which are biased by the self-selected participants, i.e. vocal and right-wing.

In commercial polling circles, a poll suffering from this kind of bias is termed a self-selecting opinion poll or "SLOP" poll. It is a common form of manipulative mechanism and fairly easy to recognise and discredit by its victims.

35.5.1.1 Pre-screening: Another hybrid of self-selection is "pre-screening", where the organisers of a poll or study deliberately or accidentally screen parts of the sample population, in order to manipulate the likely outcome of the poll or study.

Methods of polling already "accidentally" force certain pre-screening biases on the sample population. For instance, telephone polls already screen out members of the population without a telephone.

35.5.1.2 Conclusion: Self-selection makes it very difficult for a statistician to determine causation, because it is impossible for a researcher or a manipulator's victim to know whether the conclusions of a study resulted from real causes or simply from the biases of self-selected samples.

As a result of self-selection, there are often other factors affecting an outcome than just the cause itself. Self-selection bias causes problems to evaluate a product's usefulness for ordinary members of the public and researchers, and it obscures the results of market research.

35.5.2 Biased sample selection: This is the accidental or deliberately biased selection of samples by researchers, in order to support a particular hypothesis, for example, "this drug has this benefit". This is a distortion of statistical analysis, resulting from a non-random method of collecting samples. If the selection bias is accidental and is not taken into account, then the conclusions drawn may well be wrong.

When the bias is deliberate, the main objective is to prove a fraudulent proposition. The bias means that some members of the sample population are less likely to be included than others. It results in a non-random sample of a population, in which some were favoured over others, because of a particular characteristic which the manipulator knows will tend to result in a pre-ordained result.

35.5.2.1 Examples: Taking a poll about healthcare whilst standing outside a hospital would probably bias the results, because it biases the selection of participants. This is an instance of the "healthy user" and "geographical" biases (below).

In the same way, polling by fixed line telephone at dinner time every day will bias the sample, because it will only include those who have a fixed line telephone (this already biases economic status and age group).It is prejudiced by time, because it only focuses on samples who are habitually at home at a certain time, thus excluding some shift workers, certain professions and some age groups. Below is a typical case of sample exclusion bias.

A classic case of selection bias is called the "caveman effect." Much of our archaeological understanding of prehistoric man comes from caves. This includes cave paintings made tens of thousands of years ago. They survived because they were made inside protected caves. Any other evidence of this period which might have existed on trees, cliff walls, and animal skins has long been eroded by the weather. In a similar way, other structural evidence of fire pits, burial sites, etc. are more likely to remain intact up to the present day in caves. Prehistoric people are therefore associated with caves, because that is where the data still exists. But that does not necessarily mean that most of them lived in caves. This is an instance of pre-screening and geographical bias.

35.5.2.2 Types of biased sample selection: There are several ways in which sampling can be biased:

- **Healthy user bias:** This is where the sample population tends to be healthier or less healthy than the general population.

- **Exclusion bias:** This occurs when a methodology excludes certain subsets of the population on the basis of economic, social, demographic or geographical bias. It can also occur when a sample group is migratory and a study fails to follow up with the original sample group because it has left the area.

- **Pre-screening:** This is where participants are attracted to or rejected from the sample population by means of some deliberate or accidental screening mechanism. For example, looking for volunteers of a certain age group and socio-economic background to prove that smoking is bad for you, may pre-screen out younger, wealthier and healthier members of society. The conditions placed on the sample population act as an unknown screen, which can bias the sample population in unexpected ways.

- **Geographical bias:** This is where a sample is biased towards a particular geographic area. Any street poll for instance, will certainly exclude the large proportion of the population that are disabled in some way, and tend to favour sampling of those who are not. So asking a question about aid for the disabled to a sample population of able-bodied public may elicit an unrepresentative response.

35.5.2.3 Conclusion: The biased sample can lead to an over or under representation of a particular parameter in the sample population. A biased sample causes problems because any statistical conclusion based on that sample has the potential to be consistently incorrect.

In practice, almost every sample is somewhat biased, because it is almost impossible to ensure a perfectly random sample. However, if the degree of under / over representation is small, the sample can be treated as a reasonable approximation to a random sample. In addition, if the group that is under-represented isn't that different to the other groups in the variable being measured, then a random sample can still be a very similar to a truly random and completely representative sample.

The fraudulent use of deliberate bias in sample selection can lead to pre-determined results and mislead a manipulated victim. It is very difficult for a victim to determine if and where the manipulation has taken place, especially when the results look credible and the source seems respectable - like a pharmaceutical company or a large chemical corporation.

35.5.3 Lies of omission: These occur when data is deliberately ignored because it doesn't fit the manipulator's narrative. This is one of the most rampant and deliberate forms of bias in the news media and in drug and product testing. The phenomenon is often referred to as a lie of omission, rather than a lie of commission, because it doesn't deceive, it just doesn't tell the whole truth. It is also common in propaganda, where the manipulator simply filters out bits of information that contradict their chosen message.

In statistical circles, samples of data and samples of study results can be "lost"-accidentally or deliberately. When this is deliberate, it is manipulation and a type of scientific fraud. Data or test results can be deliberately lost in reports when they don't fit in with the conclusions that the manipulator wishes to convey.

Everything else in a report may be totally true and provable and highly credible but we never know what was left out of the report. There are numerous documented cases of drug trials, where trials are abandoned or studies shelved because they don't meet the pre-defined objectives. This is bad science of the most fraudulent kind.

It is a most insidious means of manipulation, because the only way it can be avoided, is to re-run the tests under controlled conditions to disprove a manipulated assertion.

35.5.4 Selecting favourable criteria: This is a deliberate or accidental bias in the criteria selected to determine if a particular sample has been affected by a particular cause. For example, in a drugs trial it is possible to choose a wide range of possible dependent variables to establish whether a drug is useful, usable, and safe under a lot of differing conditions.

Choosing favourable criteria can alter the apparent outcome of a trial. For instance, if a drug works well for a short time like 2 years, but becomes useless after 2 years of use, a trial could seek to use favourable criteria like "Effectiveness at 3 months, 6 months, 12 months and 24 months" and ignore results after that. The study would have conformed to its own terms of reference, would show excellent results for effectiveness, but it would not show the true picture because the criteria have been manipulated to suit a hidden agenda.

35.5.5 Fox guards the chickens: A very appropriate term describing how manipulative sampling bias and other statistical aberrations are possible in our heavily regulated world.

It works like this: In the Western world, the development of new drugs, chemicals, food products etc. is largely controlled by just a small number of wealthy corporations. They have the resources, technology and expertise to carry out research, test and market highly complex new pharmaceuticals, agrichemicals, and new food products. In fact, these corporations are about the only organisations that have the ability to invest in such research. Government is largely excluded from the process of research. It acts as a passive rubber stamp when all the ticks are in the right boxes. Thus control takes place by means of self-regulation.

35.5.5.1 Trust - the regulatory black hole: In a world where most governments see themselves as just supporting actors to the main corporate players, the use of self-regulation is now widespread. Government tries to keep out of the way of the corporate research efforts and the core principle in regulation is trust and "auto-control".

What this means for Big Pharma, Big Food and Big Chemical is that they are effectively charged with regulating themselves[35.1]. Given the fortunes involved in these industries, and the history of appallingly irresponsible behaviour of some corporate entities, this is really the equivalent of asking a bunch of hungry foxes to guard the chickens.

Self-regulation gives rise to a great potential for large scale statistical manipulation. Trials are not cross-checked by independent studies conducted in parallel by our governments. The quality of trials is accessed by government regulators but is based only on the final report of the corporate researchers themselves. The details of studies and trials remain largely obscured to the public or governments. Test results are often not even published because they contain so-called "corporate confidential" data.

Despite some of the past, tragic consequences of this self-regulation - as in the dreadful Thalidomide disaster - the system that allowed this tragedy to happen is still in place today for all drugs, in all countries in the world. So we end up with aberrations like negative trial result data being "lost", or inconvenient or negative reports being sidetracked. Regulators and professional bodies, whom we could reasonably expect to stamp out such manipulative practices, have basically failed us and continue to do so.

Compounding this felony, these problems are largely hidden from public scrutiny because they're too complex to convey in a single sound bite, so our politicians aren't competent to understand or to discuss them. This is one of the reasons why these regulatory issues have gone unfixed by our politicians. The other reason is that it takes a lot of time and detail to explain these issues correctly to the public.

And so we now have a situation where drugs are tested by the people who design and manufacture them, in poorly designed trials, on hopelessly small numbers of unrepresentative patients, and analysed using techniques that are flawed by design in such a way that they exaggerate the benefits of treatments. This is now the state of the modern pharmaceutical industry. Unsurprisingly, these trials tend to produce results that favour the manufacturer. When trials throw up results that companies don't like, they are perfectly likely to hide them from doctors and patients, so we only ever see a distorted picture of any drug's true effects.

Regulators see most of the trial data, but only from early on in a drug's life, and even then they don't give this data to doctors or patients, or even to other parts of government. This distorted evidence is then communicated and applied in a distorted way by the over-worked and often misled general medical profession.

35.6 Avoidance and Counteraction: This technique is very difficult to detect, avoid or counteract as a private individual. Some of the organisations that finance studies based on manipulated samples are amongst the most powerful in the world. However, if there is a suspicion that there has been sample bias, it should be possible to challenge the neutrality of the samples, and an honest researcher should be willing to be transparent about their sample populations and how they were assembled.

When a corporate organisation refuses to cooperate, it may be possible to use regulatory mechanisms to force divulgence of data, but more likely a concerned individual will have to resort to megaphone negotiations with a corporation, using the media against a background of corporate libel action. Such corporations are very sensitive to bad press about their products, and this can be used to leverage their cooperation.

---o0o---

36. Loaded questions

36.1 Definition: In statistical manipulation, a loaded question is used to manipulate the terms of reference or question, to generate a response or result that fits the manipulator's requirements.

Let us consider the question "Have you stopped beating your wife?" This query only allows for a "yes" or "no" answer, either of which entraps the respondent into an admission of either currently beating his wife or having beaten his wife in the past. Thus the question predetermines a result. The only alternative to the manipulative intention is to refuse to answer the question.

In a statistical context, the phrasing of terms of reference can be used and altered to manipulate a desired outcome or response. For instance, a sociological study could include a term of reference which states, "Determine the geographical and historical variations in violent behaviour and membership of neo-fascist organisations in the study group". The question pre-supposes that there is an incidence in violent behaviour in members of neo-fascist groups, but it doesn't attempt to compare the incidence of violent behaviour within the general population.

Thus, the loaded question, or loaded terms of reference, already limits the outcome of the study to show a desired result, which will be: X% of members of a neo fascist group were convicted of violent behaviour in years Y, in geographical areas Z.

The study isn't required to state whether the level of violence is greater than, equal to or less than the level in the general public. It isn't required to compare the level of violence in the general population of the target area. A manipulator can use almost any outcome of this study to headline "Violent crime by neo-fascists on the rise in Z" or something like "15% of neo-fascists accused of violent crime".

36.2 Persistence: Medium to Long. Strong messages tend to become embedded in the mind of victims. Unless a loaded question can be contradicted using an alternative authoritative study with different conclusions, the impression created by the loaded question will tend to prevail until it is explicitly contradicted.

36.3 Accessibility: Medium. Pretty much anyone can design and use this method to pre-determine a result, provided that they have access to some usable data.

36.4 Conditions/Opportunity/Effectiveness: Loading a question or terms of reference is available to all of us. However, anyone with some knowledge of the underlying manipulative process can unravel and publicly reveal a loaded question. Once it has been revealed as manipulative, the conclusions also collapse.

36.4.1 Examples: Poll question loading: The answers to polls and surveys are often manipulated by wording the questions in such a way as to force a certain answer or limit the choice of reply. For instance, in polling support for a war, these questions elicit very different results:

- Do you support attempts by the USA to bring freedom and democracy to other places in the world?

- Do you support unprovoked military action by the USA?

These two questions will certainly prompt different results, although they are both asking about support for some American foreign war. A more honest way of asking this question would be: "Do you support the current US military action abroad?"

Preceding the question with information that supports the "desired" answer is another way to reach a favourable outcome. It is often called "pre-loading the question". For example, more people will probably answer "yes" if asked: "Given the increasing burden of taxes on middle-class families, do you support cuts in income tax?" than the alternative, "Considering the rising budget deficit and the desperate need for more revenue, do you support cuts in income tax?"

36.5 Methodology/Refinements/Sub-species: There are no sub-types.

36.6 Avoidance and Counteraction: To personally avoid a loaded question, simply refuse to answer it, and challenge it as a loaded question.

In the public arena, loaded questions should be unravelled as publicly as possible. This dismantles the fallacy behind them and discredits any conclusions reached based on them. It also exposes and embarrasses the manipulator as a fraud.

---o0o---

37. Misreport errors

37.1 Definition: This is the deliberate misreporting or obfuscation of the "estimated error" in a statistical analysis in order to manipulate the results.

37.1.1 Errors and Probabilities: In most studies and statistical analyses it is impractical to evaluate an entire population and so a random sample is taken. The size of that sample is important, as is the randomness of the sample.

Obviously a larger sample will give us greater confidence that the results are representative of the wider population. The level of confidence can actually be determined using some well-developed and proven mathematical techniques, like the central limit theorem.

Confidence is expressed as a probability of the true result (for the larger group) being within a certain range of the estimate (the figure for the smaller sample group). This is the "plus or minus" figure often quoted in statistical surveys. The probability part of the confidence level is usually not mentioned. It is often assumed to be some standard number like 95% or 99%.

The two numbers are related. If a survey has an estimated error of +/- 5% at 95% confidence, it also has an estimated error of +/- 6.6% at 99% confidence. The actual relationship is that +/- x% at 95% confidence is always +/- 1.32*x at 99% confidence.

So, the smaller the estimated error, the larger the required sample at a given confidence level - this is pretty intuitive, really. The bigger the (random) sample, the more trustworthy is the result.

37.1.2 Confusion is easy: However, because the confidence figure is usually omitted in study results, most people assume that there is a 100% certainty that the true result is within the estimated error. This is not mathematically correct and can make a huge difference in interpreting a study result.

A poll with perfectly unbiased sampling and truthful answers has a mathematically determined margin of error, which only depends on the number of people polled. However, often only one margin of error is reported for a whole survey, whilst the survey actually also evaluates sub-groups. When results are reported for population sub-groups (with obviously smaller sample sizes), a larger margin of error will apply, but this is often not made clear in study results.

For instance, a survey of 1000 people may contain 100 people from a certain ethnic or economic group. The results which focus on that group will be much less reliable than results for the full population. If the margin of error for the full sample was 4%, say, then the margin of error for such a subgroup could be much greater, at around 13%. This can really become very significant in how results are interpreted.

Often the misreporting of errors is just sloppy work or perhaps the researcher is assuming something about the reader's knowledge (mistakenly). However, it is an easy option for a manipulator because almost no member of the public will realise that they are being manipulated.

37.2 Persistence: Long. It's unlikely that most people are going to get their head around this anytime soon.

37.3 Accessibility: Low. As a method of manipulation, misusing or allowing misinterpretation of statistical errors is only for the specialist.

37.4 Conditions/Opportunity/Effectiveness: It is highly effective, because only a statistician will realise that errors are not being properly represented or are being deliberately unreported. It is easy to translate results into headlines, because few people even read articles these days, never mind the statistical small print in a whole report.

However, it is only for use by a statistician who knows how to carefully bend the results to convey a particular message with obscure statistical caveats.

37.5 Methodology/Refinements/Sub-species: None known

37.6 Avoidance and Counteraction: To recognise this you need to understand quite a lot about statistical methods, or better still, hire an honest statistician to audit a statistical report in detail.

---oOo---

38. Data dredging

38.1 Definition: Data dredging involves creating misleading relationships in a dataset. It's the equivalent of looking for an answer (any answer) before having phrased the question. It is a misuse of the techniques of data-mining and statistical analyses, like regression analysis, with a manipulative intention.

Relationships found by dredging data might appear valid within the test set but they have no statistical significance in the wider population. It has become very popular since the advent of very large databases and the use of relational database technology.

We should note that data dredging can sometimes be a valid way of finding a possible hypothesis. But such a hypothesis must then be tested with data not in the original dredged dataset. It is misused when a hypothesis is stated as a fact without further validation and is only tested using data that actually originated the hypothesis in the first place.

Data dredging occurs when researchers browse data looking for relationships rather than forming a hypothesis before looking at the data. Another example is when subsets of data are deliberately chosen to create the illusion of significant patterns in deliberately narrowed down data sets.

In data dredging, large compilations of data are examined to find a correlation, without any pre-defined choice of a hypothesis to be tested. Since the required confidence interval to establish a relationship between two parameters is usually chosen to be 95% (meaning that there is a 95% chance that the relationship observed is not due to random chance), there is a thus a 5% chance of finding a correlation between any two sets of completely random variables.

Because data dredging exercises typically examine large datasets with many variables, it is almost certain that apparently statistically significant results will be found somewhere in the data, even though they are entirely spurious and coincidental.

This technique can be used in any field, but it is most often used in medical and other scientific research, and the financial environment, where interested parties fish the data for apparently interesting correlations and relationships.

For example, suppose that observers note that a particular town appears to have a cluster of cancers in their area, but the observers lack a firm hypothesis as to why this is. The researchers have access to a large amount of demographic data about the town and area, containing measurements for the area of hundreds of different mostly uncorrelated variables. Even if all these variables are independent of the cancer incidence rate, it is highly likely that at least one variable correlates significantly with the cancer rate. Whilst this may suggest a hypothesis, further testing using the same variables but with data from different locations is needed to confirm the hypothesis.

38.1.1 Traditional scientific methodology: For the lay reader it is important to understand the methodology used in conventional scientific research and how this provides safeguards against manipulative interference.

Conventional scientific method calls for a researcher to formulate a hypothesis, collect relevant data, use some method of statistical analysis to establish some form of correlation and then carry out a statistical significance test to see whether the results could be due to the effects of chance (the so-called null hypothesis). The results are then compared to the hypothesis to prove or disprove its truth.

A vital issue in proper statistical analysis is to test a hypothesis with data that was not used in constructing the hypothesis. This is central to the integrity of a scientific process, because every data set contains some patterns which are due entirely to chance.

If a hypothesis is not tested with a different dataset from the original study population then it is impossible to determine if the patterns found are chance patterns or whether they have some real significance. If we toss a coin 11 times and get heads 5 times and tails 6 times we could conclude a hypothesis that the coin favours tails between 6/11 - 7/11. However, testing this theory on the same data set will only confirm the theory and such confirmation will have no meaning. The statistical significance of the theory needs to be tested on a completely new, fresh dataset, using a new set of coin tossing results.

It is important to realize that proving the statistical significance of a hypothesis when it has been concluded using an incorrect procedure like data dredging is also completely spurious, and so statistical "significance tests" do not protect against data dredging. The researcher has deviated fundamentally from sound and objective scientific methods.

38.1.2 Traditional Data Mining and testing hypotheses: The process of data mining involves automatically testing huge numbers of hypotheses about a single data set by exhaustively searching for combinations of variables that show a reasonable correlation. Any apparently correlating sets are then tested for statistical significance.

But even when enough hypotheses have been tested, it is virtually certain that some will falsely appear to be statistically significant, because every data set with any degree of randomness will contain some spurious correlations. Researchers using data mining techniques are often easily misled by these apparently significant results, even though they are normal properties of random variation.

In addition, researchers often examine subsets of data which can alter the statistical tests for significance and error, in the absence of which we can arrive at misinformed conclusions. So, even in the traditional research environment, using appropriate analysis methodologies, there are many possibilities of coming to the wrong conclusion. Using illicit methods like data dredging is even more dangerous, and indeed prone to be used by a manipulator.

38.1.3 The Dangers of Dredging: Circumventing the traditional scientific approach by conducting an experiment without a hypothesis can lead to premature conclusions. Data mining can be used negatively to seek more information from a data set than it actually contains. Failure to adjust existing statistical models when applying them to new datasets can also result in the occurrences of new patterns between different attributes that would otherwise have not shown up.

38.2 Persistence: Short to Long.

38.3 Accessibility: Low. This is definitely a technique for a manipulative but well informed statistician, with access to large amounts of data and the data mining skills and dredging software to examine this data.

38.4 Conditions/Opportunity/Effectiveness: Provided you have the data, the knowledge of statistical manipulation and the necessary database technology, this is an easily used technique which can produce stunningly convincing misconceptions.

38.5 Methodology/Refinements/Sub-species: None known

38.6 Avoidance and Counteraction: The only thing a victim can do is to demand access to the data sets and sources of data, an explanation of methodology and the results of tests for statistical significance. This is a very tricky form of technical manipulation which can be very hard to circumvent, given the poor understanding of scientific method and statistics in the general population.

---o0o---

39. Data manipulation

39.1 Definition: Also called "fudging data", this practice includes selective reporting and even simply falsifying data to promote the agenda of the statistical manipulator.

Cases of selective publication are very common. The most widespread involve choosing a group of results that follow a pattern consistent with the preferred hypothesis, while ignoring other results or "data runs" that contradict the hypothesis.

Scientists generally question the validity of study results that are not peer reviewed by other investigators, or cannot be reproduced by other investigators. However, there are some scientists and organisations that refuse to publish their data and methods, some hide or "lose" data, curtail experiments etc. All of these are forms of data manipulation.

39.2 Persistence: Short to Long. Like all esoteric methods of reaching conclusions, manipulating data in a statistical way can have a very great persistence.

39.3 Accessibility: High - if you are a statistician or a designer of a study or survey; Low if you are not.

39.4 Conditions/Opportunity/Effectiveness: Any serious publication of study results should be transparent. Generally speaking, serious scientists following a particular hypothesis will publish contradictory and confirmatory results equally. They see the advancement of science as paramount to any other agenda.

However, there are those who have commercial or egotistical reasons for wishing to prove a particular case to be true or false, and who are willing to intervene to fraudulently hide data or create artificial data. Even some serious scientists have been known to engage in fraudulent and criminal behaviour.

For instance, the Piltdown skull caused a sensation in the scientific community in 1912. It took until 1953 to prove that the early "Piltdown Man" was in fact a complete forgery.[39.1]

There are plenty more contemporary examples.

39.5 Methodology/Refinements/Sub-species: Here are the main data manipulation methods:

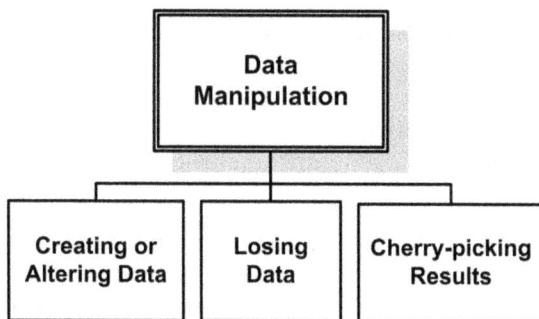

39.5.1 Creating or altering data: This is the fraudulent creation of data or alteration of existing data to achieve the desired result when subjected to statistical analysis. Creating test data is often just as simple as losing test data.

39.5.2 "Losing" data (see Discarding Unfavourable Data): This is the filtering of data which does not conform with the desired result when subjected to statistical analysis. It consists of just losing some test data. Its existence may be very easy to cover up.

39.5.3 Selective publication: Cherry-picking results: This is the publication of only selected test results which match a desired outcome. This includes the selective publication of raw sample data, the selective publication of some conclusions and the selective publication of only some of the research.

39.6 Avoidance and Counteraction: Only fully peer-reviewed, transparent and comprehensively reported study results should be taken seriously. Ideally, results should be validated against completely independent and separate investigations which seek to test "repeatability".

Any attempt to suppress data or methodology leaves the researcher open to the accusation of fraud. Arguments of commercial confidentiality are disingenuous. If a researcher wishes to publish results they must do so completely and transparently with no information held back for any reason.

If results are to be fully believed, the studies should also have been repeated by an unconnected researcher, with similar results. Anything less should be considered of dubious quality.

---o0o---

40. Discard unfavourable data

40.1 Definition: Only favourable or neutral results are used in a study and published, unfavourable results are dumped and disregarded in a study analysis.

This is a concept similar to "selective bias", but it deals with the biased selection of test results rather than test samples. It is often used in commercial circles to prove the value of a product - most often a drug or food product. Anti-GM campaigners have suggested this fraud has been used to promote GM food products, for instance. The accusation states that certain large GM research companies have deliberately suppressed unfavourable safety study results, so as not to damage their products.[40.1]

40.1.1 Users: The technique is in widespread use by organisations that are not obliged to publish every study they carry out, such as tobacco companies who, for instance, are denying a link between smoking and cancer. It is also used by anti-smoking advocacy groups and media outlets trying to prove a link between smoking and various ailments. Big pharmaceutical companies have also been accused of this stratagem in trying to sell their products[40.2]. The GM industry is riddled with accusations that unfavourable reports are hidden or "lost".

40.1.2 Proving benefit: If enough studies are conducted on a useless product, eventually some spurious correlations will demonstrate that the product is actually beneficial. Using these confirmatory study results, whilst ignoring or losing studies demonstrating its ineffectiveness, allows a manipulator to prove the value of a worthless product.

On the other hand, a manipulator can also attempt to prove that a product is dangerous. All drugs have some side effects; many products carry some risks to the user. After lots of studies and selecting only those results showing harmful side- effects or risks, one could easily (fraudulently) prove that a product is harmful. This might be helpful in damaging a competitor's product.

40.1.3 Proving safety and neutrality: It is quite easy to fraudulently prove that a product, for example a GM product, is neutral in terms of safety. All a manipulator has to do to promote the safety of a product is to find or conduct, for example, 40 studies with a confidence level of, say, 95%.

If the product is really harmless, this would on average produce one study showing the product was beneficial, one study showing it was harmful and thirty-eight inconclusive studies (38 is 95% of 40). This tactic becomes more effective the more studies there are available. Selecting the right studies thus allows the manipulator to prove, overall, that a product is neither harmful nor harmless.

40.2 Persistence: Low to High. The results can create long-lasting impressions.

40.3 Accessibility: Low: This is a domain where only those financing or managing a study have access to data and have enough power to discard parts of it. High: It can be used to carry out a study of studies by anyone with enough knowledge of the stuffy subject. Selecting only favourable study results for the evaluation will cause this summary of "all studies" to be biased.

40.4 Conditions/Opportunity/Effectiveness: It is potentially very effective and easy to hide, because no-one know what has been binned. A victim can only critique what is available; nothing can be said about the results of studies that have been effectively thrown away.

For example, in 2013 GlaxoSmithKline (GSK) announced the move to publish all its clinical trial results, eight months after it was hit with a record $3bn fine in the US in July 2012, in part for withholding safety data about its best selling diabetes drug, Avandia. In all, 26 drug companies, including eight of the 10 biggest global players, racked up fines for dishonesty of more than $11bn in the years between 2009 and 2013.

The results of clinical trials (most of which are funded by the drug industry) are frequently withheld when they are disappointing. This distorts the evidence base and raises doubts about the safety of medicines that are available on the market.

40.5 Methodology/Refinements/Sub-species: There are 5 basic sub-types of this manipulative method:

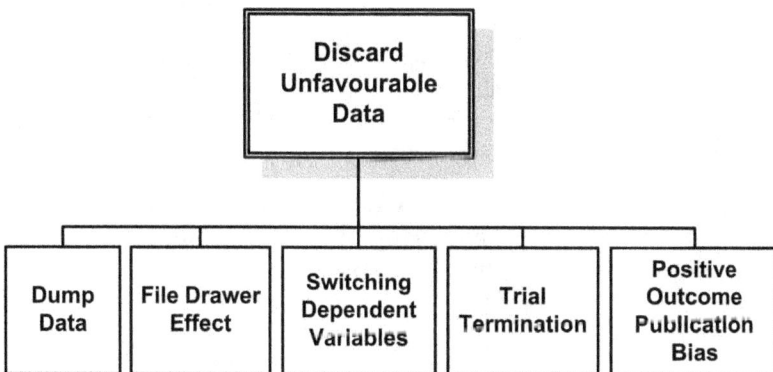

40.5.1 Dumping data: When data contradict a central theme, it is often more convenient for a manipulator to simply dump that data and pretend that they never existed. This is hard to detect since the data are not published and hardly anyone knows that the data even existed. It's a hard case to prove for a victim.

Reboxetine trials: Very often pharmaceutical companies dump unfavourable data, as in the trials of the antidepressant drug Reboxetine. Trials comparing Reboxetine against other similar drugs in three small studies (507 patients in total), showed that Reboxetine was just as good as any other drug, but 1,657 patients' worth of data was left unpublished, and these data showed that patients using Reboxetine did worse than those on other similar drugs.

Worse still was the handling of the side-effects data. The drug looked fine in the trials that appeared in headline academic literature, but the unpublished studies revealed that patients were more likely to have side-effects and withdraw from the trial, if they were taking Reboxetine rather than one of its competitor products.

Obviously, this kind of unflattering information was not for general release and was effectively "buried" by the pharmaceutical company. In the published data, Reboxetine was a safe and effective drug, but in reality it was no better than a sugar pill and, worse, it did more harm than good.

According to a systematic review and meta-analysis by IQWiG, the German Institute for Quality and Efficiency in Health Care, "published data on Reboxetine overestimated the benefit of Reboxetine versus placebo by up to 115% and Reboxetine versus (other similar drugs) SSRIs by up to 23%". It also underestimated harm, concluding that Reboxetine was an ineffective and potentially harmful antidepressant. The study also showed that nearly three quarters of the data on patients who took part in trials of Reboxetine was not published by Pfizer until much later.

By early 2007, Reboxetine was licensed worldwide in over 50 countries, including Italy, Germany and the United Kingdom. But in May 2007, however, the US FDA shockingly declined Pfizer - Pharmacia's license application for the United States market.

Data dumping by religious investigators: It's not just big corporations that get tempted to dump contradictory data. In the fundamental Christian religious hothouses of the United States, the use of selective data is quite common.

A certain infamous study on "distance healing using prayer" was "widely acknowledged as the most scientifically rigorous attempt ever to discover if prayer can heal". This was a rather incredible claim to outside observers, given that the study only had 40 participants. The study has since been discredited for improprieties in mining data.

The study was originally designed to test whether prayer could have an effect on the death rate from AIDS. However, the objective was changed after the study was completed, to see if there were any significant correlations between prayer and about two dozen illnesses associated with AIDS such as diarrhoea and oral thrush. The statistician was finally able to find about half a dozen significant correlations.

These correlations were then selected as if they were the main purpose of the study, after it was apparent that prayer had no effect on the survival of the AIDS victims.

This is the same manipulative concept as "switching dependent variables" discussed below. Normally a dependant variable is defined and fixed in the original hypothesis, like "the advance of infection of AIDS" in this case. When this didn't show any correlation with prayer, the researchers switched to another bundle of diseases, until they finally stumbled on some spurious coincidental correlations. They then used these apparently positive results to prove their original point, as if this was always the intention. They quietly dumped the "uncooperative" test results. Finally they had "evidence" that distance healing could be helped by prayer. Thank God.

40.5.2 File-drawer effect: This is the idea of burying ineffectual data. Often this happens accidentally, but sometimes it occurs for manipulative reasons, because the data doesn't appear to contribute anything to some pre-determined script.

When a study gives rise to results which find nothing of statistical significance or causal consequence, the researcher often tends to "file and lose" the offending study report, so that, effectively, it ceases to exist. The "file-drawer" effect refers to the practice of researchers in filing away and forgetting such apparently ineffectual study results.

However, this is not a scientifically valid practice and has some unfortunate consequences on a line of research. The practice of reporting and publishing only positive-outcome research creates a misrepresentation of the subject under investigation, especially if a meta-analysis of the entire data set is ever conducted on some future date. Even non-results are results and need to be added to the sum total of our dataset and knowledge of a subject.

A classic case of this phenomenon is the losing of "study non-results" in the study of parapsychology. Many studies are conducted, but only a fraction of the results ever see the light of day the rest being considered to be statistically neutral, negative to parapsychology or of no interest.

At the time of writing, the Swiss multinational Roche has been accused by the British Medical Journal of sitting on trial data for its flu treatment, Tamiflu. Governments around the world have stockpiled Tamiflu (at a great profit to the producers) against a possible pandemic, but at a cost to many governments of billions of pounds, euros and dollars[40.3].

40.5.3 Switching dependent variables: Another common technique of selective manipulation is to perform a study that tests a large number of dependent (response) variables at the same time and then only choose those that show some kind of significant correlation, dumping the rest.

For instance, a study testing the effect of a medical treatment might use as dependent variables the probability of survival, the average number of days spent in the hospital, the patient's self-reported level of pain, etc. This also increases the likelihood that at least one of the variables will, by chance, show a correlation with the independent (explanatory) variables. This is a statistically fraudulent approach, but if it is managed honestly, it could be useful in generating alternative research lines.

40.5.4 Trial termination – it's not going well: Very often, when a large-scale trial is failing to produce the expected and hoped for results, the trial is terminated. This also happens when a trial is producing results contrary to the expected results, and when a trial is producing highly negative results, in which case the trial is urgently terminated to avoid the leakage of any negative results.

Morally, unless there is an ethical risk such as a risk to human life, all planned trials should continue, regardless of how convenient the researcher finds the results.

Simply getting "inconvenient" results is not an honest reason to terminate a trial. Nonetheless, clinical trials and other scientific studies are routinely terminated because it becomes obvious that the results are not going to fit with the hidden agendas of the trial sponsors.

40.5.5 Positive-outcome (publication) bias: This is the corollary of the "File-drawer" effect.

Positive-outcome (or "publication") bias is the tendency to publish research with a positive outcome more frequently than research with a negative outcome. Negative outcome refers to finding nothing of statistical significance or causal consequence, not to finding something that (necessarily) affects us negatively.

Positive-outcome bias also refers to the tendency of the media to publish medical study stories with positive outcomes much more frequently than stories with negative outcomes. We constantly hear of medical advances, but we rarely hear of abandoned research lines.

Media bias may be due to scientific journal bias, but the latter seems to be due mainly to researchers not submitting negative outcome studies for publication (the file-drawer effect), rather than to bias on the part of a publication or peer review editor. Who wants bad news after all?

40.6 Avoidance and Counteraction: It is difficult to deal with cases of lost data, lost conclusions or lost studies. If a victim doesn't realise that a study or a data set actually exists, it is unlikely, barring an insider tip-off, that a victim will ever discover that any kind of manipulation has actually happened.

But, "information leaks" do happen, even in the most secure organisations. Good relationships between honest and ethically aware academics may give rise, not only to leaks, but also to a steady stream of revealing information.

---oOo---

41. Over-generalisation

41.1 Definition: Over-generalisation occurs when a statistic is used to arrive at a conclusion about a whole population based on data from just a particular subset which is not a representative sample of the whole population.

For instance, suppose a researcher walks past an orchard and all the apples he sees are red. It is summer. The researcher could conclude that all apples are red in summer.

The statement that "All apples are red" would be an instance of over-generalisation because the original statistic was true only of a specific subset of apples (those in summer, of a certain variety, in a certain place), which is not expected to be representative of the population of apples as a whole.

A real-world case of over-generalisation can be observed in modern polling techniques, which in some countries prohibit calling mobile phones for over-the-phone political polls. This restriction excludes an entire class of people who do not possess a fixed telephone line or are not at home very often, etc.

For example, young people are much more likely to have a mobile phone, than a fixed line. Young people are likely to be more liberal than the general population. Young people who do not have a fixed line telephone are also likely to be more liberal than their demographic group as a whole (less fixed to an address). So these polls effectively exclude many participants that are likely to be more liberal. People who are included in the poll have fixed lines. They may possibly be older, more permanent in terms of address, and more politically conservative than the "mobile-phone only" group. On the other hand, they may also be poorer and more transient than the fixed line telephone owners. At any rate, the two groups will be demographically and politically different.

Thus, a poll examining political voting preferences of young people, using only fixed line telephone polling, could not claim to be representative of true voting preferences across a whole population. It would be an "over-generalisation" because the sample used is not representative of the population as a whole, having excluded a large segment of the population who don't possess fixed telephone lines.

Over-generalisation often occurs when information is passed through non-technical sources. It is very popular with the mass media which prefer to ignore nuances in favour of good, snappy headlines.

41.2 Persistence: Low to High.

41.3 Accessibility: High - We can all over-generalise a very specific study result into huge tracts of the population.

41.4 Conditions/Opportunity/Effectiveness: Over generalisation is not that effective because it is almost always possible to find and show obvious and absurd exceptions to an over-generalisation, thus undermining the manipulative assertion and the manipulator.

Opportunities for over-generalisation abound. However, as a manipulative technique it only works properly when it is credible to the target audience.

41.5 Methodology/Refinements/Sub-species: None known.

41.6 Avoidance and Counteraction: Whenever someone attempts to generalise the particular, red lights should start to flash. Regardless of the case, anyone attempting to generalise had better have a really well-developed argument to hand and a set of data to demonstrate that a generalisation is logically and statistically valid and reasonable.

---o0o---

42. Proof null hypothesis

42.1 Definition: This is the concept that a hypothesis is true until positively demonstrated to be untrue. In reality, a hypothesis cannot always be absolutely proved to be untrue. This does not however mean that the hypothesis is actually true.

A manipulator can use this "innocent until proven guilty" concept to demonstrate that an obviously true hypothesis is untrue, simply because it hasn't been conclusively demonstrated yet, due to lack of evidence.

For instance, a tobacco producer wishes to demonstrate that their products are safe. They can easily conduct a test with a small sample of smokers versus a small sample of non-smokers. It is unlikely that any of them will develop lung cancer, and even if they do, the difference between the groups has to be very big in order to reject the pro-smoking hypothesis.

But it does not automatically follow from this that smoking is therefore harmless. The test has insufficient legitimacy to reject the hypothesis that smoking is harmless but, conversely, it doesn't have enough validity to prove the truth of the alternative hypothesis that smoking is dangerous.

Using the judicial concept of innocent until proven guilty, we can compare the test to a truly guilty defendant who is released just because the proof is not enough for a guilty verdict.

His release does not prove the defendant's innocence, only that there is not enough proof for a guilty verdict. In other words, "absence of evidence" does not imply "evidence of absence".

42.2 Persistence: Short to Long.

42.3 Accessibility: Low. This is only for the well- resourced manipulator in general.

42.4 Conditions/Opportunity/Effectiveness: Not that effective when challenged by a statistician but it can be headline grabbing in the hands of a manipulator with an agenda.

42.5 Methodology/Refinements/Sub-species: None known.

42.6 Avoidance and Counteraction: Keep your mind open to new evidence. Just because a hypothesis is still officially un-refuted, it doesn't mean that it is true. It just means that the jury is still out.

---oOo---

43. None enduring class fallacies

43.1 Definition: This is a form of manipulation that suggests that once a statistical conclusion is reached, it continues to be true.

This is obviously not so. Over time, the statistical justifications for any conclusion may change as the individuals which compose a particular statistical class also change.

For example, in the United States, the claim by congressman Bernie Sanders in 2011 that "the top 1% of all income earners in the USA made 23.5% of all income", whilst being statistically correct, may still be fallacious due to the implication that this class, composed of the top 1%, is an enduring statistical class, composed of the same individuals as in the previous year. Many of the individuals in this class may remain from the previous year, but there is no indication as to how many of these individuals do in fact continue in the original statement. This leads to the erroneous implication that all individuals in the class endured - which may not be true.

Conclusion: Things change. Today's conclusions may be tomorrow's fallacies.

43.2 Persistence: Short. Using the same examples and the same data again and again may not remain credible forever.

43.3 Accessibility: High. We all use popular street myths to demonstrate our point, despite reality.

43.4 Conditions/Opportunity/Effectiveness: It's a cheap and easy way to manipulate statistical data, but it is also very easily undermined with more up-to-date results. Using and repeating an old conclusion only works for a while... until more contemporary studies demonstrate that the world has changed.

43.5 Methodology/Refinements/Sub-species: None known.

43.6 Avoidance and Counteraction: This fallacy can easily be avoided by specifying or asking whether the statistics used refer to the same group of individuals over the period in question.

---oOo---

44. Statistical manipulation - Size Matters

44.1 Definition: Sample size manipulation is a typical abuse of statistical method in which the manipulator tries to generalise a correlation based on a small sample which is statistically insignificant. This is often done to demonstrate the statistical "truth" of a correlation which cannot honestly be generalised to the larger population because it is based on too small a sample.

As we have already mentioned, it is normal practice to look for correlations in just a sample of a huge population. It is impractical to look at entire populations to prove statistical links. So it is common to select a random sample of a set of data to research if correlations exist between various causes and a particular effect, i.e. between a group of independent variables and a single dependant variable.

For instance, if we wanted to establish if a relationship exists between bronchitis and smoking in the general population, we would first need to establish the approximate incidence of the disease and the incidence of smoking, and then use these values to determine a statistically usable and reliable sample size. This sample size determination is an important process in statistical analysis, and if it is done incorrectly, it can give rise to wildly misleading results.

So, for example, if the incidence of bronchitis is only approximately 1 in 10,000 in the general population, then using a sample group of 50 people is obviously not going to be useful, since it is statistically unlikely to demonstrate even one incidence of the disease. Therefore, obviously a larger group is required.

On the other hand, if the incidence of bronchitis is 1 in 5, then a group of 50 subjects may well yield some usable data. In general, the bigger the sample size, the more accurate will be the results of our statistical analysis.

Several mathematical techniques allow us to calculate an appropriate sample size to achieve a particular confidence level and error. In legitimate studies, before conducting a statistical analysis like Regression Analysis, we would need to calculate and define an appropriate sample size for our data set, to make conclusions in which we have a particular level of confidence (normally 95%) and a particular expectation of level error (like 5%).

Using samples which are not properly calculated can still give rise to very strong correlations, and this fact is often used by manipulators to deliver a deliberately invalid conclusion to a victim. The fact that the correlations are completely dubious does not stop the manipulator from using their conclusions to dupe a gullible public.

For instance, a headline reads, "33% of drinking water test results showed E.Coli contamination". This may be based on just 3 results, one of which showed contamination. In a larger sample, it could well be that only 1 in 1000 samples are contaminated, but the headline may be correct within the scope of the "study" of a very tiny sample. However it is disingenuous and fraudulent to extrapolate a conclusion of 33% contamination, as the generalisation was based on just 3 samples.

44.2 Persistence: Low-Medium. Surely, someone will see through a cheap trick like this? Well maybe, but the headline has delivered the message. It is much harder to erase the headline in the public perception than it is to make it in the first place.

44.3 Accessibility: High. With access to the appropriate data, assertions like these can be delivered by almost anyone. Few members of the public can authoritatively challenge the validity of such statements, so they can easily gain currency.

44.4 Conditions/Opportunity/Effectiveness: Messing around with sample size to get a different conclusion is a cheap trick, bordering on fraud. For a statistician it's a "no-brainer". Amazingly however, the press has easily sold all kinds of statistically dodgy stories, using absurdly manipulated sample sizes which later give rise to headlines. Even more amazing is that such stories persist. Some even persist although they have been challenged and proven to be ingenuous. It's hard to dislodge a good headline from the public perception, especially when the alternative is some complicated argument about confidence levels and so on. Most lay-people want simple–to-understand messages not nuanced statistical statements. And newspapers want catchy headlines that grab the readers' attention. Why let the truth get in the way of a good story?

44.5 Methodology/Refinements/Sub-species: None known.

44.6 Avoidance and Counteraction: Avoidance is simple. Just demand to see the sample size and the sample size calculation; ask for the confidence level and the standard error. If these basic calculations are not available, the headline conclusions are worthless.

---o0o---

45. The politicisation of science

45.1 Definition: The politicisation of science is the manipulation of science for political purposes. It occurs when politicians, NGOs, government, or commercial interests exert legal and economic pressures to influence the findings of scientific research or the way it is published, interpreted or reported.

The politicisation of science also affects academic and scientific freedom in a negative way. In the political arena, special-interest groups have historically conducted campaigns to promote their interests with a view to the manipulation of public policy, despite scientific consensus. Examples of this include the Climate Change deniers, the Evolution non-believers, the anti-abortionists and the family planning opponents, and many more who bizarrely deny many of the most straightforward and fundamentally self-evident elements of scientific knowledge that we have.

Extremism and science: Science tends to be politicised by extremist groups, and it is by no means a new phenomenon. The intellectual pogroms launched against early scientists by the Roman Catholic Church in Europe at the end of the medieval period are testament to this. Any contradiction of the official world vision was considered a heresy by the Church, itself steeped in ignorance and superstition. Nonetheless, the Church often inadvertently contributed to the advancement of rational scientific understanding.[45.1]

Similar politicisation of science occurred in Soviet Russia, Nazi Germany and more recently in the United States of America, during clashes over subjects as diverse as "Intelligent Design" v Evolution, Smoking versus Cancer, GMO versus non-GMO, Climate Change, etc.

Even more recently in the United States, the government of George W. Bush was found guilty of attempting to manipulate scientific expression. In 2004, a council of 9,000 concerned scientists (including 49 Nobel laureates) signed a petition with the following statement:

"When scientific knowledge has been found to be in conflict with its political goals, the administration has often manipulated the process through which science enters into its decisions. This has been done by placing people who are professionally unqualified or who have clear conflicts of interest in official posts and on scientific advisory committees; by disbanding existing advisory committees; by censoring and suppressing reports by the government's own scientists; and by simply not seeking independent scientific advice. Other administrations have, on occasion, engaged in such practices, but not so systematically nor on so wide a front.

Furthermore, in advocating policies that are not scientifically sound, the administration has sometimes misrepresented scientific knowledge and misled the public about the implications of its policies."

Contemporary examples: Today, we have new groups of extremists, many related to the far right-wing. For instance, we have the Climate Change deniers and the anti-abortionists. These groups tend to share the full gambit of scientific denial, and use the most extraordinary tactics to prove that:

- We should continue burning hydrocarbons despite overwhelming evidence of climate change

- We should force women to have babies even if their foetuses are non-viable or are the result of rape. Some of this same group also now refute that it is possible for a woman to actually conceive as a result of rape.

The tactics and arguments of this group are truly medieval, and their approach to human life and our planet mimic those of the church inquisitors of 16th century Europe. In the midst of all this folly is our main body of basic scientific knowledge, which apparently has developed more rapidly than the social capacity of some people to understand it. We do have to remember though that, within this same right-wing US anti-science grouping, there is a large number of people who also haven't yet realized that Saddam Hussein and "Obama" bin Laden are actually different people and that Iran and Iraq are in fact not the same country. So perhaps their attitude to science isn't so strange, really.

45.2 Persistence: Medium - Long.

45.3 Accessibility: Institutionally, the politicisation of science is not something most of us have any control over. This is a matter for the politicians and professional scientists. In terms of the propagation of some of the absurd scientific "facts", this is available to everyone. The manipulator relies on public ignorance for the spreading of politically driven scientific fallacies.

45.4 Conditions/Opportunity/Effectiveness: For persons of low intelligence, a dysfunctional view of human society and a poor to zero understanding of science, the manipulation of science as a political tool is indeed very effective. Interestingly, the USA hosts most contemporary cases of political manipulation of science.

The internet and right-wing media is replete with "experts" with dubious scientific qualifications, making pronouncements designed to support their bizarre moral causes. Anti-abortionists argue that abortion causes breast cancer; Creationists contend that dinosaur remains were planted deliberately to support the theory of evolution; climate change deniers refuse to take the word of the United Nations, NASA and their own insurance corporations that climate change is real and is happening now.

Even a millennial drought in the USA and a string of catastrophic weather events has thus far failed to budge this group. The stereotype of this group are Republican voting, gun-toting, xenophobic, religious fanatics. These are the same people who, with the National Rifle Association, still defended the rights of American citizens to own rapid fire assault weapons, even after 20 small schoolchildren were shot dead in the US town of Newtown, Connecticut in December 2012. This is the type which can be readily manipulated to believe pseudoscientific conclusions that support their own world view. Manipulation of science for political reasons is thus effective when used with some sections of our society, albeit the less intelligent and more thuggish members.

Here are some contemporary cases:

- **Evolution and the USA:** A 2006 article in scientific journal Science said that among the thirty-four developed countries surveyed, the U.S. ranks second from last in the number of adults who accept the theory of evolution: "The acceptance of evolution is lower in the United States than in Japan or Europe, largely because of widespread fundamentalism and the politicization of science in the United States".

- **Climate denial:** In 2006, Guardian columnist George Monbiot reported that according to data found in official Exxon documents, 124 organizations had taken money from Exxon-Mobil or worked closely with those that have. He wrote: "These organizations take a consistent line on climate change: that the science is contradictory, the scientists are split, environmentalists are charlatans, liars or lunatics, and if governments took action to prevent global warming, they would be endangering the global economy for no good reason. The findings these organisations dislike are labelled 'junk science'. The findings they welcome are labelled 'sound science'."

- **Anti-Abortion Lobbyists:** The abortion-breast cancer hypothesis is the belief that induced abortions increase the risk of developing breast cancer. This belief is in contrast to the scientific consensus that there is no evidence suggesting that abortions can cause breast cancer. Despite the scientific community rejecting the hypothesis, many pro-life advocates continue to argue that a link between abortions and breast cancer exists in an effort to influence public policy and opinion to further restrict abortions and discourage women from having abortions. While historically a controversial hypothesis, the debate now is almost entirely political rather than scientific.

45.5 Methodology/Refinements/Sub-species: None defined.

45.6 Avoidance and Counteraction: Anyone with a basic general knowledge of the main sciences, the history of science and the basis of scientific method and an average intelligence should be able to detect an attempt at moral or political manipulation of science.

Scientific manipulation is one of the easier forms of deceit to detect and dismantle. This is especially true when basically everything can be so easily researched and verified on the internet by any of us. This makes its proliferation in the USA, one of the world's richest and techno-dependant nations, all the more amazing and ironic.

Sadly, despite our technological evolution, many ordinary citizens are bereft of even a basic understanding of any of the main natural sciences.

---oOo---

46. Logical manipulation

46.1 Definition: Logical manipulation is the use of psychological biases in questions of logic to trick a victim into believing a manipulative assertion. It uses apparently logical statements to alter the conclusions of a victim.

The key feature is that statements only appear to be logical; a proper examination proves that not to be so. In a sense, these methods are also partly linguistic traps but they deserve their own category because they are exclusively employed in the abuse of a victim with a limited understanding of the principles of logic.

46.2 Persistence: Short to Long.

46.3 Accessibility: High, anyone can use this.

46.4 Conditions/Opportunity/Effectiveness: The existence of psychological biases in making logical decisions is effective as a mechanism for human manipulation.

It has little value with a victim that operates "on gut feeling", but it is effective against victims who think that they are rational and that they have a good command of the rules of logic.

46.5 Methodology/Refinements/Sub-species: There is a group of sub-species of logical manipulation, some of which we describe below:

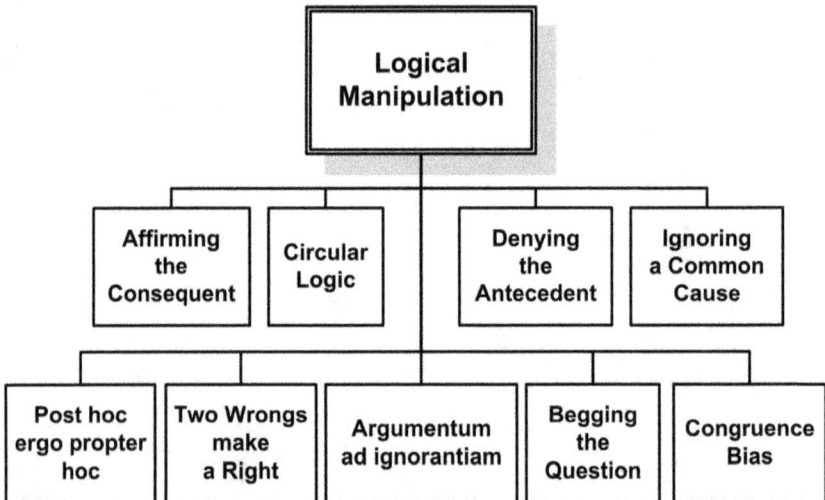

46.5.1 Affirming the consequent: This is the fallacy with a general form as follows:

- Step 1: If X is true, then as a consequence, Y will be true.

- Step 2: Y is true. Therefore X must be true.

These types of argument are a fallacy because they are invalid. Being invalid means that their conclusions do not follow from their premises, i.e., it is possible for their premises to be true and their conclusions false.

A valid argument is one in which the conclusion follows from its premises, i.e., it is impossible for its premises to be true and its conclusion false. Take for instance:

- Step 1: If a god created the universe, we should observe order and design in Nature.

- Step 2: We do observe order and design in Nature.

- Step 3: So a god created the universe.

In this example, the premise of the argument may be true but the conclusion does not follow from the premises. The invalidity of these arguments has nothing to do with their content and is due entirely to their fallacious logical form.

A statement p never follows from the statements *if p then q* and q. Even if the premises of these types of argument are true, the conclusion doesn't necessarily follow from them. Being a fallacy however, does not mean that the conclusion is false. For instance, the following examples of this phenomenon have true conclusions:

- Step 1: If President Obama is a Christian, then he is not a Muslim.

- Step 2: He is not a Muslim.

- Step 3: So President Obama is a Christian.

46.5.2 Circular Logic - A conclusion is derived from a premise based on a conclusion. A manipulator can use this tautological fraud to try to confuse a rational argument. Example: "Stripping privacy rights only matters to those who have something to hide. Therefore you must have something to hide if you oppose stripping privacy rights".[46.1]

46.5.3 Denying the antecedent: There isn't only one explanation for an outcome, so it's false to assume the cause based on the effect. Example: If you get a degree, you will get a good job. Therefore, if you don't get a degree, you won't find a good job. The manipulator fools the victim into drawing an illogical conclusion, based on a simple logical trick.

46.5.4 Ignoring a common cause: Claiming that one event caused another, when a third (unlooked for) event is probably the cause. Example: "We had the 60s sexual revolution - and now people are dying from Aids."

The manipulator is delivering a moralising payload, ignoring the fact that the 60s also brought a huge increase in international travel, human population, development of forest areas of Africa, etc. These were the real contributory factors in the development and spread of Aids, with the sexual revolution in the Western world being largely irrelevant in terms of HIV.

46.5.5 Post hoc ergo propter hoc: Claiming that because one event followed another, it was also caused by it. Example: Since the election of the president unemployment has risen, therefore unemployment is the fault of the president.

A manipulator can use this simple technique to attribute blame or credit. It plays well with people who are mentally lazy about checking the logic of what they hear or read.

46.5.6 Two wrongs make a right: This is the assumption that if one wrong is committed, another one will cancel it out. Example: "The prisoners' conditions are inhumane, but then the prisoners are inhuman criminals". A manipulator justifies a moral evil as a result of an extreme moral jeopardy.

This is similar to the way the USA, UK and their collaborators shrugged off their own roles in kidnapping, torture, detention without trial, war crimes, and deceiving their governments and electorates over the issues of Iraq, Afghanistan, and 9/11 etc.

They justified their own illegal actions on the basis of claims that the Western world was being threatened. The threats were Saddam Hussein's (fictional) weapons of mass destruction and al-Qaeda's (also fictional) global reach and alleged attack on the World Trade Centre in 2001.

46.5.7 Argumentum ad ignorantiam: An argument to ignorance. This is another logical fallacy of irrelevance, occurring when one claims that something is true only because it hasn't been proved false, or that something is false only because it has not been proved true. Some manipulators are successful delivering this fairly cheap trick with some victims and audiences.

46.5.8 Begging the question aka petitio principii: This is a type of informal fallacy in which a proposition relies on an implicit premise to establish the truth of that same proposition. In other words, it is a statement that refers to its own assertion to prove the assertion. Such arguments are of the form "A is true because A is true", though rarely is it stated like this because that really would be a bit too obvious. So, often the premise "A" is only one of many premises that go into proving that "A" is true as a conclusion.

"Begging the question" is employed by a manipulator either rhetorically, or slipped into a formal document, in the hope that it passes unnoticed and allows a bigger conclusion to be drawn. It is an old trick, with the first known definition in the West by Aristotle around 350 BC.

The following is a case of begging the question: "Paranormal phenomena exist because I have had experiences that can only be described as paranormal."

The conclusion of this argument is that paranormal phenomena exist. The premise assumes that the arguer has had paranormal experiences, and therefore assumes that paranormal experiences exist. The arguer should not be granted the assumption that his experiences were paranormal, but should be made to provide support for the claim. However, amazingly large numbers of victims don't even recognise that they are being manipulated by this obvious mechanism.

46.5.9 Congruence bias: This is a favourite in the manipulative presentation of test results by both testers and vested interests, trying to use test results to conceal a hidden manipulative payload. Congruence bias occurs because of a victim's over- reliance on direct testing results from a particular (preferred) hypothesis, whilst indirect testing has not been carried out at all.

An example will illustrate: Imagine that in an experiment a subject is presented with two buttons and is told that pressing one of those buttons, but not the other, will give a reward. The subject adopts a hypothesis that the button on the right gives a reward. A "direct test" of this theory would be pressing the button on the right and an "indirect test" would be pressing the button on the left. The latter is still a valid test, because once the result of not receiving a reward is proven; the right button is demonstrated to be the desired button.

In the case of a victim of manipulation, the manipulator can truthfully say that the button on the right will give a reward. However, this statement is only part of the truth, because it neglects to mention that only the right button gives a reward. Therefore the hypothesis is not totally proven.

This phenomenon also occurs as a result of self-delusion, where an experimenter will form a hypothesis, repeatedly get a positive test result and then naively conclude that the hypothesis is therefore completely correct. In such an experiment, a subject will test his own usually naïve hypothesis again and again, instead of trying to disprove it, or test alternate hypotheses. Not only do laboratory animals behave in this way, but also intelligent human beings.

46.6 Avoidance and Counteraction: Logical manipulation can be detected and avoided by gaining an understanding of logical analysis and by taking a little bit of time to test the statements of a potential manipulator. Incredibly, some of the most outrageous breaches of logic are accepted on trust, without anyone ever testing them. They sound OK and are therefore accepted.

---oOo---

47. Manipulation of morality

47.1 Definition: The manipulation of morality deals with the imposition or alteration of the moral rules of a victim where this benefits a manipulator. It can be personal, institutional or governmental. It is sometimes referred to as "Morality Warping".

The manipulation of moral attitudes is ancient. It has run through all mystical and religious activity since human civilisation began. But it isn't confined to religion.

Examples might include deliberate attempts to alter our perspectives on any one of a number of issues with moral criteria such as tolerance, equality, freedom, charity, mercy, self-control, friendship, modesty, honesty, hatred and aggression, pride, vanity, greed, jealousy, avarice etc.

Moral manipulation may be either "vertical" or "horizontal" in action. Vertical moral manipulation seeks to weaken or strengthen a particular moral position on a particular subject, for instance, the rectitude of the Iraq war or the use of torture. Horizontal moral manipulation seeks to weaken or strengthen our moral positions on all subjects.

Religious groups tend to use broad, "horizontal" moral manipulation to deliver a package of moral positions on everything.

Non-religious imperatives may be used to manipulate a victim or group to accept or reject a single moral principle of any kind on any vertical issue or on a wide range of horizontal moral issues. Political pressures constantly make demands on our moral judgement to accept a manipulator's assertions.

Moral manipulation is an important lever in controlling our political and social attitudes. The manipulative logic goes as follows: If you can't get someone to morally accept what you have done, then the only alternative is to alter their moral judgement.

47.2 Persistence: Short to Long. Moral manipulation can last from moments to generations. We might accidentally allow ourselves to agree with some assertion that has some unpleasant embedded prejudice within it, and then quickly reverse that moral position. On the other hand, the use of war by cultures whose moral code is based on one of the Abrahamic religions is a moral aberration that has lasted millennia and has now been boiler-plated into these religions. For instance, the Christian crusades caused centuries of violence and "legally justified" slaughter and persecution by Christianity against Islam, Judaism and any form of non-Christian voice in Europe and the Middle East; in the very name of a religion whose Messiah made the unqualified statement: "All they that take the sword shall perish with the sword". This moral contradiction continues 2000 years later.[47.1]

47.3 Accessibility: Medium to High. Moral manipulation is usually managed by a moral authority of some kind like a corporate entity, church or sect, or an agency of government. However, moral manipulation can be manifested by individuals in interpersonal relationships or in dealing with other members of our own group such as a group of colleagues or friends or a political party.

47.4 Conditions/Opportunity/Effectiveness: The manipulation of our moral beliefs is all-pervasive in modern society. From the moment we can communicate as children, we are awash with attempts to induce and alter our moral and ethical position, starting at our mothers knees, through education and into a society that worships consumption, demands more consumption, more selfishness and more individualism from us all.

The opportunities and support for altering our basic moral attitudes are firmly embedded in modern capitalism. The concept of altruism is now considered "odd" rather than "worthy and charitable". Concepts like "charity" have been nudged out by concepts like "personal success", "satisfaction", "independence", "ambition" etc.

Further up the moral hierarchy we are also expected to morally justify the immoral behaviour of our leaders and governments in waging illegal wars, using torture and kidnap, engaging in the pillage of other nations' resources and cultural heritage and in encouraging pogroms against minorities in our own countries. It all gets a bit hard to swallow for most potential victims of moral manipulation and remarkably there has yet to be any form of large-scale moral backlash, though this may yet change. The climate for the blind acceptance of the capitalist ethos has recently changed, as the moral emptiness and depravity of the capitalist system is exposed to more scrutiny and more citizens become victims of its dysfunctionality.

47.5 Methodology/Refinements/Sub-species: Here we present several sub-types of moral manipulation:

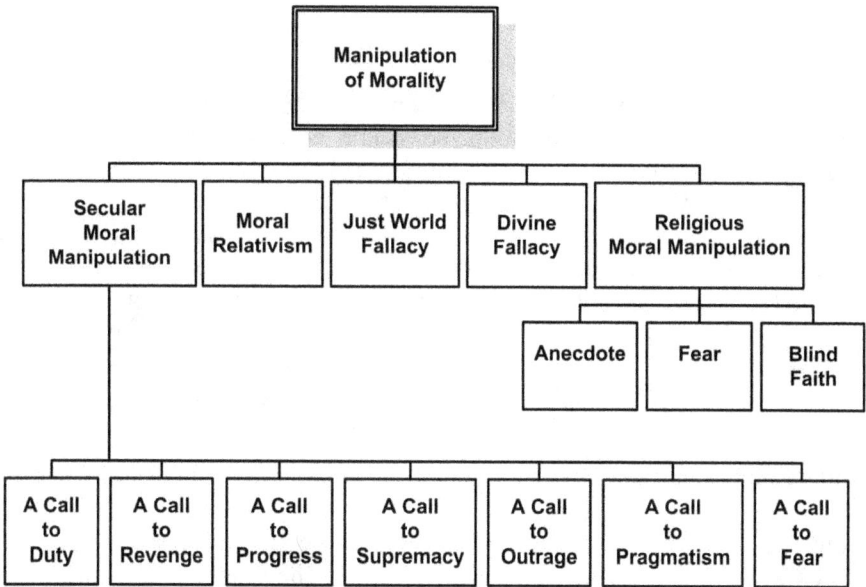

```
                    ┌──────────────────┐
                    │   Manipulation   │
                    │   of Morality    │
                    └──────────────────┘
```

Secular Moral Manipulation	Moral Relativism	Just World Fallacy	Divine Fallacy	Religious Moral Manipulation

Under Religious Moral Manipulation:

Anecdote	Fear	Blind Faith

Under Secular Moral Manipulation:

A Call to Duty	A Call to Revenge	A Call to Progress	A Call to Supremacy	A Call to Outrage	A Call to Pragmatism	A Call to Fear

47.5.1 Secular moral manipulation: Secular organisations may attempt to manipulate our moral positions to achieve some objective of their own agenda. For instance, political parties may attempt to alter our attitudes in a "vertical" sense on a single issue like war or poverty. Governments do the same and may also attempt to deliver a complete set of moral precepts in a more horizontal way, as was the case with totalitarian dictatorships like Fascist Germany, Stalinist Russia, or Maoist China where whole moral codes were being preached to populations. Corporate managements often opt to try to alter our moral attitudes to some particular issues like "progress", "wealth", "ambition", "pride" etc. Military organisations will attempt to alter the moral perspective of its members, in order to desensitise them to certain moral principles like "Thou shalt not kill" or promote concepts like a "just war". Private clubs or societies may promote or obscure certain moral priorities to promote their founding principles, as for example Freemasons will promote the concept of the existence of "a supreme being" to their members. Schools and other educational institutions constantly use moral manipulation to induce or alter particular moral premises in their pupils.

Secular moral manipulation takes place in both a horizontal and vertical sense. It may concern one issue and one moral value or it may apply across a broad range of issues and moral values. The secular moral manipulator uses a number of other manipulative methods like propaganda to trigger a moral reaction in the victim and to embed a new moral position. This is done by making an appeal or "a call" to various emotional or intellectual states in a victim. Here are some of the main calls that a manipulator will use to effect the moral manipulation:

47.5.1.1 A call to Duty: Here the victim feels strongly obliged to accept a moral position because not doing so would be a dereliction of duty. A dereliction of duty is perceived to be, morally, very bad. So, for example, every day we ask our young men to go to war on our behalf, to set aside fundamental moral commandments preached by every established religious faith - "Thou shalt not kill". We ask them to subjugate their humanistic and altruistic instincts on our behalf in order to kill, steal, and torture in our wars. We ask them to do this in order to win conflicts which are designed to give our nations, our companies and our societies more power over other nations and other people or to give us more "security" or more opportunities to steal the natural resources of other people.

But to participate in this, a psychologically "normal" soldier must accept and believe that he is fighting a "just war", otherwise he cannot morally continue. And so the manipulator appeals to the soldier's sense of duty in order to embed the concept of "just war" in the soldier's morality. The soldier gladly accepts the new moral code, because it allows him to eliminate the discomfort of conflicting moral positions (the cognitive dissonance of being a caring human being and the deliberate killing of other human beings).

47.5.1.2 A call to Revenge: A manipulator stirs a sense of offence and feeling of humiliation in a victim against some target generating in the victims a need to take revenge, to redress the wrong, and to revalidate the dignity of the victim. History is full of examples, including the success of the Nazi party as a reaction to the humiliation of Versailles [47.2], the apparently irrational US invasion of Afghanistan after 9/11, the use of torture and illegal detention by the USA after various terrorist incidents, the use of detention without trial in Northern Ireland after several IRA bombings, the Israeli massacre in the Gaza strip in 2008/9 after the kidnap of an Israeli soldier by Hamas [47.3]. A famous quote from the Vietnam War was a statement attributed to an unnamed U.S. officer by AP correspondent Peter Arnett in his writing about the destruction of Bến Tre city on 7 February 1968. Arnett cited the US major as saying in his report: "'It became necessary to destroy the town to save it'.

A call to revenge provides a victim (often the general public) with the moral cover to take an action which is disproportionate or unconnected to the original offence. The US government tried to justify the use of illegal detention and torture in Abu Graib [47.4] prison in Iraq as part of its war on terror, and based on the total fabrication that Iraq was somehow instrumental in the attack on the Twin Towers on 9/11. Not only was such an action disproportionate, it was also completely unconnected to the original event. Nonetheless, a gullible American public swallowed it hook, line and sinker.

47.5.1.3 A call to Progress: Here a manipulator makes a call to our sense of "human progress" to justify and embed a new moral imperative in the victim. For example, we have to have factory farms and keep animals in appalling conditions in order to improve the efficiency of food production. Similar calls to progress are made to justify the use of chemicals or GM technology in agriculture, designer babies - the possible genetic selection of the sex, eye and hair colouring of our offspring. More sinister are calls to progress like that of the Israeli government, after the revelation of their program of involuntary sterilisation of Ethiopian Jews arriving at resettlement camps on their way to reside in Israel[47.5]. Similar calls to progress are used to justify the continued occupation of Afghanistan by the US and NATO, when they explain that female education will be forbidden if the country falls into Taliban hands.

A call to progress makes the victim feel that it would be incorrect to stand in the way of radical actions and human development. It provides the manipulator with a lever to create a sense of discord within a group of people when there is dissention. Dissenters are forced back into line by other members of the group. For example, until recently anyone suggesting that the farming methods developed in the "Green Revolution" of the 50s and 60s are counterproductive, damaging and should be abandoned, would have been considered a Luddite crank. As it happened, the Green Revolution was overtaken by more radical and more "Green" practices such as organic and biodynamic farming.

47.5.1.4 A call to Supremacy: This is used at several levels to provide us with moral justifications for behaving in certain ways, because we believe that we know better than others, we are more developed or sophisticated than others, we are more intelligent and technologically advanced than others or that we are better organised, democratic and civilised than others. The call provides moral cover for the abuse of ethnic minorities, the abuse of the weak, for imperial interventions in other people's countries, the theft of resources or land belonging to others, the enslavement of others and a myriad other evils including misogyny and racism. A call to supremacy can be as mild as someone extolling the railway building by the British Empire in India, but it can extend to justifying active discrimination against others, murder, genocide, forced labour, forced sterilisation, theft, rape, and pillage.

A call to supremacy works by appealing to the egotistical nature of a victim or group of victims. It is appealing to many victims to be reminded how intellectually or technically superior they are to the "others". For example, in the West, we unquestioningly accept that the concept of

317

"spreading democracy in the World" is desirable, nay essential. This is despite the fact that democracy may not necessarily be a suitable system of government in all societies and that it doesn't even work very well for the Western world either. We think this way because we have morally switched off our empathy for the "others" by assuming that we are superior. The manipulator encourages this by telling us again and again that we are superior in so many ways.

47.5.1.5 A call to Outrage: This is used to alter the moral position of a victim by appealing to their sense of political or moral outrage. For example, a manipulator may appeal to a victim's empathy and horror at seeing starving children, homeless and impoverished families, victims of abuse, or casualties in a war. The victim can be made to feel partly responsible for what they see, because they are a party to the injustice or they have failed to stop an injustice. It can be used to alter the political attitudes of the victim.

Equally, a manipulator may appeal to the political outrage of a victim when confronted with certain political "facts". For example, a manipulator can induce xenophobic attitudes in a victim by appealing to the outrage felt by a victim when they start to believe that there is a connection between their poverty and the number of foreigners in the country. The number of foreigners is made to "outrage" the victim and provides moral cover for their adoption of xenophobic attitudes. We have all heard the statement which starts "I'm not a racist at all and I've got nothing against them at all, but......." The word "but" is the operative word here.

A call to outrage works by creating a justification in the victim's mind for a sense of anger and disgust at their own or someone else's situation. It is comforting to the victim to be able to feel legitimately outraged and to adopt a moral position which reflects their outrage, whether that moral position is one of empathy for the poor, the weak and the oppressed or fear and hatred of immigrants.

47.5.1.6 A call to Pragmatism: How many times a day do we hear appeals to our "Common Sense", "Objectivity", or "Pragmatism" from politicians, colleagues and friends? Somehow these words imply some kind of virtue in modern society and yet their opposites can actually be equally morally appealing: "Extraordinary Sense", "Subjectivity" and "Dogmatism".

Since when did it become a crime to be subjective (since we all are anyway)? Since when did having a moral dogma guarantee to obscure the truth (we all carry one with us)? Who wants to have just "common" sense? Despite the irrational moral tone of these appeals, many people will bend their moral position so as to be seen as pragmatic and objective.

The appeal to pragmatism is a modern one, and based on our more "scientific" approach to moral issues and decisions. Objectivity removes human emotion from a decision, common sense disallows the existence of exceptions in our moral code, and pragmatism removes any hint at spirituality from our decisions. We reason like inert machines and this is apparently good and to be encouraged. For example, we all know about the human suffering and environmental damage done to the world by the abuse of poor countries by industrialised countries and certain very immoral companies. Shell, for example, has a truly horrendous human rights and environmental record, which has been documented over decades [47.6]. Yet, despite that, we still buy Shell's products and give them profits. After all, pragmatically, we can't do anything about it anyway as individuals, so what's the point in boycotting them? Israel, in direct contradiction to numerous UN resolutions, continues to steal Palestinian land [47.7]. But objectively, we can't do anything about it, because it has US backing, so what is the point in protesting about it? There's no point, we can't change anything, can we, and common sense tells us that.

47.5.1.7 A call to Fear: Here a manipulator takes advantage of the victims' fear to alter their moral position. Fears take many forms: fear of personal security, poverty, hunger, war, loneliness or exclusion etc. A manipulator may appeal to a victim's fear of poverty to persuade them to be morally prudent. Alternatively, a manipulator may induce such a fear into a population so that it happily sacrifices its long-held civil rights in the name of preserving "homeland security". A manipulative government can make its population morally justify their xenophobia or their support for their nation's continuous war in the name of fighting "terror".

A call to fear works effectively, because fear is a very powerful and basic human instinct. Human beings have many fears and a manipulator can use any one or a combination to alter the moral perspective of a victim. For example, the US and UK governments have both maintained their countries in a state of heightened alert and fear by continuously citing terrorist threats to their countries. This is despite the fact that the statistical chance of being killed by a terrorist is much less than being hit by lightening or crushed to death by a television or piece of domestic furniture.[47.8] In this example, the public morality has been altered to accept many dubious moral positions, such as an irrational hatred for Muslims [47.9], a moral acceptance of the use of torture and the use of state kidnapping and illegal detention [47.10]. We quietly accept our own countries becoming terrorist states because it is justified by our extreme fear of "the other".

47.5.2 Moral relativism: This method of moral manipulation uses the equivocation of morality with the implication that there is no such thing as right and wrong or good and evil.

The argument plays to the advantage of regimes that desire to steal, kill, and violate the rights of people without being questioned and without consequences. The technique is used, mostly by governments, according to their imperatives at a particular moment.

For instance, Tony Blair oscillated between being highly pragmatic and relativist whilst sending troops to attack Iraq to stop "the deployment of weapons of mass destruction" the threat that he himself had invented together with George Bush. He did this against a background of moralistic Christianised babble about human rights, democracy and freedom. His behaviour was truly medieval in style; a cross in one hand and the sword in the other. The combination of the establishment Christian leader promoting a holy war as a last resort, against an evil Islamic monster dictator played well to a historically ignorant, generally apathetic and ill-informed British public. The same arguments can be equally applied to George W. Bush of course. The only difference is that Blair pretended Catholicism and Bush used Christian fundamentalism. Both used religion as a tool to justify their actions to the greater world rather than as a moral source for their actions. Such behaviour is typical of a psychopathic character where morality plays only a passing role as a tool in the achievement of "darker" objectives.[47.11]

In the wrong hands, moral relativism is a way of reversing or discrediting instinctive humanistic moral attitudes and it is implicitly evil in the sense that it darkly calls upon us to abandon human solidarity, good will and charity.

We can legitimately argue about our moralities, but we cannot deny that we are, in some sense, moral creatures in general.

The assertion that Iraq actually had weapons of "mass-destruction" was truly psychopathic, as indeed were and are Tony Blair and his co-conspirators

47.5.3 The Just-World Fallacy: This is the tendency of people to believe that the world is just and that therefore people "get what they deserve."

Here the manipulator assures the victim that the world is somehow a "just place" - that "all is for the best in the best of all possible worlds". This means that people who are losing at the game of life must have done something to deserve it and that bad people ultimately get what's coming to them.

The fallacy concludes that human actions eventually yield morally fair and fitting consequences, so that, ultimately, noble actions are duly rewarded and evil actions are duly punished. In other words, the just-world hypothesis is the tendency to attribute consequences to, or expect consequences as the result of an unspecified power that restores moral balance. The fallacy is that this implies (often unintentionally) the existence of such a power in terms of some cosmic force of justice, just deserts, stability, or order in the universe.

The reality, of course, is quite different where we see the beneficiaries of good fortune often doing nothing to earn it, and bad people often getting away with their actions without consequences whilst hard-working, generous, moral people suffer abjectly.

47.5.4 The Divine fallacy: This is also called the "argument from incredulity" and it is related to "Big Lies".

The saying goes "Tell the people that there is an invisible man in the sky that created the universe and the vast majority will believe you. Tell them "Beware - Wet Paint" and every single person will have to touch it to make sure." This is the nature of the believability of the divine fallacy.

In some circumstances a manipulator will need to argue for the existence of a divine intervention - they will often use a methodology referred to as the "Divine fallacy".

The divine fallacy, or the argument from incredulity, is a species of non sequitur reasoning which has the following form: "I can't work this out, so a God must have done it". Or, "this is an amazing fact therefore, a God did it". Or, "I can't think of any other explanation; therefore a God did it". Or, "this is just too strange; so it must be an act of God".

This is low level manipulation, generally employed against people of poor educational standards who are badly informed and emotionally weakened. It is however in constant use.

The belief in miracles and other superstitions are good examples of the divine fallacy at work. For instance, many emotionally weakened people trek to pilgrimage sites like Lourdes to be cured because they believe a miracle happened there.

47.5.5 Religious or Mystical moral manipulation: All Magico-Religious groups promote some moral manifesto which is the basis of their founding philosophy. The three Abrahamic religions Judaism, Christianity and Islam, share a broad base of common moral premises based on their common origin. Whilst there are some slight differences in the moral codes, these religions promote more similarities than differences. Non Abrahamic religions, despite their very different origins, share many of these moral principles, albeit enunciated in a rather different way. All of the virtues and vices of modern Christianity are discussed and defined in Buddhist and Hindu traditions as well. As would be expected, the list of human virtues and vices considered by all the ancient religions is common to all, simply because the moral issues are common to all humanity, regardless of religion, race or economic status.

Religions manipulate the morality of adherents by different means and address the subject of morality in a "horizontal" way to deliver a complete and complex set of moral lessons:

- **Anecdote:** A religion demonstrates a moral principle by telling a story and showing that a certain moral position causes a desirable or undesirable outcome. This makes the listener believe that a particular moral message is true and adopts the underlying moral position. Very often the anecdotes used are contained in "Holy" Books which have mystical significance and have unchallengeable sources and esoteric origins.

- **Fear:** A religion, using unchallengeable assertions like the existence of "hell", may threaten adherents with "eternal hell fires" if they fail to adopt a particular moral position. They may threaten expulsion (ex-communication) from the group for failing to conform morally.

- **Blind Faith:** Most religions have origins and moral principles developed in very ancient times. Their histories are often poorly documented, not very reliable and prone to be elaborated down the ages. Therefore, adherents are often required, as a first step, to accept some esoteric or mystical assertions as fact based only on blind faith. Thus "faith" is often the first "virtue" that an adherent must learn. For adherents, this tautological connection between faith-religion-morality relies at some point on unquestioning faith. Many religions use highly emotive manipulative methods to induce blind faith in their followers including grand and impressive visual and symbolic displays.

47.6 Avoidance and Counteraction: Manipulation of morality can only be really be avoided by having a dynamic, honest and open moral approach to human attitudes and behaviour, centred on the concept that most human beings are basically good but that many of them often make moral mistakes.

A humanistic view of morality is straightforward, practical and reasonable. It also defends against external attempts to manipulate our moral attitudes.

Understanding the games that manipulators play to get us to alter or erode our moral positions provides the main defence against moral manipulation.

---oOo---

48. Emotional manipulation

48.1 Definition: Emotional manipulation covers a wide range of manipulative methods used in close personal relationships with members of one's family and close friends. Having a close personal relationship doesn't guarantee that we won't be manipulated even by our closest and most intimate contacts. The subject of emotional manipulation also applies to those who are likely to, or trying to, become close to us.

People who think they have very close and trusting relationships with family members and very good friends are often shocked to realise just how superficial and manipulative those relationships really are.

There is actually no place in a healthy, balanced, open relationship for serious manipulation of any kind. On the other hand, there are occasions when we all employ some very low-level manipulation on our loved ones, frequently with their own interests at heart, I hasten to add. This often happens without any conscious thought and is generally harmless. However, the inclination to "manipulate" instead of "discuss" is a dangerous tendency, which may have seriously destructive consequences for a relationship. In a proper, open relationship, manipulation should not be a method which we consciously use to achieve personal objectives contrary to the wishes of our loved ones.

Sadly, there are many who live in manipulative relationships with their husbands, wives, and close family. The misery they suffer "trying to keep the peace" with their controlling family members is often tragic and seemingly inescapable.

Emotional manipulation is an emotive issue, close to the hearts of many psychologists and social workers. It is a difficult and sensitive subject.

Here we will define the basic mechanisms of emotional manipulation, but in truth it is a subject requiring much more specialist attention, especially for the victim. We don't seek to advise anyone suffering seriously from this phenomenon.

48.2 Persistence: Short to Long. It can last any time: from just a few seconds to an entire lifetime.

48.3 Accessibility: High - we can all do this and we can all suffer from this.

48.4 Conditions/Opportunity/Effectiveness: Emotional manipulation works because a manipulator finds and exploits vulnerabilities in the victim's personality or situation. This is also similar to other forms of manipulation where the "cost" to the victim to avoid the manipulation is greater than the *benefit* that the manipulator *enjoys*.

However, it is important to note that some of these vulnerabilities can be managed or eliminated by the victim at almost zero cost so we have listed all these very human vulnerabilities into the categories used by the psychologists who first defined them (Braiker, Simon & Kantor). Few of us could honestly say that we never suffered from any of these vulnerabilities:

48.4.1 The "Braiker" List of vulnerabilities:

Addiction to earning the approval and acceptance of others.

Lack of assertiveness and ability to say no.

Unclear sense of personal identity.

Low self-reliance.

A desire to please.

Emotophobia - a fear of negative emotions like frustration, anger, or distaste.

External locus of control - feeling helpless.

48.4.2 The "Simon" List of vulnerabilities:

- Low self-confidence - The victim is self-doubting, lacks confidence and assertiveness, and is likely to go on the defensive too easily.

- Emotional dependency - The victim has a submissive/dependent personality. The more emotionally dependent the victim is, the more vulnerable they are to being exploited and manipulated.

- Naïveté - Here the victim finds it too hard to accept the idea that some people are cunning, devious and ruthless, or is "in denial" that they are actually being victimized.

- Over-intellectualisation - The victim tries too hard to understand and believe in the manipulator, accepting the manipulator has some valid reason to be hurtful.

- Over-conscientiousness - The victim is too willing to give the manipulator the benefit of the doubt and see their side of things.

48.4.3 The "Kantor" List of vulnerabilities:

- Too impulsive - makes snap decisions about what to buy or whom to marry, for instance, without consulting others.

- Too naïve - cannot believe there are dishonest people in the world, assuming that if there were they would not be allowed to operate.

- Too trusting - people who are honest often assume that everyone else is truthful too. They are more likely to commit themselves to people they hardly know without checking credentials, etc., and less likely to question so-called experts.

- Too immature - has impaired judgment and believes the exaggerated advertising claims.

- Too narcissistic - narcissists are prone to falling for unmerited flattery.

- Too greedy - the greedy and dishonest may fall prey to a psychopath who can easily entice them to act in an immoral way.

- Too impressionable: easily seduced by charmers. For instance, they might vote for the seemingly charming politician who kisses babies.

- Too dependent - dependent people need to be loved and are therefore gullible and liable to say yes to something to which they should say no.

- Too masochistic - lack self-respect and so unconsciously let psychopaths take advantage of them. They think they deserve it out of a sense of guilt.

- The elderly - the elderly can become fatigued and less capable of multi-tasking. When hearing a sales pitch they are less likely to consider that it could be a con. They are prone to giving money to someone with a hard-luck story.

- Too lonely - lonely people may accept any offer of human contact. A psychopathic stranger may offer human companionship for a price.

- Too altruistic - the opposite of psychopathic: Too honest, too fair, and too empathetic.

- Too frugal - cannot say no to a bargain even if they know the reason why it is so cheap. They can't resist buying the cheapest shoes that fall apart after one week even though he knows a more expensive pair will last ten times as long…..a victim of false economy.

- Too materialistic: easy prey for loan sharks or "get rich quick" schemes.

48.5 Methodology/Refinements/Sub-species: There are an almost infinite number of methods of emotional manipulation. Here we will present just a few commonly experienced methods and variants. We have divided the methods into 2 groups for clarity.

```
                    ┌─────────────────┐
                    │   Emotional     │
                    │  Manipulation   │
                    │      (I)        │
                    └─────────────────┘
```

Lying-Partial Deceit	Denial	Rationalisation	Diversion	Evasion	Shaming

Vilify Victim	Play Servant	Projecting the blame	Play Confused	Reverse Dependency	Seduction

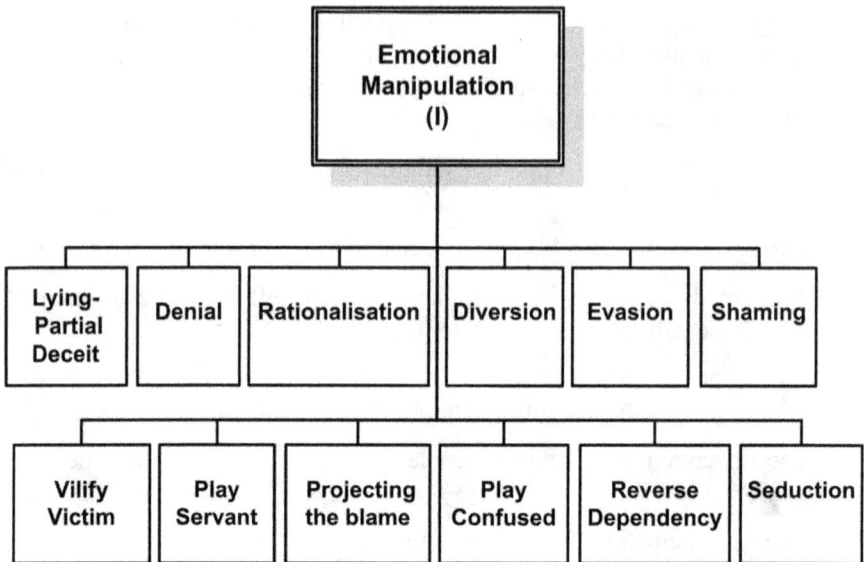

48.5.1 Lying and partial deceit: It is sometimes hard to tell if somebody is lying at the time. Generally the truth becomes apparent later. One way to minimize the chances of being successfully deceived is to understand that some personality types, particularly psychopaths, are experts in the art of lying and cheating and betray no signs of guilt or conscience.

48.5.2 Partial Deceit also known as Gaslighting: Partial deceit is a subtle form of lying where the deceiver withholds a significant amount of the truth, but mixes some facts with the lies. It is used by propagandists, but it is also often used in domestic emotional manipulation. When this happens consistently over a period of time it may cause a victim to question their sanity, since they are never quite sure what is true and what is a lie.

This type of abuser often accuses their partner of doing something wrong to justify their own actions or to mislead their partner about why they are being mistreated. Alternatively, the goal of such abusive accusations is to blame the partner for their anger, irritation or insecurity, and thus prove that the anger or abuse the victim is suffering is actually justified because the victim is really at fault.

No psychologically healthy partner wants to see his or her spouse feeling bad or hurt, plainly he or she would prefer to comfort or heal their pain.

48.5.3 Denial: Here the manipulator refuses to admit that they have done something wrong.

48.5.4 Rationalisation: This is an excuse made by the manipulator for inappropriate behaviour. Rationalization is closely related to "spin".

48.5.5 Diversion: Here, the manipulator is not giving a straight answer to a straight question and instead is being diversionary, steering the conversation onto another topic.

48.5.6 Evasion: This technique is similar to diversion, but instead irrelevant, rambling, vague responses are given, so called "weasel words".

48.5.7 Shaming: Shaming tactics come in many forms: a fierce look or glance, unpleasant tone of voice, rhetorical comments, and subtle sarcasm are but some. Manipulators can make one feel ashamed for even daring to challenge them.

It is an effective way to foster a sense of insecurity in a victim. The manipulator uses sarcasm and "put-downs" to increase fear and self-doubt in the victim. Manipulators often use this tactic to make others feel unworthy and therefore defer to them.

48.5.8 Vilifying the victim: More than any other, this tactic is a powerful means of putting the victim on the defensive.

48.5.9 Playing the servant role: This method cloaks a self-serving agenda in the guise of a service to a more noble cause. For example, claiming that one is acting in a certain way for "obedience" and "service" to God or some human authority figure.

48.5.10 Projecting the blame (blaming others): Here the manipulator finds a scapegoat, often using subtle, hard-to-detect ways.

48.5.11 Play confused: Here the manipulator tries to play dumb by pretending that he doesn't know what the victim is talking about, or he pretends to be confused about an important issue brought to his attention.

48.5.12 Reverse dependency: Most of us believe that we tend to do nice things for the people we like and bad things to the people we hate. In fact, it doesn't quite work like this. The reality is that we grow to like people for whom we do nice things and we tend to hate people whom we have harmed.

This is a readily used manipulative opportunity. A manipulator can co-opt a victim by giving them an opportunity to help the manipulator. As soon as the victim has done some favour for the manipulator, the victim begins to form an emotional attachment towards the manipulator. It is almost as if the victim begins to form affection for his "emotional investment" which will then grow with time.

The reverse is also true. An inadvertent injury can cause the rapid development of full-scale enmity between two otherwise neutral parties. In this scenario, a manipulator can deliberately cause this injury and bring about an entirely artificial rift.

48.5.13 Seduction: Here the manipulator uses charm, praise, or flattery to get the victim to lower their defences and give their trust and loyalty to them.

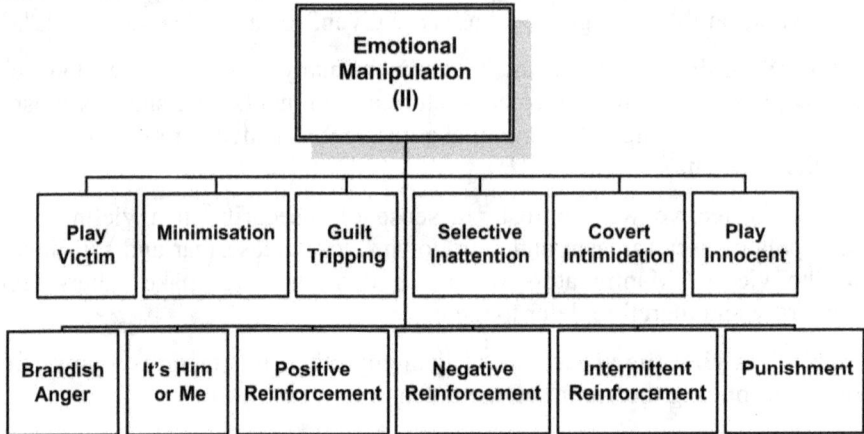

```
                    Emotional
                    Manipulation
                        (II)

Play      Minimisation   Guilt      Selective    Covert        Play
Victim                   Tripping   Inattention  Intimidation  Innocent

Brandish   It's Him   Positive        Negative        Intermittent     Punishment
Anger      or Me      Reinforcement   Reinforcement   Reinforcement
```

48.5.14 Play Victim: Playing the victim role ("poor me"): The manipulator portrays themselves as a victim of circumstance or of someone else's action in order to gain pity, sympathy or compassion and thus get something they want from the listener. Caring and conscientious people are moved by suffering and the manipulator often finds it easy to play on their sympathy to get their cooperation.

- Play Victim: You're Sick, I'm dying: This is an extreme variant of the "Play Victim" method. Emotional manipulators will try to make themselves look more of a victim than their victim. They crave attention and when their victim starts to lose interest, the manipulator acts up by playing victim in a more extreme way to regain the attention.

- Play Victim: Vulnerability: This is a variant on the basic play victim method. It involves pretending to be vulnerable in some way to control a victim: "I don't know what I would do if you left me" etc.

48.5.15 Minimization: This is denial coupled with rationalization. The manipulator asserts that their behaviour is not as harmful or irresponsible as someone else was suggesting, for instance saying that a taunt or insult was "just a joke".

48.5.16 Guilt tripping: Guilt tripping is a special kind of intimidation tactic. A manipulator suggests to the conscientious victim that they do not care enough, are too selfish or have it "too easy". This usually results in the victim feeling blame-worthy, keeping them in a self-doubting, anxious and submissive mode.

48.5.17 Guilt tripping Favours: "I'll Do You This Favour, But Don't Forget You Owe Me": It's really difficult to ask someone for a favour when you know they're going to exploit you as payment for it.

In reality, it's quite normal to ask a favour from a friend. But there are people who will do you one favour and then milk you for every little thing afterwards. When you put your foot down, they will go on a tirade about how you have no sense of gratitude. To avoid this kind of manipulation, be careful whom you ask for favours. Remember, with some people, there is a price for everything.

48.5.18 Selective inattention: (aka selective attention): In this method a manipulator refuses to pay attention to anything that may distract from their own agenda, saying things like "I don't want to hear it."

48.5.19 Covert intimidation: This is the technique where the manipulator throws the victim into a defensive position by using veiled threats. These can be subtle, indirect or implied threats of many kinds, e.g." If you keep saying that there will be consequences".

48.5.20 Play Innocent: The manipulator feigns innocence. They suggest that any harm done was unintentional or they in fact did not do what they are accused of. The manipulator may put on a look of surprise or indignation. This tactic makes the victim question their own judgment and possibly their own sanity.

48.5.21 Brandishing anger: Here the manipulator uses anger to stir up sufficient emotional intensity and rage to shock the victim into submission. The manipulator is not actually angry, he simply pretends to be. He just "wants what he wants" and gets "angry" when he is denied it.

48.5.22 It's Him or Me: Some people like to make their friends choose between them and another person. The victim is pressured to choose the manipulator for fear of losing their friendship.

A true friend would never force such a decision. This is a manipulative method that even small children use in the playground. To avoid making a decision the victim should "walk away".

48.5.23 Positive reinforcement: This method includes praise, superficial charm, approval, fake sympathy, excessive apologies, gifts, money and attention. Facial expressions such as a forced laugh or smile are common characteristics.

48.5.24 Negative reinforcement: This method involves removing someone from a negative situation as a reward. "If you do this awful job, you will not be punished for your previous crime".

48.5.25 Intermittent or partial reinforcement: Partial or intermittent negative reinforcement creates an effective climate of doubt and fear. Partial or intermittent positive reinforcement can encourage the victim to persist. For example, in most forms of gambling, the gambler is likely to win now and again, but still lose money overall.

48.5.26 Punishment: This method of manipulation combines and includes shouting, nagging, intimidation, the guilt trip, threats, swearing, emotional blackmail, sulking, crying, and playing the victim.

48.6 Avoidance and Counteraction:

It is difficult to generalise about avoidance and counteraction on a subject as particular and powerful as emotional manipulation. As always, emotional manipulation depends on some kind of cost-benefit differential between manipulator and victim. Emotional "costs" are hard to evaluate for a victim, but an emotionally "strong" victim can beat a manipulator in several ways, primarily by removing the manipulator's "reward", and then by increasing the cost to manipulate the victim.

Generally speaking, it is pretty much impossible to live together with a seriously manipulative personality as a partner or family member. The only exception to this is when the manipulator has already realised that they have a problem and when they are actively and honestly trying to change or control their feelings and behaviour.

However, anyone who really believes that they have some superior right to manipulate other people (especially a loved one), is pretty much beyond help by friends or family. They are almost certainly beyond the help of their intimate victim. The serial emotional manipulator needs specialist psychotherapy.

48.6.1 Knowledge is Power: The key to the avoidance of emotional manipulation is that intangible concept "self-knowledge".

If we can acknowledge and understand our own vulnerabilities, then we can possibly prevent manipulators from using these weaknesses against us. We have listed the most likely vulnerabilities above.

However, understanding our vulnerabilities isn't actually the solution to the problem, (which is the personality of the manipulator), but at least we can avoid the worst excesses of the manipulator and perhaps manage a relationship in which a victim may be trapped.

48.6.2 Know "the enemy": Manipulators come in different forms, so as victims of emotional manipulation we need to know our manipulators.

Bear in mind that a manipulator can be unconscious about what they are doing. In effect they are manipulators by accident. Most of us manipulate each other a little, generally with our partner's interests at heart and this is mostly harmless.

However, a manipulator has various possible motivations, including:

- The need to advance their own purposes and personal gain at virtually any cost to others.

- A strong need to attain feelings of power and superiority in relationships with others - this is a need to feel in control (aka. "The control freak").

- A desire to gain a feeling of power over others in order to raise their own self-esteem.

48.6.3 Cut and Run: Really serious emotional manipulators can be extremely difficult individuals to deal with. They may be perfectly reasonable, balanced and charming to the rest of the world. Their manipulative agenda may be targeted at just a single victim.

Again, in this arena it is impossible to generalise or advise. However, instinct should play a part in the strategy of the victim. If the behaviour of the manipulator seems excessive, then it probably is excessive, and if there is no visible sign of change or attempt at self-analysis, then it might be safer to leave a relationship than to try and engineer a personality change in the manipulator.

---oOo---

49. Manipulation of bias and heuristics in decision making

49.1 Definition: In this section we are going to consider manipulative methods based on common psychological biases and our use of heuristics (mental shortcuts) to take advantage of our sometimes irrational actions and attitudes.

Over the years, many biases which affect judgment and decision making have been defined by psychological and sociological research. These predispositions appear as systematic deviations from a standard of rationality and good judgment.

Here is a general visualisation of psychological biases:

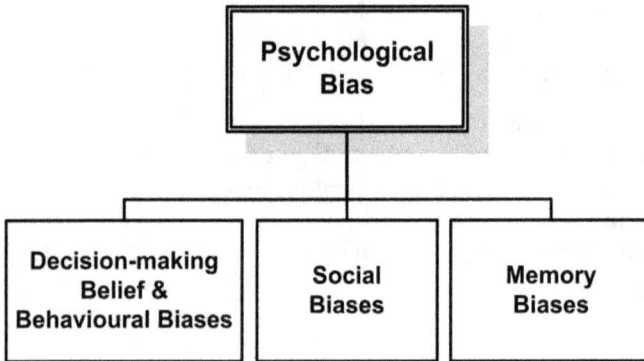

```
                    ┌─────────────────┐
                    │  Psychological  │
                    │      Bias       │
                    └─────────────────┘
                             │
        ┌────────────────────┼────────────────────┐
┌───────────────────┐ ┌─────────────┐ ┌─────────────┐
│  Decision-making  │ │   Social    │ │   Memory    │
│     Belief &      │ │   Biases    │ │   Biases    │
│ Behavioural Biases│ │             │ │             │
└───────────────────┘ └─────────────┘ └─────────────┘
```

In this section we will deal with the first of these biases which affect personal decision-making, belief and behaviour (also referred to as cognitive biases). We will see how they are used in manipulative strategies. Later chapters will deal with forms of manipulation which use the various social and memory biases.

49.1.1 Heuristic origins: Some biases stem from our use of heuristics to process information when making a decision. Heuristics are experience-based techniques for problem solving, learning, and discovery. Heuristics are also mental short cuts, used to speed up problem solving and human data processing when a complete evaluation of the data is impractical.

49.1.2 Manipulative opportunities in cognitive biases: There are many decision making, belief and behavioural biases and the list continues to grow as more are discovered. These psychological "tendencies" offer fertile grounds for a manipulator to operate. Using subtle psychological means, a manipulator can exploit these unrecognised weaknesses in a victim.

The use of cognitive biases in the interests of a manipulator is generally considered exploitative, abusive, devious, and deceptive. However, this form of manipulation is not necessarily intended to have negative consequences. For instance, doctors can try to persuade patients to change unhealthy habits by taking advantage of one or more of these psychological inclinations, for example a desire to "fit in". This kind of influence is generally felt to be harmless when it respects the right of the subject to accept or reject the attempted persuasion, and if it is not unduly coercive. Depending on the context and motivation, this kind of psychological influence may or may not constitute manipulation.

49.2 Persistence: Short to Long.

49.3 Accessibility: High. There are so many biases involved in how we make decisions that their manipulative use is very common. Many of us use these propensities in those around us to manipulate them in an entirely sub-conscious way. We don't even know we are doing it.

49.4 Conditions/Opportunity/Effectiveness: We are all subject to cognitive biases and the inappropriate use of heuristics, but many of us are entirely unaware of the effects they have on our decisions. We tend to make decisions, but we rarely think about how we reach them. The decisions we make seem to fit in with our view of the world, and we are generally happy with them.

49.5 Methodology/Refinements/Sub-species: The range of manipulative possibilities is almost infinite, but the following list gives an indication of the range and manipulative opportunities of the known cognitive biases. The list defines first the bias and then the potential for manipulative uses. We have divided this large list alphabetically into seven parts simply to aid readability.

```
                    ┌─────────────────────────┐
                    │      Manipulation       │
                    │   of Bias / Heuristics in │
                    │    Decision Making (I)   │
                    └─────────────────────────┘
```

Ambiguity Effect	Attentional Bias	Availability Heuristic	Availability Cascade	Base rate Fallacy	Belief Bias

Blind spot Bias	Choice-Supportive Bias	Cognitive Dissonance	Confirmation Bias	Conjunction Fallacy

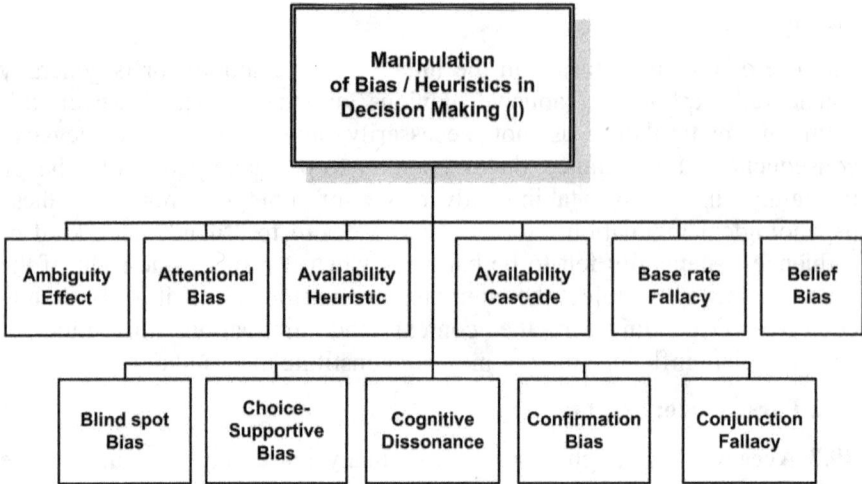

49.5.1 Ambiguity effect: This is the propensity to avoid options for which missing information makes the probability seem "unknown". We tend to prefer options where we know the probability of a favourable outcome, rather than those options where we do not know the probability of a favourable outcome. For example, "I know that there is at best a moderate chance of my winning a local competition as the local players are good. There is a competition in the next town, but I do not know how good the players are there. Rather than 'risk it', I just enter for the local competition". A manipulator uses this tendency to force inaction or alternative decisions by depriving a victim of information on probable outcomes of particular options.

49.5.2 Attentional bias: People often pay attention to emotionally dominant stimuli in their environment, whilst neglecting relevant data. A manipulator can use emotive data or imagery to divert the victim's attention from the rational evaluation of data.

49.5.3 Availability heuristic: We frequently overestimate the likelihood of events with greater "availability" in our memory. Recent, unusual or emotionally charged memories may play an important role. A manipulator can keep an event or subject at the front of the victim's mind (memory) by constantly reminding him of it, or vice versa, keep it at the back by ignoring it completely.

49.5.4 Availability cascade: This is a self-reinforcing tendency in which a collective belief gains more and more plausibility through its increasing repetition in public discourse (or "repeat something long enough and it will become true"). A manipulator can use continuous repetition of a theme or belief to increase plausibility.

49.5.5 Base rate fallacy or base rate neglect: This is the inclination to base judgments on specifics, ignoring general statistical information. The manipulator cites specific cases to a victim to prove the value of their case, despite generally accepted trends to the contrary.

49.5.6 Belief bias: Someone's evaluation of the logical strength of an argument is influenced by the believability of the conclusion. The manipulator appeals to the common sense and "obviousness" of a conclusion to prove that the argument is valid.

49.5.7 Bias blind spot: This is the tendency to see ourselves as less biased than others and to be able to identify more cognitive biases in others than in ourselves. The manipulator appeals to the obviously "completely rational and unbiased nature" of the victim to inflate their sense of superior rationale.

49.5.8 Choice-supportive bias: We often remember our choices as better than they actually were. The manipulator appeals to the past wisdom of the victim who may be reluctant to make a decision.

49.5.9 Cognitive dissonance is a term used in psychology to describe the feeling of discomfort when simultaneously holding two or more conflicting ideas, beliefs, values or emotional reactions. Cognitive dissonance is one of the most influential and extensively studied theories in social psychology.

In a state of dissonance, people may sometimes feel a sense of "disequilibrium", which may manifest itself as uneasiness, frustration, dread, guilt, anger, embarrassment, anxiety, etc. It is often experienced by cult followers when a long predicted apocalyptic event does not happen. The sense of great expectation followed by total disappointment creates a cognitive dissonance.

This dissonance may cause the victims to behave in different ways. In our cult example, the disappointed may find theological reasons to explain the non-event, perhaps claiming to have been spared. The initial disappointment may thus make them more fervent in their belief. Others may leave the cult and look for alternative explanations to calm their feelings of discontent.

The theory of cognitive dissonance in social psychology proposes that people have a motivational drive to reduce dissonance by altering existing cognitions, adding new ones to create a consistent belief system, or, alternatively, reducing the importance of any one of the dissonant elements. A manipulator may use a sense of cognitive dissonance in a victim to persuade them to alter or drop a particular opinion, or to behave in a certain way. For instance, someone can be encouraged to take professional short-cuts at work because "getting the job done is more important than breaking the rules a little".

49.5.10 Confirmation bias: This is the propensity to search for or interpret information or memories in a way that confirms one's preconceptions. The manipulator reminds us of the "good old days" or "the good old friends" we knew and trust.

49.5.11 Conjunction fallacy: This is the inclination to assume that specific conditions are more probable than general ones. The manipulator cites precise cases of past events to prove the likelihood of a future event, and deliberately ignores general trends which may have an impact.

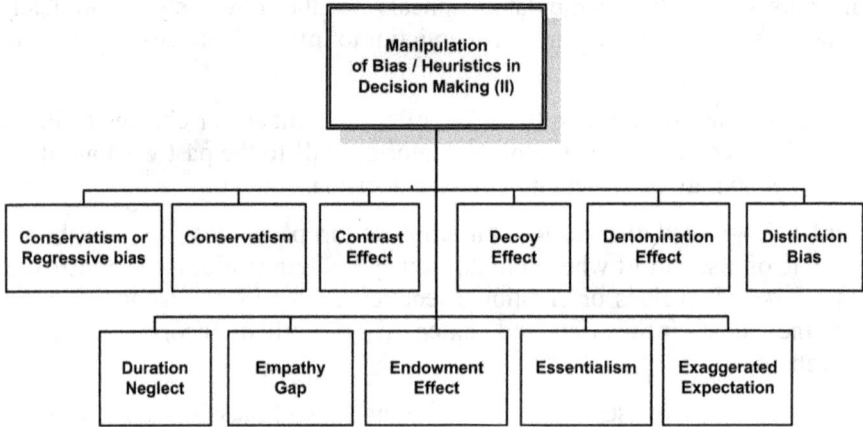

49.5.12 Conservatism or regressive bias: People frequently underestimate high values, likelihoods/probabilities/frequencies and overestimate low ones. Often their estimates are not revised appropriately even after the receipt of new evidence. This is because of the general bias to conservatism. The victim prefers to ignore new evidence. It is more comfortable.

The conservatism bias in some ways is similar to the "Base Rate bias", in that it has to do with the revision of opinion with the receipt of new information. The "Base Rate bias" has the effect of overweighing new data. Conservatism has the opposite effect.

Under conservatism, people do not revise their judgements on receipt of new data. Conservatism acts to protect the waste of the prior cognitive effort in making a decision. This is irrational. A manipulator can take advantage of conservative bias to direct a victim's decisions towards low risk / low return and more mediocre, less revolutionary options.

For example, in times of political upheaval a manipulator may argue to maintain the "comfortable" status quo. Many victims feel attracted to this argument because they are biased to maintain the status quo, not for any rational reason, but simply because it is more comfortable and seems to require less effort from them.

49.5.13 Conservatism (Bayesian): This is the tendency to revise belief insufficiently when presented with new evidence. This results in our estimates of probabilities being conservative. The manipulator uses the inherent conservatism of the victim to provide support to conservative postures (see above).

49.5.14 Contrast effect: This is the enhancement or diminution of a weight or other measurement when compared with a recently observed contrasting object. So, asking someone to estimate the weight of a chair by comparing it with that of a feather or a car will illicit firm comparisons. Asking a victim for a weight estimate of two similar chairs will illicit uncertain responses.

Here, weight is a synonym for any form of measurement, like time, distance, difficulty, beauty even. People living in countries where the citizens tend to be tall, find their fellows to be of normal height, and everyone of more average height is seen as "short". This is because "tall" is normal for them. The manipulator can use the recent quantitative experiences of a victim to prejudice their judgment of their present experience.

49.5.15 Decoy effect: This is a change of preferences where a third option is asymmetrically dominated. A manipulator introduces an inferior option to lead the victim to one of the more dominant options. This is a favourite trick in sales and marketing. For example, if there are 2 models of a hard disk available, of different sizes and prices, some customers will go for size, some for price. If a third model then is introduced which is less good value than either and has a size in between that of the original two models, most customers will ignore the decoy (obviously) and tend to buy the more expensive, larger capacity model from the original options.

49.5.16 Denomination effect: This is the susceptibility to spend more money when it is denominated in small units rather than large units. So, for example, we can be persuaded to spend more in coins rather than notes.

A manipulator uses this tendency to price in small amounts and delivery quantities to create the impression of cheapness. For example, strawberries may be priced at €0.99 for a 200g pack rather than in €4.95 for a 1kg tray. The customer needs 1kg and so will probably buy 5 packs, because, after all "they are only €0.99 each".

49.5.17 Distinction bias: This is the inclination to view two options as more dissimilar when evaluating them simultaneously, rather than separately. A manipulator selects the options for evaluation, (together or apart), depending on the outcome required.

For example, when televisions are displayed next to each other, the difference in quality between two very similar, high-quality televisions may appear great. A consumer may pay a much higher price for the higher-quality television, even though the difference in quality is imperceptible when the televisions are viewed in isolation. Because the consumer will probably be watching only one television at a time, the lower-cost television would have provided a similar experience at a lower cost.

49.5.18 Duration neglect: This is the neglect of the duration of an episode in determining its value. The manipulator "glosses over" or trivialises the period of a bad experience in order to minimise its importance to the victim.

49.5.19 Empathy gap: This is the likelihood to underestimate the influence or strength of feelings, in either oneself or others. The manipulator plays down the emotional issues at stake and gives priority to practical matters.

49.5.20 Endowment effect: People often demand much more when selling an object than they would be willing to pay for it. A manipulator can intentionally inflate the price of an object by trying to procure it from a victim. This may make the object too expensive to sell thereafter, or make the victim value the object more.

49.5.21 Essentialism: This is the categorisation of people and things according to their essential nature, in spite of variations. The manipulator lumps a lot of similar candidates together and refuses to indicate which candidates show some exceptionally good or bad qualities.

49.5.22 Exaggerated expectation: Frequently, real-world evidence turns out to disappoint our expectations (this is the inverse of the conservatism bias). A manipulator takes advantage of the expectations of the victim that "all will be well", despite pessimistic projections.

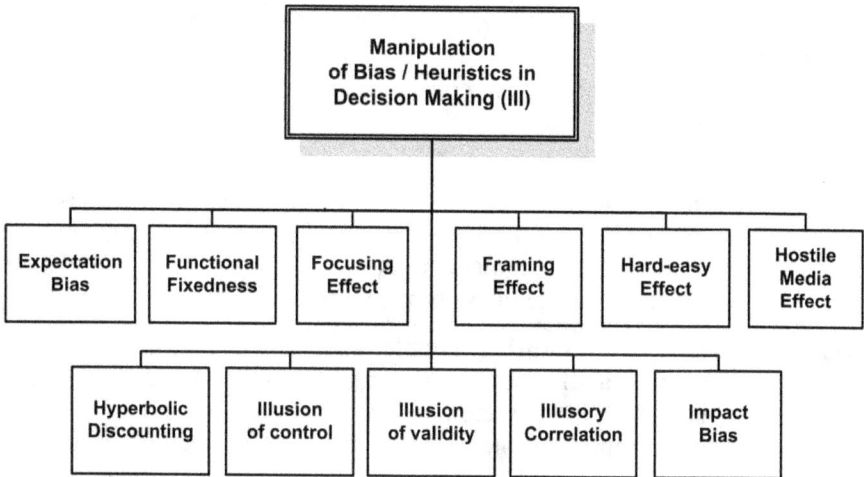

```
                    ┌─────────────────────┐
                    │    Manipulation      │
                    │ of Bias / Heuristics in │
                    │ Decision Making (III)   │
                    └─────────────────────┘
```

| Expectation Bias | Functional Fixedness | Focusing Effect | Framing Effect | Hard-easy Effect | Hostile Media Effect |

| Hyperbolic Discounting | Illusion of control | Illusion of validity | Illusory Correlation | Impact Bias |

49.5.23 Experimenter's or expectation bias: This is a predisposition for experimenters to believe, certify, and publish data that agree with their expectations for the outcome of an experiment, whilst disbelieving, discarding, or downgrading the corresponding weight of data that appear to conflict with those expectations. A manipulator may trap an experimenter into defending an indefensible result, simply because the experimenter feels responsible for the data and the result. Alternatively, a manipulator may co-opt a willing experimenter into conspiring to alter results and data to confirm a pre-defined expectation.

49.5.24 Functional fixedness: This is the acceptance of functional limits placed on the use of an object only in the way it is traditionally used. A manipulator forces the victim back into a "functional box" by reiterating that a door of a burning house can only be opened with a key whilst ignoring the sledge hammer, crow bar or mechanised digger standing nearby.

49.5.25 Focusing effect: This is the tendency to place too much importance on one aspect of an event. The manipulator makes the victim focus on a single cause without allowing an honest evaluation of what really happened.

49.5.26 Framing effect: This is the inclination to draw different conclusions from the same information, depending on how or by whom that information is presented. The manipulator alters the opinion of a victim by delivering information to them via a pre-determined and biased route. Individuals tend to give more credibility to data presented in different ways. A highly polished, professional presentation may impress some people, but may make others suspicious.

49.5.27 Hard-easy effect: Based on a specific level of task difficulty, we naturally overestimate our ability to complete simple tasks whilst underestimating our ability to complete complex tasks. A manipulator can take advantage of this bias by deliberately under or overestimating the difficulty of a victim's task.

49.5.28 Hostile media effect: This is the tendency to see a media report as being biased, depending on one's own partisan views. A manipulator can direct a victim towards certain media outputs to generate an angry reaction, based on the known factional views of the victim.

49.5.29 Hyperbolic discounting: People often have a stronger preference for more immediate payoffs rather than for later reward. A manipulator can augment an incentive for a victim by moving the reward closer to the effort. This is a primary principle of "Payment by Results" incentive schemes which state "keep the reward close at hand".

49.5.30 Illusion of control: This is the propensity to overestimate one's degree of influence over external events. A manipulator can put a victim at risk by bolstering their confidence in managing a situation over which they have little control.

49.5.31 Illusion of validity: This is the likelihood that very consistent but weak data will lead to confident predictions. A manipulator delivers an invalid argument by emphasizing only the consistency of the data and correlations, without also describing the weaknesses of the data - e.g. a small sample size, or a non-random sample.

49.5.32 Illusory correlation: This is the tendency to inaccurately perceive a causal relationship between two unrelated events. A manipulator can create an illusion in some victims that a causal relationship exists between two or more events, when actually a more thorough evaluation proves that the events are unrelated or are not directly related.

49.5.33 Impact bias: This is the tendency to overestimate the intensity/length of impact of future feelings. This bias tends to make us expect that we will feel worse than we actually do when things go wrong. Fear is a powerful emotion and people's imagination often gets the better of them, leading to an exaggerated dread of the future.

A manipulator may use this trait to maintain a victim in a state of fear of some particular consequences, by implying that things will be much worse than they actually are or will be, even when things go wrong.

```
┌─────────────────────────┐
│     Manipulation        │
│ of Bias / Heuristics in │
│  Decision Making (IV)   │
└─────────────────────────┘
```

Information Bias	Insensitivity to Sample size	Irrational Escalation	Less-is-better Effect	Ludic Fallacy	Mere Exposure Effect

Money Illusion	Moral Credential Effect	Neglect of Probability	Normalcy Bias	Observer Expectancy Effect

49.5.34 Information bias: Often people seek more information even when it cannot affect the situation. A manipulator can send a victim off on wild goose chases for information to help in a crisis, whereas, in reality, the information is worthless and contributes nothing to solving a crisis.

49.5.35 Insensitivity to sample size: This is the tendency to under-expect variation in small samples. A manipulator can use a victim's ignorance of sample size in order to prove a case based on small sample sizes.

49.5.36 Irrational escalation: This is the phenomenon where people justify increased investment in a decision based on the cumulative prior investment, despite new evidence suggesting that the investment decision was probably wrong. A manipulator uses this predilection to continue milking a victim, already committed to a cause, to pledge even further. Related to the "Gambler's fallacy".

49.5.37 Less-is-better effect: This is a preference reversal where a dominated smaller set is preferred to a larger set. For example, a 300g portion of ice cream overflowing a small cup is preferred to a 400g portion of ice cream in much larger cup. A manipulator can use this bias to persuade a victim to buy a small but valuable object instead of a larger but less valuable object, even if the real unit value is lower for the manipulated choice. Putting delicacies (like truffles or caviar) in small expensive looking packages allows a retailer to get a higher price per kilogram.

49.5.38 Ludic fallacy: This is the misuse of comparisons between games and real-life situations. It is also described as "basing studies of chance on the narrow world of games and dice". A manipulator can appeal to a victim using narrow game analogies instead of real life comparisons. For instance, he says: "Well, it's just the luck of the draw", to describe one's job prospects, whereas we know that there are several ways of improving our job prospects.

49.5.39 Mere exposure effect: People often express undue liking for things, merely because of familiarity with them. A manipulator can appeal to a victim by referring to familiar objects, attitudes and surroundings, rather than a rational evaluation of appeal.

49.5.40 Money illusion: This is the tendency to concentrate on the nominal (face value) of money rather than its value in terms of purchasing power. A manipulator can make an amount of money sound very large or very small, without actually making any real comparisons to what it will buy the victim.

49.5.41 Moral credential effect: This is the tendency of a person's track record of non-prejudice to increase the likelihood of them developing prejudices in the future. Recent studies have lead to the paradoxical conclusion that the act of affirming one's egalitarian or pro-social values and virtues might subsequently facilitate prejudiced or self-serving behaviour; an effect also referred to as "moral credentialing." A manipulator dealing with an ethically virtuous victim can use their ethical track record to persuade them to tend away from their previously unprejudiced attitude. For example, a manipulator may persuade a victim to lie or cheat, in order to achieve something which is morally justified - "the end justifies the means".

49.5.42 Neglect of probability: This is the inclination to completely disregard probability when making a decision under uncertain conditions. When in doubt, people are often unable to calmly consider the options. A manipulator may leverage a victim's inability to make a rational estimate of the probabilities of various events to persuade the victim to think or behave in a certain irrational way. A victim may prefer an illogical decision to trying to make a reasonable estimate of probability.

49.5.43 Normalcy bias: This is the refusal to plan for, or react to, a disaster which has never happened before. A manipulator can use this complacency, thinking that "everything will be OK", to lull a victim into a false sense of safety. It can also be used by a manipulator to expose the lack of preparedness of a victim who has not considered what might go wrong.

49.5.44 Observer-expectancy effect: This occurs when a researcher expects a given result, and therefore unconsciously manipulates an experiment or misinterprets data in order to reach that outcome. A manipulator can use this bias to encourage a researcher to illicitly seek out or alter a particular result.

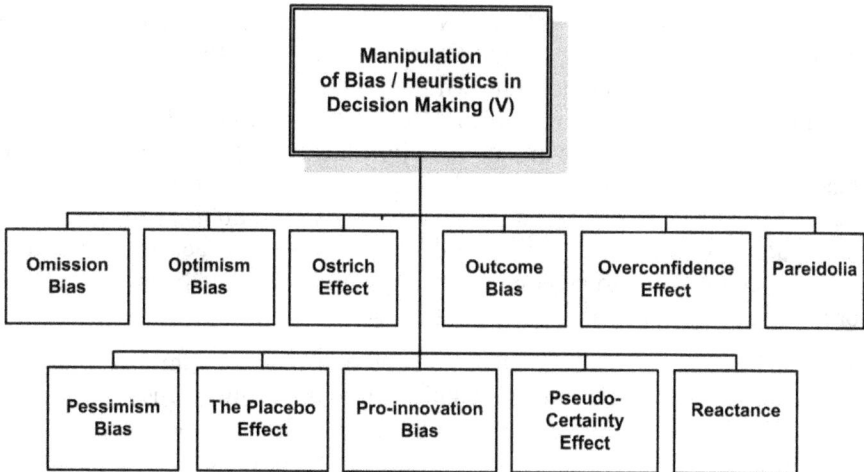

```
                    ┌─────────────────────┐
                    │    Manipulation      │
                    │ of Bias / Heuristics in │
                    │  Decision Making (V) │
                    └─────────────────────┘
```

| Omission Bias | Optimism Bias | Ostrich Effect | Outcome Bias | Overconfidence Effect | Pareidolia |

| Pessimism Bias | The Placebo Effect | Pro-innovation Bias | Pseudo-Certainty Effect | Reactance |

49.5.45 Omission bias: We frequently judge harmful actions as morally worse than equally harmful omissions (inactions). The manipulator can help a victim justify turning a blind eye to a crime or deceit as less morally repugnant than actually committing the crime or guile. The crimes of child abuse committed by the Roman Catholic clergy in Ireland, for example, under the noses and in plain sight of the general public, escaped detection and punishment because the population "turned a blind eye" to it.

49.5.46 Optimism bias: This is the inclination to be over-optimistic, overestimating favourable and pleasing outcomes (see also wishful thinking, valence effect, positive outcome bias). A manipulator can take advantage of over-optimism to alter a victim's behaviour or decision making.

49.5.47 Ostrich effect: This is the propensity to ignore an obvious (negative) situation by adopting an attitude of "Ignorance is bliss". The manipulator takes advantage of the desire of the victims not to know something by not informing them. It is also known as "No news is good news". Governments constantly withhold bad news to keep us "blissfully ignorant".

49.5.48 Outcome bias: This is the inclination to judge a decision by its eventual outcome, instead of basing it on the quality of the decision at the time it was made. It is also referred to as: "the beauty of hindsight". A manipulator can heap information onto a victim about what happened after the event so as to alter the perception of a decision, even though that information was not available at the time the decision was made. He may say, for example, "Well, of course, we expected that to happen when we made the decision."

49.5.49 Overconfidence effect: This is the tendency towards excessive confidence in our answer to questions. For example, for certain types of exam questions, studies have shown that answers that people rate as 99% certain turn out to be wrong 40% of the time. Overconfidence has been called the most "pervasive and potentially catastrophic" of all the cognitive biases to which human beings fall victim [Plous, S. (1993)]. It has been blamed for lawsuits, strikes, wars, and stock market bubbles and crashes. A manipulator can trick an overconfident victim into an action or position which then turns out to be completely ill-judged - it could be an investment or a military action or a political strategy etc.

49.5.50 Pareidolia: This is when a vague and random stimulus (often an image or sound) is perceived as significant, e.g. seeing images of animals or faces in clouds, the man in the moon, or hearing non-existent hidden messages on records played in reverse. A manipulator can persuade a gullible victim to believe something, based on completely irrelevant visual coincidences or images he has created for the purpose. For instance, in July 2012, in New Jersey, a knot in a tree trunk was discovered. "Believers" claimed it resembled the Virgin Mary. The tree trunk drew large crowds of people who came to pray and lay flowers and place votive candles by the tree. Yes, this was in 2012. [N.Y. Times 22/7/2012].

49.5.51 Pessimism bias: This is the tendency for some people, especially those suffering from depression, to overestimate the likelihood of negative things happening to them. A manipulator can use this bias to persuade a victim to act in a certain way, buying unnecessary insurance for instance, or selling stocks or property at a loss when convinced of impending economic doom around the corner. This is a favorite of equity market manipulators, who force a market down in order to buy stock at low prices.

49.5.52 The placebo effect: "The physician's belief in the treatment and the patient's faith in the physician exert a mutually reinforcing effect; the result is a powerful remedy that is almost guaranteed to produce an improvement and sometimes a cure."

The placebo effect is the measurable, observable, or felt improvement in health or behaviour not attributable to any medication or invasive treatment that has been administered. It has become a catchall term for a positive change in health, unrelated to medication or treatment. The change can be due to many things, such as spontaneous improvement, reduction of stress, misdiagnosis in the first place, patient's expectations, patient conditioning, etc.

A manipulator can use the placebo effect to alter a victim's perception of an illness by making them feel better, making them feel that something is being done, when in fact it isn't. Alternatively, a placebo effect may undermine a victim's trust in another treatment.

49.5.53 Pro-innovation bias: This is the inclination to prefer invention/innovation, while ignoring limitations, weaknesses or risks of failure in the innovation: "It's new, therefore it's good." A manipulator can use this bias to promote a new product to a victim, despite its lack of track record or quality. This is a favourite marketing trick. Consumers are constantly enjoined to buy the latest PC or mobile phone even when the one they have is still perfectly good. Consumers will often tend to buy the new model even though it has almost no track record.

49.5.54 Pseudo-certainty effect: This is the propensity to make risk-averse choices if the expected outcome is positive, whilst making risk-seeking choices to avoid negative outcomes. A manipulator can point a victim in a certain direction by altering the perception of the outcome. For example, an investment advisor can influence the investments of a client by emphasising higher or lower risk levels of investment alternatives.

49.5.55 Reactance: This is the urge to do the opposite of what someone wants you to do, out of a need to resist a perceived attempt to constrain your freedom of choice (also known as "Reverse psychology"). A manipulator can use this tendency to persuade a victim to act in a certain way, simply by encouraging them to do the contrary. The victim, in a reactive attempt to show that they are "free", ends up being manipulated.

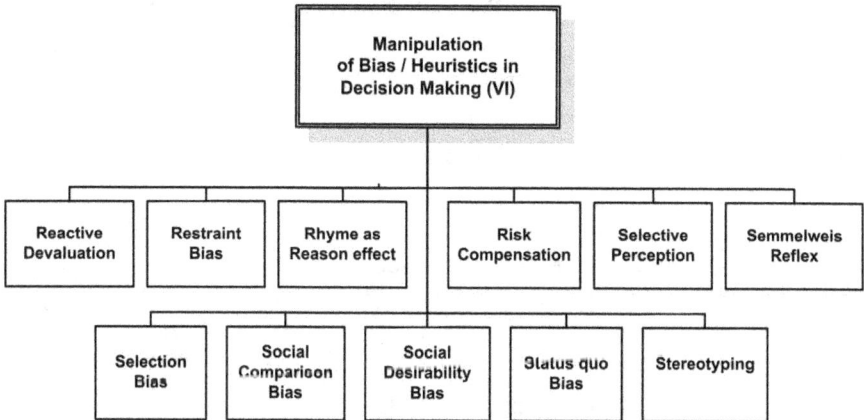

49.5.56 Reactive devaluation: This is the propensity to devalue proposals that are no longer hypothetical or purportedly originated with an adversary. A manipulator can discredit a proposal in the eyes of a victim by attributing them (truthfully or falsely) to an adversary of the victim.

49.5.57 Restraint bias: Humans often overestimate their ability to show restraint in the face of temptation. A manipulator can use this inaccurate self-image to entice and tempt a victim, despite the confidence that the victim exhibits in their ability to resist temptation. Marketing specialists use this inclination to determine the placing of tempting goods or offers in certain locations in a shop. The "restrained" customer walks past them and then returns later to buy one!

49.5.58 Rhyme as reason effect: This is the strange phenomenon where rhyming statements are perceived to contain profound truths. A famous case was the O.J Simpson trial with the defence's use of the phrase "If the gloves don't fit then you must acquit." A manipulator might use this bias to phrase statements to rhyme to increase their acceptability by a victim.

49.5.59 Risk compensation / Peltzman effect: This is the predilection to take greater risks when perceived safety increases.

A manipulator can persuade a victim to take greater risks when the victim thinks that some kind of safety net exists, whether it does or not.

For example, a bank official or real-estate salesman may say, "You can't lose with property. Whatever happens you always have your house". Here, their "safety net" is completely fictional, but the perception makes the victim take more risk.

49.5.60 Selective perception: This is the tendency for expectations to affect perception. A manipulator can use this inclination to deliver messages to a victim based on the manipulator's knowledge of the victim's expectations.

49.5.61 Semmelweis reflex: This is the inclination to reject new evidence that contradicts a paradigm. A manipulator can use this bias to make a victim reject new information, simply because it doesn't conform to their existing practice or norms.

49.5.62 Selection bias: This is the distortion of a statistical analysis resulting from a biased method of collecting samples. If the selection bias is not taken into account, then the conclusions which are drawn may be wrong. A manipulator can use this bias to persuade a victim to use a particular sample, and thus alter the results of a study or statistical analysis.

49.5.63 Social comparison bias: This is the propensity, when recruiting staff, to favour potential candidates who don't compete with one's own particular strengths. A manipulator can use this bias to alter the type of employees that are hired, simply by always presenting innocuous candidates.

49.5.64 Social desirability bias: This is the tendency to over-report socially desirable characteristics or behaviour, whilst under-reporting socially undesirable characteristics or behaviour. A manipulator can use this trait to change the responses of victims by phrasing questions with a desirable or undesirable slant.

49.5.65 Status quo bias: This is the inclination to like things to stay the same (see also: loss aversion, endowment effect, and system justification). The manipulator can use this preference to alter a victim's actions or expectations by appealing to their desire to maintain the status quo.

49.5.66 Stereotyping: This involves expecting a member of a group to have certain characteristics, without having any actual information about that individual. A manipulator can use this tendency to malign or compliment another person or group in the eyes of a victim, simply by referring to a common stereotype.

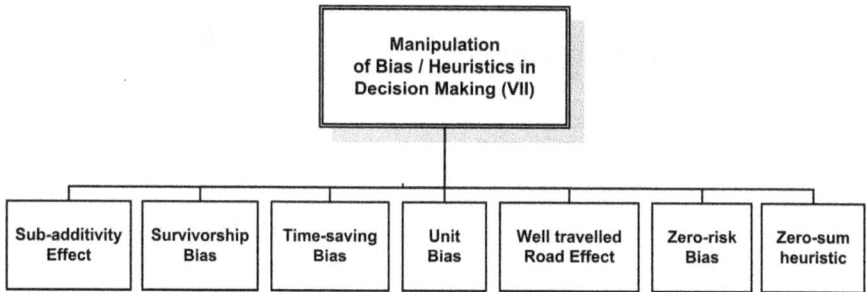

49.5.67 Sub-additivity effect: This is the susceptibility to estimate that the likelihood of an event is less than the sum of its (more than two) mutually exclusive components. A manipulator can use this tendency to confuse a victim in their risk or chance evaluations.

49.5.68 Survivorship bias: We tend to concentrate on the people or things that "survived" some process, whilst inadvertently overlooking those that didn't, because of their lack of visibility. A manipulator can use this trait to alter a victim's conclusions by only presenting information about the candidates that succeeded, whilst ignoring data about the ones that failed some selection process.

49.5.69 Time-saving bias: This bias is concerned with underestimations of the time that could be saved when increasing from a relatively low speed, and overestimations of the time that could be saved when increasing from a relatively high speed. "Speed" can be seen as a synonym for pace or performance of work, progress, investment, development, etc. A manipulator can use this bias to alter a victim's perception of the benefits of accelerating or decelerating, by making appropriate comparisons of possible changes in "speed". For example, a driver in a hurry may accelerate from 100km/h to 110km/h to save time. But in fact this only saves 10% or less of the journey time. A driver accelerating from 30km/h to 60km/h will save 50% of their journey time. We tend to ignore the relativity of the benefit we gain (or lose).

49.5.70 Unit bias: This is the inclination to want to finish a given unit of work, or task. We prefer to finish off logical units, in general, because it appeals to our sense of order, rather than any rational objective.

The bias extends as far as the consumption of food where some of us will try to finish off a particular (less favourite) component before starting to eat another part of our dish (children are adept at it). In a work environment, we tend to try to process our task list one item at a time. Even when we are delayed in processing one of the tasks, instead of moving on to the next item, we will tend to wait until the current task is completed.

A manipulator can use this bias to persuade a victim to process tasks in a serial way rather than in parallel. A manipulator can use this inclination to alter the way in which work is prioritised.

49.5.71 Well-travelled road effect: This is both the underestimation of the time taken to traverse oft-traveled routes, and the overestimation of the time needed to traverse less familiar routes. A manipulator can use this flaw in estimation to trick a victim into making poor approximations of the time required to reach a particular destination. A "route" can also be seen as a synonym for a process, like a project plan, or a development plan, etc. A familiar activity will be underestimated, whilst an unfamiliar activity will be overestimated in terms of effort, time and resources required.

49.5.72 Zero-risk bias: This is the preference for reducing a small risk to zero over the option of a greater reduction in a larger risk. A manipulator may use this bias to persuade a victim to alter their investments to eliminate a small risk completely whilst simultaneously not addressing a much larger risk.

49.5.73 Zero-sum heuristic: This is intuitively judging a situation to be zero-sum (i.e. that gains and losses are correlated). The name derives from the zero-sum game in the game theory, where wins and losses sum to zero. The manipulator uses this tendency to persuade a victim to act (or not act) in a certain way, because, after all, alternative actions will be a case of "swings and roundabouts" - a zero-sum outcome, anyway.

49.6 Avoidance and Counteraction: To avoid being manipulated by your own cognitive biases, you need to become aware of these common predispositions when making decisions or deciding to believe something. Decision making is a minefield of psychological bias and a "land of plenty" for the manipulator.

---oOo---

50. Self-delusion - the manipulation of self

50.1 Definition: Self-delusion involves convincing oneself of a truth (or lack of truth), without regard to a rational, objective evaluation of the facts. "Humans tend to see what they want to see" is a statement which defines the phenomenon very well. Self-deception is the process or fact of misleading ourselves to accept claims as true or valid when they are actually false or invalid. Self-deception, in short, is a way in which we justify false beliefs about ourselves to ourselves.

Self-deception works by using a process of denying or rationalising the relevance, significance, or importance of opposing evidence and logical argument.

We include this subject in a discussion of manipulation because it relates to us all as victims of our own delusions. However, it is also relevant to the special character of both the manipulator and manipulated.

This is a subject of intense interest in psychology and we won't attempt a complete analysis of all possible forms of self-delusion here. But there are some important aspects of self-delusion which make it highly relevant to the subject of human manipulation in general, and we will focus on these here.

50.1.1 The self-deluded victim: One of the most interesting and important aspects of self-delusion is that a manipulator relies on his victims being, in some sense, already deluded. This may take the form of the victim's intellectual laziness, or it may be the result of years of accruing unquestioning assumptions by the victim. Either way, an intellectually weak or passive victim is fertile ground for a manipulator.

The target group for this kind of manipulation includes people or groups with strongly held views based on unchallenged assumptions and, conversely, those who have no views at all because of an intellectual disinterest or a lack of intellectual faculty.

Very often, a manipulator will seek out people who are, to some extent, intellectually lazy and incurious. For the predator, these are the natural equivalent of the weaker members of a species and therefore singled out for attention by the "hunter".

50.1.2 The deluded manipulator: It's not just the manipulator's victims that are self-deluded. Very often the perpetrator is also suffering from some serious delusions. The obvious delusion is that the manipulator has more power than they actually possess. This is typical of the bully who uses and abuses weaker members of a group.

The fallacy of strength and invincibility is only revealed when a stronger influence challenges the delusion of the bully. In another instance, the manipulative "control freak" justifies his own behaviour as being "necessary in the best interests" of the victim. This particular self-delusion is only challenged when the victim finally leaves, and the manipulator is confronted with the reality of having no-one left to control.

50.1.3 How self-delusion encourages manipulation: This seeming contradiction of a deluded victim and a deluded manipulator gets close to the heart of why and how human manipulation actually works in reality.

The coexistence of the delusional intellects of both victim and manipulator is only possible under certain conditions. It requires that both parties lack interest in self-analysis and that at least the victim is also intellectually lazy. None of us are capable of completely honest self-analysis, as we will see from the self-delusional types we describe below. However, an honest attempt at an intellectual understanding of ourselves and our context on this planet does reveal some interesting and useful dichotomies and lessons which we should try to learn, if we care at all about being semi-autonomous individuals.

The most potent of these lessons are:

Don't believe your own propaganda

Don't abide rigidly by any assumption, whatever its origin.

These mantras can simultaneously guard us against both becoming a manipulator and being manipulated.

50.1.4 How widespread is self-analysis? Only a small percentage of the world's population makes a real and consistent attempt at self-analysis. Most of us don't have the time. However important self-analysis may be, we are all mostly too busy with practical issues of survival. So, we are therefore, to some extent, all capable of being manipulated or indeed, of manipulating (consciously or unconsciously) our fellow human beings. It is part of the modern human condition that can only be mitigated, but never "cured".

50.1.5 Good science and bad science: Thomas Gilovich, the Cornell psychologist, describes the details of many studies which make it clear that we must be on guard against the tendencies to:

Misperceive random data and see patterns where there are none.

Misinterpret incomplete or unrepresentative data and give extra attention to confirmatory data while drawing conclusions without attending to or seeking out non-confirmatory data.

Make biased evaluations of ambiguous or inconsistent data, tending to be uncritical of supportive data and very critical of unsupportive data.

It is because of these tendencies that advocates of "good science" demand clearly defined, controlled, double-blind, randomized, repeatable, publicly presented studies.

Without such safeguards, we run a great risk of deceiving ourselves and others into believing things that are not actually true, based on our own delusions: bad science, in other words.

Because of these tendencies, non-scientists must try to imitate the methodologies of "good science", whenever possible, in trying to establish theories and beliefs. In fact, scientists must keep reminding themselves of these tendencies and guard against pathological science and self-delusion.

As potential victims of manipulation, the general public should insist on the same, high standards of evidence and interpretation from all sources which impact our decision making. That includes demanding our own honest evaluation and the avoidance of self-delusion in personal decision making.

50.2 Persistence: Long. Self-delusions become embedded in our personalities and start to become conditioned responses to the extent where we don't even think about the issues any longer. The longer a delusion is allowed to persist, the more traumatic it becomes when the delusion is finally exposed.

50.3 Accessibility: High, we all suffer from self-delusion.

50.4 Conditions/Opportunity/Effectiveness: There is no manipulation as effective as Self-delusion. It requires no external reinforcement and it is very difficult to dislodge, particularly since the victims (ourselves) are firmly convinced that the basis of the delusion is actually fact.

We all suffer from some delusions. It is common to the human condition.

50.5 Methodology/Refinements/Sub-species: There are many sub-types of self-delusion, the most important of which we present here. They are divided into two groups to assist readability:

```
                    ┌─────────────────────────────┐
                    │        Self-delusion         │
                    │            & the             │
                    │  Manipulation of Self (I)    │
                    └─────────────────────────────┘
```

Introspection Myth	Personal rebellion Selling out	Confirmation Bias	Frequency Illusion	Selective Bias	Fatalism of Disadvantage

Procrastination	Backfire Effect	Inattention Blindness	Anchoring Effect	Loss Aversion	Asymmetric Insight

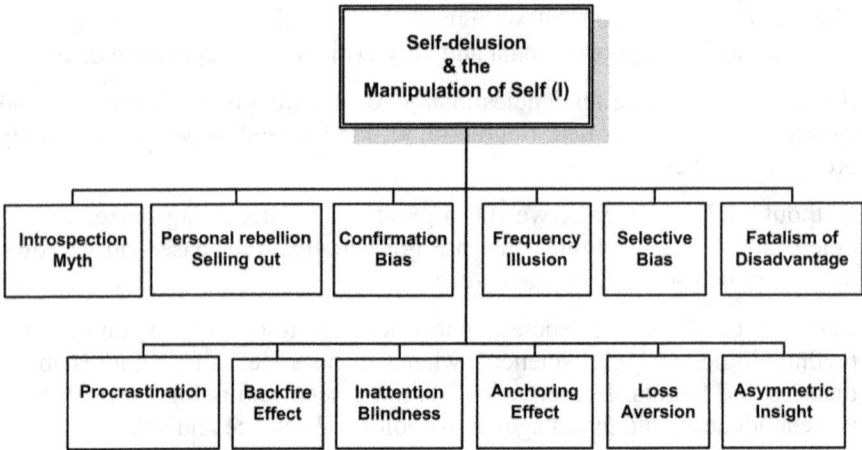

50.5.1 Introspection myth: Most of us will claim that we are capable of honest introspection and emotional self-analysis. However, in reality, the origins of certain emotional states which we experience are completely unavailable to us. Therefore, large parts of our personality cannot be intellectually analysed by us alone.

Furthermore, when we are challenged to say why we like or hate certain things, like a work of art or a piece of music, or even a person or place, for instance, we will often find it extremely difficult to honestly describe why we feel attracted or repelled. Generally, we will just make up something which is actually not true at all, simply to give an answer, whereas the reality lies deeply buried in emotional states which are largely invisible to our intellectual self.

The complex emotional associations which determine our own preferences can often be associated with completely unconnected events, like a cast of light and shadow reminding us of some long forgotten, but pleasant, childhood experience. Conversely, a sound may be inexplicably terrifying for no apparent reason. The pits of emotional reaction are bottomless and for most of us, they are completely opaque at an intellectual level.

Completely "honest" introspection is almost impossible for most of us. That doesn't mean that we shouldn't try however. But "fishing" in our own "emotional ponds" carries risks. Honest reflections (where they can be verbalised) reveal things about our personalities which may endanger our own image in the eyes of others. Few people are willing to take such risks with raw emotions of this sort, even if we were capable of communicating them.

To overcome this emotional "inexplicability", we solve the problem by inventing simpler intellectual explanations for many of our stronger emotional reactions. In this sense, we manipulate ourselves to believe one (invented) reality, because of our inability to understand or confront a much more complex, perhaps darker, truer reality. By communicating these "invented emotions" to others we perpetuate these self-delusions.

One way of dealing with this particular form of delusion is to at least attempt a better, more personally honest, understanding of one's own emotions. That need not involve a discussion with anyone else but oneself - or as the Shakespeare enjoins in Hamlet, "To thine own self be true".

50.5.2 Personal rebellion - selling out: There is a common misconception that consumerism and capitalism are sustained only by immoral corporations, profit motives, advertising and defrauding workers and consumers.

In reality, much of modern consumerism and capitalism is driven by competition among ordinary consumers (you and me) for status.

Every generation has produced its own counter-culture of rebellion, of raging against the establishment, often from the confines of the relatively comfortable middle-classes. This rebellion has generally manifested itself in some relatively harmless acts of "defiance", in terms of dress, music, hairstyle or social behaviour. Rarely do any of these generational "rebels" fully engage in an attack on the economic system or ruling establishment.

Social networking may become the latest highpoint of this delusion of rebellion. Now we can rebel at the click of a button by signing a petition to save the rainforests (whilst being sold an Apple iPad on the same page), without realising that the iPad was probably manufactured by destroying some rainforest. We delude ourselves by ignoring such great contradictions between our "rebellious self image" and our "non-rebellious self reality". On the contrary, when it comes to being rebellious, it is a much milder affair for most of us.

Having a dissenting opinion on movies, music or clothes, or owning clever or obscure possessions is about as rebellious as most of us get. This is the way that middle-class people fight each other for status. They can't out-consume each other, because they can't afford it, but they can out-do each other in terms of taste or attitude. For the capitalist world, this represents less of a threat than a selling opportunity, and it is rarely long before the capitalist machine cranks into action to capitalise on these new markets of the "rebellious middle-class".

In this respect, many middle-class "rebels" have sold out over the years since the end of the Industrial Revolution. They wear the clothes, use the symbols and language and cluster in groups with other "rebels". They may even demonstrate on the streets for this or that. But, rarely do any of them step outside of the ring of acceptable behaviour and enter into a serious, revolutionary challenge to the establishment of which they are part.

The self-delusion of being "rebellious" sustains the victim's ego and self-esteem, but does nothing to advance any real cause for social change. There is no cure for this particular self-delusion, except to be honest enough to admit one's own moral limitations, stop wearing silly clothes and falling for every single conspiracy theory, (stick with the credible ones). The alternative, of course is to get really serious about bringing about fundamental changes in our society, and put a laborious effort into this process by joining forces with other committed activists. But selling out is easier for most people.

50.5.3 Confirmation bias, also referred to as self-reinforcement: We all believe that our opinions are the result of years of rational, objective analysis. The reality is that our opinions are the result of years of making assumptions, paying attention only to information that confirms what we already believe, and ignoring information which challenges our preconceptions.

Confirmation bias refers to a type of selective thinking, whereby we tend to only look for and notice that what confirms our beliefs, and to ignore, not look for, or undervalue the relevance, of what contradicts our beliefs.

Mostly we don't even realise that we are involved in a kind of self-manipulation because we feel comfortable with our own value system. Our personal value system was evolved by us to explain the world. Undermining our own value system is psychologically disturbing. It may be catastrophically damaging to us, because it may create uncomfortable cognitive dissonances. Therefore, we have strong reasons to maintain our own core opinions, even against the most coldly accurate contradictions. In the case of such conflicts, we will likely find all kinds of alternatives to support our views, rather than re-examine our core opinions.

Without confirmation bias, many conspiracy theories would fall apart. Did we really put a man on the moon? Is there really a God? Are we ruled by aliens? If you are personally looking for proof of any wacko theory, you can certainly find evidence for almost anything, if you set the standards of data quality to satisfy your own biases.

That doesn't imply that there really are no conspiracies out there - it simply serves to illustrate that some conspiracy theories are just pure inventions, designed to confirm our existing moral biases, rather than us altering our moral biases based on an honest evaluation of the facts. Just because it is a conspiracy theory doesn't make it either right or wrong. It is just a theory. Just because we are paranoid doesn't mean that "they" are not after us! We need to keep an open mind and not allow ourselves to be manipulated in either direction.

50.5.4 Frequency illusion: A sub-type of confirmation bias is the so called "frequency illusion". This is that apparently strange occurrence when once you've noticed a phenomenon, it then seems to happen a lot, all the time in fact.

For instance, some book or movie you haven't heard of for years suddenly starts to be mentioned all the time. If you are thinking about buying a new car, you suddenly see people driving them everywhere. If you've just ended a long-term relationship, suddenly every song you hear seems to be written about love - your love, or it has been a favourite of your ex-partner. If you are having a baby, you start to see babies everywhere.

It can seem that this constant appearance has a supernatural significance. In reality it has a very simple psychological explanation. The reason this happens is because the subject is close to your recent memory, and suddenly you subconsciously start noticing its presence in the random world around you, giving the illusion that an awful lot of coincidences are occurring. This leads you to the suspicion that something more profound is happening. Such events can lead an unwitting person to suspect that some deeper, almost supernatural event is happening to them, when in fact it is just the mind playing tricks.

50.5.5 Selective bias: At the level of personal opinion, this type of delusion is endemic. We all tend to filter out opinions which differ from our own, and seek out opinions which coincide with our own.

Over time, by never seeking the antithetical, and by only reading magazines, books and watching television programmes that confirm our belief system, we can become so confident in our worldview, that no one could dissuade us of any part of it. Everything we know seems to confirm it.

This is a potentially dangerous form of delusional self-manipulation because it denies the concept of "keeping an open mind" or "thinking outside the box". In science, we move closer to the truth by seeking evidence to test the contrary of our hypothesis. Perhaps the same method should inform our personal opinions as well.

This bias is also often used by external manipulators, like advertisers or media outlets. There's always someone out there willing to sell "eyeballs" to advertisers, by offering a guaranteed audience of people looking for validation of their own vision. This is precisely the business model of Fox News. They are the channel of choice for the right-wing Republican voters of the USA, and Fox News gives these people exactly what they desire -

hard right-wing opinions.

50.5.6 Fatalism of disadvantage: This is the delusion that if we are in a very bad situation, we have and can use some personal, heroic reserve of energy and strength to help us overcome our situation. In fact, most people, when they feel that they have lost control of their destiny, will give up and accept whatever situation they are in.

Both of these attitudes represent a form of self-manipulation, because, in fact, both positions are inadequate responses to an unfavourable personal environment.

There are many tragic cases of human beings being beaten into submission by personal circumstances to the point at which they simply accept their awful situation and position in life. The current world and history is full of such cases. There are also numerous cases where individuals in the most appalling conditions have survived and recovered in some way. An absolute belief in universal fatalism or heroism is equally mistaken. Only the individual can decide which role they will play.

Most of us who haven't experienced such violence or disadvantage, believe that we have a hidden store of resilience to fight back. However, in fact, when driven to absolute submission, few of us would have enough emotional or physical resources to completely recover control of our lives, were we to have been so roundly beaten and demoralised.

What we can do is accept our inability to immediately recover control of our lives, and we can attempt to control those aspects of our lives which we can manage. Apart from death, all physical disadvantages can be managed, somehow, even if they cannot be completely overcome. In this way, the absolute destruction of an individual can be avoided by the individual focusing on those aspects of life still within their control.

Using this mechanism, it is possible, with time, to overturn the most disadvantaged personal situation by simply learning how to effectively manage periods of helplessness. Supporting concepts from people who have confronted the despair of total helplessness are "Thought is free", "Our time will come" etc.

50.5.7 Procrastination: This is one of the most common forms of self-manipulation. We think we procrastinate because we are lazy and that we can't manage our time well. The reality is a bit more complicated. In terms of personal procrastination, we are really dealing with the internal conflict we have between our childish human predilection for pleasure and fun versus our "adult obligations" to utterly boring, uninteresting and unpleasant tasks.

We tend to delay because we are sometimes weak in the face of this impulsive "child" within us. The real way to deal with procrastination is actually to learn how to manage this constant conflict between these two personalities and tendencies.

This involves learning to think about how we actually think and then finding ways to manage the procrastinating "child". So, when we see signs of weakness we can, with practice, trick ourselves into behaving in an adult way, instead of just slipping into a constant round of guilt and more procrastination. It's not easy.

50.5.8 The Backfire Effect: It's a generally accepted fact that when our deepest convictions are challenged by contradictory evidence, our beliefs may actually get stronger.

When people with opposing views interpret new information in a biased way, their views can move further apart. Research in Stanford observed a group of volunteers with strong views on the death penalty. They were given mixed experimental research on the use of the death penalty - both pro and con. After reading the research material, 23% of the group reported that their views had become even more extreme, no-one had changed sides.

This hardening of attitudes happens despite the fact that we like to believe that we are quite rational. We would like to believe that when our beliefs are challenged with new facts, we alter our opinions and incorporate the new information into our thinking. But very often we do the opposite.

This is an unfortunate and perverse aspect of human behaviour, because it has created an easy prey for the manipulator: A rational person can be radicalised and made to be seen as extremist by the intervention of a simple gain-saying challenge.

This phenomenon is seen in many contexts, including the scientific, political communities, but also in inter-personal relationships.

50.5.9 Inattention blindness: This is sometimes called "Change blindness". It is a delusion which refers to the idea that we see and take in everything that is happening around us, processing it all like a camera. In fact, most people are aware of only a tiny fraction of what is happening around them, and even less of this information is actually ever processed. This applies just as much to things which are happening in plain sight, as to events or objects not directly visible.

A normal person's attention cannot be focused on everything, therefore everyone experiences inattention blindness. Inattention blindness has an effect on people's perception. This is because they are unaware of the unnoticed stimuli.

This inattention effect can also be employed by an external manipulator or used by the subject themselves to reinforce a perception they find more comfortable than reality.

There have been multiple experiments performed to demonstrate that this phenomenon is universally prevalent. The "invisible gorilla" experiment conducted in the 1990s showed that 50% of a group of people watching a basketball video, failed to notice a woman, dressed in a full gorilla suit carrying an umbrella, walk through the game several times. The focus of the volunteers was on watching the basketball, so the gorilla woman just didn't register.

The important thing about this phenomenon is that we cannot always trust what we see. In fact, we can never completely trust what we see. We can relate what we saw with some accuracy, but we cannot of course, report on or interpret what we did not see.

This should lead us all to adopt a healthy suspicion of our own sensory perceptions. In other words, we should learn to assume that we probably have not actually seen the entire picture of what happened or what was said or done.

By keeping an open mind on our own sensory perceptions, it may be possible to uncover more important facts about a particular event. Having said that, most people take what they "see" and "hear" at face value and will argue that what they think they have seen and heard, is the absolute and complete truth of a scene.

The old adage should really be applied: "Believe nothing you hear and only half of what you see."

50.5.10 Anchoring effect: This is the tendency to rely too heavily, or "anchor," on a past reference, or on just one piece of information, when making decisions.

Most of us think that when we make a decision, we do so as a result of a rational analysis of all known factors. However, it is now recognised that very often our decisions can be heavily biased by initial impressions or other bits of patchy information which influence our rational decision making ability.

Anchor points can be something as innocent as the original price on an object in a sale. Your first perception lingers in your mind, affecting later perceptions and decisions. So if something appears to have been originally cut in price from 200€ to 70€, the perception of the true value of the item is fixed at 200€. This is despite the fact that, without having known about the 200€ original price, you may rationally have valued the item at a much lower price. The anchor in this case is 200€ and this value influences all further decisions about whether to buy the item or not.

Anchoring is not only a form of self-delusion; it is also a phenomenon that is used by manipulators to persuade a victim to act in a certain way, or to believe a certain thing. In the above example, a shopkeeper has used the technique to create an anchor point of 200€ and is manipulating customers who see the sale price as an excellent price reduction.

50.5.11 Loss aversion and the sunken cost effect: Despite the fact that we are all pretty much convinced that we make rational decisions about future value, risk of loss and investment, the reality is that most people are highly emotional in their investment decisions. Phrases like "can't lose", "guaranteed returns", "cast-iron investment", etc. are commonplace in conversations amongst laymen about money and "where to put it".

What's more, existing investments very often become emotional attachments, which make them harder to sell or abandon, even when, rationally speaking, the facts dictate that the investment should be sold or abandoned.

The classic case of this phenomenon is when someone buys a ticket for a concert or movie in advance. Prior to the performance they learn that it is a disappointing event and has received very bad reviews....: "a waste of time". However, even ticket holders who are totally convinced of the worthlessness of the event will attend the event anyway, because they have already paid for the ticket.

Logic would demand that the ticket be thrown away because of the huge weight of negative criticism, but the emotional fear of loss obliges the victims to attend the event anyway.

They do this because they are "loss averse", and despite the fact that they are effectively "throwing good money after bad" by wasting time and money in attending something that everyone else thinks is rubbish. This irrational attachment to the original investment (i.e. the ticket) clouds their judgement, and they are unable to rationalise the idea of discarding the ticket and saving their time by not going to the event.

This is delusional behaviour; it is widespread, and it was most spectacularly seen in the collapses of property or investment bubbles such as the famous internet bubble of the 1990s and the property market collapses of the 1980s and 2007.

In these and many similar financial and economic collapses, ordinary investors, including corporate investors, tended to hang on to their investments, even after there was ample evidence that their investments were unlikely to gain value and were already seriously overvalued.

The late 1990s produced some spectacular corporate failures in the internet sector. Many internet companies build on poor business models experienced huge gains and cataclysmic losses in share value. And yet many investors stayed in the market until their investments became literally valueless. Such was their "emotional" attachment to their "pet" investments.

Around 2007-2008, the housing markets of many parts of Western Europe suffered a similar fate, triggered off by the panic over US "sub-prime" mortgages, where huge amounts of credit had been extended to borrowers of poor credit-worthiness.

Ordinary investors had been previously encouraged to borrow money to "invest" in domestic property because of the street myth that "property always gains and can never lose value". The important caveat missing was "if it is bought at a price close to its fundamental value".

Huge speculative prices were indeed paid for relatively modest properties, as investors fought to get a share of "the action" and get onto the "property ladder". Very soon property prices were absurdly inflated against their fundamental value as "just a place to live".

When the bubble did start to deflate, it was clear enough to any rational investor that it was time to leave the field. However, again, the loss aversion delusion kicked in and many ordinary people couldn't bring themselves to accept a break-even price or even a small loss. Many small investors decided to wait - until they had a really big and completely unmanageable loss on their hands.

Many investors simply couldn't contemplate the idea that their beloved investment was failing. This emotional attachment to an investment has cost many ordinary people their life savings, and brought untold misery to millions of ordinary, naïve people and their families.

The phenomenon is clearly a form of self-delusion but it also provides fertile ground for external manipulators who know that ordinary "punters" will always tend to buy at the top of market and sell at the bottom.

The financial manipulators of the capitalist world understand this delusional behaviour very well, and take advantage of it to time their departure from and entry into a market; the rule of the professional investor being to sell at the point of maximum public optimism and buy at the point of maximum public pessimism.

In the case of the so-called "Euro crisis", the point of maximum pessimism was probably around February 2009, the point at which European stock markets started drifting upwards again after 2 years of severe falls.

The opposite of loss aversion is "efficient investment". A central principle of efficient investment was put very succinctly by one of the old

Rothschild dynasty who, when asked about when to sell, said "Don't be too greedy, sell when you have a profit, and leave the last 10% (before the peak of a market) for the people... ".

Even in those days, the delusion of loss aversion amongst ordinary punters was well understood and manipulated by various capitalists to generate and protect profit.

50.5.12 Asymmetric insight: This particular delusion makes us believe that we are generally happy to tolerate diversity and respect others' points of view. In reality, most people are quite insular and motivated to form small groups of like-minded people with similar backgrounds and opinions whilst excluding everyone else.

The original delusion of being tolerant and open is based on the belief that we know everyone else far better than they know us, and not only that, we know them even better than they know themselves.

We believe the same thing about groups of which we are members. As a whole, our group understands outsiders better than outsiders understand our group, and we understand our group better than the rest of its members understand themselves.

This sad, un-utopian conclusion about our lack of real unity as a species, is the result of years of experimentation in behavioural science. The behaviour of tribal societies has demonstrated, (including our own bloody history as a species), that we tend to form groups which rapidly become exclusive to any others who are even slightly different from us, or who come from outside our own group.

Apart from the delusional belief in our tolerance of diversity, the fallacy also opens up a door to the outside manipulator, particularly when it suits the purpose of the manipulator to create division and antagonism where there would normally be harmony and warmth.

As an illustration, two groups that normally coexist in an apparently stable and friendly way, can be rapidly driven into open warfare by a very small intervention by an outside manipulator. The manipulator knows that the division between two different groups will be disproportionate to the reason for the conflict. This is why murderous family and "tribal" feuds can be started over the most trivial of issues, such as an overhanging tree, a barking dog, an annual historical or religious parade, or a few metres of land. Ireland's recent history is a tragic example of how a manipulator can set two previously tolerant groups at each other's throats in the space of just a few years[50.1].

```
                    ┌─────────────────────┐
                    │    Self-delusion     │
                    │       & the          │
                    │  Manipulation of Self│
                    │         (II)         │
                    └─────────────────────┘
```

Cathartic Venting	The Affect Bias	Barnum Effect	Buyer's Stockholm Syndrome	Recency Bias	Wishful Thinking

Selective Thinking	Continued Influence Effect	Motivated Reasoning

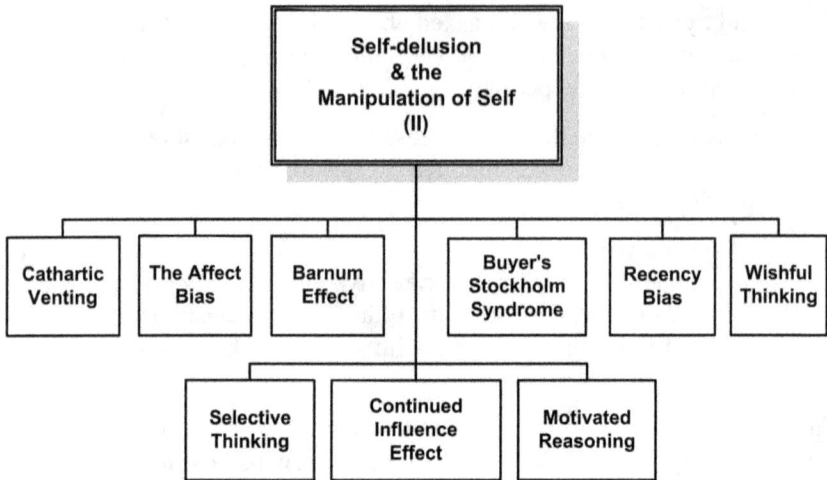

50.5.13 Cathartic venting: The advent of modern psychology has brought some important advances in our understanding of our emotions and the nature of repressive behaviour.

We have, for instance, come to believe that all forms of repressive behaviour are counter-productive. Included in this is the widely-held belief that anger should never be "bottled-up" and that such feelings can and should be healthily vented in the "usual" way. This might be the slamming of doors, storming out of a meeting, or whatever angry people do at a particular moment. Venting one's anger is generally considered to be an effective way to reduce stress and prevent lashing out at friends and family.

This generally held view is, however, a delusion. In fact, venting anger in this way actually increases aggressive behaviour over time. There is a very simple reason for this: Catharsis will make you feel good, but it's an emotional "roundabout" and not an end in itself. The emotion which leads us to catharsis will still be there afterwards, and if it made you feel good, you will seek it out again in the future. So, in a sense, cathartic venting becomes a form of emotional addiction with some strongly negative effects.

Anger tends to originate in some form of frustration. This frustration can either be channelled into corrective action or it can develop into anger. The anger can still be managed by calming down and rationalising the problem. This requires some effort and may give few immediate results in terms of the original problem.

Alternatively, anger can be vented in a cathartic way. This will give an instant gratification but will do nothing at all about the original issue. Giving in to the use of cathartic venting in this way tends to make us become catharsis junkies, using this "vent" more and more frequently as an apparent "solution" to all frustrations. This is a destabilising and invariably destructive route.

One of the risks of this particular delusion is that a manipulator can use this commonly accepted view of catharsis to encourage its public use by a victim. Over time, a victim's behaviour (under the tutelage of the manipulator), can be made to degenerate. It may reach the point where a victim becomes completely isolated from colleagues and friends who find the victim's tantrums intolerable.

Groups of victims can be encouraged to vent their anger in this way, and it gets really serious when groups of angry, inarticulate, "venting" people hit the streets!

The mechanism for the manipulator is simple: it is akin to making bullets for the victim to fire. The manipulator simply has to vent his anger, together with the victim in private, against some particular targets. Thus, a victim is encouraged to do the same thing whenever the case arises. All that is left is for the manipulator to ensure that the victim has plenty of opportunities for public anger. Once the addiction is established, the victim's behaviour becomes self-reinforcing and ultimately self-destructive.

Extreme racist parties use cathartic outbursts of xenophobia and extreme anger to convert their political message into menacingly violent demonstrations.

50.5.14 The Affect bias: This is defined as basing a decision on our emotional reactions rather than on a rational calculation of risks and benefits. This is a form of self-delusion. However, it can become a manipulative method, when the delusion of the victim is used by an external agency with a particular agenda to affect the behaviour of the victims.

This is often manifested as a decision based on emotions generated by very recently seen images or words. A typical case of the "affect bias" is the reaction of people when a food product claims to reduce incidence of cancer, heart disease, etc. In such a case, the use of the emotive word "cancer" is enough to alter the buying decision of the victim in favour of the product. The word "cancer" has acquired such demonic status, that no further proof is required - the product is a "must have".

On the other hand, associating a product with beautiful celebrities sends signals of success, health and wealth. These signals can be so powerful that a victim feels obliged to buy, simply to be seen to be associated with a product endorsed by such socially powerful icons Success may be "contracted" in this sense by some form of associative osmosis, because the celebrities and the victim use the same after-shave.

The "Affect bias" is constantly used in a more sinister and political way. For instance, if you want to scare people into voting for you, you could use the following expressions every opportunity you get: terrorist, weapons of mass destruction, bioterrorism, and nuclear holocaust. Just make sure that you associate all risks of these bad things with your opponent's political weaknesses.

You can also let people know that you stand for homeland security, protection, adequate defence, increased safety, family, community and prosperity. Keep reminding the voters that you're strong on national defence and you are a patriot, while your opponent is weak on national defence and some kind of unknown "socialist".

This combination of negative affect bias warnings and positive affect bias attractions is almost guaranteed to herd your target subjects into your voting camp.

50.5.15 The Barnum Effect: This is the phenomenon where individuals believe descriptions of themselves to be tailor-made for them, but in fact, they are vague and general enough to apply to a wide range of people. This effect provides a partial explanation for the acceptance of some beliefs and practices, such as astrology, graphology, and some types of personality tests.

A related and more general phenomenon is that of subjective validation. Subjective validation occurs when two unrelated or even random events are perceived to be related, because a belief, expectation, or hypothesis demands a relationship. Thus, people seek a correspondence between their perception of their own personality and the contents of their horoscope.

Studies have shown that the Barnum effect is quite universal. It has been observed in many cultures. However, these studies have also found that victims tend to trust their manipulators if any of the following conditions are true:

The subject believes that the analysis applies only to him or her, and thus applies their own meaning to the statements.

The subject believes in the authority of the evaluator.

The analysis lists mainly positive traits.

Sex has also proven to play a role in how accurate the subject believes the description to be: Studies have shown that women are more likely than men to believe that a vague statement is accurate and about them.

The method in which the Barnum personality profiles are presented can also affect the extent to which people accept them as their own. Barnum profiles that are more personalized - perhaps containing a specific person's name - are more likely to yield higher acceptability ratings than those that could be applied to anyone.

50.5.16 Buyer's Stockholm syndrome: Also known as "Post-purchase rationalization", is the self-delusion whereby someone who buys an expensive product or service overlooks any faults or defects in order to justify their purchase.

Many purchasing decisions are made emotionally, based on factors such as brand-loyalty and advertising pressures, and so these buying decisions are often rationalized retrospectively in an attempt to justify the choice.

When a person has clearly made a poor purchasing decision, they will still attempt to justify the decision by trying to convince themselves and their peers that it was a good decision.

This rationalization is based on the so-called "Principle of Commitment" and the psychological desire to stay consistent to that commitment. It is related to the concept of loss aversion where the victim cannot face the possibility that they have made a wasteful purchase. So, they create an artificial reality to justify the bad decision.

The phenomenon is well known to marketers who rely on slick marketing and image to persuade customers to buy their product, knowing that any shortfall in product quality, value or usefulness will be made up for by the buyer's insistence that it was a good purchase.

Victims of this manipulation actually become instrumental in the plot of the manipulator by aggressively promoting the product as a means of justifying their own bad decision.

50.5.17 Recency bias: This is the tendency to think that trends and patterns we observed in the recent past will continue into the future. Predicting the future in the short term, even for highly changeable events like the weather or the stock market, based on events in the recent past, may work fine most of the time.

However, predicting the future in the long term according to what has recently occurred has been shown to be no more accurate than flipping a coin. This is especially true in fields like meteorology, demographics, economics, investment, technology assessment, futurology, and organizational planning.

Nonetheless, the general public is constantly exposed to poorly formulated predictions based on data from the recent past. These predictions very often turn out to be catastrophically wrong. Looking back over the last 30 years, few of the really large events that affected the world have been accurately predicted; for instance the end of the Cold War, the fall of the Berlin Wall, the Arab Spring, Global Warming, the rise of the internet, the wars of the Middle East, etc.

Why do we make such poor predictions and why does the public believe these dodgy forecasts?

Recent events and trends are much easier to remember and discern than either events in the distant past or unknown events that will occur in the future. So, rather than do the hard work of studying the long term past, we tend to use recent events to make our predictions. It is easier. But we also refuse to accept that many areas of human interest are beyond our ability to predict at levels better than chance.

So, because of the difficulties in making accurate long-term predictions based on long term historical data and trends, the public is fed a poor quality diet of fairly random attention seeking headlines, few of which actually represent reliable predictions of the economic, social, technological or political future.

Apparently, we even find it hard to make accurate predictions of our own population growth, despite the fact that we have a wealth of fairly accurate historical data to work with. So we lurch from doom predictions of global starvation to demographic time bombs, predicting catastrophic population decline. Amazingly, these entirely contradictory arguments are dished out to us simultaneously with no apparent embarrassment by the media.

Regarding population issues, the contradictory conclusions are shamelessly used by a politically manipulative press to justify particular short-term political agendas, such as legalising GMO crop products to feed the starving, or delaying the retirement age of workers to maintain the creaking social welfare system.

So we may be sure that the motivation driving these predictions is entirely political, wholly short-term, and based on demographic predictions of very dubious quality. Indeed, the predictions are no more than politically motivated statements, often designed to frighten us. They should not really be given the grand title of "prediction".

The recency bias of the general public makes the selling of these "end of nose" projections much easier for the manipulator, because everyone knows the population is ageing - they can see it with their own eyes.

50.5.18 Wishful thinking: Wishful thinking is interpreting facts, reports, events, perceptions, etc., according to what one would like to be the case rather than according to the actual evidence. It is a primitive and very common form of self-delusion.

Commercial and political manipulators often play up to this particular delusion by telling their victims what they think they want to hear.

50.5.19 Selective thinking: Selective thinking is the process whereby one chooses to remember favourable evidence for a belief, while ignoring and forgetting unfavourable facts.

This kind of selective thinking is the basis for most beliefs in the psychic powers of so-called mind readers and mediums. It is also the basis for many, if not most, occult and pseudoscientific beliefs.

We should note that selective thinking works independently of wishful thinking and should not be confused with biased thinking whereby one seriously considers data contrary to one's belief but one is much more critical of such data than one is of supportive data.

50.5.20 Continued influence effect: This is a form of self-delusion, which can also be used to the advantage of an external manipulator.

This effect happens when a victim learns "facts" about an event that later turn out to be false, but the discredited information continues to influence the victim's reasoning and understanding, even after the information has been discredited and corrected.

There are many cases where the general public continues to believe completely untrue stories, despite the "facts" behind the story being completely and comprehensively discredited.

Manipulators take advantage of this phenomenon because they know that it is more important to tell a good story with a strong political message than to be accurate.

The manipulator knows that any inaccuracies in their narrative are less important than the message delivered, simply because the corrections will be ignored by their audience. The influence of the original story will continue more strongly than any correction of inaccuracies.

50.5.21 Motivated reasoning: Motivated reasoning leads people to confirm what they already believe, whilst ignoring contrary data. In addition, it drives people to develop elaborate rationalisations to justify holding beliefs that are obviously wrong, both logically and evidentially. Motivated reasoning is confirmation bias taken to a more extreme level.

Motivated reasoning responds defensively to contrary evidence, actively discrediting such evidence or its source, without logical or evidentiary justification. Clearly, motivated reasoning is emotionally driven.

It is assumed by social scientists that motivated reasoning is driven by a desire to avoid cognitive dissonance. Self-delusion, in other words, feels good and motivates people to vehemently defend obvious falsehoods.

Examples of motivated reasoning:

- The Apollo moon landing was a hoax.

- Climate change is a hoax.

- Evolution is a hoax.

- Saddam Hussein was involved in 9/11.

- The Holocaust didn't happen.

- AIDS is not caused by HIV.

- Vaccines cause autism.

- Barack Obama was not born in the United States.

50.6 Avoidance and Counteraction: The only way to avoid self-delusion is to learn how to be reflective, self-analytical and self-critical. This requires some self-knowledge, some self-discipline and perhaps some professional help.

---oOo---

51. Fear is the enemy

51.1 Definition: Fear is used to manipulate people by inducing victims to alter their behaviour with threats of potentially unpleasant consequences. These threats and fears may be for something which is real, imagined or fraudulent.

Fear is one of the few innate human emotions and it has an extremely powerful influence on our behaviour. A basic survival mechanism, it is the human reaction when danger is detected or pain is felt. Fear can cause many reactions, such as a desire to hide or flee to avoid a danger.

However, fear can be conditioned into human behaviour by traumatic experiences and it can also be learned and taught by people or institutions. Religions teach fear to reinforce moral concepts by implying the existence of hell and Satan, for instance.

In a similar way, theocratic or militaristic regimes can also induce fear in their populations as a means of control. There are many ways in which fear in a population can be used in a manipulative way, as part of a conditioned response by a regime or political elite.

Fear can be counter-productive for the victim when it is artificially conditioned by a manipulator. A victim can made paranoid, irrationally afraid of the most mundane circumstances or even whole classes of other human beings.

For example, a victim can be conditioned to be frightened of black people or Muslims. Such unfounded fears benefit neither the victim nor the subject of the fear. They benefit only the manipulator.

There are many forms of fear, each of which has its own potential for manipulative use against a victim or group.

51.2 Persistence: Short to Long. Fears can last for just a few seconds or for generations.

51.3 Accessibility: High. Everyone is subject to some fears.

51.4 Conditions/Opportunity/Effectiveness: Fear can be an effective manipulative tool to use against individuals, groups and even against the whole of society.

Politicians, regimes and the media use fear to induce secondary emotions in their victims, which they then channel into actions to achieve some pre-planned manipulative objective. Here are just a few examples:

Xenophobia in war: During the Second World War in Britain, the British government used various propaganda channels to induce a fear in the general population that the Nazi government of Germany had sent many spies and saboteurs to Britain. This created a climate of general suspicion, convincing people to keep an eye on their neighbours and any strangers in their area, and to report anything remotely suspicious to the authorities. This induced paranoia, causing some unpleasant and occasionally absurd and hilarious incidents.

Death and Religion: The Roman Catholic Church (and other religions) has created a hugely elaborate system of religious and social rules which members must strictly adhere to in order to achieve eternal life, and thus avoid the inevitability of mortal death.[51.1]

The rules are strictly exclusive, meaning that only members of the faith will be allowed to enter heaven. This would generally act as a powerful recruiting tool, was it not that every other religion also uses a similar exclusive condition, thus making the consumer's choice of which religion to join a difficult decision!

Frightened Nation: In the United States, there is a general fear of a whole range of possible threats such as invasion, terrorism, the federal government, murderous neighbours, "crazies", Muslims, socialists, alien invasion etc. This has given rise to the highest gun ownership rates in the world and some of the highest murder rates in Western society (600% higher than Germany, for example). The media and language of the US is highly militaristic, over-burdened with a mandatory patriotism.

The murder by a woman of a young Indian (Hindu) man pushed under a subway train in 2012 seemed to personify the attitude of some members of the public. The murderess said she "had hated Muslims and Hindus ever since the 9/11 attacks". Her reference to "Hindus", who are not even remotely implicated in the 9/11 attacks, makes her action even more tragic, but it also makes the pervasive use of fear by the US administration even more shocking and dangerous.[51.2]

Social Exile for non-conformity: Many of the liberties which allow European citizens to live more freely or in alternative ways have been gained since the advent of democracy in Europe. But these freedoms are gradually being eroded by increasingly right-wing and intolerant governments, insisting that we conform to a pattern of behaviour and economic productivity.

Social welfare systems are now designed to keep citizens in regular employment as "productive units". Failure to conform means expulsion from society into a sub-class of poverty and exclusion.

Whilst in past centuries, the poor or eccentric were just a normal part of every village or town, and indeed often a large percentage of the population, now they are ostracised to the very margins of our society. They are "non-people", invisible to the rest of us, except when seen crouching in the shadows or being pursued by our police for begging or busking.

51.5 Methodology/Refinements/Sub-species: Here we define the three main categories of fear: Existential Fears, Social Fears and Phobias. Within these categories we will then define some common types of fear.

Existential Fears

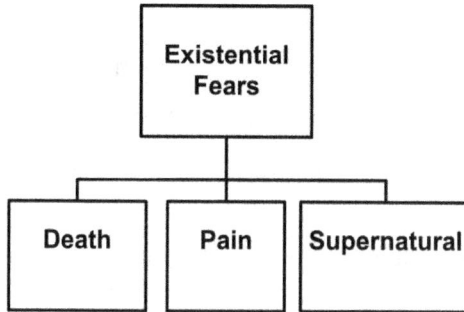

Social Fears:

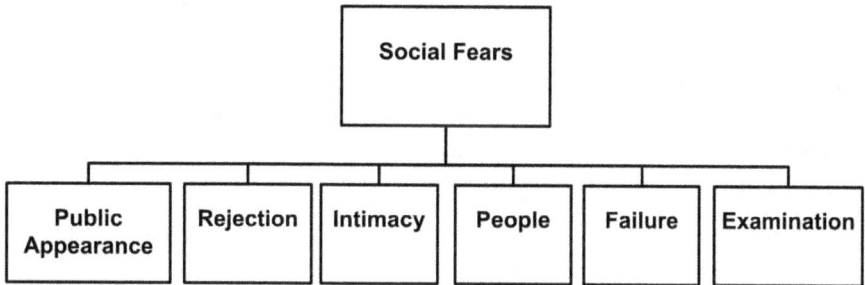

Phobias:

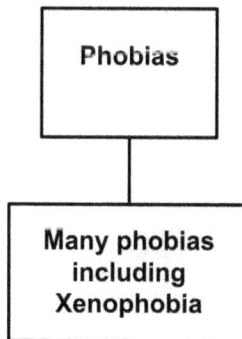

Existential Fears

- Fear of death: Fear of losing one's life.

- Fear of pain: Fear of physical or emotional pain.

- Fear of the supernatural: Fear of inexplicable, unnatural forces.

Social Fears

- Fear of social rejection: Fear of being rejected by a peer group

- Fear of intimacy: Fear of being too close to other people.

- Fear of people: Fear of contact with other people.

- Fear of failure: Fear of failing in a task or objective.

- Fear of public appearances: Fear of appearing in front of an audience.

- Fear of examinations: Fear of being tested or examined.

Phobias

There are dozens of phobias. Here are just a few common examples: Fear of certain animals, insects, heights, water, open spaces, closed spaces, bridges, tunnels, needles, hospitals, flying, driving.

- Xenophobia fear of anything or anybody foreign. This is a commonly manipulated fear.

51.5.1 Examples of emotions and potential actions which can be manipulatively induced by fear: Here is a list of common fears and the secondary emotions which are generated, along with actions which can be induced in the victim by a manipulator.

Existential Fears	Secondary Emotions	Induced Actions
Fear of pain	Fear of violence against victim or family, suspiciousness, faith in law enforcement.	Carrying of weapons, reluctance to interact with strangers, aggressive-defensive behaviour to others.
Fear of Death	Desire for eternal life via magico-religious agents, hope for supernatural intervention, compulsive religious behaviour.	Belief in one or more "all-powerful" Gods, adherence to a structured religion, a refusal to accept non-believers or allow other religions or atheism. Theocratic attitudes in politics, holy wars, inquisitions and crusades.
Fear of the Supernatural	Reinforcement of religious faith to protect against the supernatural. Fear of the dead and artefacts connected with death.	Ritualistic and compulsive behaviour to drive away "evil spirits", devils etc. Strict adherence to religious rules of living.
Social Fears	Secondary Emotions	Induced Actions
Fear of rejection	A desire to conform to group behaviour - group think. A reluctance to be seen as strange or exceptional.	Dress and behave like the rest of the group. Buy what the group buys and eat what the group eats, live where the group lives and work where the group works, vote and think like the group.
Fear of intimacy	A reluctance to open up with others, form close relationships, feel empathy or trust others.	Become a "loner", operate outside of the group, seek isolation, blame others for one's isolation, and punish others in the group.

Social Fears	Secondary Emotions	Induced Actions
Fear of the public / groups of people	A fear of social contact or being around people. Fear of people, antagonism towards groups of people.	Refusal to participate in social events. Violent action against public institutions and large groups of people.
Fear of failure	Economic and social ambition, admiration for wealth and success, abhorrence of failure and poverty.	Striving for material wealth, hard work, economic prudence, pride in material wealth. Disdain poor people.
Fear of examination	Nervousness when interrogated or tested by any institutions.	Refusal to participate in formal academic or examinations of skills, knowledge or events. Exclusion from education.
Phobias	**Secondary Emotions**	**Induced Actions**
Xenophobia	Disdain for strangers and foreigners, nationalism, patriotism, desire to defend the homeland, national arrogance.	Inhospitality, violence against strangers, foreigners, supremacist membership, join military to fight foreign wars.

51.5.2 How do politicians use fear to manipulate people? According to a study which has appeared in a recent issue of the American Journal of Political Science, politicians are very likely to try to use fear as a mechanism of social conditioning to oblige members of the public to agree with decisions that they would normally reject. This conditioning is very obvious during elections in many parts of the world, but especially, some say, in the United States, where fear is constantly in use to persuade the population to vote for one party or the other.

In contemporary US politics, the population is constantly being frightened and bullied into accepting breaches of their constitutional and civil rights and the human rights of others without any possibility to protest at judicial oversight (such as Guantanamo inmates, torture victims and kidnap victims of the CIA).

The best examples of this are documents such as the Patriot Act. The levels of manipulation achieved by this dystopian bill are truly astonishing. They severely limit the average citizen's right to privacy on the very vague basis of protecting their security. This is the equivalent of saying that we have to lock you up in order to protect your freedom!

And what's even worse is that individuals sheepishly allow these breaches of their basic human rights, hoping to gain the illusion of security. If before 9/11 the government had proposed such a measure, then all groups protecting individual rights would have had a field day, calling the measure unconstitutional and abusive. But, in the context of "9/11" and "the war on terror", protest has become muted. The protestors themselves are frightened by their own government.

Nowadays if a person or an organization objects to the Patriot Act, they are immediately labelled as "un-American", a term that seems to be used more and more in the US, although not many people know exactly what it means. And therein lies the problem with the manipulation of fear. Because politicians on TV after September 11, 2001 kept repeating the word "terrorist" and "terrorism" time and again, the population started feeling at risk; well, more at risk than they did before 9/11.

And sociological studies have shown that there's no better moment to deceive the public if you're a politician, than when it's scared to death. It was in such times that the Patriot Act was passed, whilst the invasions of Afghanistan and Iraq were taking place, without many people knowing exactly what was really going on, just trusting blindly in the government, like frightened children clinging to their parents.

The bottom line resulting from all these developments is that US and other citizens are now deprived of many of their constitutional and human rights; they can be arrested and held without charge, treated like common criminals, and body searched at airports as if they are murder suspects.

"A greater understanding of when fear can and cannot be used to scare citizens into supporting bad policies can help journalists and scholars more effectively interpret important historical events. It can help them think about whether, and to what extent, elite manipulation of citizen emotions contributed to initial public support for these kinds of government actions," Arthur Lupia and Jesse O. Menning, the authors of a new study of the subject, argue.

When the public is not afraid and knows exactly what the politicians are talking about, they are much less likely to fall for these political tricks. But, by keeping people in a state of fear, telling them that attacks are inevitable, the population ends up supporting decisions they would otherwise dissent against.

And America is starting to look more and more like a police state with every passing year. This country is no longer the beacon of democracy in the world. Fear has truly become the enemy.

51.6 Avoidance and Counteraction: Fear is an important mechanism of survival when allowed to operate in a natural way. However, when fear is used in manipulative ploys, it can rapidly become more dangerous to the victim than the threats themselves.

Actions are curtailed by fear, freedoms may be lost by fear and violence may result from the manipulation of fear. Fear can truly be an enemy of the people. We should never accept fear of an external threat unless we can rationally determine that it is a real threat and that it may actually harm us. We need to realise that the more generalised the threat, the less likely is it to affect us.

For instance, the chances of someone living in Europe or the USA being killed by a terrorist are infinitely smaller than the risks of being hit by lightening or being shot by one of our gun-toting neighbours. When one puts these risks into proportion, the fear and the potential for political manipulation disappears [47.8].

---o0o---

52. Manipulation of Memory

52.1 Definition: We all suffer from various memory biases where our recollections are unreliable or subject to external manipulation. The manipulation of memory is a technique whereby a manipulator takes advantage of the various common heuristic errors and biases in the memory of a victim.

As George Orwell remarked in his book 1984, "He who controls the past, controls the future. He who controls the present, controls the past."

The manipulation of memory is vital in many other forms of controlling activity, whether it is control of the individual, a group or a whole nation. This is a politically important concept because our perceptions of the past may alter our attitudes and actions in the future.

52.2 Persistence: Medium - Long. This method shows a high level of persistence. This, coupled with the fact that the victim's memory can be used as a platform to endorse other manipulative acts, makes this a particularly potent form of control.

52.3 Accessibility: Low to High.

52.4 Conditions/Opportunity/Effectiveness: Manipulation of memory is important because it allows a manipulator to set the backdrop for other forms of manipulation. Certain events can be air-brushed away and new events or impressions added.

Memory is not a static phenomenon; a memory changes every time it is recalled. The changes to our memories occur because of the experiences we have in the meantime.

Manipulating a victim's memories is a technique that is widely available to us all. After all, how often have we sat around with old friends remembering childhood scenes of idyllic happiness when we all know that it really wasn't always that happy? All kinds of psychological memory biases alter our memories and can be used to trigger alterations in our recollections

Manipulation of memory is also quite effective and long lasting because, as far as the victim is concerned, he remembers what happened "perfectly". In fact the only perfect thing one can say about memory is that it is perfectly unreliable.

52.5 Methodology/Refinements/Sub-species: There are many so-called memory-biases or errors which can be manipulated to someone else's advantage. Here are some common ones:

```
                    ┌─────────────────┐
                    │   Manipulation  │
                    │    of Memory    │
                    │       (I)       │
                    └─────────────────┘
```

Bizarreness Effect	Choice Supportive Bias	Change Bias	Childhood Amnesia	Regression Bias	Consistency Bias

Context Effect	Cross race Effect	Cryptomnesia	Egocentric Bias	Fading Affect Bias	False Memory

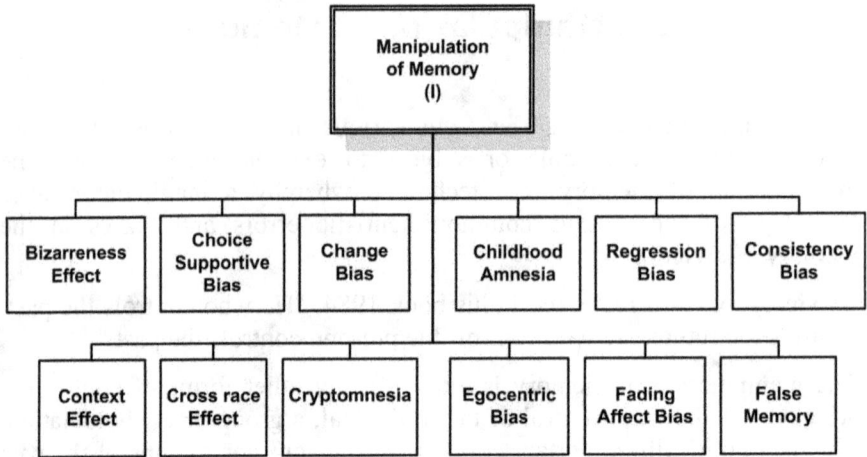

52.5.1 Bizarreness effect: This is the effect that bizarre, unusual or extraordinary events or material are better remembered than common occurrences.

A manipulator can use this bias to underline how an event is remembered in the future. This is often used by advertisers to make us remember their product because of the bizarre associations in their advertising, like the use of cartoon characters etc.

52.5.2 Choice-supportive bias: This happens when we remember chosen options as having been better than rejected options.

A manipulator may use this bias to persuade a victim that they have made a correct choice and that the decision was better than the choices rejected by the victim. For instance, a manipulative investment advisor may cover up previous bad advice to a client by focusing only on the good advice he has given.

52.5.3 Change bias: This occurs after using a lot of effort to produce change and remembering past performance as more difficult than it actually was.

A manipulator can persuade a victim that such "a huge investment in effort" ought not to be repeated again and that it is better to do nothing.

52.5.4 Childhood amnesia: This is the retention of few memories from before the age of four and relatively poor adult recollection of events before the age of ten.

A manipulator can persuade a victim of actions or events that occurred when the victims were children but which a victim can no longer recall, e.g. "you were such a lovely quiet baby", or "you were so fond of him when you were a child". The victim has no recollection of the period so cannot contradict the manipulator.

52.5.5 Conservatism or **Regressive Bias**: There is a tendency to remember high values and high likelihoods/probabilities/frequencies as being lower than they actually were, but not the low ones higher than they actually were. Based on the evidence, memories are not extreme enough. Memories tend towards a mediocre recollection rather than recollecting extremes in a more accurate way.

A manipulator can appeal to this conservative memory bias in persuading a victim that something which happened in the past was not quite as good or bad as it really was.

52.5.6 Consistency bias: This is the inclination to incorrectly remember our past attitudes and behaviour as resembling our present ones, e.g. "I have always felt the same about this."

A manipulator can use this tendency to persuade a victim to act on their "long-held" beliefs (which may actually be very newly acquired beliefs).

52.5.7 Context effect: This is a bias in which memories are dependent on context. It means that out-of-context memories are more difficult to retrieve than in-context memories. For instance, the recall time and accuracy for a work-related memory will be lower at home, and vice versa.

A manipulator can take advantage of this disposition by referring a victim to home related memories whilst at work and vice versa, to trip the victim into showing poor recall.

52.5.8 Cross-race effect: This is the tendency for people of one race to have difficulty identifying members of a race other than their own.

Manipulators in a racist environment use this unfortunate propensity to identify all members of a particular ethnic background as "all looking the same". This horrible statement is designed to denigrate people of other races in the eyes of a manipulative victim. However, it does work in all directions, including in the direction of the racist manipulator's own ethnic background.

52.5.9 Cryptomnesia: This is a form of misattribution where a memory is mistaken for imagination. It occurs when a forgotten memory returns without being recognised as an existing memory by the subject. The subject believes it is something new and original; he or she is experiencing a memory as if it were a new inspiration.

A manipulator can use this tendency to make a victim believe that they have just originated something new and wonderful, whereas they are just remembering something from their own past.

52.5.10 Egocentric bias: This is the recollection of the past in a self-serving manner, e.g. remembering one's exam grades as being better than they were, or remembering a caught fish as bigger than it really was.

A manipulator can use this to deliver credible memories and exaggerations of their own past to a listening victim.

52.5.11 Fading affects bias: This is the bias in which an emotion associated with unpleasant memories fades more quickly than the emotion associated with positive events.

A manipulator can use this tendency to persuade a victim or group of victims that something awful from the past "wasn't that bad after all". It's a personalised re-writing of history encouraged by a third party.

52.5.12 False memory: This is a form of misattribution where imagination is mistaken for a memory.

A manipulator can deliberately use this bias to make a victim believe that they were involved in something which was actually just a figment of their imagination.

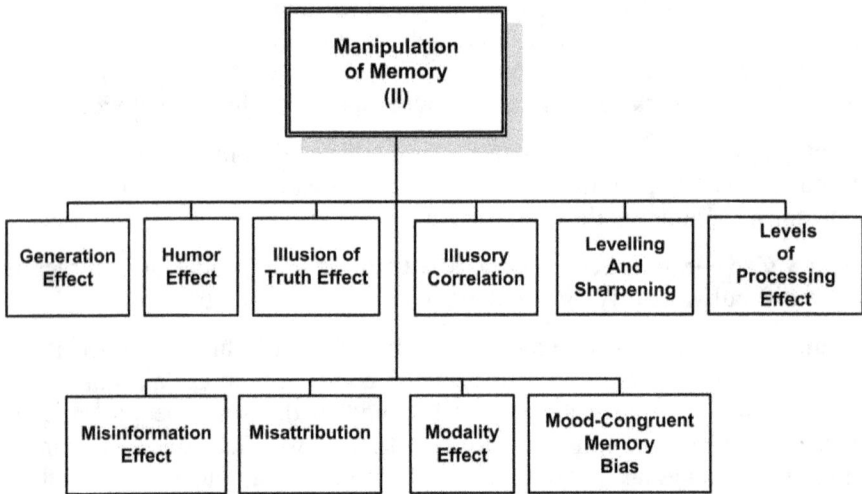

```
                    ┌─────────────────────┐
                    │   Manipulation      │
                    │   of Memory         │
                    │      (II)           │
                    └─────────────────────┘
```

Generation Effect	Humor Effect	Illusion of Truth Effect	Illusory Correlation	Levelling And Sharpening	Levels of Processing Effect

Misinformation Effect	Misattribution	Modality Effect	Mood-Congruent Memory Bias

52.5.13 Generation effect (Self-generation effect): This is the psychological bias whereby self-generated information is remembered best. For instance, people are better able to recall memories of statements that they have made than similar statements made by others.

Manipulators make use of this bias by carefully remembering statements made by their victim. They then re-use these statements in a persuasive context with the victim. The victim recognises their statements and endorses them with little further persuasion.

52.5.14 Humour effect: This is the bias that humorous items are more easily remembered than non-humorous ones. This might be explained by the distinctiveness of humour, the increased cognitive processing time to understand wit, or the emotional arousal caused by comedy.

This is a technique much in use by the manipulator; they use humour to deliver some fairly unpleasant and manipulative payloads to a victim. It is often used to deride other people or to create an impression of camaraderie between a victim and the manipulator whilst covering a more sinister motive. These moments of humour reinforce the victim's manipulated attitudes.

52.5.15 Illusion-of-truth effect: This is the bias that people are more likely to identify statements previously heard as true, (even if they cannot consciously remember having heard them), regardless of the actual validity of the statement. In other words, a person is more likely to believe a familiar statement than an unfamiliar one.

This is another technique in constant use by the manipulator; the victim hears the same "common sense" arguments again and again. After a while, the familiar language and sentiment of the argument become powerful reasons to endorse the manipulator's views, regardless of the victim's objective view.

52.5.16 Illusory correlation: This is the bias of inaccurately remembering the relationship between two events.

A manipulator can easily take advantage of the fact that victims often forget the details of a cause and effect. This bias extends into historical memory as well as into one's personal experiences. The technique is used by propagandists and works because we tend to be selective in what we remember.

For example, the peoples of the Allied nations in WWII were persuaded by a large propaganda effort after the war to quickly forget the enormous sacrifices of the Soviet armies and citizens in dismantling the Nazi Eastern offensive and destroying much of the Nazi war machine.

Despite such large and well-documented facts, Western history books rarely indicate the true extent of Soviet human, economic and military sacrifice in World War II.

52.5.17 Levelling and Sharpening: These memory distortions are introduced by the loss of detail in a recollection over time, often concurrent with the sharpening or selective recollection of certain details that take on exaggerated significance in relation to the experience lost through levelling. Both biases may be reinforced over time, and by repeated recollection or re-telling of a memory.

This tendency can be used by a manipulator to alter a victim's recollection of events, and create new conclusions or reinforce existing conclusions about events in the past. Already, few of us can remember the details of how Tony Blair lied to the British Parliament to persuade MPs to sanction the use of military force in Iraq. We remember it was immoral and illegal but we don't quite remember the details anymore.

The manipulator hopes that this "dulling" effect will give them time for things to blow over, hoping and expecting that time will "wash all things clean". It doesn't usually work over the long term because historians and survivors often wish to determine the truth.

52.5.18 Levels-of-processing effect: Different methods of encoding information into memory have differing levels of depth and recall. The shallower the level of consideration, the slighter the memory and vice versa: deeper intellectual consideration leaves a more profound memory.

Manipulators often use deliberate trivialisation of some subjects as a means of "rapidly moving along" when it comes to an issue they prefer to be forgotten as quickly as possible.

Conversely, a manipulator can also focus on issues they wish to be given undue consideration, so that it establishes a foothold in the pubic memory.

52.5.19 Misinformation effect: Misinformation affects people's reports of their own memory.

This is an important phenomenon because it refers to the way misinformation can actually affect our own memories. Misinformation, well presented, and repeated often enough, can develop its own life, allowing a victim to start to re-invent the past based on a tainted memory, overwhelmed by many forms of misinformation. This can be used by a manipulator to alter an entire historical narrative for a single victim, a group or an entire society.

The US war in Vietnam, which led finally to the ignominious scenes of the last US officials fleeing from the roof of their embassy in Saigon by helicopters to a waiting aircraft carrier, are a piece of factual and well documented history of US military defeat and humiliation.

However, the words "defeat" or "retreat" are impossible to use for many Americans, even to this day. And so, gradually, the defeat of the USA by Vietnam has been altered with waves of US misinformation to the point that popular opinion is that the USA left the country voluntarily as part of a strategic "Vietnamisation". This is an amazing contention and hard to digest when one watches the documentary films of panicky US marines desperately holding back the crowds on the roof of the US embassy in Saigon as selected citizens scramble up rope ladders to escaping helicopters. Meanwhile US marines dump escape helicopters into the sea to make space for more on the deck of the aircraft carrier standing off in the China Sea. It is hardly a scene from a "planned and dignified withdrawal", really.[52.1]

52.5.20 Misattribution: Information is retained in the memory but the source of the memory may be forgotten. This is one of the "Seven Sins of Memory": Misattribution is divided into Source Confusion, Cryptomnesia and False Recall/False Recognition.

Manipulators frequently take advantage of this bias to attribute an action or statement to some person or organisation that wasn't actually responsible for it.

This is done either to attract blame or credit to that person or agency. It works fine until someone checks the facts and reveals the misattribution. But in the meantime it has done the manipulator's job of influencing his victims, and the misinformation generally "sticks".

52.5.21 Modality effect: The modality effect refers to the higher level of recall of the last few items of a list when presentation is auditory as opposed to visual. It is usually attributed to echoic memory.

This memory bias is used by advertisers and speech-writers in the design of how they deliver information being verbally delivered to an audience. They place the key points late in the list to ensure that they are remembered best.

52.5.22 Mood-congruent memory bias: This bias involves the improved recall of information congruent with one's current mood. A manipulator detects the mood of a group and delivers messages to that group which correspond with their mood.

An antagonistic subject will tend to remember a statement or sentiment if it is in line with his own animosity whilst the reverse also holds true, a manipulator addressing a highly positive person or group will be remembered if their message is also positive and upbeat.

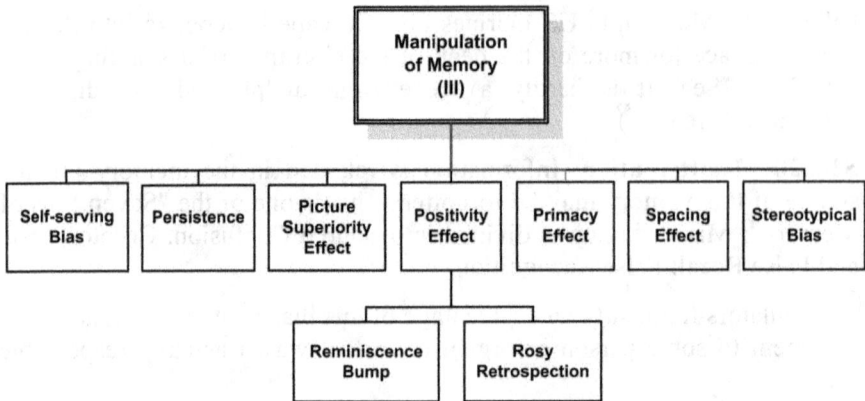

52.5.23 Self-serving bias: In this instance we perceive ourselves to be responsible for desirable outcomes but not responsible for undesirable ones.

A manipulator will often appeal to this bias when addressing a victim or victim group. By only referring to the good actions of the victim and ignoring the bad behaviour of the victim, a manipulator can engender a favourable reaction from his victim(s). See also "Social Manipulation".

52.5.24 Persistence: This is the tendency to experience unwanted recurrences of memories of a disagreeable event.

Manipulators use this tendency to remind victims of unpleasant experiences, thereby influencing a victim's actions or attitudes, for example, "Remember what happened the last time I did the cooking..."

52.5.25 Picture superiority effect: Concepts are much more likely to be remembered if they are presented in picture form than if presented in the written word.

For the manipulative advertiser or propagandist, "A picture speaks a thousand words".

52.5.26 Positivity effect: This is the tendency of older adults to favour positive information over negative information in their memories. It is related to the phenomena of:

-   "Rosy retrospection": the remembering of the past as having been better than it really was.

-   "Reminiscence bump": the recalling of more personal events from adolescence and early adulthood than personal events from later lifetime periods.

384

Many adults look back at their childhood and early adulthood with fond memories, mostly because they have filtered out the unpleasant or negative memories. This is partly a method of psychological self-preservation. Accumulating a large amount of negative memories cause an unpleasant and de-motivating sensation and so we just filter out the unpleasant recollections and hold on to the comfortable memories.

Advertisers take advantage of this to portray images of idyllic childhood scenes in order to sell their products to adults. Other manipulators appeal to this bias to convince victims of the joys of a previous era or of "a more ordered and happy world" when trying to deliver conservative manipulative payloads.

52.5.27 Primacy effect, Recency effect and Serial position effect: This effect describes the tendency that items near the end of a list are the easiest to recall, followed by the items at the beginning of a list; items in the middle are the least likely to be remembered.

This effect is in use by advertisers and by political speech writers. Anything they wish to hide is placed in the middle of a list. Anything they wish to emphasise is at the beginning and end. See also: "Modality effect".

52.5.28 Spacing effect (Lag effect): This is when information is better remembered when exposure to it is repeated over a longer period of time.

This is another pillar of the advertising industry and the propagandist. They use this effect to deliver strong manipulative payloads over long time periods.

The opposite is also true: messages delivered to the victim in a short period are much less memorable. So anything that needs to be said but forgotten should not be repeated.

52.5.29 Stereotypical bias: This is the bias in which the memory is distorted towards stereotypes (e.g. racial, gender etc.). For example, "black-sounding" first names being deliberately associated with criminal activity by a racist manipulator. The idea is that the victim builds up and uses the stereotype designed and delivered by the manipulator.

Advertisers and social and political manipulators constantly use stereotyping to trigger a "memory" in their victims. The stereotypes are built up over a period and then used repeatedly. Stereotypes can be something as relatively harmless as "the happy middle-class family on holiday" but they can equally be some derogatory racist slur.

```
                    ┌─────────────────┐
                    │   Manipulation  │
                    │    of Memory    │
                    │      (IV)       │
                    └─────────────────┘
```

Suggestibility	Telescoping Effect	Testing Effect	Verbatim Effect	Tip of the Tongue	Von Restorff Effect

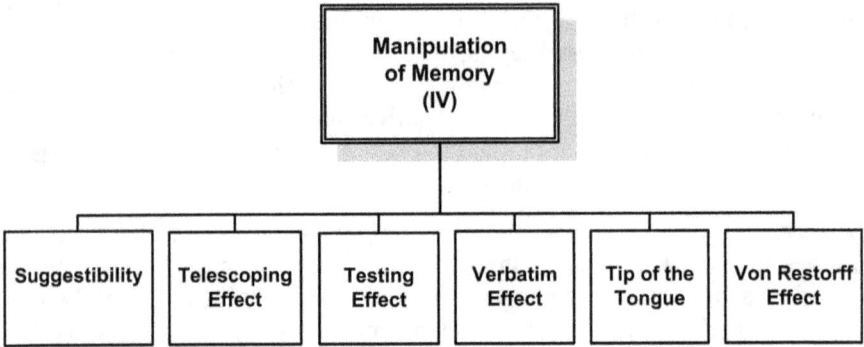

52.5.30 Suggestibility: This is a form of misattribution where ideas suggested by a questioner are mistaken for memory.

A manipulator uses this bias to suggest concepts to a victim as being already part of their remembered understanding. Finally a victim believes that these ideas are actually their own, rather than having been implanted by the manipulator.

52.5.31 Telescoping effect: This is the tendency to move recent events backwards in time whilst conversely fast-forwarding remote events forward in time. The result is recent events appear more remote whilst far off events seem more recent.

In politics, a manipulator may wish to refer to historical events as being more recent than other more up-to-date events. For instance, a biased view of events in Israel's history would tend to focus on the Nazi atrocities and European pogroms against the Jews of 70 years ago, rather than on the war crimes by the state of Israel against Palestinian civilians committed in the last few months.

52.5.32 Testing effect: Frequent re-visiting or re-examination of particular memories improves their recall.

The constant repetition and re-examination of material in our memory by a manipulator can be used to maintain this material close to the top of the victim's memory, for example, "Don't forget what happened the last time...."

52.5.33 Verbatim effect: Often the "gist" of what someone has said is better remembered than the verbatim wording.

"The devil is in the details", is a common lament but very often we only remember the essential message of a statement. We tend to neglect the details because of time constraints or just too much stimuli at that moment.

A political manipulator can take advantage of this to deliver un-noticed payloads in the details of a message or statement. None of the details will be remembered later, but yet these details will form part of the public record. This can be very useful for "covering one's tracks".

52.5.34 Tip of the tongue: This is the phenomenon where a subject is able to recall parts of an item, or related information, but is frustratingly unable to recall the whole item. This is thought to be an instance of "Memory blocking" where multiple similar memories are being recalled and interfere with each other.

A manipulator can cause this to happen to a victim by bombarding the victim with memory requests of a similar type. The victim gets confused and is unable to fully recall the whole details of any one memory. It's a tactic used in aggressive interrogation and cross-examination to undermine the credibility of a defendant or witness.

52.5.35 Von Restorff effect: This is the bias where a conspicuous item is more likely to be remembered than other items.

This effect is used by advertisers and political manipulators to draw attention to one point or message by making it "stick out" more than the others.

For example, a politician can make a particular point more memorable by making it very funny, strange, frightening, disturbing etc., in comparison with the rest of their message. An advertiser does the same thing by, say, using a very pretty actress to deliver a message in an advert, with the rest of the cast is deliberately very boring or unattractive.

52.6 Avoidance and Counteraction: Memory biases are difficult to control because a lot of them are unconscious and we therefore have little control over when they are influencing us.

However, with some training, we can learn to carefully evaluate our memories to see if we are allowing a bias to alter the rationality of how and what we recall. In this way we can sometimes avoid the use of manipulation of memory by outside influences.

---o0o---

53. Social manipulation

53.1 Definition: This is the manipulation of a victim by taking advantage of common social biases in one or more victims. Some of these biases may be considered to be weaknesses in a victim's ability to make rational judgements about their true position in society.

Social manipulation is normally considered to be abusive and negative towards a victim. However, it can be used with the best interests of the victim in mind, or it can be neutral to the victim's interests. It is usually very secretive, but there are cases where the victim may be aware of some parts of the manipulative play. Therefore, depending on the context and motivations, social influence may or may not constitute underhand manipulation.

53.2 Persistence: Short to Long.

53.3 Accessibility: Low to High.

53.4 Conditions/Opportunity/Effectiveness: Social manipulation may apply to an individual or a group. It may be carried out by an individual or a group. It can be motivated by interpersonal, social, economic or political objectives. Some forms of social manipulation are very effective, some are less credible. Some of the types are long lasting and some are of only short duration.

All of us are subject to social biases, so there is fertile ground for their use in a manipulative action.

53.5 Methodology/Refinements/Sub-species: There are several so-called social biases which can be used by a manipulator against one or more victims. Some are more useful to the manipulator than others. Here are some common social biases:

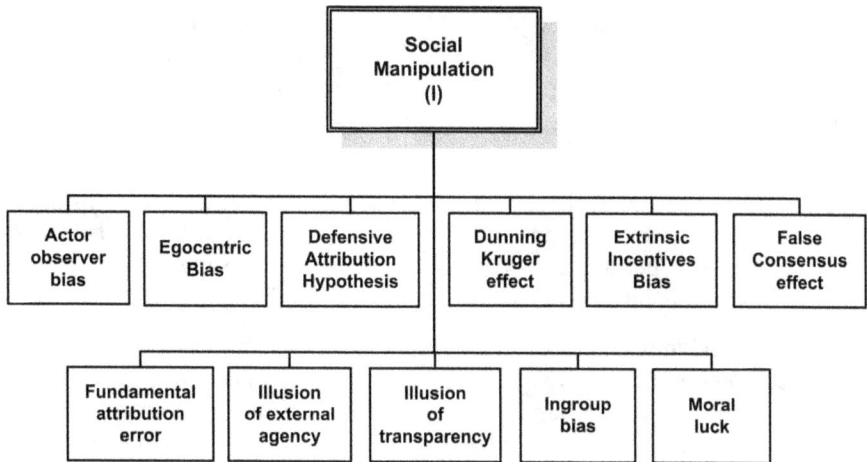

```
                        ┌─────────────────┐
                        │     Social      │
                        │  Manipulation   │
                        │       (I)       │
                        └─────────────────┘
```

| Actor observer bias | Egocentric Bias | Defensive Attribution Hypothesis | Dunning Kruger effect | Extrinsic Incentives Bias | False Consensus effect |

| Fundamental attribution error | Illusion of external agency | Illusion of transparency | Ingroup bias | Moral luck |

53.5.1 Actor-observer bias: This is a tendency to explain the behaviour of other people as the result of their personality rather than their environment. On the other hand we frequently exaggerate the influence of our own environment and downplay the influence of our own personality on our own behaviour.

This tendency blames others for their behaviour because they are inherently "bad", but excuses our own behaviour because we are just helpless victims of a poor environment.

A manipulator uses this bias to alienate and demonise victims by attributing their bad behaviour to their inherent evil selves. The manipulator remains above such blame by claiming a damaging environment for any of his particular personal moral offences.

53.5.2 Egocentric bias: This occurs when people claim more personal responsibility for the results of a joint action than an outside observer would credit them. It is also an inclination to overstate changes between the present and the past to make people look better than they actually are.

This rather annoying bias occurs quite often when one partner takes more credit than is due to them, or when someone deliberately talks up their accomplishments despite the reality that many people were responsible for that achievement.

Despite the unpleasant aspect of this bias, it does have its uses to a manipulator. Very often an egocentric person can be very useful, for instance, when a manipulator wants to "hedge their bets" in taking a particular action.

If things don't work out as expected, it can be very useful to have an egocentric type around who is willing to boast of their responsibility for the undertaking. For the manipulator, this provides a useful insurance policy if things go wrong. The egocentric victim becomes a ready and willing fall-guy, the scapegoat having already boasted of his responsibility for the success-turned-failure.

This is related to the Self-serving bias, which is a tendency to claim more responsibility for successes than for failures. It may also manifest itself as a tendency for people to evaluate ambiguous information in a way beneficial to their interests (see also group-serving bias).

53.5.3 Defensive attribution hypothesis: This bias makes us more likely to attack someone for a mishap when it is serious. When it is less serious, the tendency is lower. When a mishap is more serious then the tendency to blame is higher.

This tendency to attribute responsibility is also increased by any similarities between an outside observer and the victim of the mishap. So, in general, more responsibility will be attributed to a harm-doer by the observer when the outcome becomes more severe, and the victim is more similar to the observer.

Example: Men are statistically more likely to apportion some responsibility to a rape victim than are women because some men tend to sympathise less with the victim than do most women.

Manipulators use this bias to generate antagonism towards either the object or subject of a mishap, or both. The stirring up of antagonism amongst a particular group is a powerful source of manipulative influence.

For instance, when a young woman dies during a miscarriage in a country which forbids abortion, then the reaction of many women in that country is understandably to attack the laws that allow this to happen. Other outsiders (men and women) will blame the woman's husband for allowing her to give birth in such a morally backward country. Yet another group will use the event to strengthen their anti-abortion views and the definition of the guidelines for allowing termination. The case is very serious, so there has to be blame. A manipulator can use such an event to fan the flames of an argument in favour of allowing legal termination of pregnancy to save a mother's life. Regardless of the moral issues at stake here, the bias is a powerful force in persuading victims to take up a particular moral stance.

53.5.4 Dunning–Kruger effect: Unfortunately, incompetent people often fail to realise that they are incompetent because they lack the skills to distinguish between competence and incompetence. People frequently mistakenly rate their ability much higher than average.

Many of us will have noted the peculiar coincidence which manifests itself in some people, namely the potentially dangerous combination of ignorance and arrogance. The Dunning-Kruger effect is the name given to this phenomenon. It causes the often puzzling combination whereby a person may know almost nothing about a subject but yet proclaim great confidence in their knowledge about that field.

A manipulator can take advantage of this phenomenon when they find and encourage an appropriate victim to take on more than they can manage, in a subject area where they really have little knowledge. This can clearly place the victim at the risk of making a big mistake, being discovered and suffering the consequences.

This obviously won't work for every potential victim. Some of us know our limitations and will not be persuaded to pretend more knowledge than we actually have. However, there are plenty of suitable cases who can and will adopt a mantle of confidence, despite almost total ignorance.

53.5.5 Extrinsic incentives bias: This is the phenomenon where people assume that they themselves are motivated by intrinsic motivations, (i.e. pure academic interest), but that everyone else is only driven by extrinsic motivations (money, status etc).

Types of motivation: Intrinsic motivation refers to motivation that is driven by an interest or enjoyment in the task itself, it exists within the individual rather than relying on any external pressure. Intrinsic motivation is based on taking pleasure in an activity rather than working towards an external reward.

Extrinsic motivation refers to the performance of an activity in order to attain an outcome. Common extrinsic motivations are rewards like money and status, and / or threats like physical punishment, exclusion etc. Competition is generally considered extrinsic, because it encourages the performer to win and beat others.

Manipulative uses: A manipulator can take advantage of this particular bias by convincing a victim that they are morally superior to others because their motivation is driven by higher motives. The willing victim can thus be persuaded to ignore their interests in more material rewards like money and status.

53.5.6 False consensus effect: This is the tendency for people to overestimate the degree to which others agree with them.

In a manipulative sense, this is a readily usable bias where a confident victim can be persuaded to enter an antagonistic "lion's den" with complete confidence that the lion will agree with him.

53.5.7 Fundamental attribution error This is a propensity for people to blame a bad situation on a personality rather than external circumstances. When something goes wrong we are inclined to seek out a person to blame rather than accept that it just happened because of a combination of circumstances in a particular situation.

Politicians are often blamed for economic downturns, whereas in fact many economic declines are often merely cyclical. For example, commodity prices move through long cycle changes due to long-term global supply and demand changes. To blame a local politician for these economic events is obviously unfair. Nonetheless, it is common practice in Western politics to depose a regime which fails to deliver, whether or not it is within their control.

Manipulative uses of this are fairly obvious. A political opposition will always release its "attack dogs" to find a scapegoat if there is a scandal, an economic problem or some form of organisational problem or natural catastrophe, much to the applause of the most supposedly rational public. The sound of logical arguments about long-cycle commodity price trends is drowned out in the calls for blood.

53.5.8 Illusion of external agency: This is the effect where people see a personal experience as being the result of some "external influence", "insight" or "benevolence". This is the confusion between "the magic in here" and "the magic out there" illusion. In this illusion, a victim sees a "moving hand" or an unknown external influence, rather than their own personal influence on actual events.

The illusion provides fertile ground for a manipulator. Any victim suffering this illusion can be persuaded that what is happening is the result of some unspecified external influence, which can be spiritual or mystical in some way .This can alter the attitude and behaviour of a victim. For instance, a victim can be persuaded that the reason they have inherited a small fortune is a divine act, and has happened so as to help a religious sect financially with a donation, etc.

53.5.9 Illusion of transparency: This is an illusion in which we overestimate other people's ability to know us and overestimate our own ability to know other people. We tend to believe that we are an "open book" to others and that they are similarly transparent to us. In fact, some will say human beings are often inscrutable.

Even when quite distressed or rather happy, we may not necessarily demonstrate any obvious physical signs of emotion. Human beings are actually not very transparent in terms of emotional expression.

A manipulator may use this phenomenon to deceive a victim into believing that the manipulator is not experiencing a strong emotion of some kind. In the same way a manipulator can pretend to be experiencing intense emotions simply to fool the victim.

53.5.10 Ingroup bias: This is a tendency for people to give preferential treatment to others they perceive to be members of their own group.

Manipulators use this preference to control a group and to maintain unity. Naturally, victims of such a manipulation will tend to protect members of their own group.

53.5.11 Moral luck: This is the propensity for people to ascribe blame or praise to someone even when it is clear that the person had little or no control over the action or its consequences.

A manipulator can use this bias to gain acceptance to a group of victims simply by winning their praise for something the manipulator didn't actually do.

A manipulator can also encourage blame against someone who was not actually responsible for some misdeed.

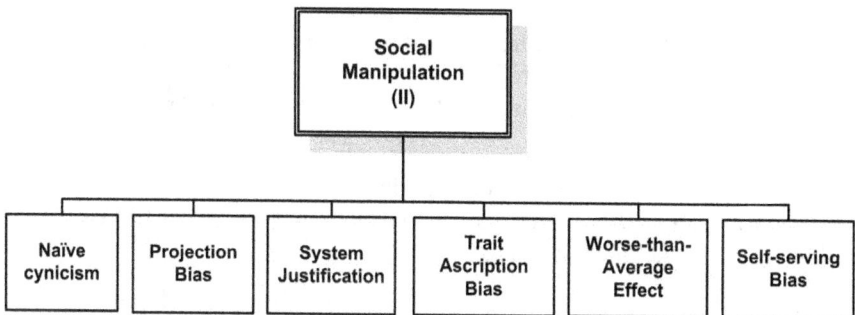

```
                    ┌─────────────────┐
                    │     Social      │
                    │  Manipulation   │
                    │      (II)       │
                    └────────┬────────┘
   ┌────────┬────────┬───────┼────────┬─────────┬──────────┐
┌──┴───┐ ┌──┴────┐ ┌─┴─────┐ ┌┴─────┐ ┌┴───────┐ ┌┴────────┐
│Naïve │ │Projec-│ │System │ │Trait │ │Worse-  │ │Self-    │
│cyni- │ │tion   │ │Justi- │ │Ascrip│ │than-   │ │serving  │
│cism  │ │Bias   │ │ficat. │ │tion  │ │Average │ │Bias     │
│      │ │       │ │       │ │Bias  │ │Effect  │ │         │
└──────┘ └───────┘ └───────┘ └──────┘ └────────┘ └─────────┘
```

53.5.12 Naïve cynicism: This is the expectation of more egocentric bias in others than in oneself. Of course, most of us are egocentrically biased in a similar way, but this bias is useful to manipulate a victim into believing that they are more rational than those around them.

Thus a manipulator can create the false impression in a victim that they are in full control of a situation, when in fact they are not.

53.5.13 Projection bias: This is the tendency to unconsciously assume that others share one's current emotional states, thoughts and values.

This is often a means of projecting undesirable thoughts, motivations, desires, and feelings onto someone else as some means of deflecting the subject's own feelings of guilt. It provides a function whereby a person can protect themselves from a feeling that is otherwise repulsive.

Some psychologists describe projection as "the operation of expelling feelings or wishes the individual finds wholly unacceptable, or too shameful, too obscene, too dangerous, by attributing them to another person."

Manipulators have used the phenomenon of projection to divert attention away from themselves to others.

Historically, concepts of bewitchment could be attributed to the exercise of projection. This was not limited to adult manipulators. Projection is one of the medical explanations that attempt to diagnose the behaviour of the afflicted "bewitched" children at Salem in 1692[53.1].

53.5.14 System justification: This is the inclination to defend and bolster the status quo. Existing social, economic, and political arrangements tend to be preferred and alternatives disparaged, sometimes even at the expense of individual and collective self-interest.

Manipulators constantly use this bias to maintain the status quo by appealing to the victim's fears of change in the current social, economic and political position.

53.5.15 Trait ascription bias: This is the tendency for people to view themselves as relatively variable in terms of personality, behaviour and mood whilst viewing others as being much more predictable.

Manipulators may use this bias to persuade a victim to act outside "the norm", in order to carry out some agenda of the manipulator. The victim is gratified because they see themselves as being more "wild" or more "flexible" than the general population.

53.5.16 Worse-than-average effect: A susceptibility to believe ourselves to be worse than others at tasks which are difficult.

A manipulator may use this to deter a victim from practical intervention in complex situations or involvement in complex problem solving.

53.5.17 Self-serving bias: This is the bias which makes us perceive ourselves responsible for desirable outcomes, but not responsible for undesirable ones.

A manipulator will often appeal to this bias when addressing a victim of victim group. By only referring to the good actions of the victim whilst ignoring the bad behaviour of the victims, a manipulator can engender a favourable reaction from his victims. See also "Manipulation of Memory".

53.6 Avoidance and Counteraction: Central to remaining aloof from social conditioning and manipulation is the sense that, generally speaking, we are all pretty much the same from a sociological point of view. Few of us are either saints or sinners, and most of us are fools sometimes.

Social manipulation relies on emphasising social differences rather than on encouraging unity. It works by encouraging disparity rather then seeking similarity. To avoid the plague of social manipulation, ordinary people need to work in the opposite direction to the manipulator. We can do this by encouraging social solidarity and by being honest and sensible about social biases which are common to us all.

---oOo---

54. Group manipulation

54.1 Definition: This chapter deals with manipulation of a group and manipulation by a group. Manipulation of a group is often linked to manipulation by a group whereby a controlling manipulator co-opts a group to act as proxies for the manipulator. The group, in their turn, become the active manipulators. Manipulation of a group is a common and potent form of persuasion which most of us have experienced at some time in our lives.

Manipulation of a group is not always malicious or particularly secretive. For instance, the training and conditioning of nurses or other groups of medical professionals to adhere to certain protocols of hygiene is not malicious.

However, in the wrong hands and with evil intentions, group manipulation can have some appalling consequences. Some of the most disgraceful crowd violence and racist behaviour has resulted from the external manipulation of suitably impressionable groups.

54.2 Persistence: Short to Medium.

54.3 Accessibility: Medium.

54.4 Conditions/Opportunity/Effectiveness: Manipulation of a group or "crowd" is a highly effective method of social control because it is self-perpetuating and self policing. Once a group has been persuaded of a manipulator's arguments, the group can be made to act as proxies. They will self-reinforce the manipulative payload against any dissenting members within the group.

Anyone can be the initiator of a group manipulation providing they are credible to a sufficiently large part of the group.

54.5 Methodology/Refinements/Sub-species: There are three basic methods of group manipulation:

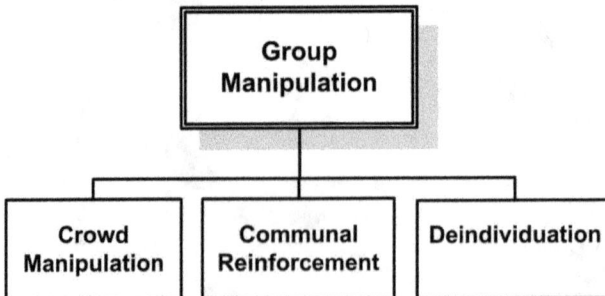

54.5.1 Crowd manipulation: This is the use of techniques based on the principles of crowd psychology to engage, control, or influence the desires of a crowd, in order to direct its behaviour toward a specific action.

This practice is common to politics and business and can facilitate the approval, disapproval or indifference to a person, a policy, or a product by a crowd. Whether there are any ethical uses of crowd manipulation is debatable.

Comparison with propaganda: Crowd manipulation differs from propaganda, although they may reinforce one another to produce a desired result. Propaganda can be defined as a consistent, enduring effort to create or shape events to influence the relations of the public to an enterprise, idea or group. But crowd manipulation is a relatively short call to action once the seeds of propaganda have been sown, and the public is organised into a crowd.

A propagandist appeals to everyone in a population over a longish period of time (weeks, months or years). The crowd manipulator appeals to a particular segment of the masses assembled in a crowd in real time. In situations such as a national emergency, a political manipulator may use methods of mass media to address and incite the general public as if speaking directly to a crowd.

Crowd manipulation differs from "crowd control". Crowd control serves as a security function. Local authorities use crowd control techniques to contain and defuse crowds and to prevent and respond to unruly and unlawful acts such as rioting and looting.

54.5.2 Communal reinforcement: Communal reinforcement is the manipulative process by which a claim becomes a strong belief through repeated assertion by members of a community or group.

The process is independent of whether the claim has been properly researched, or is supported by empirical data significant enough to warrant belief by reasonable people. Often, the mass media contribute to the process by uncritically supporting a claim. More often, the mass media provide tacit support for untested and unsupported claims by saying nothing sceptical about even the most outlandish claims.

Communal reinforcement explains how entire nations can pass on some of the most amazing gibberish from generation to generation. It also explains how testimonials, reinforced by other testimonials within a community of therapists, sociologists, psychologists, theologians, politicians, talk show hosts, etc., can supplant and be more powerful than scientific studies or accurate gathering of data by disinterested parties.

Communal reinforcement explains, in part, why about half of all American adults deny that evolution occurred and believe that Abraham's god created the universe in six days, made the first man and woman out of clay, and a snake talked the woman into disobeying an order from Abraham's god, thereby causing all of our problems.[54.1]

It also explains how otherwise rational and intelligent people can be persuaded to accept such stories as true when they are provided by a comforting community in a time of emotional need. Every cult leader knows the value of communal reinforcement combined with isolating cult members from contrary ideas.

Example: The Myth of Antioxidants: In pseudo-medicine there are lots of completely nonsensical assertions which are completely without scientific foundation, but which are constantly repeated as if they were self-evident facts. For instance, the use of the word "Antioxidants" to denote a group of foods and food supplements which are said to reduce the risk of cancer. In reality, there is no evidence at all to support many of the claims about these foods or supplements. But despite this lack of evidence, the "benefits of antioxidants" is believed by millions of people in the Western world and is constantly reinforced by those believers.

54.5.3 Deindividuation: In certain heightened states of social upheaval, individuals in groups or crowds can be induced to lose their self-awareness. Theories of deindividuation propose that it is a psychological state of decreased self-evaluation and this provides an explanation for a variety of abnormal collective behaviour such as violent crowds, lynch mobs, etc. The manipulative use of de-individuation has also been attributed as explanations for acts of apparently spontaneous genocide. It has also been suggested as an explanation for abnormal antisocial behaviour in computer-internet based communications like social networks etc.

Although generally considered in the context of negative behaviour such as mob violence and genocide, de-individuation has also been found to play a role in positive behaviours and experiences where team cohesion and single-mindedness is important.

There are many cases in which the effects of deindividuation can be seen in real-world groups. Deindividuation occurs in varied instances like the police force, criminal and other gangs, the military, religious cults, sports teams, and social organizations. Although they may seem very different on the surface, these groups share many traits that make them conducive to deindividuation and therefore useful to the manipulator.

All of these examples share a strong drive towards group cohesion. Police officers, soldiers, religious adherents and sports teams all wear uniforms that create a distinct in-group image whilst reducing the distinctive characters of a group's individual members.

54.6 Avoidance and Counteraction: The primary protective method against group manipulation is not to participate too much in groups that have a shared sociological objective and which demand absolute allegiance.

This means that any group which fails to tolerate discussion or dissention should be avoided. As soon as a group starts to silence its members by dictating "party policy" or "group policy", it's time to leave. The wearing of uniforms is almost always a manipulative act although there are a few tolerable exceptions such as the police force and army. A group that behaves in any of these ways has generally ceased to be healthy and is becoming manipulative.

---oOo---

55. Induced animosity

55.1 Definition: Induced animosity is the manipulative technique whereby a perpetrator creates a strong and emotional dislike in a victim for another individual victim or group. The objective is to place victims in a position of conflict, which will ultimately damage their interests and/or will benefit the interests of the manipulator.

The traditional name for this tactic is "divide and rule" and the strategy has an ancient lineage in many imperial traditions, including the Roman Empire and the Napoleonic Empire. It has been in constant use and continues, to this day, to be a most popular method of political and social manipulation.[55.1]

55.2 Persistence: Short to Long.

55.3 Accessibility: High. Creating antagonism is available and practiced at all levels of society.

55.4 Conditions/Opportunity/Effectiveness: Virtually everyone has access to this method of exploitation, albeit that their effectiveness depends upon their knowledge of a victim. A perpetrator is also limited in the range of their victims by barriers such as social status and position. Also, no one is immune from this type of manipulation, whether they are the potential "antagonists" or "antagonised".

Once a conflict has been initiated, it takes some level-headed intervention to detect a manipulator at work, to get the antagonist parties back together again, and re-establish a peace.

55.4.1 Motivation: There are a number of reasons why it may be beneficial to engender animosity in a victim:

- To engage the time and energy of a victim.

- To consume the time and energy of two victims (as opponents).

- To discredit a victim.

- To gain sympathy for a victim's opponent.

- To create discord in a previously co-operative group.

55.4.2 Mechanism: In order to induce animosity in a victim, a manipulator must rely upon other manipulative techniques. The prime objective is to contrive that a victim's opponent be made to represent a threat to the victim. For this the manipulator must engender fear and hatred in the victims which he does by means of deceit, propaganda, rhetoric etc.

A victim's opponent (also a victim) is partly a latent feature of this manipulative plot. It may be necessary for a manipulator to acquaint the enemy with the primary victim's feelings and possible intentions. This serves to engender distrust and fear between the two.

This distrust, if a manipulator's plans go well, soon becomes self-perpetuating. The whole process takes off independently at a certain point, the moment when there is no possibility for the victim and his opponent to compromise or negotiate. Once the fires of animosity are lit, the manipulator only needs to intervene occasionally to change its direction or to increase its intensity according to his plans.

The pitch at which a conflict is played out by his victims is totally determinable by the manipulator. The manipulator decides with what information and provocations to provide the victims in order to maintain the conflict.

The levels of the provocations provided by the manipulator determine the aggressive behaviour engendered in the victims. It is this flexibility in controlling the induced level of animosity that makes this form of manipulation especially attractive to governments and management. Sometimes they want to create a small political rift; sometimes they need a full-scale war (as in the animosity deliberately created between religious groups in Northern Ireland and different religions in many parts of the Middle East).

55.5 Methodology/Refinements/Sub-species: There are nine main sub-types of Induced Animosity:

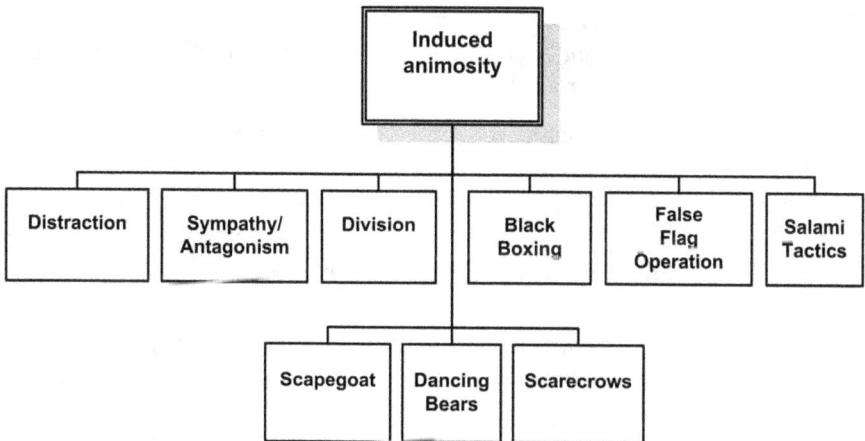

55.5.1 Distraction: Using distraction, a manipulator creates a conflict between one or more victims to turn their attention away from some activity he doesn't wish to be scrutinized, or to delay or stop an action by the victims.

In this scenario, the victim's energies are channelled towards the contrived discord in which they suddenly find themselves. Consequently, they become less available for their own normal activities, are weakened and are also distracted from the manipulator's activities.

There are many cases in government and industry where this technique is useful. A competitor can, for example, distract a chief executive from his objectives by initiating industrial disputes or personal conflicts amongst a management-team or between a manager and a director.

All forms of contention are energy depleting, the victim will, by necessity, be "tied up" by the conflict and this benefits the manipulator's agenda.

55.5.2 Sympathy/antagonism: Should a manipulator wish to gain support for themselves or for another individual or group which they support, the manipulator may prey upon the natural sympathy which most people will exhibit towards the so-called underdog.

Firstly though, the manipulator must create this status, either for themselves or for a subject. There is generally no better way to gain sympathy than to make a subject the target of irrational aggression.

Here the real victims are those who give their sympathy to the party being attacked, not realizing that they are being manipulated. Once this sympathy has been gained, an aggressor is discredited, along with their opinions, whilst the opinions of the besieged subject are upheld by the manipulator.

This is irrational behaviour, of course, but it works, because most people, when they condemn, condemn absolutely. They don't qualify their distaste for an aggressor on the grounds of the aggression only.

55.5.3 Division: Manipulators may have no specific reasons for wishing to create enmity in a group, except to bring about its ultimate disintegration and the final destruction of the group. The group may perhaps be an obstacle of some sort for the manipulator. The manipulator wishes to cause serious infighting between members of the group to predicate its destruction.

Creating internal division is a fairly rough method of creating conflict. It does not require much advance planning or consideration, because the direction and intensity of the conflict need not be predetermined. Animosity can be allowed to rage uncontrollably. A manipulator's only objective is to create an irreconcilable split within a group.

In order to bring this about, the manipulator needs some knowledge of the personalities and internal political bickering of the member victims. The manipulator can then choose any one of these background disputes to kindle and fan a fire of destructive factionalism.

55.5.4 Black-boxing: This is institutional manipulation where antagonism is induced by systematic means. It works by requiring that citizens or other people divide themselves into predetermined groups.

One case is the mandatory classification of Americans by race, ethnicity, religious affiliation and the like in government forms such as the census.[55.2]

This "black boxing" reinforces people's self-identification as belonging to racial or other groups (often artificially), as opposed to part of a generic American citizenry.

In a country respecting the rule of law, such classifications should be irrelevant to the state. But reinforcing such divisions may keep Americans at odds with each other, and divide liberal thinking voters by colour, class, and ethnicity, rather than uniting them via their socio-economic similarities as citizens of the "United" States of America.

55.5.5 False flag operations: This is the staging of an event or secreting of evidence in order to create the appearance that one's opposition is responsible for some scandal or atrocity.

This manipulative method is often used as a justification for repression or for more power and authority. The Reichstag fire that ushered the Nazis to power is one famous example.[55.3]

55.5.6 Salami tactics: This method of manipulation was developed by Mussolini and named by the Hungarian communist Rakoszci. Salami tactics are a way to foster internal strife within an opposition group and then to slice the members off.

If, for instance, the Tea Party movement could be separated from the Republican Party, this would be a good example of salami tactics.

55.5.7 The Scapegoat: This method involves placing an inordinate amount of blame on a person or group, usually in order to distract attention away from the true underlying causes of a problem or failure. It is also used to target a specific group for criticism, abuse or even destruction. It's a favourite manipulative weapon of the political right-wing to blame some other victim or victim group for the economic or political problems of one's society.

For instance, the Nazis, in their propaganda, blamed the Jewish population of Europe for the dreadful economic state of the continent during the mid and late 1930's. This scapegoat was used (and believed) by many ordinary Europeans, despite the obviously dysfunctional nature of the global securities markets at the time which had triggered the Wall Street Crash and the economic depression that followed.[55.4] The poverty and misery being endured by "ordinary" Germans was manipulatively transferred to the "ordinary" Jewish population with tragic consequences.

55.5.8 Dancing Bears: This is the use of political "operatives" to foment or sustain opposition to a person, movement, or party. It is used by a political operator who having infiltrated a group, then acts as an extreme caricature of that group in order to reduce that group's attraction to the general public. The tactic often plays on people's tendency to make a bivalent (either-or) choice. It was pioneered in Russia.

One example is the use of the ultra-nationalist Vladimir Zhirinovsky of the party LDP, his purpose was to marginalize ultra-nationalism and make politicians like Vladimir Putin look "moderate" by providing a foil.

A possible consequence of this tactic may be the public's sentiment that "politics is just a circus", disenchanting citizens and dissuading them from any interest or activity in politics.

55.5.9 Scarecrows: This describes the method by which an "operative" infiltrates an opposing party, movement or group and wards off potential members.

This can be done in many ways - social media, being unpleasant, expressing extreme views, stereotyping the worst aspects of a movement, anti-social behaviour etc.

55.6 Avoidance and Counteraction: "Divide and rule" and other strategies of induced antagonism are always at play somewhere in party politics, government and management. This means that many internal divisions are either manipulated or encouraged by external provocateurs.

Machiavelli, the great Renaissance specialist in manipulation, didn't approve of the "divide and conquer" principle, though not for any moral reasons. He simply felt that conflict used up too much of the citizens' energy. He believed that the public would be better employed in the propagation and protection of the state. He felt that in times of hardship, factionalism was negative and undesirable because at those moments the state most needs its citizens undivided attention, unity and dedication. Despite Machiavelli's views, the technique is in constant use in modern Western society.

The way to avoid induced antagonism is to seek consensus and refuse to be drawn into conflicts with those we would consider allies or to accept unsubstantiated assertions which are antagonistic. Easier said than done.

---oOo---

56. Induced unity

56.1 Definition: The manipulator seeks to unite a group of victims in a common cause. It has the opposite effect of induced animosity which seeks to divide its victims. In "induced animosity", the objective is to weaken the victim group. In "induced unity", the objective is to strengthen a group of victims.

At first glance "induced unity" may seem an unlikely form of manipulation, but in fact it's a lot more commonplace than one would think. There are many reasons why a manipulator would wish to unite a group of people to work and cooperate together.

56.1.1 Examples: The military ethos seeks to encourage large numbers of people to live and work together as a cohesive unit, motivated by a common cause. Religious groups like monastic orders of monks or nuns have a similar objective. Political institutions, like the houses of a parliament will claim to share a common interest in the government of their country. Political parties, secret societies, brotherhoods, clubs and academic institutions all seek to create solidarity of purpose and action.

56.1.2 The manipulative element: Individuals that join a large organised group do so for various reasons such as poverty, insecurity, ambition, common interest, or a shared philosophy or shared experience. Very often, members appear to join of their own free will. They then stay in the group for the same reasons that they joined, at least apparently so. However, in reality it is very rare that an individual actually joins a group without the intervention of some outside manipulation. The military recruit by appealing to patriotic sentiment, camaraderie and an offer of security and a steady job. The religious orders appeal to spirituality, religious principles and a particular model of the world. Political organisations make similar philosophical appeals to individuals to unite in a common cause. Members are kept in by the manipulative use of fear of the "insecure life outside" of the group.

At a political level, huge parts of a population can be persuaded to unite under a common banner, particularly in times of war where other manipulative techniques (like propaganda) are also used to raise patriotic sentiment.

In times of peace, a politician can "peel off" social sub-groups that can then be encouraged to unite for a political or philosophical cause. Examples in the last 30 years would be the extreme right-wing groups like the US Tea Party, or the hard left-wing British Militant Tendency of the 1990s, the right-wing English Defence League and the more recent global anti-capitalist movement "Occupy".

56.2 Persistence: Short to Long.

56.3 Accessibility: Medium.

56.4 Conditions/Opportunity/Effectiveness: In times of heightened social tension or serious threats to the security of a society, country or just one social group, the tendency is for human beings to cling together and form groups to defend themselves.

However, this tendency to form a group and the sentiments of its members can be manipulated by an outside agency to gain control of the group for entirely ulterior motives.

56.5 Methodology/Refinements/Sub-species: There are two main methods used to manipulatively unite victim groups:

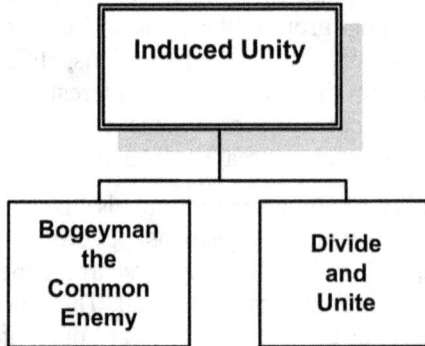

```
          ┌─────────────────────┐
          │   Induced Unity     │
          └─────────────────────┘
          ┌──────────┴──────────┐
┌──────────────┐      ┌──────────────┐
│  Bogeyman    │      │   Divide     │
│    the       │      │    and       │
│  Common      │      │   Unite      │
│  Enemy       │      │              │
└──────────────┘      └──────────────┘
```

56.5.1 Bogeyman - the common enemy: This is a manipulative technique which focuses victims' attention on external groups that are considered to be communal enemies, and encourages the victims to act in unison to defend themselves against their common enemy. The technique uses the principle that "My enemy's enemy is my friend" to unite otherwise disunited groups.[56.1]

Examples of groups that can be seen as common enemies include members of certain religions, secret organisations, political parties, social establishments, and racial groups, ethnic and social minorities.

This tactic works by oversimplifying political reality: it misleads and radicalises members of similar ideological affinities so that they act towards a certain common objective. It works because it uses the common currency of fear, which unites even ideologically dissimilar groups against an enemy more threatening than their normally antagonistic parochial competitors.

During the early Christian crusades, the Arab fiefdoms of the time were also generally at war with each other. However, these local wars were always suspended as soon as the word went out that "the Christians are coming". The principle that my enemy's enemy is my friend, as always, prevails.

56.5.2 Divide-and-Unite: This method of "inducing unity" involves firstly sowing the seeds of discord among various groups and then the manipulator arrives to reunite them and appear as their "saviour".

Unifying influences are seen as positive, peace-givers and pro-social. A manipulator can easily adopt this role. However, first the manipulator may need to artificially create social divisions in order to then resolve them.

56.6 Avoidance and Counteraction: Beware of too much cheering for communal causes, especially when the cheering seems to be orchestrated and centred on a party, group or individual.

In an un-manipulated society, unity and solidarity are hard won sentiments which take much time, contact and trust to build up. They are not sentiments which can be switched on and off.

---oOo---

Notes

Note 1.1 Literacy: Literacy in the Western world was remarkably low until the 19th century. In 1841 33% of all Englishmen were still illiterate. In France in the 18th century, 70% of the population were illiterate. Public education during and after the Industrial Revolution started to improve the situation. According to UNESCO, global illiteracy halved between 1970 and 2005. The present estimates are that illiteracy affects 15% of the world's population.

Note 2.1 Ancient examples of political manipulation:

- **Ancient Greece:** The ancient Greeks used sport to enhance the fitness of their citizens for war and to demonstrate their superiority over other city-states; they used a complex religion to underpin their moral superiority and justify the actions of their government.

- **Ancient Rome:** The patron-client system was a unique feature of Roman society. Citizens formed relationships that acted as an important link in the political and social systems and served to influence political support. Patrons, usually a patrician, would take "clients", young patricians or plebeians, under their wings and provide them with advice, money, business opportunities or representation in court. In turn, clients would help to enhance their patron's status by providing certain services, such as working on political campaigns, appearing with their patron in public as part of a group of faithful retainers, or using their specialized skills or training to enhance their patron's status. Clients ranged from freed men and businessmen to artists and writers. It was a common practice in Republican Rome for a patron-politician to either ally themselves with prominent writers or patronize them publicly. It was not so different from the way in which modern politicians ally themselves with a sympathetic newspaper or television station.

Note 2.2: Iraq War and the US lies that led to it: The war that began on March 19, 2003, was justified to the people of the US and UK by claims that Iraqi leader Saddam Hussein had weapons of mass destruction and connections to al-Qaeda terrorists - almost all of these turned out to be false. Some of the most senior officials in the U.S. government, including President Bush himself, Vice President Dick Cheney and Secretary of Defence Donald Rumsfeld, asserted these claims in public with absolute confidence, even while privately, high-ranking U.S. military officers and intelligence professionals were voicing their doubts.

WMD lies: Anthony Zinni, the former commander in chief of U.S. Central Command, stated that on August 26, 2002 in an award ceremony in

Tennessee, Dick Cheney said, "Simply stated, there is no doubt that Saddam Hussein now has weapons of mass destruction, there is no doubt he is amassing them to use against our friends, against our allies and against us." Zinni, sitting next to Cheney's lectern, says he "literally bolted" when he heard the Vice President's comments. Zinni stated that "In doing work with the CIA on Iraq WMD [weapons of mass destruction], through all the briefings I heard at Langley, I never saw one piece of credible evidence that there was an ongoing program." He recounted going to one of those CIA briefings and being struck by how thin the agency's actual knowledge of Iraqi weapons programs was. "What I was hearing [from Bush administration officials] and what I knew did not jive," Zinni said in an interview with Rachael Maddow. Zinni was later replaced by Gen. Tommy Franks, who succeeded Zinni as commander of the Centcom, to plot the "decapitation" of the Iraqi government, according to the now declassified talking points from the session. Meanwhile "Curveball", an Iraqi defector, later confirmed that he had fabricated the claims about Iraq's weapons of mass destruction which were quoted as "facts" by former US Secretary of State Colin Powell when he presented the case for war to the United Nations.

Al-Qaeda connection lies: Mark Rossini was then an FBI counter-terrorism agent detailed to the CIA. He was assigned the task of evaluating a Czech intelligence report that Mohammed Atta, the leading 9/11 hijacker, had met with an Iraqi intelligence agent in Prague before the attack on the World Trade Towers. Cheney repeatedly invoked this report as evidence of Iraqi involvement in 9/11. "It's been pretty well confirmed that he [Atta] did go to Prague and he did meet with a senior official of the Iraqi intelligence service in Czechoslovakia last April," Cheney said on 'meet the press' on Dec. 9, 2001. But the evidence used to support the claim, a supposed photograph of Atta in Prague the day of the alleged meeting, had already been debunked by Rossini. He analyzed the photo and immediately saw it was bogus: the picture of the Czech "Atta" looked nothing like the real terrorist. It was a conclusion Rossini relayed up the chain, assuming he had put the matter to rest. Then he heard Cheney endorsing the discredited report on national television. "I remember looking at the TV screen and saying, 'What did I just hear?' And I - first time in my life, I actually threw something at the television because I couldn't believe what I just heard," Rossini said in an interview published in February 2013.

These examples of the manipulation used, showed that Cheney, Rumsfeld, Wolfowitz and others were determined - probably from the moment they came into office - to invade Iraq. Paul Pillar, one of the CIA's top terrorism analysts stated in 2012 that the 9/11 attacks "made it politically possible for the first time to persuade the American people to break a tradition of not launching offensive wars." But to achieve that goal, secret intelligence was twisted, massaged, and wildly exaggerated. "It wasn't a matter of lying about this or lying about that," Pillar says, "but rather, through the artistry of speechwriters and case-presenters, conveying an impression to the American people that certain things were true." But those things were not true and the perpetrators of these lies knew this all along.

Note 6.1 Disabled persons travelling by air: European Regulation (EC) No. 1107/2006 of the European Parliament and of the Council of 5 July 2006, concerning the rights of disabled persons and persons with reduced mobility when travelling by air.

Note 6.2 Tesco accused of using slave labour. Tesco was one of a number of companies that were accused of using unpaid labour to carry out menial tasks. Burger King and Poundland were also participants in the so-called "Work experience program" along with many other companies. All three of these companies withdrew from the government scheme. Tesco said it has asked British Department of Work and Pension officials to make the work experience scheme voluntary after thousands of angry customers wrote in and posted messages on Twitter and the company's Facebook site, accusing the multinational of profiting from hundreds of thousands of hours of forced unpaid work. In February 2013, the British Court of Appeal declared most of these involuntary work-schemes illegal, forcing the UK government to pay huge rebates to those denied social welfare for refusing forced labour.

Note 9.1 None of the above: In some jurisdictions or organisations there is an option to allow the voter to indicate disapproval of all of the candidates in the voting system. It is based on the principle that consent requires the ability to withhold consent in an election, just as they can by voting "no" on ballot questions. Spain, Greece, Ukraine, Columbia, Bangladesh provide this option as standard procedure.

Note 11.1 Big Lies: Afghanistan under control of ISAF: In 2013, the following official statement appeared on the NATO website: "As part of the international community's overall effort, ISAF is working to create the conditions whereby the Afghan government is able to exercise its authority throughout the country. To achieve this goal, ISAF conducts security operations to protect the Afghan people, neutralise insurgent's networks and deny sanctuary in Afghanistan to extremists."

Despite the upbeat military assessments by NATO and the US government of an improving security situation in Afghanistan, a leaked report in February 1st 2012 had the following content according to the London Times, Reuters and Huffington Post, which was then confirmed by a US military commander:

"The U.S. military said in a secret report the Taliban, backed by Pakistan, is set to retake control of Afghanistan after NATO-led forces withdraw from the country, raising the prospect of a major failure of western policy after a costly war". Lieutenant Colonel Jimmie Cummings, a spokesman for the NATO-led International Security Assistance Force, confirmed the existence of the document, reported by Britain's Times newspaper and the BBC.

Note 12.1 British colonial war crimes: The British armed forces have a considerable history of war crimes, stretching from the 18th century right up to the present day.

Recent discoveries in the Hanslope Park archive of the British Foreign Office have shown that a concerted attempt was made to destroy evidence of British war crimes as the empire began to collapse in the 1950s and 1960s. Many of the most sensitive papers from Britain's late colonial era were not just hidden away, but simply destroyed.

Amongst surviving papers was the original instruction for the systematic destruction of evidence, issued in 1961 after Iain Macleod, Secretary of State for the Colonies, directed that post-independence governments should not get any material that "might embarrass Her Majesty's government", that could "embarrass members of the police, military forces, public servants or others e.g. police informers, that might compromise intelligence sources.... ".

Also surviving were some essential papers relating to atrocities committed by the British army during the Mau Mau uprising, and complaints from victims of these atrocities, which arrived before the High Court in 2012.

Here are some notable examples of British atrocities up to the 1960s, for which all evidence was not entirely destroyed:

a/ During the Second Boer War (1879-1915), the British Empire ordered the civilian internment of the Afrikaner population into concentration camps, one of the earliest uses of this method by modern powers. Women and children were rounded up and transported to the camps under the most brutal, inhuman and appalling conditions, i.e. being transported in open cattle trucks in freezing rain during winter, without being given adequate food and water. Many children died under these conditions, even before getting to the camps. Most of these camps were badly organised and suffered from poor hygiene and little food. Most of the children in these camps died, many mothers losing all their children. A significant portion of the adults also died. Some Afrikaners consider this to be a war crime, ending with the deaths of at least 34,000 people.

b/ Irish war of Independence, 1920: Numerous cases of atrocities committed against civilian populations included the Croke Park massacre where British troops opened fire on the crowd, killing many civilians in retaliation for an earlier IRA attack.

c/ The 1919 Amritsar Massacre in India: On 13th April 1919 on hearing that there was an illegal meeting of 15,000 to 20,000 people, including women, senior citizens and children, assembled at Jallianwala Bagh public park in Amritsar, Northern India, Brigadier-General Reginald E.H. Dyer went with fifty riflemen to a raised bank and ordered them to shoot at the crowd. Dyer ordered the firing to continue for about ten minutes until the ammunition supply was almost exhausted, with approximately 1,650 rounds fired. Official Government of India sources estimated that fatalities were 379 with 1,100 wounded. The casualty number estimated by Indian National Congress was more than 1,500 with approximately 1,000 dead.

As recently as 2013 the British government still refused to apologise for the atrocity: David Cameron, British Prime Minister, defended his decision to stop short of delivering a formal British apology for the Amritsar massacre. As relatives of the victims expressed disappointment, the prime minister said it would be wrong to "reach back into history" and apologise for the wrongs of British colonialism. Cameron was speaking shortly after becoming the first serving British Prime Minister to visit the scene of the massacre.

d/ Iraqi revolt 1920: During the first years of British rule in Iraq, numerous attacks on civilians were carried out, including village burning and indiscriminate bombing.

e/ Malaya 1948: Massacre of 24 unarmed villagers in Malaya by soldiers of the Scots Guards.

f/ Aden 1960s: Army's Intelligence Corps operated a secret torture centre for several years in the 1960s.

h/ Abuse of Mau Mau insurgents (1952 -1960):Detained by British colonial authorities, they were tortured and sometimes murdered.

Note 15.1: Suppression of the Irish Language by Britain: In an attempt to enforce complete subjugation, the English passed laws to suppress the native Irish language. First, the authorities had to deal with their own people.

In 1366, the Statutes of Kilkenny required that all Englishmen in Ireland retain their English surnames and continue to speak English. After this, various attempts were made to suppress the use of the Irish language by the native population. At first these met with little success; when Irish Catholics were forbidden to teach in schools, illegal schools were opened. Eventually though, the Irish could read the writing on the wall. In order to prosper in business or politics, you had to speak English.

The Irish language increasingly became associated with poverty and backwardness. In the National School system established in 1831, children were beaten with what became known as a 'tally stick' if they were caught speaking Irish. Far from being upset by this, many parents enthusiastically endorsed it, feeling that the future of their children depended on their ability to speak English. Because of this, Ireland experienced a steady decline in the number of native Irish speakers. It has been estimated that there were five million people living in Ireland at the end of the eighteenth century. Of these, two million were exclusively Irish speakers, one and a half million spoke both Irish and English, and one and a half million spoke English exclusively. A hundred years later, there were only about 600,000 Irish speakers left, with only 3.5% under the age of 10 able to speak the language.

Note 17.1 Reading the Riots - The Guardian LSE study: Widespread anger and frustration at the way police engaged with communities was a significant cause of the summer riots in every major city where disorder took place, the biggest study into their cause has found. Hundreds of interviews with people who took part in the disturbances which spread across England in August revealed deep-seated and sometimes visceral antipathy towards police.

In a unique collaboration, the Guardian and London School of Economics (LSE) interviewed 270 people who rioted in London, Birmingham, Liverpool, Nottingham, Manchester and Salford.

The project collected more than 1.3m words of first-person accounts from rioters, giving an unprecedented insight into what drove people to participate in England's most serious bout of civil unrest in a generation. Rioters revealed that a complex mix of grievances brought them on to the streets, but analysts appointed by the LSE identified distrust and antipathy toward police as a key driving force.

Note 20.1 Ryanair plan for standing-only plane tickets foiled by regulator. In February 2012, the airline announced that an unnamed regulator has thwarted its plan to sell standing-only tickets, by refusing an application for test flights. Under the scheme, a Boeing 737-800 would be fitted out with 15 rows of seats and 10 rows of standing berths. Michael O'Leary, the budget airline's chief executive, said: "We have asked the question could we run some trials on this and the immediate response is somewhat negative."

O'Leary has claimed in the past that the carrier was looking at charging passengers for using the toilet, in a bid to limit loo facilities on planes and replace them with extra seats. Ryanair has also suggested it would put passengers in the hull - in bunks - and has called for flights with only one pilot instead of the usual two.

Note 21.1 Ban on showing US coffins: In February 2009 the Obama administration lifted an 18-year ban on coverage of the return of military members killed in war, by allowing families of dead soldiers to decide whether the news media may photograph the flag-covered caskets.

As President Bush's Defence Chief Gates said, he had looked into lifting the ban on coffins at Delaware's Dover Air Force Base, where dead troops arrive for transfer to their hometowns. The ban had been in place since George W. Bush's father implemented it, Bush jr. continued to renew the ban during the Iraq and Afghanistan wars.

Note 21.2: Israeli air strikes hit media centres in Gaza City, November 2012. Six people were injured when Israeli air strikes targeted buildings housing media organisations including Sky News, al-Arabiya and al-Quds TV.

Israeli military planes struck two media headquarters in Gaza City in the early hours of the morning of 18th November 2012, injuring six people, including a cameraman who lost a leg. A number of media organisations were based in the al-Shawa building, including al-Quds television which is associated with Islamic Jihad. Khader al-Zahhar, a cameraman with al-Quds TV had his leg amputated as a result of injuries sustained in the attack.

A second air strike struck another media complex in the city, the al-Shuruq building. It housed Sky News, the al-Arabiya news network, Dubai TV and an office of al-Aqsa TV which is affiliated with Hamas. The attacks effectively silenced the media reporting from within the Gaza strip. It was seen as a way for the Israel military government to control reporting of their attack on Gaza.

A statement from the Israeli military stated: "The IDF calls on international journalists and correspondents who operate in the Gaza Strip carrying out their duties, to stay clear of Hamas's bases and facilities – which serve them in their activity against the citizens of Israel."

Note 21.3 Nazi and Israel tactics bear a shocking similarity: The similarities in the behaviour of the regimes of Nazi Germany and the modern state of Israel are stunning: Here are some of the common tactics: 1/ The use of fenced ghettos, poverty and economic isolation to physically exclude those people considered to be racially inferior. For the Nazis it was the Jews, for the Israelis it is the Palestinians. The erection of 700km fences around Palestinian areas by Israel has been condemned by the United Nations. 2/ The use of collective punishment by the Nazis against the communities of resistance fighters (including Jewish fighters) was designed to undermine resistance by punishing many unconnected civilians. Lately the same tactic has been used by Israel. It uses the demolition of houses of Palestinian fighters, and mass arrests of whole communities to intimidate civilian populations. Israel even resorted to the bombing and invasion of Lebanon in 2006 (with the death of over 1000 civilians) because 3 Israeli soldiers had been killed in a Hezbollah incursion. Racial segregation by the Nazis included the stripping of many basic rights of Jewish populations in "occupied territories". The Israelis use similar tactics against Palestinians, with restrictions in movement, segregated public transport, segregated schools, and denial of land rights to Palestinians etc. Meanwhile, Israel has forced non-white Jewish settlers from Ethiopia arriving in Israel to receive contraceptive injections, whilst condemning them to almost universal poverty. Israel has 700 outstanding and unexplained complaints for torture awaiting investigation. The UN and Red Cross have commented on all of the above and the state of Israel is considered in breach of several articles of the Geneva Conventions.

For example, in 2010, the ICRC says that Israel is punishing the whole civilian population of Gaza: "The whole of Gaza's civilian population is being punished for acts for which they bear no responsibility. The closure (of the border) therefore constitutes a collective punishment imposed in clear violation of Israel's obligations under international humanitarian law," the agency said in the statement.

And again, many Palestinians rounded up and held by Israel are never charged and are held in an illegal "limbo" of "administrative custody" with no rights of recourse. According to the Palestinian Centre for Human Rights, from the Six Day War (1967) to the First Intifada (1988), over 600,000 Palestinians were held in Israeli jails for a week or more. Rory McCarthy, The Guardian's Jerusalem correspondent, estimates that one-fifth of the Palestinian population has at one time been imprisoned since 1967.

Note 22.1 The Halo effect - studies: Multiple studies of the halo effect in jury outcomes have shown that attractive individuals both receive lesser sentences and are less likely to be convicted than unattractive ones. Efran in 1974 found that subjects were more lenient in sentencing attractive individuals than unattractive ones, even when exactly the same crime was committed. This has been attributed to people with a high level of attractiveness being seen as more likely to have brighter futures in society, thanks to socially desirable traits they are believed to possess. Monahan, in 1941, studied social workers accustomed to interacting with people from all types of background; his findings showed the majority found it very difficult to believe beautiful people were guilty of a crime.

Note 22.2: Organic food and health halos: There is little evidence that organic foods are more nutritious than conventionally grown foods, according to the most comprehensive study to address the question to date. However, the findings by researchers at Stanford University, California, do suggest that eating organic foods can reduce the likelihood of consuming pesticides and antibiotic-resistant bacteria. Lead author Crystal Smith-Spangler and a team of researchers looked at 240 published studies of the nutrient and contaminant levels in organic and conventionally grown foods, as well as studies of humans consuming the two types of food.

The researchers reviewed 17 studies (six of which were randomised clinical trials) of populations consuming organic and conventional diets, and 223 studies that compared either the nutrient levels or the bacterial, fungal or pesticide contamination of various products (fruits, vegetables, grains, meats, milk, poultry and eggs) grown organically and conventionally. The duration of the studies involving human subjects ranged from two days to two years. Smith-Spangler wrote in the Annals of Internal Medicine: "Despite the widespread misperception that organically produced foods are more nutritious than conventional alternatives, we did not find evidence to support this perception."

They found no consistent differences in the vitamin content between the two types of produce, or that conventional foods pose any greater health risk than organic ones. However, their analysis did find that conventional produce carries a 30% higher chance of pesticide contamination when compared with organic foods.

Note 23.1 United Nations FAO disputes need for GM crops to feed the future world: Can the world produce enough food to meet global demands without GM technology? The answer is yes, according to a report from the UN's Food and Agriculture Organisation's (FAO) Global Perspective Studies Unit completed in 2012 (**http://www.fao.org/economic/esa/esag/en/**) . This conclusion is reached by FAO experts whose quantitative analysis specifically does NOT allow for any production improvements from genetically modified (GM) crops. These are not factored in by FAO due to the ongoing uncertainties regarding the technical performance, safety and consumer acceptance of GM crops (p.2). Therefore the FAO projections are based on 'present-day' technical knowledge only (p.1, 2, 95, 117). Ignoring the impact of any future developments in genetic engineering, and using a FAO report emphasises that: "Concerning the future, a number of projection studies have addressed and largely answered in the positive the issue whether the resource base of world agriculture, including its land component, can continue to evolve in a flexible and adaptable manner as it did in the past, and also whether it can continue to exert downward pressure on the real price of food (see for example Pinstrup-Andersen et al., 1999). The largely positive answers mean essentially that for the world as a whole there is enough, or more than enough, food production potential to meet the growth of effective demand, i.e. the demand for food of those who can afford to pay farmers to produce it." (p.109). The Food and Agriculture Organisation is the largest autonomous agency within the United Nations. The report "Agriculture: Towards 2015/30" is published at **http://www.fao.org/es/ESD/at2015/toc-e.htm** .

Note 23.2: The Seralini studies: Seralini and his team were heavily criticised, mostly by vested industry interests. Finally in January 2013, they issued a detailed 300 page defence of their study, which can be found at **http://gmoseralini.org/category/critics-answered/**. The defence effectively counters hundreds of individual criticisms made against the original study.

Note 23.3 Google Effect on Memory: This study was carried out by researchers Betsy Sparrow, Jenny Liu, and Daniel M.Wegner and the report is available at: **http://www.wjh.harvard.edu/~wegner/pdfs/science.1207745.full.pdf**

Note 24.1 Racism in the USA: In November 2012, an AP Poll showed that racism in the USA has increased since 2008. According to the poll, "51% of Americans now express explicit anti-black attitudes, compared with 48% in a similar 2008 survey." The three percentage point rise is not large, and within the poll's margin of error. But, at the very least, it indicates that there is no decline in racism, on the contrary in fact. And the prejudice isn't limited to blacks: 52% openly express anti-Hispanic sentiments.

The numbers go up when measured by an implicit racial attitudes test. That is, when the survey takes into account the "dog-whistles," the new word for coded racist language only those "tuned in" will hear, anti-black sentiment is 56% and anti-Hispanic sentiment is 57%.

Given that only 78% of the population is white and 63% of the US population is white and non Hispanic (according to the National Census Bureau 2011) this means that a very large percentage of White Anglo Saxon Americans have racist attitudes, somewhere between 65% and 89% depending on which figures are used and assuming that black people are not prejudiced against black people.

Note 24.2: Sarkozy and Racism in France: In September 2010, during a debate in the European parliament, MEPs expressed grave concerns over Mr. Sarkozy's policy of returning the Roma from illegal camps to Eastern Europe. Social Democrat, Labour and Liberal MEPs voted a European Parliament resolution condemning the French President's policy to expel Bulgarian and Romanian gipsies. They expressed "deep concern regarding the recent measures taken by the French government to repatriate and return thousands of Roma EU citizens to their countries of origin". MEPs also criticised the European Commission for failing to enforce freedom of movement rights for EU citizens. Martin Schulz, the German leader of Social Democrat MEPs accused President Sarkozy of carrying out "a witch-hunt against a minority" in order to boost his flagging popularity at a time of economic crisis.

Sarkozy initiated the French ban on face covering, "prohibiting concealment of the face in public space" in an Act of Parliament passed by the Senate of France on 14 September 2010, resulting in the ban on the wearing of face-covering headgear, including niqabs and other veils covering the face, in public places, except under specified circumstances. The ban also applies to the burqa, a full-body covering, if it covers the face. It is believed that less than 2000 Muslim women actually wear any of these face covering garments in France. But Sarkozy felt the need to make a political statement about the subservience of France's Muslim population.

Note 24.3 Persecution of the Romani in Europe: Persecution of Romani people reached a peak during World War II in the Porajmos, the Nazi genocide of Romanis during the Holocaust. Because the Romani communities of Eastern Europe were less organized than the Jewish communities, it is more difficult to assess the actual number of victims, though the U.S. Holocaust Memorial Research Institute in Washington puts the number of Romani lives lost by 1945 at between 500,000 and 1.5 million. Former ethnic studies professor Ward Churchill has argued that the Romani population suffered proportionally more genocide than the Jewish population of Europe and that their plight has largely been sidelined by scholars and the media.

The extermination of Romanis by the German Nazi authorities in the Protectorate of Bohemia and Moravia was so thorough that the Bohemian Romani language became extinct. The policy of the Nazis varied across countries they conquered: they killed almost all the Romanis in the Baltic countries, yet they did not attempt to eliminate the Romanis in Denmark or Greece. Romanis were also persecuted by the fascists in Croatia, who were allied to the Nazis. As a result, there were hardly any Romanis left in Croatia after the war.

According to a report issued by Amnesty International in 2011, "...systematic discrimination is taking place against up to 10 million Roma across Europe. The organization has documented the failures of governments across the continent to live up to their obligations". Antiziganism has continued in the 2000s, particularly in Germany, France, England, Romania, Bulgaria, Slovakia, Hungary, Slovenia and Kosovo.

Note 25.1 Britain's New Labour more right-wing than the Conservative Party: Here are a few indications of how Tony Blair's New Labour became more right-wing than the Conservative party, starting with two comments of former Conservative Prime Ministers about New Labour:

a/ "Blair more conservative than me": Sir John Major, Conservative Prime Minister from 1990 to 1997, rightly remarked to the Leveson Inquiry that leader Tony Blair was more right-wing than he. Sir John told the Inquiry that he once joked about Mr Blair who led Labour to victory in 1997, stealing his clothes. He also said he was not surprised that "The Sun" (a right-wing newspaper) switched its backing from the Conservatives to Labour in the run-up to the 1997 election.

b/ Chilcot Inquiry: "Establishment Stitch-up": The British Conservative party leader David Cameron in June 2009, referred to the Inquiry into the Iraq invasion by New Labour's Tony Blair. He referred to the dubious independence of the inquiry as "an establishment stitch-up." He was joined in his condemnation of the bias of members of the inquiry by the Liberal Democrat party. Coming from the main "establishment party", this was a damning attack on honesty and integrity of New Labour.

c/ Independence of the Bank of England: The first policy U-turn of Blair's New Labour occurred almost immediately on the party entering office in 1997, with the surprise move (dominated by Blair and Brown) to grant operational independence to the Bank of England. The policy continued the Thatcherite approach. Whilst the initiative itself was not in place under previous Conservative governments, the motive behind the decision was identical to the Conservative commitment to the New Right approach that economic growth depended less on high rates of unemployment and demand than it did on stable economic conditions characterised by low levels of inflation (Bevir 2005:107 & Aimee Oakley, Polis Journal 2011/2012)

d/ The Private Finance Initiative (PFI): As part of the new "modernisation" agenda, New Labour leaders recognised a need to move away from old Labour's approach and towards a pro-business stance. In order to show their commitment and favourable approach, on entering office in 1997, new Labour agreed to continue the private finance initiative (PFI) that had been introduced by the Conservative party. Private sector involvement in public services had long been anathema to most in the Labour party, yet on entering office New Labour enthusiastically picked up and expanded the policy" (McAnulla 2006: 125). As a Treasury official closely involved with the PFI told Keegan, "it was a way of demonstrating they [New Labour] could do business with the City" (Keegan 2003: 269 cited in Shaw, 2007: 91). Although renamed as "public private partnerships" (PPP), the idea was synonymous with the private finance initiative of the Conservative government. Aimee Oakley, Polis Journal 2011/2012

e/ Welfare-to-work; The New Deal: As part of New Labour's "third way", this program was a continuation of the Thatcherite agenda on social welfare. New Labour shifted their emphasis towards an "Anglo-American model, extolling the virtues of flexible labour markets and building welfare around the needs of a flexible workforce, with training and education to deal with job insecurity" (Driver and Martell 1998: 50).

But did "the third way" offer any real differences to previous Conservative commitments? The "endorsement of conditionality" whereby benefits would be withdrawn should participants of the scheme fail to comply, drew similarities with the ideology of the New Right (Dwyer 2000: 90). The New Deal scheme had clear similarities with the Job Seeker's Allowance under previous Conservative governments. Seamus Milne and Richard Thomas state that "the sanction regime for the under 25s who refuse to take part in the [so-called] New Deal programme is essentially the same as that introduced as part of the Tory government's Job Seekers' Allowance" (1997 cited in Hay 1999: 122). Under this scheme, those reliant on welfare would "lose 40% of their benefit indefinitely if they refused to accept one of the welfare-workfare options presented to them" (Hay 1999: 121). The similarities between the New Deal and the Conservative's "Project Work" programme, is also striking. As Gray describes, Project Work was "the first post-war compulsory work programme in the UK, involving 13 weeks" compulsory work in return for benefit." (Aimee Oakley, Polis Journal 2011/2012).

Note 25.2 Think tanks and Iraq invasion: A prime example of the involvement of various think tanks in illegal actions was that of the organisation "Project for the New American Century", a conservative, Washington-based think tank. On September 20, 2001 (nine days after the September 11, 2001 attacks), the PNAC sent a letter to President George W. Bush, advocating "a determined effort to remove Saddam Hussein from power in Iraq", or regime change:

"...even if evidence does not link Iraq directly to the attack, any strategy aiming at the eradication of terrorism and its sponsors must include a determined effort to remove Saddam Hussein from power in Iraq. Failure to undertake such an effort will constitute an early and perhaps decisive surrender in the war on international terrorism. "

From 2001 through 2002, the co-founders and other members of the PNAC (mostly members of the Bush administration) published articles supporting the United States' invasion of Iraq. On its website, the PNAC promoted its point of view that leaving Saddam Hussein in power would be "surrender to terrorism." In 2003, during the period leading up to the 2003 invasion of Iraq, the PNAC had seven full-time staff members in addition to its board of directors. Despite the fact that there never was a connection between Saddam Hussein and Osama bin Laden, the PNAC think tank tried to persuade the population to believe that there was.

Note 25.3 Think tanks and anonymity: In February 2013 it was revealed that Conservative billionaires used a secretive funding route to channel nearly $120m to more than 100 groups casting doubt about the science behind climate change. The funds, doled out between 2002 and 2010, helped build a vast network of think tanks and activist groups working to a single purpose: to redefine climate change from neutral scientific fact to a highly polarising "wedge issue" for hardcore conservatives.

The millions were routed through two trusts, Donors Trust and the Donors Capital Fund, operating out of a generic town house in the northern Virginia suburbs of Washington DC. Donors Capital caters to those making donations of $1m or more. Whitney Ball, chief executive of the Donors Trust said that her organisation assured wealthy donors that their funds would never be diverted to liberal causes. "We exist to help donors promote liberty which we understand to be limited government, personal responsibility, and free enterprise," she said in an interview. By definition that means none of the money is going to end up with groups like Greenpeace, she said. "It won't be going to liberals." Ball won't divulge names, but she said the stable of donors represents a wide range of opinion on the American right. Increasingly, over the years, those conservative donors have been pushing funds towards organisations working to discredit climate science or block climate action. Donors exhibit sharp differences of opinion on many issues, Ball said. They run the spectrum of conservative opinion, from social conservatives to libertarians. But in opposing mandatory cuts to greenhouse gas emissions, they found common ground.

"Are there both sides of an environmental issue? Probably not," she went on. "Here is the thing. If you look at libertarians, you tend to have a lot of differences on things like defence, immigration, drugs, the war, things like that compared to conservatives. When it comes to issues like the environment, if there are differences, they are not nearly as pronounced."

By 2010, the dark money amounted to $118m distributed to 102 think tanks or action groups which have a record of denying the existence of a human factor in climate change, or opposing environmental regulations. The money flowed to Washington think tanks embedded in Republican Party politics, obscure policy forums in Alaska and Tennessee, contrarian scientists at Harvard and lesser institutions, even to buy up DVDs of a film attacking Al Gore. [Guardian 2013]

Note 26.1 Britain and Northern Ireland: Internment without Trial: Operation Demetrius was a British Army operation in Northern Ireland on 9-10 August 1971, during "The Troubles".

It involved the mass arrest and internment (without trial) of 342 people suspected of being involved with Irish republican paramilitaries (the Provisional IRA and Official IRA). Armed soldiers launched dawn raids throughout Northern Ireland, sparking four days of rioting that killed 20 civilians, two Provisional IRA members and two British soldiers.

About 7,000 people fled their homes, of which roughly 2,500 fled south of the border. No loyalist paramilitaries were included in the sweep and many of those who were arrested had no links with republican paramilitaries, which caused much anger. The policy of internment was to last until December 1975 and during that time 1,981 people were interned.

Its introduction and the abuse of those interned, led to numerous protests and a sharp increase in violence. The interrogation techniques used on the internees were described by the European Court of Human Rights as "inhuman and degrading", and by the European Commission of Human Rights as "torture".

Note 26.2 United States a pariah state: On December 13th, 2012 the European Court of Human Rights ruled in the case of Mr. Masri and his forcible disappearance, kidnapping and covert transfer without legal process to United States custody nine years earlier. The court ruled that the action by the United States violated the most basic guarantees of human decency. Notably, the court found that the treatment suffered by Mr. Masri in 2003 "at the hands of the special C.I.A. rendition team,at an airport in Skopje, the capital of the former Yugoslav republic of Macedonia, amounted to torture." Although the case was filed against the Macedonian government and the court does not have jurisdiction over the United States, the ruling is a powerful condemnation of improper C.I.A. tactics and of the abject failure of any American court to provide redress for Mr. Masri or the other victims of Washington's discredited policy of secret detention and extraordinary rendition. The 17 judges in the European Court's Grand Chamber, several of whom grew up under Communism, have done what the United States Supreme Court has declined to do, namely condemn egregious abuse of an innocent man by out-of-control security services. Many more cases are expected to follow and are currently being heard by the court.

Note 26.3 Guantanamo military commissions: These are military tribunals created by the Military Commissions Act of 2006 for prosecuting detainees held in the United States Guantanamo Bay detainment camps. The Military Commissions act of 2006 was a response by the Bush government to the US Supreme Court ruling that the detention and trial of detainees in Guantanamo under existing legislation was illegal under the terms of the Geneva Convention and was in fact a war crime. The act of the Bush regime effectively legalised an internationally defined war crime into US statute. It continues to this day and has drawn widespread international criticism, providing moral motivation for various global terrorist activities.

Note 26.4 Show Trials - Goldman Sachs: Rajat Gupta, a board member of Goldman Sachs received a sentence of just 2 years for serious insider trading crimes, carrying penalties of up to 105 years. The penalty he received was considered by many to be inappropriately lenient. In January 2013 he also initiated a procedure to have his conviction reversed, which at the time of writing is pending in front of a federal judge.

Note 27.1 Common misconceptions: There were and are literally thousands of commonly held misconceptions. Many misconceptions have been corrected and many more have been adopted. For example, the concept that Columbus discovered America is patently nonsense (since it was already populated when he arrived), but it is still described in most primary school books as "a fact". If you want to see just how many commonly held misconceptions really do exist just search the internet for "list of common misconceptions" and prepare to be surprised.

Note 27.2 Trolls - intellectual honesty: Professional trolls very often do not have a profound understanding of the subject they are attempting to disrupt. Generally they have only an armoury of manipulative gainsays and insulting rhetoric.

To detect if someone is a troll you can examine them on some innocuous piece of information regarding the subject. If they demonstrate some insight, then delve a little further. A troll will usually be unable to answer a question or discuss an issue as soon as you deviate from their rehearsed narrative. A real person will simply admit they just don't know or have no understanding of a particular topic; a troll will ignore the question and look for another person to intimidate.

Note 28.1 Companies with skeletons in the cupboard: Many companies which are household names now, have a disreputable past which they would prefer to forget about. Here are a couple of examples:

Holocaust gas chambers: IG Farben was a company formed by a merger of BASF, Bayer, Hoechst, Cassella and Agfa in 1925. IG Farben held the patent for the chemical Zyklon B used in Holocaust gas chambers, and owned 42.2% of Degesch, the company which manufactured it. 24 directors of IG Farben were indicted in the Nuremberg trials (1947–1948) and 13 were sentenced to prison terms of between one and eight years.

Some of those indicted in the trial were subsequently made leaders of the post-war companies that split off from IG Farben, including those who were sentenced at Nuremberg. In 1951, the Allies split the company up into its original constituent companies. The four largest quickly bought the smaller ones. Today only Agfa, BASF, and Bayer remain. Hoechst in 1999 de-merged its industrial chemical operations to Celanese AG and merged its life-sciences businesses to form Aventis. IG Farben was officially put into liquidation in 1952 but this did not end the company's legal existence. As of 2012, it still exists as a corporation "in liquidation", meaning that the purpose of the continuing existence of the corporation is being wound up and dissolved in an orderly fashion. As of 2012, its shares are still traded on German markets.

Ikea and slave labour: Ikea, the Swedish based international company is famous for its inexpensive furniture. In 2012, the company admitted that political prisoners in the former East Germany provided some of the labour that helped it keep its prices so low. A report by auditors at Ernst & Young concluded that Ikea, a Swedish company, knowingly benefited from forced labour in the former East Germany to manufacture some of its products in the 1980s. Ikea had commissioned the report in May 2012 as a result of accusations that both political and criminal prisoners were involved in making components of Ikea furniture and that some Ikea employees knew about it. "Even though Ikea Group took steps to secure that prisoners were not used in production, it is now clear that these measures were not effective enough," the company said in a statement. Accusations against Ikea started to appear around 2011 in news media reports in Germany and Sweden. Ikea's admission has given new impetus to efforts by victims' groups to receive compensation for work they were forced to perform under the communist government in East Germany. At least two well-known mail-order companies in the former West Germany, Neckermann and Quelle, which have since run into financial trouble, have also been accused of using forced labour.

Note 28.2 Saddam Hussein, Bin Laden and their relationship with the USA: Both Saddam Hussein and Osama bin Laden received significant economic and political support from the USA and the West in the years prior to the 9/11 attacks:

Saddam Hussein: In 1980, Iraq invaded Iran with the support of the Arab states, the United States, and Europe, and heavily financed by the Arab states of the Persian Gulf. Saddam Hussein had become the "defender of the Arab world" against a revolutionary Iran, acting as a proxy for the United States. The blatant disregard of international law and violations of international borders were ignored. Iraq received economic and military support from its allies, who overlooked Saddam's use of chemical warfare against the Kurds and Iranians, and Iraq's efforts to develop nuclear weapons. These chemical weapons were developed by Iraq from materials and technology supplied by West German companies. The Reagan administration of the United States supplied Iraq with "satellite photos showing Iranian deployments" and advised Hussein to bomb civilian targets in Tehran and other Iranian cities. France sold 25 billion dollars worth of arms to Saddam.

Osama bin Laden: A Saudi citizen from a wealthy, well connected family. In 1979 he went to Pakistan to assist in training mujahideen resistance fighters engaged against the Soviet army in Afghanistan. This training program was financed by both the Saudi government and the CIA of the United States to the value of $3 billion in total. Under Operation Cyclone from 1979 to 1989, the United States provided financial aid and weapons to the mujahideen through Pakistan's ISI. Bin Laden met and built relations with Hamid Gul who was a three-star general in the Pakistani army and head of the ISI agency. Although the United States provided the money and weapons, the training of militant groups was entirely done by the Pakistani Armed Forces and the ISI, including Osama bin Laden.

Note 28.3 Official textbook is Euro-sceptical: Taken from the Guardian, February 2013: A-level history students are using a textbook that teaches a highly partisan, strongly Eurosceptic view of Britain's entry into the European Union, MPs have claimed. The book, which is entitled Britain 1945-2007, by the respected historian Michael Lynch, has been criticised for a biased view of Britain's first steps towards the common market.

In one section, it devotes five lines to the advantages of Britain having joined the European Economic Community and 26 lines to the disadvantages. The book is thought to be taught in large numbers of British schools, part of a bestselling series for A-level students.

It says of Britain's 1973 entry into the Common Market and subsequent referendum: "The British people were never given the full story ... the people were kept in the dark. They were constantly told there were no political implications attached to Britain's joining, that it was purely an economic arrangement." The book goes on to call that reasoning a "deception". Earlier, the book says of the 1975 pro-entry campaign, "Stress was laid on the economic advantages Britain would gain. But these proved illusory."

Julian Huppert, the Liberal Democrat MP for Cambridge, has said that the book is "clearly" very alarming. "People should be taught a fair and balanced view of history to make up their own minds what they think of it. It is deeply worrying that a recognised text book should be presenting a one-sided Eurosceptic account such as this," he said. Stephen Dorrell MP, former cabinet minister and patron of the pro-European Tory Reform Group, said that the book was biased, but that most teenagers would be able to see through its arguments, "That is a tendentious version of events, but I would hope that most 17- and 18-year-olds are perfectly able to see that line of argument for what it is. The one sure way of creating a reaction in a 17-year-old is to pump a line that is not supported by an open mind," he said.

Note 30.1 Machiavelli and Religion in government: To quote: "No institution is firm or lasting if it rests on man's strength alone. History and reason combine to show that the roots of all great institutions are to be found outside this world. Sovereignties, in particular possess strength, unity, stability, only to the degree to which they are sanctified by religion." Note the interest which Machiavelli had in religion and the qualities he lists …. "Strength, unity, stability".…..and note the absence of words or sentiments of "morality", "divinity". Religion, for Machiavelli was just an adjunct to state power.

Note 30.2 Apartheid in South Africa: Some of the more trivial examples of apartheid included the following rules: Blacks were not allowed to run businesses or professional practices in those areas designated as "white South Africa" without a permit. They were supposed to move to the black "homelands" and set up businesses and practices there. Transport and civil facilities were segregated. Black buses stopped at black bus stops and white buses at white ones. Trains, hospitals and ambulances were segregated. Because of the smaller numbers of white patients and the fact that white doctors preferred to work in white hospitals, conditions in white hospitals were much better than those in often overcrowded and understaffed black hospitals. Blacks were excluded from living or working in white areas unless they had a pass. A pass was issued only to a black person with approved work. Spouses and children had to be left behind in black homelands. Police vans patrolled the white areas to round up illegal blacks found there without passes. Black people were not allowed to employ white people in white South Africa. More serious forms of apartheid resulted in the total disenfranchisement of black people in their own country until 1994.

Note 30.3 McCarthyism: During the McCarthy era (1950-1956), thousands of Americans were accused of being communists or communist sympathizers and became the subject of aggressive investigations and questioning before government or private-industry panels, committees and agencies. The primary targets of such suspicions were government employees, those in the entertainment industry, educators and union activists. Suspicions were often given credence, despite inconclusive or questionable evidence, and the level of threat posed by a person's real or supposed leftist associations or beliefs was often greatly exaggerated. Many people suffered loss of employment and/or destruction of their careers; some even suffered imprisonment. Most of these punishments came about through trial verdicts later overturned, laws that would be declared unconstitutional, dismissals for reasons later declared illegal or actionable, or extra-legal procedures that would come into general disrepute.

The most famous examples of McCarthyism include the speeches, investigations, and hearings of Senator McCarthy himself; the Hollywood blacklist, associated with hearings conducted by the House Un-American Activities Committee (HUAC); and the various anti-communist activities of the Federal Bureau of Investigation (FBI) under Director J. Edgar Hoover. McCarthyism was a widespread social and cultural phenomenon that affected all levels of society and was the source of a great deal of debate and conflict in the United States.

Note 31.1 Olympic Games and British military exhibitionism: In July 2012, the British government placed missile batteries at six sites around London in advance of the upcoming Summer Olympics, including on top of two apartment buildings where residents had previously expressed reservations about hosting the anti-aircraft weapons. "Whilst there is no reported threat to the London Olympics," said Defence Secretary Phillip Hammond in a statement, "the public expects that we put in place a range of measures aimed at ensuring the safety and security of this once-in-a-generation event. Ground-based air defence systems will form just one part of a comprehensive, multi-layered air security plan which, I believe, will provide both reassurance and a powerful deterrent." In addition to the Rapier and High-Velocity missile batteries, the government also stationed a Royal Navy helicopter carrier in the River Thames and station Royal Air Force jets and army helicopters nearby.

Note 31.2 Gaelic Athletic Association was founded on Saturday, 1 November 1884, in the billiards room of Lizzie Hayes' Commercial Hotel, Thurles, Co. Tipperary. All present that day had come in response to a circular published in the national press, or had been invited privately by Michael Cusack and Maurice Davin, both of whom were leading figures in Irish athletics. From its beginning the GAA was considered to be no mere sporting organisation, with their first historian noting that the association was founded by men who wished to "foster a spirit of earnest nationality" and as a means of "saving thousands of young Irishmen from becoming mere West Britons". A police report written in the mid-1880s claimed that the GAA had been founded by the Irish Republican Brotherhood with the intention of getting "the muscular youth of the country into an organisation, drilled and disciplined to form a physical power capable of over-awing and coercing the home rule government of the future".

Note 33.1 Pharmaceuticals - Off-label use: This is the practice of prescribing pharmaceuticals for an unapproved indication, or an unapproved age group, with an unapproved dose or using an unapproved form of administration.

In the USA, the Food and Drug Administration Centre for Drug Evaluation and Research (CDER) reviews a company's New Drug Application (NDA) for data from clinical trials to see if the results support the drug for a specific use or indication. If satisfied that the drug is safe and effective, the drug's manufacturer and the FDA agree on specific language describing dosage, route of administration, and other information to be included on the drug's label. Off-label use of medications is very common. Generic drugs generally have no sponsor as their indications and use expands, and incentives are limited to initiating new clinical trials to generate additional data for approval agencies to expand indications of proprietary drugs. Up to one-fifth of all drugs are prescribed off-label and amongst psychiatric drugs, off-label use rises to 31%.

Note 35.1 Self-regulation in the food industry: According to a study published in 2013 in the Lancet, food, drink, and alcohol companies are using similar strategies to the tobacco industry to undermine public health policies, and they should be regulated, say public health experts in Australia. Negotiating with multinational companies on salt, fat and sugar levels, including calorie and alcohol amounts on labels in the way the UK government had done will not work, say the authors of the study. "Self-regulation is like having burglars install your locks," said Professor Ron Moodie of the University of Melbourne, Australia. "You feel you're safe, but you're not."

The paper is one of a series published by the medical journal on the large and growing threat of what are known as non-communicable diseases (NCDs) across the globe - namely cancer, heart disease and stroke, diabetes and respiratory diseases. All are caused partly by our lifestyles - smoking, eating processed food, drinking and taking less exercise - in response to a world where energy-dense food, sugary drinks and alcohol are cheap and heavily marketed.

In 2010, 34.5 million people around the world died from these diseases, 65% of all deaths that year. That number is expected to rise to 50 million deaths a year by 2030 as the NCD epidemic spreads. The World Health Organisation has set a target to reduce these deaths by 25% by 2025.

Moodie and colleagues say that the food and drink industries should be treated like the tobacco industry - as companies with too much of a vested interest in the sale of unhealthy products to help curb the epidemic of disease. They must have no role in the formulation of national or international policy, they say. "Regulation, or the threat of regulation, is the only way to change these trans-national corporations. The industry must be put under pressure if it is to change."

The researchers were unable to find any health benefit to industry involvement in voluntary regulation or public-private partnerships. Industry documents, they say, reveal how companies shape public-health legislation and avoid regulation. They build "financial and institutional relations" with health professionals, non-governmental organisations, and national and international health agencies, says the paper. They distort research findings and they lobby politicians to oppose health care reform.

Huge multinational companies dominate sales worldwide. "The frequently used term 'competitive market' suggests a wide variety of traders; however, the most powerful corporate sectors of the world's food system are increasingly concentrated to the point of oligopoly.

"For example, in the USA, the 10 largest food companies control more than half of all food sales. Worldwide, this proportion is about 15% and is rising rapidly. More than half of global soft drinks are produced by large trans-national companies."

The multinationals are now moving in on the developing world, the researchers say. "Saturation of markets in high-income countries has caused the industries to rapidly penetrate emerging global markets, as the tobacco industry has done. Almost all growth in the foreseeable future in profits and sales of these unhealthy commodities will be in low-income and middle-income countries where consumption is currently low."

The Food and Drink federation said: "We agree that action is required to tackle the worldwide health burden of obesity and diet-related diseases. However we believe that collaboration between a very wide range of organisations can successfully address the multi-factorial causes of non-communicable diseases."

Note 39.1 Piltdown man frauds: The Piltdown man was a hoax in which bone fragments were presented as the fossilised remains of a previously unknown early human. These fragments consisted of parts of a skull and jawbone and are said to have been collected in 1912 from a gravel pit at Piltdown, East Sussex in England. The significance of the specimen remained the subject of controversy until it was exposed in 1953 as a forgery, consisting of the lower jawbone of an orang-utan deliberately combined with the skull of a fully developed modern human. The Piltdown hoax is perhaps the most famous paleoanthropological hoax ever to have been perpetrated. It is prominent for two reasons: the attention paid to the issue of human evolution, and the length of time (more than 40 years) that elapsed from its discovery to its full exposure as a forgery.

Note 40.1 Monsanto product safety data: An acrimonious dispute erupted between Monsanto and the Seralini research team, with Seralini's team showing apparent correlations between cancers in rats and Monsanto's GM maize NK603. Seralini rebutted all the industry's criticisms of his study and challenged Monsanto to publish the full results of its product safety tests for the active ingredient of its "Roundup" herbicide, glyphosate. Until this impasse, Monsanto had failed to publish such data for reasons of public interest and was not obliged to do so under US and European product licensing legislation. At the time of writing, Monsanto has still failed to publish this data. Therefore one can only surmise what information Monsanto are hiding about this omni-present herbicide.

Note 40.2 Big Pharma loses data all the time: "Bad Pharma: How drug companies mislead doctors and harm patients". This study of pharmaceutical companies and how they play tricks with data was published in 2012 by Ben Goldacre. Here you can find a complete description of how trial data can be "lost" in order to manipulate pharmaceutical trial results.

Note 40.3 Tamiflu, Roche, British Medical Journal and statistical transparency: In November 2012, the leading British Medical Journal asked the drug maker Roche to release all its data on Tamiflu, claiming there is no evidence the drug can actually stop the flu. The drug has been stockpiled by dozens of governments worldwide in case of a global flu outbreak and was widely used during the 2009 swine flu pandemic.

At the same time, one of the researchers linked to the BMJ called for European governments to sue Roche. "I suggest we boycott Roche's products until they publish missing Tamiflu data," wrote Peter Gotzsche, leader of the Nordic Cochrane Centre in Copenhagen. He said governments should take legal action against Roche to get the money back that was "needlessly" spent on stockpiling Tamiflu.

Last year, Tamiflu was included in a list of "essential medicines" by the World Health Organization, a list that often prompts governments or donor agencies to buy the drug. Tamiflu is used to treat both seasonal flu and new flu viruses such as bird flu or swine flu. WHO spokesman Gregory Hartl said the agency had enough proof to warrant its use for unusual influenza viruses like bird flu. "We do have substantive evidence it can stop or hinder progression to severe disease like pneumonia," he said.

In the U.S., the Centres for Disease Control and Prevention recommend Tamiflu as one of two medications for treating regular flu. The other is GlaxoSmithKline's Relenza. The CDC says such antivirals can shorten the duration of symptoms and reduce the risk of complications and hospitalization.

In 2009, the BMJ and researchers at the Nordic Cochrane Centre asked Roche to make all its Tamiflu data available. At the time, Cochrane Centre scientists were commissioned by Britain to evaluate flu drugs. They found no proof that Tamiflu reduced the number of complications in people with influenza. "Despite a public promise to release (internal company reports) for each (Tamiflu) trial...Roche has stonewalled," BMJ editor Fiona Godlee wrote in an editorial.

In a statement, Roche said it had complied with all legal requirements on publishing data and provided Gotzsche and his colleagues with 3,200 pages of information to answer their questions. "Roche has made full clinical study data ... available to national health authorities according to their various requirements, so they can conduct their own analyses," the company said. Roche says it doesn't usually release patient-level data available due to legal or confidentiality constraints. It said it did not provide the requested data to the scientists because they refused to sign a confidentiality agreement.

Roche is also being investigated by the European Medicines Agency for not properly reporting side effects, including possible deaths, for 19 drugs including Tamiflu that were used in about 80,000 patients in the U.S.

Note 45.1 The Paris Condemnations of 1210 to 1277: The Condemnations of 1210-1277 were enacted at the medieval University of Paris to restrict certain teachings as being heretical. These included a number of medieval theological teachings, but most importantly the physical treatises of Aristotle. The investigations of these teachings were conducted by the Bishops of Paris. The Condemnations of 1277 are traditionally linked to an investigation requested by Pope John XXI, although whether he actually supported drawing up a list of condemnations is unclear.

Approximately sixteen lists of censured theses were issued by the University of Paris during the 13th and 14th centuries. Most of these lists of propositions were put together into systematic collections of prohibited articles.

Of these, the Condemnations of 1277 are considered particularly important by historians as they allowed scholars to break from the restrictions of Aristotelian science. This had positive effects on the development of science, with some historians going so far as to claim that they represented the beginnings of modern science.

Note 46.1 If you have nothing to hide, you have nothing to fear: This saying has been attributed to George Orwell and Goebbels, although it is not certain who the author is. It has gained some currency in recent years as governments around the world have launched new attacks on our privacy, particularly with the use of the internet. The problem with the premise of holding huge citizen databases is that a/a liberal regime may become illiberal at some future time and use personal data to incriminate political enemies, b/ despite living a blameless life you may still be inadvertently implicated in criminal activity, simply because of a pattern of behaviour which triggers an automatic red flag to the authorities, c/ you never know if the data they hold is correct, d/ sometimes laws must be broken for the good of society, take the legalisation of homosexuality for example, e/ privacy is a fundamental need and right.

Note 47.1 Christian crusades: The term "crusade" is used to describe religiously motivated campaigns conducted between 1100 and 1600. Rivalries among both Christian and Muslim powers led to alliances between religious factions against their opponents, such as the Christian alliance with the Islamic Sultanate of Rûm. The crusades had a major political, economic, and social impact on Western Europe. They resulted in a substantial weakening of the Christian Byzantine Empire, which fell several centuries later to the Muslim Turks and included a long period of wars in Spain and Portugal, where Christian forces conquered the peninsula from Muslims in an event closely tied to the crusades.

The crusades and the "just war" doctrine: The papacy of Pope Gregory VII had struggled with reservations about the doctrinal validity of a holy war and the shedding of blood "for the Lord" and had, with difficulty, resolved the question in favour of justified violence. More importantly to the Pope, the Christians who made pilgrimages to the Holy Land were being persecuted. Saint Augustine of Hippo, Gregory's intellectual model, had justified the use of force "in the service of Christ" in his book "The City of God".

Note 47.2: The humiliation of Versailles and the Nazi party: Hitler gained popular support by attacking the Treaty of Versailles and promoting Pan-Germanism, anti-Semitism, and anti-communism with charismatic oratory and Nazi propaganda.

Together with many other Germans, Hitler was convinced that the Treaty of Versailles was completely unjust and a serious humiliation for the German nation; especially article 231 that blamed Germany as the country primarily responsible for the First World War.

One of the reasons for Hitler's rise in the 1930s was the popular consent within Germany that Versailles was unjust and was a form of collective punishment and humiliation to the whole of Germany.

Many historians believe that if Versailles had made a more honest and just settlement for WWI, it is quite likely that Adolf Hitler and the Nazis may never have risen to power in Germany.

Note 47.3: Gilad Shalit, an Israeli soldier, was abducted inside Israel by Hamas militants in a cross-border raid via underground tunnels near the Israeli border with Gaza on 25 June 2006. The Hamas militants held him for over five years until his release on 18 October 2011 as part of a prisoner exchange deal. He was freed in exchange for 1,027 prisoners - mainly Palestinians and Arab-Israelis.

Note 47.4: Abu Ghraib torture and prisoner abuse: During the war in Iraq, human rights violations, committed from late 2003 to early 2004, in the form of physical, psychological, and sexual abuse, including torture, reports of rape, sodomy, and homicide of prisoners held in the Abu Ghraib prison (also known as Baghdad Correctional Facility) came to public attention beginning in early 2004 with Department of Defence announcements. These acts were committed by military police personnel of the United States Army together with those of additional US governmental agencies. It is believed (and there is some evidence to demonstrate this) that the abuses at Abu Ghraib were ordered by and condoned at the highest military and political levels of the United States government, as high as President George W. Bush.

Note 47.5 Depo Provera - Sterilisation of Ethiopian Jews in Israel: In 2010, certain members of the feminist movement accused Israel of a "sterilisation policy" aimed towards Ethiopian Jews, for allowing the prescription of contraceptive drugs like Depo-Provera in the community. They stated that the Israeli government deliberately gives female Ethiopian Jews long-lasting contraceptive drugs like Depo-Provera. Jewish agencies involved in immigration said that Ethiopian women were offered different types of contraceptives and that "all of them participated voluntarily in family planning". Dr. Yifat Bitton, a member of the Israeli Anti-Discrimination Legal Center "Tmura" said that 60 percent of the women receiving this contraceptive were Ethiopian Jews, while Ethiopians made up only 1 percent of the population and "the gap here is just impossible to reconcile in any logical manner that would somehow resist the claims of racism."

Note 47.6 Shell and human rights abuses: In September 2011, an industry watchdog accused Royal Dutch Shell of funding armed gangs in Nigeria and said this had fuelled human rights abuses. Platform, a London-based non-government organisation monitoring the oil and gas industry, said in a 75-page report that the Anglo-Dutch major paid government forces that have attacked, tortured, and killed Nigerians living in the creeks and swamplands of the Niger Delta.

"Basic company errors have exacerbated violent conflicts in which entire communities have been destroyed. Billions have been lost in revenues to the government and oil companies, sending shock waves through the global economy," the report said. While primary responsibility for human rights violations falls on the Nigerian government and other perpetrators, Shell has played an active role in fuelling conflict and violence in a variety of forms," Platform said.

It says Shell regularly assisted armed militants, in one case in 2010 transferring large amounts of money to a group credibly linked to militia violence. The report says Shell sided with clashing gangs, picking the more powerful group to help protect its oil infrastructure.

Again in August 2012, Platform accused Shell of financing violent human rights abusers in Nigeria. The data is analysed in a new Platform briefing, "Dirty work: Shell's security spending in Nigeria and beyond", which shows that a substantial amount of Shell's security spending went into the hands of known human rights abusers in the volatile Niger Delta region.

Note 47.7 Illegal settlements in occupied territories: The consensus view in the international community is that the existence of Israeli settlements in the West Bank including East Jerusalem and the Golan Heights is in violation of international law. The Fourth Geneva Convention includes statements such as "the Occupying Power shall not deport or transfer parts of its own civilian population into the territory it occupies".

At present, the view of the international community, as reflected in numerous UN resolutions, regards the building and existence of Israeli settlements in the West Bank, East Jerusalem and the Golan Heights as a violation of international law. UN Security Council Resolution 446 refers to the Fourth Geneva Convention as the applicable international legal instrument, and calls upon Israel to desist from transferring its own population into the territories or changing their demographic make-up. The reconvened Conference of the High Contracting Parties to the Geneva Conventions has declared the settlements illegal as has the primary judicial organ of the UN, the International Court of Justice.

Note 47.8 The statistical chances of being hurt by a terrorist - Americans are as likely to be killed by their own furniture as by Terrorism: In 2010 (the latest report of the US Nation Counterterrorism Centre), 15 Americans were killed in terrorist attacks; nine died in 2009; 33 in 2008; 17 in 2007; 28 in 2006; and 56 in 2005. The vast majority of private U.S. citizens killed in terrorist attacks died in the war zone countries of Iraq and Afghanistan. So the tally of Americans killed by terrorists around the world since 2005 comes to a total of 158, yielding an annual rate of 16 Americans killed by terrorists outside of the borders of the United States. Taking these figures into account, a rough calculation suggests that in the last five years, your chances of being killed by a terrorist are about one in 20 million. This compares to the annual risk of dying in a car accident of 1 in 19,000; drowning in the bath at 1 in 800,000; dying in a building fire at 1 in 99,000; or being struck by lightning at 1 in 5,500,000. In other words, in the last five years you were four times more likely to be struck by lightening than to be killed by a terrorist. Indeed, a comparable number of Americans are crushed to death by their own televisions or other domestic furniture each year.

Note 47.9 Islamophobia on the rise according to CAIR (Council on American-Islamic Relations, University of California, Berkeley): According to the latest report of CAIR in 2010 "Islamophobia and Its Impact in the United States", there is a continuing increase in fear and hatred for Muslims in the United States:

- The public's favourable rating of Islam sank from 40 percent in November 2001 to 30 percent in August 2010 according to the Pew Research Centre.

- According to those interviewed for this report, on a scale from 1 (best situation for Muslims) to 10 (worst possible situation for Muslims) Islamophobia in America stands at a 6.4. Interviews were conducted in September and October of 2010.

- In late November 2010, the Public Research Institute found that 45 percent of Americans agree that Islam is at odds with American values.

- A Time magazine poll released in August 2010 found, "Twenty-eight percent of voters do not believe Muslims should be eligible to sit on the U.S. Supreme Court. Nearly one-third of the country thinks adherents of Islam should be barred from running for President...."

- In terms of anti Muslim incidents the 2009 CAIR report informs that for the 2008 calendar year, CAIR and its affiliate chapters processed a total of 2,728 civil rights complaints. This number represents a 3 percent increase in reported cases from 2007 (2,652 reports) and an 11 percent increase over cases reported in 2006 (2,467 reports).

- The occurrence of reported civil rights complaints by Muslims continues to increase at mosques and Muslim organizations, rising from 221 cases in 2006 to 564 cases in 2007 to 721 cases in 2008. This represents a 28 percent increase from 2007 to 2008. There were 118 reported cases of discrimination in schools in 2007 and 153 in 2008. This represents a 31 percent increase. (2009 CAIR report)

Note 47.10 The acceptance by US citizens of the use of torture: A Huffington Post survey of surveys in 2009 found that in 30 polls taken since September 11, 2001, the average public approval for American use of torture is 44 percent, ranging as low as 15% and as high as 49%, depending on the vagaries of the question.

Note 47.11 Tony Blair - Psychopathological use of religion: In an interview with Michael Parkinson broadcast on ITV1 on 4 March 2006, Blair referred to the role of his Christian faith in his decision to go to war in Iraq, stating that he had prayed about the issue, and saying that God would judge him for his decision: "I think if you have faith about these things, you realise that judgement is made by other people ... and if you believe in God, it's made by God as well."

A longer exploration of his faith can be found in an interview with "Third Way Magazine". There he says that "I was brought up as [a Christian], but I was not in any real sense a practising one until I went to Oxford. There was an Australian priest at the same college as me who got me interested again. In a sense, it was a rediscovery of religion as something living that was about the world around me rather than some sort of special one-to-one relationship with a remote "Being" on high. Suddenly I began to see its social relevance. I began to make sense of the world".

Cherie Blair's friend and "spiritual guru", Carole Caplin is credited with introducing her and her husband to various bizarre New Age symbols and beliefs, including "magic pendants" known as "BioElectric Shields". One of the Blairs' New Age practices occurred when on holiday in Mexico, where the couple, wearing only bathing costumes, took part in a "rebirthing" procedure, which involved smearing mud and fruit over each other's bodies while sitting in a steam bath.

At one point Alastair Campbell, Blair's director of strategy and communications gave away the regime's real attitude to religion when he intervened in an interview, preventing the Prime Minister from answering a question about his Christianity, explaining, "We don't do God".

Note 50.1 Manipulation of sectarian war in Ireland: Despite the sectarian violence between Catholics and Protestants displayed in the last 30 years in the Irish conflict, this sectarian hatred is generally felt to be manipulated, mostly by interests close to the British government. Despite the propaganda and stereotypes, Ireland's nationalist, "freedom fighting" history is replete with examples of well-healed Protestants, many of them part of the aristocracy. The modern history of Ireland is not one of sectarian violence and the latest in-fighting appears to have been triggered off and promoted by agents provocateurs working with British military intelligence such as the UVF and UFF, both virulently anti-Catholic groups. Evidence of this manipulative relationship is now beginning to emerge. The damage to Catholic and Protestant relations however will take years to correct.

During the 18th and 19th century, many of Ireland's most vocal nationalists seeking separation from the rest of Britain were Protestant landowners, educated, wealthy and definitely not the typical poor Irish Catholic nationalist stereotype of today. People like Wolf Tone, a Protestant tutor from Kildare, organised the 1798 Rebellion which even managed to declare a Republic for a short time in County Mayo. In October 1791 Tone had founded the Society of the United Irishmen. The original purpose of this society was no more than the formation of a political union between Roman Catholics and Protestants which conspired to establish an Irish republic by armed rebellion. The membership consisted of many Protestants prominent in Irish society. W.B. Yeats and Lady Gregory were instrumental in saving the Irish language and forming the Gaelic league together with Douglas Hyde (another Protestant and later first President of Ireland). Into the 20th century, many of Ireland's Nationalist rebels were Protestants and many were members of the aristocracy. Sir Roger Casement was executed by the British for his part in the Easter rising. Irish history has many examples of Protestant nationalists and republicans, including several Protestant Presidents of the Irish Republic in modern times.

Note 51.1 Purgatory and Hell: Purgatory, according to Catholic teaching, is the state or place of purification or temporary punishment by which those who die in a state of grace are believed to be made ready for the Beatific Vision in Heaven. Only one who dies in a state of grace can be in Purgatory, and therefore no one who is in Purgatory will remain there forever or go to Hell. Hell is a place of eternal suffering and punishment in an afterlife. Hell is sometimes portrayed as populated with demons that torment those dwelling there. Hell is traditionally depicted as fiery and painful, inflicting guilt and suffering.

Note 51.2 Fear and a Frightened Nation: Some politicians in society incite fear in the general public to achieve political goals, for example Herman Göring, the Nazi leader, commented that: "The people don't want war, but they can always be brought to the bidding of the leaders. This is easy. All you have to do is tell them they are being attacked, and denounce the pacifists for lack of patriotism and for exposing the country to danger. It works the same in every country."

The term "culture of fear" is also used in contemporary reports to describe fears about Islamic terrorism which, it can be easily argued, are fears that are exaggerated or irrational in nature. The term has also been used to describe irrational fear in other contexts, such as citizens fearing persons of different ethnic backgrounds, or neighbourhood residents fearing retribution if they assist police in identifying criminals.

Note 52.1 The fall of Saigon - Vietnam War, April 30, 1975: The fall of the city was preceded by the evacuation of almost all the American civilian and military personnel in Saigon, along with tens of thousands of South Vietnamese civilians associated with the southern regime. The evacuation culminated in Operation Frequent Wind, which was the largest helicopter evacuation in history. In addition to the flight of refugees, the end of the war and institution of new rules by the communists contributed to a decline in the population of the city. Most of the South Vietnamese helicopters were dumped into the ocean to make room on the decks for more aircraft.

Note 53.1 The Salem witch trials: The Salem witch trials were a series of hearings and prosecutions of people accused of witchcraft in colonial Massachusetts, between February 1692 and May 1693. Despite being generally known as the Salem witch trials, the preliminary hearings in 1692 were conducted in a variety of towns across the province: Salem Village, Ipswich, Andover and Salem Town. The episode is one of the most notorious cases of mass hysteria, and has been used in political rhetoric and popular literature as a vivid, cautionary tale about the dangers of isolationism, religious extremism, false accusations and lapses in due process.

It was not unique, being an American example of the much larger phenomenon of witch trials in the Early Modern period. Many have considered the lasting impressions from the trials to have been highly influential in subsequent American history, including manifestations of blind, violent, fundamental Christian fanaticism in America, as well as the kidnap, abuse and torture of foreign prisoners during the ongoing "war on terror", both abroad and in Iraq's Abu Ghraib prison and Afghanistan's Baghram bases.

Note 54.1 God created man, who created God? According to a 2001 Gallup poll about 45% of Americans believe that "God created human beings pretty much in their present form at one time within the last 10,000 years or so."

Another 37% believe that "human beings have developed over millions of years from less advanced forms of life, but God guided this process".

Finally, 14% believe that "human beings have developed over millions of years from less advanced forms of life, but God had no part in this process".

Belief in creationism is inversely correlated to education; of those with postgraduate degrees, 74% accept evolution. In 1987, Newsweek reported: "By one count there are some 700 scientists with respectable academic credentials (out of a total of 480,000 U.S. earth and life scientists) who give credence to creation-science, the general theory that complex life forms did not evolve but appeared 'abruptly.'"

Note 55.1 Divide and Rule examples from history:

Example 1: The Romans invaded Macedonia from the south and defeated King Perseus of Macedon in the battle of Pydna in 168 BC. Macedonia was thus divided into four republics that were heavily restricted from relations with one another and other Hellenic states. A ruthless purge occurred, with allegedly anti-Roman citizens being denounced by their compatriots and deported in large numbers.

Example 2: Following the October revolution, the Bolsheviks engaged at various times in alliances with the Left Socialist-Revolutionaries, some anarchists, and various non-Russian ethnic nationalist groups against the conservative White Russian movement, Right Socialist-Revolutionaries, and other anarchist and ethnic nationalist groups. This was done to establish the Communist Party of the Soviet Union (the Bolshevik party) as the sole legal party in the Soviet Union.

Example 3: In an attempt to stem the passion for Irish sovereignty in the early part of the 20th century and afterwards, the British government sought to create enmity between Catholics and Protestants, many of which shared a desire to be free from British rule. Many of these artificial hatreds continue to this day.[50.1]

Note 55.2 Segmentation of population in United States: The pervasive division of all US citizens by various criteria like "Ethnicity" and "Colour" by the US government and the media is very noticeable to observers from outside of the USA. A glance at the results published by the US Bureau of Census gives a typical indication of the divisions. Apparently there is no such thing as just a plain citizen of the "United" States of America. Here are the categories of division used by the census and other branches of government: White, Black or African American, American Indian or Alaska Native, Asian, Native Hawaiian or Other Pacific Islander, Hispanic, White alone not Hispanic.

Note 55.3 False Flag - The Reichstag Fire: This was an arson attack in 1933 on the German parliament. The police conducted a thorough search inside the building and found Marinus van der Lubbe, a young, mentally handicapped Dutch communist and unemployed bricklayer who had recently arrived in Germany, ostensibly to carry out political activities. The fire was used as evidence by the Nazis that the communists were beginning a plot against the German government. Van der Lubbe and four communist leaders were subsequently arrested. Hitler, who was sworn in as Chancellor of Germany four weeks before, on 30 January, urged President Paul von Hindenburg to pass an emergency decree to counter the "ruthless confrontation of the Communist Party of Germany". With civil liberties suspended, the government instituted mass arrests of communists, including all of the communist parliamentary delegates. With them gone and their seats empty, the Nazis went from being a plurality party to the majority; subsequent elections confirmed this position and thus allowed Hitler to consolidate his power. Meanwhile, investigation of the Reichstag fire continued, with the Nazis eager to uncover Comintern complicity. In early March 1933, three Bulgarian men were arrested who were to play pivotal roles during the Leipzig Trial, known also as the "Reichstag Fire Trial". The Bulgarians were known to the Prussian police as senior Comintern operatives, but the police had no idea how senior they were. Historians disagree as to whether Van der Lubbe acted alone or, as seems more likely, the arson was planned and ordered by the Nazis, then dominant in the government themselves, as a false flag operation.

Note 55.4 Hyperinflation in the Weimar Republic, the Depression and the rise of Nazism: The hyperinflation of the Weimar Republic lasted between 1921 and 1924, during which time the nation's currency turned to junk. Although the inflation ended with the introduction of the Rentenmark and the Weimar Republic continued for a decade afterwards, hyperinflation is widely believed to have contributed to the Nazi takeover of Germany and Adolf Hitler's rise to power. Hitler himself, in his book Mein Kampf, made many references to the German debt and the negative consequences that brought about the inevitability of "national socialism". Some economists, however, point out that Hitler's rise was immediately preceded by the 1931 economic crisis, which, while also being partially triggered by Germany's debt, was, unlike the hyperinflation crisis of 1923, characterized by massive deflation created by a government austerity program. It also produced resentment from bankers and speculators, whom the government and the press blamed for the inflation crisis. Some Germans called the hyper-inflated Weimar banknotes "Jew confetti", thus consolidating Hitler's propaganda assertions that the economic woes of Germany were the fault of the Jewish population.

Note 56.1 My enemy's enemy is my friend: Examples in modern national history include:

- Long-term enemies Britain and France uniting against Germany during World War I.

- The Western capitalist democracies aiding the Soviet Union following the Nazi invasion during World War II.

- U.S. supporting anti-communist dictatorships during the Cold War.

- The United States backing Saddam Hussein during the Iran-Iraq War due to the anti-American Iranian Revolution of 1979.

- The Soviets backing India to counter both the pro-American Pakistani government and the People's Republic of China, following the Sino-Soviet split.

When George W. Bush was gathering his "coalition of the willing", in an address to a joint session of Congress on September 20, 2001 he paraphrased Jesus Christ when he said: "Either you are with us, or you are with the terrorists."

---oOo---

About the author and editor

Malcolm Coxall, the author, is a management consultant and systems analyst with more than 30 years experience. Starting with a career in industrial dispute arbitration for the International Labour Organisation, Malcolm later became a free-lance systems consultant, working in mainland Europe and the Middle East.

With experience working for many of the world's largest corporate and institutional players, as well as several government agencies Malcolm has acquired a ringside view of the human, organisational and management methodologies used by medium and large businesses in industries as diverse as banking, oil, defence, telecoms, manufacturing, mining, food, agriculture, aerospace, textiles and engineering.

Malcolm has published articles on politics, human system design, political manipulation, environmental economics, sustainable agriculture, organic food production, forest biodiversity, and environmental protection. Malcolm is the author of "Machiavellian Management - A Chief Executive's Guide" and of a series of textbooks dealing with relational database design ("Oracle Quick Guides"). He is active in European environmental politics and was the successful private complainant in the European Court of Justice in several cases of national breaches of European environmental law. He now lives in southern Spain from where he continues his consultancy work and writing, whilst managing the family's organic farm.

Guy Caswell, the editor, was born in Southampton, UK in 1955. He spent his formative years in Nigeria and worked in various jobs in England before leaving for Thailand in 1992, where he divides his time between teaching English in Bangkok and the family farm in the north-east of Thailand.

Guy graduated from Ramkhamhaeng University majoring in Thai language. As an English tutor, Guy claims to have the longest serving student in the world, a prominent Thai politician whom he has tutored in English continuously for 17 years. Guy's interests include politics, farming, playing guitar and Thai culture.

---oOo---